Visions
of the
Modern

Visions
of the
Modern
John Golding

with 38 illustrations

Thames and Hudson

To James, yet again

British Library Cataloguing-in-Publication Data

A catalogue record for this book is available from the British Library

ISBN 0-500-23674-7

Printed and bound in Slovenia

Contents

Introduction

THE ESSAYS contained in this volume span a period of three decades and are some of the products of a lifetime spent in looking at works of art and trying to make them. I grew up in Mexico, so my first experience of contemporary art was that of Mexican mural painting; apart from the wealth of pre-Columbian material and of beautiful Spanish Colonial architecture, not much other art was to be seen. However, at a relatively early age I encountered the expatriate Surrealist community which had congregated in Mexico during the Second World War. This included such figures as Benjamin Péret, Wolfgang Paalen and Leonora Carrington, while at times other luminaries such as André Breton (whom I never met), Max Ernst and Echaurren Matta visited the country. The Surrealists widened my horizons at a time when I wasn't even aware I had any. I was fascinated by their work (although possibly less than by their personalities); and the visual enthusiasms they passed on to me, combined with my own admiration for the great Mexican masters, may account for the fact that, when I encountered the new revolutionary American art of the 1940s and 1950s, I at once felt so completely at home with it.

At the same time, during university days in North America, I began to visit New York whenever I could and, like so many others of my generation, it was at the Museum of Modern Art that I received further artistic education. I subsequently came to realize that the scope of its collections and the displays and exhibitions it mounted provided a far more coherent overview of the development of twentieth-century art than could be seen in any European museum.

In 1951 I came to Europe for the first time, primarily to look at all the great art of the past which I had been studying and reading about but which I had not yet seen. I enrolled at the Courtauld Institute as a graduate student during what in retrospect has come to look like possibly its most distinguished period. There I was fortunate enough to work under Anthony Blunt and Johannes Wilde, both teachers of genius. The bias of the teaching at the time, as at almost every other art historical centre in the world, was towards a formalistic analysis of works of art, although there were also compulsory courses on Renaissance texts. Connoisseurship as such has never greatly attracted me, but I enjoyed the emphasis on visual concentration and analysis. I did badly at the end of my first year there because I had spent most of my time in museums and galleries, both in this country and on the continent. My own response to art has always been primarily instinctive, and visual images still have the ability to absorb and hold me instantly. The process of trying to understand them and to place them in history has always followed on from their initial impact.

In Paris in 1953 I saw the large exhibition of Cubist painting mounted at the Musée d'Art Moderne, then still housed in the Palais de Tokyo. I responded directly to the works and almost at once came to realize that I could never fully appreciate much subsequent modern art, that had already come to mean so much to me, until I had come to terms with Cubism. My immersion in Cubism, on which I wrote a PhD dissertation, became the initial basis of my own teaching career at the Courtauld, although I taught across a wide spectrum. My attraction to art that combines innovation and experiment with strong formal values ensured my bias towards French art of both the nineteenth and early twentieth centuries, and most of the essays in this book are concerned with French art, or with art that was being produced in France, in the first three decades of this century. German Expressionism, for example, invigorates me but is fundamentally alien to my temperament. American Abstract Expressionism, on the other hand, has always appealed to me both because of my own visual origins but also because in so much of it a feeling for purely pictorial considerations goes hand in hand with the metaphysical concepts and ideas the artists sought to convey. Although I have written about American art, only essays on Gorky and Stella are included here. The former is the artist who formed a bridge between European art and European sensibilities and the new, rawer emergent American art. The latter perhaps more than any other living American artist has sought to come to terms with European art of the past.

The volume is perhaps inevitably dominated by Picasso, simply because he looms so large in the art of our century and because his output is so enormous – greater than that of any other recorded artist. The 1992 Matisse retrospective in New York demonstrated that he was Picasso's only genuine rival in terms of visual power and invention; but despite his more intellectual bent of mind he is a more difficult artist to write about; a discussion of his art can so easily become meaningless unless it is accompanied by large numbers of high quality reproductions. Because of that there is less Matisse here than I would have wished. Then again, by the 1920s Matisse had retreated into a more private and conventional artistic world while Picasso continued to evolve and astound; the 1920s and 1930s produced some of his greatest work. Despite this and my own intellectual debt to Surrealism, I still feel that the art of the 1920s and 1930s lacks the sheer visual exhilaration and incandescence that characterized French art in the first two decades of this century. Braque, Léger, Gris, Derain and Brancusi all contributed to making this one of the most exciting moments in the history of art, and their names, together with those of many of their friends and colleagues, appear frequently on these pages.

When I was doing research in the archives of the Museum of Modern Art in the mid-1950s I was fortunate enough to interview Marcel Duchamp on two occasions and came under his legendary spell. Here the process of involvement was for me reversed and it was his ideas and the elegance and originality of his intellect that led me into his work. He taught me indirectly much about French literature and thought of both the late nineteenth and early twentieth centuries. His influence on a large proportion of later twentieth-century art has been incalculable, although I still do not think he was an artist who lived his life with visual intensity and joy. His example has produced a great deal of work that is primarily cerebral and that for my own taste gives too little visual stimulus and delight.

One of the artists whom I most admire but about whom I have not written is Mondrian. When I try to analyse why this is I can only say that because I find the pictures are so formally perfect and because they so totally embody the philosophical concepts underlying them, to talk about them seems unnecessary. Then again, it is impossible for me to get interested in an artist's work without becoming involved in that artist's mind and personality and there is a sense in which Mondrian painted himself out of his pictures. On the other hand, the unpredictable vitality of Malevich's work and the irresistible force of his artistic personality invite engagement of a more confrontational kind. Like most of the artists whose work is discussed in these pages – Derain and Duchamp are the possible exceptions – his vision was essentially forward looking and optimistic, and his modernity lay in part at least in his belief that art no longer had any frontiers, and that in practice anything and everything was possible.

All the original texts have been left virtually intact although a few passages dealing with detailed examinations of individual works have been eliminated or compressed. A few factual errors have been corrected and the corrections acknowedged in the notes. In some of the pieces which originated as reviews of books or exhibitions, a few passages that were of topical interest at the time have been suppressed.

The dialogue between myself and my friend Richard Wollheim is included here as a kind of epilogue only because I feel it says something new and original about the nature of abstract art and about the way artists have felt their way into it.

JOHN GOLDING
London, April 1993

1

Guillaume Apollinaire:
the Painters' Friend

ALTHOUGH Guillaume Apollinaire was the most influential art critic writing in France during the decade before the outbreak of war in 1914, many of his painter friends felt that he possessed almost no visual sensibility; Picasso; Braque, Jacques Villon and the visionary dealer D. H. Kahnweiler, among others, felt that Apollinaire had no eye. And yet the difficulties which confronted and often overcame him in his capacity as critic illuminate the problems facing the critic of today, and a study of his criticism continues to deepen our understanding of the art of his time. For no other man reflected so completely every facet of the artistic temper of his age. He was a weather-vane which responded to the slightest intellectual vibration; he was a net which caught and gathered up every new aesthetic trend. Artists loved his company, and he made them aware of themselves and of each other. Above all, he was a cardinal figure in creating the artistic climate of Paris early in this century – a climate in which anything and everything was thought possible. It was this belief that made the early twentieth century one of the most exciting periods in the entire history of the visual arts, and Apollinaire, for all his failings, remains its spokesman and its most representative critic.

Apollinaire's first serious pieces of art criticism were two articles dedicated to Picasso which were published in 1905.[1] These are also among the first notable references to Picasso's art to appear in the French press, and they show Apollinaire at his critical best. The articles are poetic and light in tone, sensitive and perceptive. Apollinaire shows himself aware of the socially conscious art which Picasso was producing when he writes: 'Beneath the tawdry finery of these slender acrobats one senses very strongly that they are young people of the people, inconstant, wily, cunning, poor and lying.' He distinguishes between the early work of the 'blue' period and the more recent canvases, rightly observing that Picasso's art was becoming calmer and more detached. Then, most prophetically and

11

impressively, he refutes a statement made by the critic Charles Morice who had accused Picasso of harbouring 'a precocious disenchantment'.[2] Apollinaire says, 'I think the opposite. Everything enchants him, and his undeniable talent seems to me to be at the service of a fantasy that is a balanced combination of the delicious and the horrible, the abject and the delicate.'

All in all, the Picasso articles make a good beginning to Apollinaire's career as an art critic, and in at least one respect he lived up to this early promise: no other critic has ever helped and encouraged such an impressive number of gifted and, for the most part, unknown young painters. Picasso did not show his early Cubist work publicly; if by 1914[3] the public was becoming aware of the fact that here was a genius who had already altered the course of Western art, it was Apollinaire's doing. Apollinaire never did Braque full justice; but if Braque's name was known to the public at all during the early years of Cubism, this was due to Apollinaire's frequent references to him in his columns.[4] Apollinaire was largely responsible for organizing the minor Cubists into a militant group with a strong public image. He 'invented' Marie Laurencin; it was he who made Delaunay famous. He helped to consolidate the reputations of Matisse, Derain and Vlaminck and was perhaps the only critic in France who was fully alert to the activities of the *Blue Rider* group in Germany. He realized that Mondrian's highly personal approach to Cubism was leading him toward total abstraction and he recognized at once that Boccioni was the most gifted of the Futurist painters. He was the first critic to take Chagall seriously, and within the space of a year he had raised de Chirico from obscurity to a position very close to celebrity.

And yet, despite the galaxies of now famous names which are scattered over so·many pages of Apollinaire's writings, he still disappoints as a critic, even at his best. Throughout his life, Apollinaire insisted that an artist's approach to his work should be intuitive, and the works of art that attracted him most were those which he felt to be most spontaneous. Apollinaire saw himself – rightly – as a poet first of all, and only secondarily as a critic. He therefore never felt obliged to explain or justify his artistic judgments. A highly intelligent man, he was perfectly capable of sustained argument, but he deliberately avoided it because intellectual reasoning went against his artistic beliefs. So, apart from the fact that his powers of visual comprehension were limited, the

expressions of his enthusiasms in retrospect tend to seem superficial, his conclusions often contradictory and hollow.

The second reason why Apollinaire fails to satisfy as a critic is
bound up with the problem of art criticism today, for in many
respects Apollinaire is the prototype of the modern journalist critic.
He wrote about painting in order to make a living. To fill his
columns he had to write about the indifferent and second-rate, as
well as about the original and truly creative His job was to give the
public an overall picture of what was to be seen in Paris, month by
month, week by week. This he did – without any historical regard
for the past and with little concern for an accurate transcription of
the present. His desire to produce, in haste, criticism that sounded
provocative and profound led him to invent the sort of pseudo-
metaphysical jargon that is found all too frequently in writings
about present-day art. Conversely he was, if not the originator of
what might be called the 'gossip' school of art criticism, at least one
of its greatest popularizers.

How was it possible that, given these limitations, his judgments
on contemporary paintings could have been as sound as they were?
The answer to this is that whereas he had very little feeling for
painting, he had a passion for novelty in any sphere and an almost
uncanny gift for recognizing what was original and significant, even
when he was unable fully to understand it. Furthermore, he knew
personally most of the artists he wrote about and was perfectly
capable of detecting a genuine artistic personality when he
encountered it. A case in point is his treatment of the Douanier
Rousseau. His first references to Rousseau were slighting, but when
Apollinaire had come to know him and had seen him at work (and
also, one cannot help suspecting, when he had heard Picasso and
Rousseau's other painter friends talking about him) he became an
ardent champion of Rousseau's art. Apollinaire was a man who
loved painters more than he loved painting. He was a brilliant
propagandist for them, and, still more important, he was an inspired
friend.

Apollinaire was born in Rome (in Trastevere) in 1880 – a year
before Picasso. He was an illegitimate child, and it is not completely
certain who his father was, although the likelihood is that he was
the son of a picaresque nobleman from Saint Moritz, Francesco Flugi
d'Aspermont. Apollinaire himself liked to hint that his father had
been a prelate of great importance; and a cartoon by Picasso shows

13

Apolliniare crowned by a papal tiara.[5] His mother was a grand
courtesan called Olga Kostrowitzky, and Kostrowitzky was the
name used by Apollinaire until 1902 when he adopted the
pseudonym by which we now know him. In 1887, Madame
Kostrowitzky moved her sons to Monte Carlo and the gambling
tables. It was at this moment that the culture of Monaco was
swinging away from Italy toward France, and Apollinaire thus
received his education in French rather than in Italian. By the turn
of the century, he was more or less settled in Paris. He earned his
living by working as a tutor and a bank clerk, and occasionally he
ghosted stories and articles for better-known writers. Soon he was
frequenting advanced literary gatherings where he met the older
generation of Symbolist poets whose work he already knew and
admired; Verlaine had died in 1896, but he become acquainted with
Moréas, Paul Fort, Francis Jammes and the American, Stuart Merrill.
At this time he also met the literary eccentric, Alfred Jarry, who was
to have an important influence, not only on his work, but also on his
way of life. Jarry was also to become identified in Apollinaire's mind
with an equally important mentor: Rimbaud.

In 1903, together with the young poet, André Salmon, and a man
known as the Baron Mollet,[6] Apollinaire founded *Le Festin d'Esope*,
a magazine which made a genuine attempt to detach itself from
Symbolism, which a younger generation of poets, in love with
contemporary life, were beginning to find too aristocratic and
remote from the new world of the twentieth century. It is worth
quoting from Apollinaire's editorial in the first issue which serves to
define his aesthetic attitude at the time when he first came into
contact with contemporary painting: 'We are anxious, unsatisfied,
blasé about everything we are shown, for everything bears the stamp
of a past we no longer love, of which we wish to retain only those
aspects which will help us to live, to prepare for the future.' This is a
call to arms that heralds not so much the classical, formalistic and
rational revolution effected by the Cubists, as the passionate,
turbulent and aggressive world of the Italian Futurists.

A few months later, early in 1904, Apollinaire met Vlaminck and
Derain. He still had very little knowledge of Post-Impressionist
painting and their work seemed to him enormously bold and daring.
At this moment, Fauvism was exactly right for Apollinaire; it was
violent, colourful, immediate and not too difficult to understand. In
fact, early twentieth-century painting was in a position not unlike

that of early twentieth-century writing. In both arts there was a sense of excitement and the desire to produce something entirely new to meet the needs of the new epoch, but young painters and writers felt somehow disoriented and were uncertain how to proceed. The Fauve painters realized that the art of Van Gogh, Gauguin and Cézanne held the key to something completely new, but they were not quite sure what it was; and in the last analysis, the art of the Fauves was not so very different from what had gone before. The statements made public at that time by the Fauves are few and contradictory. Apollinaire could have performed a valuable service for posterity had he recorded what they said about earlier artists and what they felt were their own achievements and goals. But the closest he ever comes to discussing the nature of Fauvism is to tell us that it was a prelude to Cubism, which it was only in so far as the Fauve painters were detaching themselves to a certain extent from naturalistic appearances.

It is characteristic, however, that when Apollinaire met Matisse in 1905, he realized at once that here was the most important artist of the Fauve group. He tended to see painting very much in terms of personalities, and on this level his instinct seldom let him down. 'Le Fauve des Fauves', he calls Matisse in 1907,[7] and a few years later he remarks that Matisse was one of the few artists who had successfully eliminated all traces of Impressionism from his style. This was perfectly true, for it was Matisse, and Matisse alone, who extracted the logical conclusions from the Fauves' desire to release colour from its representational role, and who saw the movement for what it was: a transitional period between Post-Impressionism and the great new styles of the twentieth century. Henceforth, Matisse's name appeared in Apollinaire's columns with greater frequency than that of any other artist except Picasso.

There is evidence, too, that Apollinaire listened carefully to what Matisse had to say about contemporary painting. In 1907 Apollinaire interviewed Matisse for *La Phalange*,[8] and Matisse used his statements to Apollinaire as a sort of trial run for his more important *Notes of a Painter*, which appeared a year later. Certain passages from *Les Trois Vertues Plastiques* (a short article of 1908[9] in which Apollinaire talks about painting in general terms, rather than simply reviewing a particular exhibition) read like quotes from Matisse. On the whole, the article would not be worth remembering were it not for a Bergsonian insistence on the importance of intuition and a general feeling of excitement at the possibility of a new, anti-naturalistic art.

If Fauvism retained strong links with the past, Cubism belonged only to the twentieth century. For Apollinaire the two movements remained closely associated; and this is one of the reasons why he was never able to appreciate the real significance of the Cubist achievement. One cannot help suspecting that subconsciously he was trying to reconcile the approach of Matisse, an intellectual artist in the French tradition, with that of Picasso, whose utterances on painting were anarchistic and occasionally humorous or deliberately provocative. In his writings Matisse stresses the importance of intuition, but what he really wanted to obtain was a carefully calculated effect of spontaneity. Picasso, on the other hand, proceeding truly intuitively, produced in his early Cubist phases paintings that must have appeared studied and intellectual when compared to the colourful immediacy of Matisse's work of the same period.

The meeting with Picasso took place in the summer of 1904, probably in the bar known to the painters as *Le Fox* (a name that appears as the title of a 1911 Cubist etching by Braque). The friendship between the two men was immediate and intense, and there can be no doubt that Apollinaire put Picasso in touch with the most recent aesthetic trends in French literature. Certainly the first wave of Neo-Classicism that appears in Picasso's work of 1905 corresponds to the shift toward Neo-Classicism in French literature during the first years of the century.

The *Demoiselles d'Avignon*, 1907 (Museum of Modern Art, New York) a painting which Apollinaire must have known and which has a fair claim to being the most important single pictorial document the twentieth century has yet produced, is not mentioned in his critical writings. However, he may have commemorated it in a poem called *Lul de Falentin*, written in 1907, the same year the *Demoiselles* was painted.[10] The poem is very difficult to understand and has always baffled Apollinaire scholars. It is strongly erotic in flavour, taking the form of an invocation to some sirens who attract men, specifically oarsmen and sailors, to their cave. In one stanza, Apollinaire refers to their 'terrible mute mouths', while their eyes are described as 'bestial stars' (*étoiles bestiales*). The main argument in support of the idea that the poem may relate to the *Demoiselles* is that in the original sketches, Picasso included figures of two men, one of which he subsequently identified as a sailor.[11] Since the sailor image appears in Picasso's work specifically in connection with the *Demoiselles*, it is tempting to assume that it is part of an iconography which he and Apollinaire shared. If the hot, over-charged atmosphere of the poem calls to mind the sinuous siren paintings of Böcklin with their literary connotations, rather than the angular and savage nudes of the *Demoiselles*, it is worth remembering that while with this painting Picasso was making a final break with the past, he was also looking back for the last time to his early work, which had grown out of a late nineteenth-century idiom with strong literary overtones.

And Apollinaire did play an important, if indirect, part in the painting of the *Demoiselles*. He had a friend, Géry-Piéret, who one day in March of 1907 stole three Iberian stone heads from the Louvre.[12] Apollinaire suggested that they might interest Picasso; Picasso bought two of them and used them as models for the heads of the two central figures of the *Demoiselles*. The male head is particularly close to a sketch of a sailor's head which is either a study for the *Demoiselles* or a postscript to it. Legend has it that it was Apollinaire who introduced Picasso to Braque towards the end of 1907, thus initiating the collaboration between the two painters that was to result in the birth of Cubism the following year. (In fact the artists may have met sooner: a sketch-book of Picasso's containing drawings dating to the early spring of 1907 mentions Braque's name twice.)

It is as a champion of Cubist painting that Apollinaire achieved critical fame. *The Cubist Painters*, published in 1913, has long been considered his major critical work, and it was on this little book of some 12,000 words that his reputation as a critic depended until the publication of his collected criticism in 1960.[13] We know that Apollinaire supported Picasso and Braque wholeheartedly in their creation of a new style, and he certainly became the movement's greatest propagandist. But of all the art movements he knew and promoted, Cubism was, in fact, the one he least understood. If we examine *The Cubist Painters* in detail, it emerges as a sadly undistinguished work. It is, as a matter of fact, only a compilation of various short, journalistic articles, most of which had appeared in newspapers and periodicals in previous years.[14]

The book contains some of the most cloudy and confusing passages of criticism that Apollinaire ever produced. There is only one cursory reference to Cézanne and only one direct allusion to tribal art, the second great formative influence on Cubism – and tribal art is mentioned in the same breath as Egyptian art which affected the painters very little. Apollinaire believed above all in an intuitive approach, and he must have realized from talking to Picasso and Braque, and from seeing them at work, that these artists proceeded in precisely this way, and yet he posited a deep metaphysical basis to their art. At the same time he was impressed by the talk of the minor figures in the movement, who drew scientific parallels with Cubist painting; so he tried to give the movement importance and weight by references to the fourth dimension, a concept that was beginning to fascinate artists but which was still little understood. At another point he actually referred to Cubism as a new kind of religious art.

But Apollinaire's main problem, which prevented him from giving a convincing picture of the Cubist revolution, was even more complex. The most recent works of Picasso and Braque looked to him nearly abstract, but both painters insisted that their works were realistic. As a result, Apollinaire continually contradicts himself. In one paragraph he states that 'the subject matter no longer counts, or hardly counts at all' while in the next he declares that it is the artist's function always to refer to nature and to reinterpret it. A passage in which he makes the point that modern art is striving toward 'pure art', 'pure abstraction', is immediately followed by the remark: 'Picasso studies the object like a surgeon dissects a corpse.' Apollinaire's mystification is understandable. For in their total reconstruction of the grammar of painting, Picasso and Braque had come very close to total abstraction. Their own realistic intentions, however, are confirmed not only by their contemporary statements but by all their subsequent work which used the discoveries of Cubism to produce a new, anti-naturalistic but figurative or representational style. And in a sense the dualism of Apollinaire's approach is prophetic, because it was the classical Cubism of Picasso and Braque that posed boldly and for the first time to many artists the problems of abstraction versus representation. The twentieth-century see-saw had been set in motion, and, ever since, the weight of artistic production has been now on the side of abstraction, now on the side of the figurative image.

Much has been written about parallels between Apollinaire's poetry and Cubist painting. Apollinaire's poetry had certainly been an influence on the imagery of Picasso's 'rose' period and he was also influential in encouraging the painters to introduce 'found' objects – theatre programmes, cigarette packets and so forth – into their work, although his own poems which relate most closely to Cubist painting (and which use analogous technical devices) are perhaps his *Poèmes Conversations*, which were written after Cubism had become a fully developed style. It is true that from the start Apollinaire showed himself dissatisfied with the conventional concepts of space and time; and we know that he applauded the Cubists in their rejection of traditional perspective. But his own ideas about time and space were entirely different from theirs. He was always fascinated by the idea of being able to fade back into the past, of seeing into the future, of being in several places at once. All this has very little to do with the cool, lucid and balanced world of the Cubists; rather, it projects us forward to the dream fantasies of the Surrealists.

The passages in *The Cubist Painters* which deal with the peripheral and minor figures of the movement are the ones most frequently attacked. One has to admit that Apollinaire's description of Marie Laurencin as a 'scientific' Cubist, along with Picasso and Braque, is rather ridiculous. This, however, must be regarded as an act of real gallantry, as Laurencin, who had been Apollinaire's mistress for some years, had cruelly rejected him before the book was published. Nevertheless, Apollinaire's classification of the painters into groups is still valid.

And his dealings with the minor artists attached to the movement revealed his extraordinary talents as an impresario. It was largely his idea that the painters Léger, Delaunay, Le Fauconnier, Metzinger and Gleizes should band together in 1911 to overthrow the installation regulations of the *Salon des Indépendants* in order to exhibit as a group. The result was the first, great Cubist manifestation and scandal, and Apollinaire's long review of the exhibition established him as the spokesman of the group.[15] A few months later when the same group of painters showed in Brussels, Apollinaire, in a preface to the catalogue, graciously accepted the name 'Cubists' on their behalf. From then on he attended their gatherings, encouraged and publicized them in his columns, and in private spurred them on to ever greater efforts. Apollinaire also played a part in the organization of the important *Section d'Or* exhibition of 1912, planned as a retrospective to explain Cubism to the public.

Apollinaire

It was in a lecture delivered at this exhibition that Apollinaire first distinguished four types of Cubism. The first was Scientific Cubism. If we omit from his category Laurencin and consider Léger's work an independent variant of the style, the painters Apollinaire included are those whom today we would call true Cubists: Picasso, Braque, Gris, Metzinger and Gleizes. The second category, Physical Cubism, was designed to fit artists such as Le Fauconnier, who had taken the first steps toward Cubism but then refused to break with traditional perspective. The third section, Orphic Cubism, was the one which most interested Apollinaire, for it contained his favourite painters of the moment: Delaunay, Marcel Duchamp and Picabia. A fourth category, Instinctive Cubism, Apollinaire generously extended to anyone who felt like climbing on the bandwagon.

Orphism was very much Apollinaire's invention, and in promoting this movement he played his most important and creative role as an art critic. Looking back on Orphism, it is now obvious that the style had two separate aspects: if identified with Delaunay's painting it meant pure, lyrical abstraction; used in connection with Duchamp and Picabia it meant something quite different. Apollinaire's statement in *The Cubist Painters* that 'the subject no longer counts', while not applicable to Picasso's and Braque's work, is certainly true in reference to Delaunay's paintings of that period. In 1912 when Delaunay was entering his first abstract phase, Apollinaire's relationship with Picasso had temporarily cooled. At the same time he was seeing Delaunay almost daily and for a short while even lived in his apartment. It was then that he wrote his poem, *Les Fenêtres*, which (although this has been disputed) is certainly a tribute to Delaunay's series of paintings bearing the same title. Towards the end of 1912, Delaunay published his own first writings on art,[16] and his ideas are strongly reflected in that part of *The Cubist Painters* which Apollinaire added while his book was already in proof.[17] Perhaps we are justified in thinking that if Apollinaire encouraged Delaunay toward his new, brightly coloured and completely abstract style, Delaunay in turn succeeded in persuading Apollinaire that his latest paintings were the logical outcome of the Cubism of Picasso and Braque, whose attitude toward nature he considered to be timid and vacillating. This impact of Delaunay on Apollinaire is, in part at least, the reason why *The Cubist Painters* is such a tortuous and contradictory book. Early in

1913 Apollinaire accompanied Delaunay to Berlin to hang an exhibition of his work and to lecture at the opening, thus contributing to the opinion held by many Germans that Delaunay was the most important French artist of his generation.

The Orphism of Duchamp and Picabia was a very different matter. Here we leave the Cubist world completely, and it is at this moment that Apollinaire becomes a truly significant influence on contemporary painting, the inspiration of a new generation of artists and the key figure to an understanding of their work.

Apollinaire's aesthetic position, as it emerges from his poetry, had for some time been as close to that of the Futurists as to that of the Cubists. Though he always treated Marinetti, the founder of the Futurist movement, rather casually and distrustfully, their artistic developments had, in fact, been very similar. Both were foreigners who came to artistic maturity in Paris through direct contact with the Symbolist poets. Both knew Jarry well and used him as a means of reacting against the more rarefied aspects of the Symbolist world. Like Marinetti – and indeed like every young intellectual in Europe – Apollinaire was deeply influenced by Nietzsche, and he shared with Marinetti and the Futurists an anarchistic and destructive attitude toward the past and a passion for every aspect of modern life. Like them, he loved speed and machines and the heady atmosphere of a big city at night. The famous lines from the *Chanson du Mal Aimé*, written in 1903/4, in which Apollinaire describes the Paris evenings as 'drunken on gin, flaming with electricity', might well have inspired Boccioni's *The Laugh of 1911* (Museum of Modern Art, New York). Further on in another stanza he speaks of a trolley car, rattling down the tracks, emitting green sparks and making a sort of *musique concrète*, an image that also reappeared in Boccioni's art.

Apollinaire extensively reviewed the large Futurist exhibition held in Paris in 1912.[18] He had played a part in it himself; by showing works of Picasso and Braque to Marinetti he had influenced Marinetti's decision to finance the Futurist painters' trip to Paris so they could brush up on developments there before risking a Paris show.[19] Apollinaire's attitude toward Futurist painting was a bit condescending, but he admired it for its breadth of conception, choice of subject matter and stimulating use of titles. By 1913 he had been persuaded to try his hand at a Futurist manifesto which was published in June as *L'Anti-tradition Futuriste*.

Apollinaire

Futurist manifestos hitherto had been wild and impassioned in tone, sometimes breathless and staccato, sometimes decidedly heavy-handed. The major feature of Apollinaire's manifesto is a bar of music to which should be sung, very loudly, the single word MERDE. Below this are listed the categories of people and places to which he wishes this epithet to be applied. These include: art critics, pedagogues, professors, historians, Venice, Versailles, Pompeii, Bruges and Oxford. At the end a rose is gracefully proffered to the Cubists, the Futurists and to himself.

With this manifesto we are in a very different world from the romantic sphere of the Futurists with its strong reliance on nineteenth-century formulas of rhetoric. We have entered the world of Dada. And if the Futurists taught the Dadaists how to publicize themselves and how to use the techniques of shock and outrage, it was Apollinaire who showed them how to get away with it. The mad lyricism, the crazy humour and the lightness of touch which raised the best of the Dada attacks on art from mere intellectual protests to the level of works of art in their own right were qualities that first appeared in Apollinaire and in his Orphist friends, Duchamp and Picabia.

Seen in its broadest sense, Dada was a movement aimed at sabotaging the values of middle-class society which, from the nineteenth century on, had become prevalent all over Europe and America. Young intellectuals felt that bourgeois smugness and materialism had succeeded in divorcing art from life; artists had become isolated, a class apart. To reinstate the artist's importance in society, bourgeois attitudes and standards of good taste had to be destroyed.

Apollinaire's campaign of subversion had been going on much longer than is usually recognized. In an article on *Forgeries*, published in 1903,[20] Apollinaire wrote: 'Contempt is a liberating sentiment. It exalts a noble spirit, and incites to great enterprises.' During the following years Apollinaire perfected his own techniques of contempt and ridicule. For example, in 1907, the year of the first Cézanne retrospective, he wrote an hilarious parody[21] in which Franz Jourdain (the somewhat reactionary President of the advanced *Salon d'Automne*) is influenced by a crafty dealer in his selection of paintings for the Cézanne exhibition. Another time he published, as a straightforward piece of reporting, a completely fictitious account of a completely fictitious *Congress for the Liberty*

Duchamp, *Apolinère Enameled*, 1916–17

of Art, which gave him the opportunity to satirize the type of convention attended by what we would now call the 'artistic establishment'.[22] Sometimes Apollinaire's style reads like a parody of itself, so that it is occasionally hard to tell whether he is serious or whether he is joking, as for instance in this quotation from a review of a group exhibition: 'Miss Jane Poupelet shows a bronze *Cow Returning to the Stable*, which is a lovely work, worthy of the greatest sculptor. It is the key work of this exhibition and in this gifted artist's development. Miss Poupelet also shows a daring nude . . .'[23]

Dada was not so much an attempt to reform art as an attempt to reform life. Art was rather the weapon that was used, and occasionally it became the target. The Dadaists hit out not only in their writings and paintings, but also in their personal behaviour. Apollinaire himself was leading a Dada life long before the movement got going. Picabia tells the story[24] of going to Apollinaire's flat to take him to an important literary banquet. Since Apollinaire could not find his black tie, Picabia painted a black tie on his neck and the two set off. This was, of course, less shocking than painting a moustache on a reproduction of the Mona Lisa and exhibiting it publicly[25] but it stemmed from the same attitude. In an attack on 'good taste' he bought a cheap, over-decorated inkwell and carried it around with him, presenting it to his friends as an object of beauty, a work of art. The exact date of this occurrence is unknown, but I think the inkwell may have been the first Dada 'ready-made'.

There are countless other similar gestures, all small and insignificant in themselves, but they made Apollinaire a legendary figure in the eyes of young artists who, during the years 1914–18, sought ways of expressing their disgust with a society which they held responsible for the war, its horrors and atrocities. Apollinaire himself remained in constant contact with the movement, contributing to Dada periodicals and corresponding with the leaders of Dada in New York and Zürich.

Much of the Dada side of Apollinaire's personality had been awakened by Alfred Jarry. In an article on Jarry, published after the latter's death in 1907, Apollinaire attempted to assess Jarry's achievements, and succeeded in defining an important aspect of Dada aesthetics. He wrote: 'There is no word that can really describe that particular kind of mirth, through which lyricism becomes satire, through which satire, applied to reality, goes so far beyond its object that it destroys the object itself. Then it rises so high that it goes almost beyond the reach of poetry, while vulgarity, emanating from good taste itself, is transformed by some unimaginable phenomenon into a necessity.'[26] But whereas Jarry, living in comparative artistic isolation, was an eccentric whose protests against religion and society were largely personal, Apollinaire and his friends quite consciously embarked on a campaign denouncing publicly what they believed to be false moral standards and hypocritical aesthetic attitudes, a campaign that was to result in the first truly international art movement the world had ever known.

Toward the end of 1912, Apollinaire, together with Duchamp and Picabia, took a trip to the district in the Jura Mountains known as Zone.[27] It was during the punning sessions enjoyed by the three friends that Duchamp began to imagine how the concepts and contradictions implicit in linguistic acrobatics, and the often disturbing psychological implications inherent in them, could find an equivalent in the manipulation of visual images. Few painters can have had their career so transformed by jest.[28] Visual punning became an essential feature of Dada art, and from 1912 on,

Duchamp and Picabia gave their works deliberately humorous and equivocal titles such as *Catch as Catch Can*, *Physical Culture* and *The Passage of the Virgin to the Bride*. In 1914 Duchamp signed his first 'ready-made' and visual Dada was truly launched.

Had Apollinaire lived (he died in 1918) I think he would certainly have taken part in the great Dada manifestations which were staged in Paris after the war – despite the fact that the war in which he served[29] had transformed him in many ways, and he would have been, so to speak, Dada with a difference.

On 26 November 1917, Apollinaire gave a lecture entitled *L'Esprit Nouveau et Les Poètes* at the Vieux Colombier theatre in Paris. By then he was one of the most famous and controversial artistic personalities of the day, and a list of guests in the audience reads like a roster of the artistic élite of the time. In the front row sat the rising generation of poets and writers, men such as André Breton, Soupault, Eluard and Aragon. They had come with the hope of being shocked, and shocked they certainly were, but in a quite different way than they expected. Apollinaire opened the lecture with the following words: 'The new spirit which will dominate the entire world has nowhere else come to light in poetry as it has in France . . . it claims to have inherited from the classics solid good sense, a confident spirit of criticism, a wide view of the world and the human mind, and that sense of duty which limits or rather controls manifestations of sentimentality.' Some listeners waited for no more. This was a call to order, and, by proclaiming it, Apollinaire had betrayed them.

The lecture was indeed a call to order, but not to the order of a classical and traditional past. Apollinaire, who to a large extent had invented Dada, was now helping to invent Surrealism. What he suggested, in effect, was a discipline that would enable poets and artists to investigate the world and to find in it new truths which would lead to a deeper understanding of contemporary life. This discipline, this technique, would in Apollinaire's words 'open up new vistas into the exterior and interior universes, which are not inferior to those which scientists in all fields discover every day, and from which they extract endless marvels'. Although he never actually mentioned the world of the subconscious, this was what he meant when he referred to 'interior universes'. Throughout his life Apollinaire had preached the doctrine of intuition; now he suggested, perhaps paradoxically, that intuition, if investigated

25

scientifically and methodically, could yield new results. The new methods of investigation upon which he insisted throughout the lecture and by which, he felt, old myths, old truths could be revalidated for modern men, became in the hands of the Surrealists the techniques of analysis and psychic automatism. Apollinaire denied, as the Surrealists did later, that in art there was any distinction between the beautiful and the ugly; like them, he emphasized that art was to be renovated, not for its own sake, but as a tool for living. For Apollinaire the war had been a sobering experience. He understood that if Dada was trying to wipe the aesthetic slate clean by a destruction of traditional values, it must also begin to see itself as the starting point of a new, positive and progressive epoch. This is exactly what Breton in effect proclaimed with his first Surrealist manifesto of 1924, a document which sounded the final death knell for Dada and which was dedicated to the memory of Guillaume Apollinaire.

From a technical point of view, the key passages in Apollinaire's lecture were those dealing with the doctrine of surprise. 'Everything,' he says, 'depends on the effect of surprise . . . Surprise is the greatest source for what is new . . . it is through the important position given to surprise that the new spirit distinguishes itself from the preceding literary and artistic movements, and in this respect it [surprise] belongs exclusively to our time.'

The first reference to what we might call the 'technique of surprise' occurs in a review of 1914, when, speaking of de Chirico, Apollinaire says: 'The painter uses that modern recourse – surprise.'[30] In another review of the same year, Apollinaire contrasts the work of Chagall with that of de Chirico, whose work he describes as 'barer, subtler, closer to the past but more truly new'.[31] Once again Apollinaire's instinct had led him to a prophetic utterance, for while the art of Chagall remained at the service of a purely personal fantasy, de Chirico became one of the three major formative influences on visual Surrealism. Moreover, he is, perhaps, the painter to whom Apollinaire in his latest poetry is most akin. The sense of nostalgia and desolation enhanced by colourful images shown in a strange, clear light, the pathos underlying a carefully balanced classical structure, the deliberate disregard of logic, and the startling confrontations of seemingly unrelated ideas and objects – all these are qualities characteristic of Apollinaire's poetry and of the best of de Chirico's contemporary paintings.

Indeed, Apollinaire's poetry and prose writings are a storehouse of Surrealist images. To quote from his *Onirocritique*[32] which was first published in 1908: 'I had an awareness of the different eternities of man and woman. Two animals of different species were coupling and the rose trees trailed vines heavy with clusters of moons. From the mouth of an ape emerged flames which branded the world with *fleurs de lis.*' After having fathered innumerable children, the protagonist (Apollinaire) is killed by a band of sailors who run away when he assumes the frightening aspect of a lion. Passages such as these might well have inspired the early and best canvases of Dali, and they show how close Apollinaire was to the world of the Surrealists long before the movement came into existence. He lived as close to his subconscious as was humanly possible, and he was fearless about facing it in his art.

The other two great influences on visual Surrealism were Marcel Duchamp and Picasso. From 1912 onwards, Picasso too had been using the technique of surprise. It might be said that it is this that distinguishes his Synthetic Cubism from that of Braque and Gris. Whereas they tended to use new Cubist techniques and procedures logically, Picasso delighted in using them paradoxically, extracting unexpected meanings out of forms by combining them in new ways. And in this context it is worth noting that it was in his programme notes for the Diaghilev ballet *Parade*, designed by Picasso, that Apollinaire first coined the word 'Surrealism'.[33]

On 9 November 1918, when Picasso heard the news of Apollinaire's death,[34] he produced not a posthumous portrait of Apollinaire, but one of his own last realistic self-portraits.[35] Henceforth, he appears in his own work, mostly symbolically, as the painter, the sculptor, the jester, the bull. In 1918 Picasso was well-established and already regarded by many as the greatest artist of his age. Certainly in this self-portrait, he was not searching for his own identity, for he was one of those fortunate artists who had known from the start of his career exactly who he was. But since his immediate reaction to Apollinaire's death took the form of looking at himself, it is perhaps not too fanciful to suggest that Picasso was also looking back at his years of poverty and struggle, and with this self-portrait paid homage to his friend who for fourteen years, even during a brief period of estrangement, had believed in him, had encouraged and promoted him with unswerving loyalty. It was the greatest tribute that could have been paid to Apollinaire.

Sérusier,
The Talisman, 1888

Derain,
Three Trees, L'Estaque, 1906

2

Fauvism and the School of Chatou:
Post-Impressionism in Crisis

EARLY in October 1888 a young painter staying at the Pension Gloanec in Pont Aven was ushered into the presence of Gauguin, clutching a canvas which he submitted for criticism. The following morning, in the Bois d'Amour, just outside the town, one of the most famous painting lessons in history took place. 'How do you see those trees?' Gauguin asked. 'They are yellow. Then paint them yellow. And that shadow is bluish, so render it with ultramarine. Those red leaves? Use vermilion.'[1]

The direct result of the lesson was not Derain's *Three Trees, L'Estaque*, 1906 (The Art Gallery of Ontario) of the summer of 1906, but Sérusier's *The Talisman*, 1888 (Collection of J. Fr. Denis, France), painted that momentous morning, a work that was to transform the art and lives of his young Nabi colleagues when he showed it to them on his return to Paris, accompanying it as he did with the verbal message from Gauguin of 'the concept, still unknown to us of the painting as a flat surface covered in colours assembled in a certain order'.[2] This concept was to be elaborated by Sérusier's friend and fellow Nabi, Maurice Denis, in his celebrated essay of 1890 which opened with the sentence: 'Remember that a picture before being a battle-horse, a nude woman or some anecdote or other, is essentially a flat surface covered in colours arranged in a certain order'[3] – a formulation which brought him instant fame. The confrontation between these two paintings is deeply revealing for it would suggest that although the literature on Fauvism invariably presents it as the first of the twentieth-century pictorial revolutions, the difference between these two paintings is in fact one of degree and intensity rather than of kind, one of realization rather than of intention.

The school of Chatou comprised two painters, Vlaminck and Derain, and it was born on the suburban railway line that links St Germain-en-Laye with the Gare St Lazare in Paris. It was a journey that in those days took exactly forty-seven minutes; and by one of those gratifying coincidences of history Sérusier and Denis had met on the same line some ten years earlier. On a June morning in 1900 Vlaminck and Derain climbed into the same railway compartment; they already knew each other by sight, but on this occasion Derain had a folio of drawings on his lap and they struck up a conversation. They caught the same train back that evening; it was derailed at La Garenne and they walked back to Chatou, striding from railway-sleeper to railway-sleeper, discussing not only art but their private and secret lives and ambitions.

The following morning they met at the ferry to La Grenouillère, and set up their easels on the island with Derain, so Vlaminck tells us, facing the more conventional view back to Chatou with its bridge and clock-tower, while he turned aside to paint a thicket of poplars.[4] La Grenouillère had already been immortalized by Monet and Renoir in the late 1860s (and it has as fair a claim as any other place to being the birthplace of Impressionism) and the territory covered by Vlaminck and Derain on their subsequent painting expeditions was one very familiar to the Impressionists. Indeed, the local antiquarian and historian of Chatou, M. Maurice Catinat, in a charming book entitled *L'Ecole de Chatou*,[5] has made a case for there being two schools of Chatou, with Monet and Renoir as representatives of the first. Derain once observed that in so far as the term Fauves was apposite, Chatou was their jungle. If so, it was a bosky, willowy jungle. Vlaminck was still finishing his army service at the time of his meeting Derain, but he came out in September 1900, and during the following year the two painters shared a studio in what had been the Restaurant Levaneur, next door to the even more famous Café Fournaise, patronized by, among others, Flaubert and de Maupassant, and the terrace of which had been the setting for Renoir's *Déjeuner des Canotiers* of 1881 (Phillips Memorial Gallery, Washington DC). The prospect had in the meantime altered slightly – between 1873 and 1903 the population of Chatou had doubled – but though threatened it was still pleasant.

The inhabitants of Chatou still talk of the 'bras vif' and the 'bras mort' of the river as it stands divided by the island, and in 1901 Vlaminck, appropriately enough in view of his rumbustious lifestyle and his stormy pronouncements on art, moved to Reuil, on the noisy bank (although Chatou was still his station) while Derain remained in Chatou itself on the quiet side until the autumn of 1906 when he took a studio in Paris. A splendid apocryphal story has it that one day the artists were painting on the banks of the Seine. Derain called across, 'Today I am painting all in blues,' and Vlaminck shouted back, 'And I all in reds'; and there is a sense in which Vlaminck is the red Fauve and Derain the blue. The two men work marvellously well as complementary characters: Vlaminck passionate, emotive, somewhat violent and purely instinctual; Derain much colder, more self-questioning, very much the intellectual.

Vlaminck complained about his time in the army, but he seems nevertheless to have extracted a certain amount of profit from it. He educated himself by reading French nineteenth-century classics – the writers, above all Zola, who were to influence his own style as a writer – and it was also at this time that he began to read Max Stirner and Nietzsche, the thinkers who more than any others fostered his anarchist propensities. He began publishing in the anarchist press, and he tended to see Fauvism very much in terms of anarchy: 'I wanted to revolutionize habits and contemporary life, to liberate nature, to free it from the authority of old theories and classicism which I hated as much as I hated the general or the colonel of my regiment . . . I heightened all my tonal values and transposed into an orchestration of pure colour every single thing I felt. I was a tender barbarian filled with violence.'[6] He had had no real training as an artist, and he always made a great point of the fact that he never went to museums, although he once remarked, more significantly than he realized: 'I lie when I say that "I never go to museums." I lie for the same reasons which make me say I never go to a brothel.'[7] In fact we find the hero of his *Tout Pour Ca* (1903), who bears a strong resemblance to both himself and Derain, visiting the Louvre, and studying Mantegna, Ghirlandaio, Holbein and Rembrandt. At the same time, with the exception of his excursions into the territories of Van Gogh and Cézanne, for the most part he consciously tried to avoid being influenced by other artists; and this was to give his work during the Fauve years its peculiar ebullience and agressiveness, and ultimately to prove a source of tremendous weakness to his art.

The discovery of Van Gogh came early in 1901, when he visited the great Van Gogh retrospective at Bernheim Jeune's. It was on this occasion that the nucleus of the Fauve movement first came together, for it was here that Derain introduced Vlaminck to Matisse. Of the exhibition he said: 'I wanted to cry with joy and despair. On that day I loved Van Gogh more than my father.'[8] The picture known as *L'Homme à la Pipe* or *Le Père Bouju* (Musée

Nationale d'Art Moderne, Paris) is signed and dated 1900, and this date has always been accepted. However, Vlaminck made a point of later buying back the few early works which he had sold, including this one, and these were almost all subsequently redated. This one I would readily accept as a work of 1901: it doesn't look much like Van Gogh, but it looks exactly like the way in which an untutored young artist would look *at* Van Gogh; and the thick impasto and whirling, emotive brush strokes probably reflect the 'joy and despair' experienced on that first encounter. The identity of Père Bouju has to my knowledge never been disclosed, but Vlaminck allowed the painting to be shown as a self-portrait at an exhibition entitled *L'Ecole de Chatou*, organized by the Galerie Bing in 1947, to which he contributed a preface. I suspect it was almost certainly a nickname used during the famous escapades which he and Derain got up to during the early years of their association.

Derain was in turn conscripted in September 1901. We can keep track of his movements and ideas through his letters to Vlaminck, although these are mostly undated and the sequence is at times unclear.[9] Unfortunately, Vlaminck's side of the correspondence has not been preserved, but the one-sided exchange remains one of the most important existing set of documents for an understanding of the intellectual and aesthetic currents informing young painting in the early years of the century. Almost from the start we find Derain writing about his desire to produce a synthetic art (synthesis is a recurrent word), valid for all time, not just the present. He distinguishes between 'feeling' and 'expressing',[10] anticipating Matisse's better-known writings on the subject. Presumably in a vein of slight attack on Vlaminck he insists that expression is not the result of the desire to convey simple sensations, but the synthesis of a sum of experiences and sensations, although he also suggests that greater simplicity of expression is the aim to which a new art must aspire. The painters he mentions most frequently are Van Gogh, with Cézanne coming a close second; and if by common consent of both of the painters of Chatou Van Gogh was the artist who more than any other initiated or provoked their Fauvism, Cézanne was to be the painter who ultimately disrupted it.

For an understanding of Derain's character, most significant, perhaps, is the frequent recurrence of the word 'doubt'. In a letter of 1902 he writes: 'Doubt is everywhere and in everything. Some people, those, with a talent for synthesis, declare themselves openly

Vlaminck, *Landscape with Red Trees*, 1906

for form. But behind it all, doubt subsists.'[11] And what was to characterize his work in the years following his release from the army in September 1904 was precisely a desire for synthesis, which led him to explore in turn a multiplicity of sources, tempered by that all-pervading doubt that led him to reject a particular source or combination of sources the moment he had given them pictorial expression. More than any other artist of his generation in the first six years of the century Derain was to act as an aesthetic barometer and his works as premonitions of events to come. He was to give both Picasso and Matisse a nudge at significant moments in their careers; and if Vlaminck represents most compellingly the extrovert immediacy that was to give Fauve painting its urgency and vitality, Derain's restlessness, his style-searching, his doubt – these qualities were to make him the artist who reflected what Fauvism ultimately was most truly about. He painted many self-portraits but none so revealing as that of 1904 (now in a Los Angeles Private Collection), probably executed immediately after his release from the army, showing him as it does torn between the conflicting influences of Gauguin and Cézanne, and conveying as it does the all-consuming doubt that was to characterize his art until his death in 1954.

Derain produced relatively little while he was in the army, but he painted with Vlaminck on leaves of absence spent in Chatou, mostly landscapes of the district. Many are slight, and it would be dangerous to deduce too much from them; but surviving canvases of the period are extremely hard to see and because of this they are important documents. The Vlamincks are still clumsy and he has difficulty handling the heavy impasto which owes something, at a distance, to Van Gogh. The Derains are defter, although the handling is tentative. In painting, it was Derain who almost invariably took the lead, but in view of the fact that he never refuted Vlaminck's frequent claims to primacy during the early years of their association, perhaps we should ascribe the freedom of handling and the subsequent move into thicker, more physical paint effects to Vlaminck's influence, if not necessarily to his example. Derain, we know from contemporary sources, already had great presence and he was formidable in argument, but the letters make it patently clear that for a period at least, Vlaminck held him in total thrall.

Vlaminck's next move, and this was something with which he struggled for the next twelve months, was an attempt to separate colour from drawing in an attempt to come to terms with the component elements of painting. In Van Gogh, draughtsmanship and colour are often synonymous – or, to put it differently, he draws with the loaded brush; this is something which looks easy and exciting but is in fact extremely hard to achieve, and hence, I think, Vlaminck's repeated false starts. But he was learning fast, and the works which he showed at the Indépendants of 1905 have a brooding, windswept quality which is prophetic of later developments.

Derain meanwhile had turned to Gauguin, and if Van Gogh was undoubtedly the painter who meant most to Vlaminck during the years of Fauvism, Gauguin was to cast an equally potent spell on Derain, off and on, between late 1904 through to the autumn of 1906. Derain appears to have discovered Gauguin immediately on his release from the army (there is no mention of Gauguin in the letters) and he paid what amounts to an overt tribute to him in the Old Tree (Musée d'Art Moderne, Paris), one of his exhibits at the 1905 Indépendants; it is perhaps indicative of his character that he should always have been attracted to the moodier, darker Gauguins, whereas Matisse, for example, preferred the blonder, higher-keyed Tahitian works. And for all the immediate pleasure afforded by

34

Chatou Fauvism, an undercurrent of loneliness and unease in works executed in the vicinity is never far beneath the surface.

Le Pont du Pecq, 1905 (Private Collection) another of Derain's exhibits at the Indépendants, shows him combining the lessons learnt from Gauguin (the organization of the picture surface in curving bands of colour that in Derain's work have become increasingly unnaturalistic) with a more broken stroke that may owe something to Van Gogh and possibly already something to Divisionism, an attempt at the all-desired synthesis that results here in those stylistic inconsistencies – the playing off of flatter colour areas against more broken ones, of thick paint effects against thinner ones, of relatively naturalistic colour against artificial or arbitrary notes – which were to be so fundamental to Fauvism during its first fully developed and mature style. It could be argued that this was the first truly Fauve work.

Matisse remembered making several trips out to Chatou. One of these was almost certainly towards the end of 1904, or early in 1905; it was on this occasion that he persuaded Derain's father to finance Derain's trip to the south the following summer. Afterwards Derain took him round to Vlaminick's. According to Vlaminck he returned the following day and his visits led to Vlaminck's showing for the first time, shortly afterwards, at the Indépendants – Matisse was chairman of the hanging committee.[12] Matisse had a poor head for dates and when talking about his first meeting with Vlaminck, through Derain, at the Van Gogh exhibition of 1901, he went on to say that he visited them at Chatou and wasn't surprised by what he saw because he was working in a similar vein. On the grounds of the visual evidence he was almost certainly telescoping the two events into one, because in 1901 neither of the younger painters (and certainly not Vlaminck) could have shown him anything that could have interested him, whereas by late 1904 their work did have quite a lot in common with his own proto-Fauve experiments of the late 1890s, and in the case of a work like Le Pont du Pecq had actually opened up certain possibilities that he was subsequently to explore.

The Indépendants of 1905 featured a large Van Gogh retrospective, and this would suggest that Derain's Mountains at Collioure (National Gallery of Art, Washington), one of the most Van Goghian of all Derain's works, was also one of the first paintings to be executed in the south when he arrived there with memories of Van Gogh fresh in his mind. In a letter to Vlaminck dated 28 July 1905, after he had been in Collioure some weeks, he claimed to have already learnt two points from the visit:

(1) 'A new concept of light which consists in this: the negation of shadow. Here light is very strong, shadows very faint. Every shadow is a world of clarity and luminosity which contrasts with the sunlight. Both of us have overlooked this, and in future, where composition is concerned it will make for a renewal of expression.' At first glance this goes very little beyond Impressionism, but within the concept of a simplified form of painting there is the implication that not only do shadows contain light but that they can be as colouristically and hence as compositionally dominant. However, in relationship to the Fauvism of Chatou, the statement is of enormous importance, because from the autumn of 1905 through to that of 1906 it was to rely for its effects on the intense light sensations of the south imported to the north and arbitrarily grafted on to the northern countryside with a resultant heightening of colouristic abstraction and artificiality.

(2) 'Have come to know when working near Matisse that I must eradicate anything to do with division of tones. He goes on but I've had my fill . . . it's a logical means to use in a luminous and harmonious picture. But it only injures things which owe their expressiveness to deliberate disharmonies.'[13] And I think that the words 'deliberate disharmonies' are probably more revealing and prophetic than any that Derain had used before. The statement also confirms the fact that with the possible exception of a handful of strongly Van Goghian paintings, Derain's first Collioure paintings were the most purely Divisionist. And here a point that has never been made must be stressed: for the Fauves the Divisionist sketch was more important than the Divisionist painting, for the simple reason that in their paintings the Divisionists were forced to grade their pure colours out or reduce them to paler tints where they meet, while in the sketches, which allow a lot of white ground to come through, each colour mark or area stands much more purely for itself and acts on the colours around it in a much more independent and autonomous fashion.

There follows in Derain's work a reversion to a more banded, colouristically orchestrated sort of painting of the *Pont du Pecq* type, although the new Collioure canvases are more tapestry-like in effect – the result almost certainly of a visit undertaken by Derain and Matisse, in the company of Maillol, to Daniel de Montfried's country estate nearby. Gauguin's South Seas canvases had been seen in fairly large quantities in Paris during the preceding years, but de Montfried's collection was one of the finest; furthermore he was Gauguin's executor, and the Gauguin estate was at this time in his hands. It must have been a particularly moving and thrilling experience for young painters to see so many still virtually unknown works by this mythical master. Certain works by Derain which combine a synthetist or cloisonist structure with touches of Divisionist-derived strokes should logically come between the more purely Divisionist canvases and the more Gauguinesque paintings; but what one can learn from Derain's working methods from the contemporary sketch-book now in the Musée d'Art Moderne in Paris (1903–5) is that the first statements of an individual theme are often the most fully developed and assured, while they tend to tail off in a series of afterthoughts, metaphorical aesthetic question marks which challenge or question the initial theme or else comment on it in terms of earlier idioms.

Derain's entries to the famous Fauve 'cage' at the *Salon d'Automne* showed him working in a variety of styles and consulting a variety of sources wide enough to have preoccupied a young painter over a period of many years, although they had been painted during the space of a few brief months. Vlaminck's exhibits, on the other hand, showed him still faithful to his first great mentor and love, and one of them, *La Maison de Mon Père* (Private Collection), shows him closer to Van Gogh than anything that he had produced before. He now appears to have been looking at Van Gogh's drawings as well as his paintings (he certainly knew those owned by Matisse which had been shown at the retrospective mounted within the *Indépendants* earlier in the year). The design is sketched in dark outlines on a primed but raw canvas support and paint is then applied in rhythmic strokes that resemble in a simplified way the ripples, eddies and whirlpools of Van Gogh's markings. It is revealing to compare details of the Vlaminck with others from paintings by Van Gogh because the comparison demonstrates how much more inconsistent Vlaminck's technique is. The confrontation also makes the point that whereas the surface rhythms evoked by Van Gogh's brush strokes are very insistent, they also have a strong directional thrust backwards and forwards through space, while by contrast Vlaminck's strokes are much more purely two dimensional in emphasis.

Vlaminck's rejection of all theory (and he even hated discussions about painting) would have put Divisionism beyond the pale for him; but he assimilated a certain amount of it indirectly through Derain and Matisse and in the autumn of 1905, when his two friends had returned from Collioure with their summer's work, he produced a group of paintings which made use of a white ground to achieve a separation of colour markings or touches that in *La Maison de Mon Père* had been separated by a drawn black outline, with a resultant heightening of luminosity. Vlaminck was to speak very emotionally of his use of primary colours; in fact he seldom relied on them exclusively for his effects. He once remarked more factually, 'I used only seven colours [in my Fauve painting] almost without intermediaries'[14] – and in these works they can be counted.

Derain is said to have made two visits to London and he was certainly there in March 1906. Dorival, who knew Derain personally, states categorically that he came over for the first time in the autumn of 1905, although he gives no supporting documentary evidence.[15] The most recent American scholarship has suggested that a first visit was made in the spring of 1905 and that the brilliant Divisionist-inspired London works were executed then and are the result of Derain having seen Matisse's major work in that idiom, his famous *Luxe, Calme et Volupté* (Private Collection).[16] But it is hard to believe that Derain could have achieved the colouristic saturation and luminosity, which characterize all the London paintings, without the experience of Collioure behind him. It is possible, too, that the first channel crossing was simply a reconnaissance trip to sound out the terrain and that all the London paintings belong to 1906. We know that Derain came to England on the instigation of Vollard, who wanted a latter-day sequel to Monet's Thames paintings which had been shown with such success at Durand-Ruel's in 1904. Derain spoke of nine paintings done for Vollard; in fact approximately twice that number are known, but we know from his letters that he was working all out, and he had produced a greater number still during his months at Collioure. Derain's paintings of *The Houses of Parliament* punctuate the series. Thus one might suggest tentatively a progression from the first works with references to both Divisionism and Impressionism, through to the softer examples with echoes of Monet and Turner (a letter dated March 1906 mentions a visit to look at the National Gallery Turners), on to works where the technique is more mixed and the colour more arbitrary and personal and which tend to be characterized by exceptionally high viewpoints and by exciting ellisions of lines and forms. But once again, on the evidence of the sketch-book, it would be dangerous to try to construct too logical a sequence. However, what can be said with conviction is that the London series contains works that are the most liberated, the most spontaneous and the most truly enjoyable and hedonistic that Derain ever produced. Working in a new and stimulating environment, free temporarily from the competition of his colleagues in Chatou and Paris and from the ever-constant anxiety about what the next step should be, he achieved a quality of physical and optical exhilaration he was never again to recapture.

The London paintings were understandably enough to affect Vlaminck deeply. Through them he was in turn to be influenced indirectly by other artists whose impact upon his own work, and most particularly that of Gauguin, he would have violently denied. The year 1906 was to be, on the visual evidence of his painting, the happiest and most relaxed of his career. And it was in the spring, summer and early autumn of that year that for a brief spell of approximately four months the two painters of Chatou held together in perfect balance the divergent currents and streams that had been informing Derain's art during the past two years. The spiritual harmony which reigned between them is demonstrated by the canvases painted by the two men during the summer and autumn months of 1906.

This brings us back to the starting point of this essay. Writing on Gauguin's death in 1903 Maurice Denis remarked that the secret of his ascendance over young painters was: 'That he furnished us with one or two ideas, very simple, of a necessary truth, at a moment when we were totally without instruction.'[17] Elsewhere in his obituary he made the point that the Nabis, the representatives of the most avant-garde tendencies in young art in the early 1890s, knew virtually nothing of Impressionism. And I think that deprived of the retinal disciplines of Impressionist procedures to which Gauguin had submitted himself, and of the direct contact with the literary experiments and achievements of the 1880s which had informed his aesthetics – and on which young writers were already turning their backs (and here Moréas is perhaps the classical case in point) – the teachings of Gauguin could indeed be dangerously simplistic. By the middle of the 1890s Bonnard and Vuillard, the most gifted of the

Nabis, who had briefly used Gauguin and oriental art to produce work that was unprecedently simple and straightforwardly decorative in its effects, had reverted to what could perhaps best be described as a latter-day, somewhat conceptualized, indoor Impressionism. Sérusier and Denis were following paths that closely parallel those of the writers of the Catholic revival, those authors who had partaken of and in some instance contributed to the literary innovations of the 1880s, but whose subsequent production belongs to what a literary historian of the period has aptly called 'The Reactionary Revolution'.[18] And in painting the rhythm of the previous decades, whereby artists of a new generation adapted or examined the style of a previous one and almost immediately turned it into something different – this rhythm was broken.

Contemporary critics of the 1880s, baffled by the diversity and novelty of the painting created in its second half, saw it as a confused time; and yet in retrospect the decade looks marvellously rich and diverse, but full of clarity of purpose. In the succeeding decade the heroic figures of the 1880s who survived were undoubtedly consolidating their achievements. But if we isolate the work of the younger generation of painters, after 1892 the 1890s become dappled and shadowy, full of nuance which immediately evades historians when they try to ascribe to the period an optimistic, forward-looking pictorial face.

It seems to me deeply significant that we can learn as much (and indeed, I think, possibly more) about the aesthetic problems and cross-currents of the time by examining the work of the painters who retrenched or who tacitly admitted failure – painters like Emile Bernard, Sérusier and Denis – as we can by looking at the works of their more gifted colleagues. Matisse, we have to keep reminding ourselves, was the same age as the Nabis, but he had chosen to serve an exceptionally long apprenticeship, while Bonnard, the most deeply talented of the Nabis, when he emerges as a truly great artist in the first decade of the twentieth century, but above all in the 1920s and 1930s, had become in a sense historically displaced, a rare example of a major artist who tells us little of the times in which he lived. It is significant that in the closing years of the century the artist working in Paris who was extracting the most compelling visual conclusions from Gauguin's Post-Impressionism and from the symbolist aesthetic which had helped to provoke it was Scandinavian and a bird of passage. I refer to Edvard Munch.

It was probably towards the mid-1890s, when they were closest, that Pissarro said to Sérusier: 'We have been the destroyers. It is now the turn for the builders to come forward'[19] – a statement which poignantly underlines the dilemma facing the Nabis. They were intelligent and sensitive enough to see and understand that the great pioneers of the previous generation had to a certain extent cleared away the burden of the Renaissance tradition, and that a new painting was necessary and possible. But the 'too great liberty'[20] of which Sérusier spoke with fear, and the responsibility it implied, placed an intolerable burden on a group of young artists in their early twenties, deprived by circumstances of the personal support and encouragement of their artistic fathers and mentors. It is possible, as Denis implied, that if Gauguin had remained in France the situation might have been different. The premature deaths of Van Gogh and Seurat, and the fact that Neo-Impressionism failed to produce an artist of true genius, must obviously be taken into account. The Nabis paid lip-service to Cézanne, but he was becoming increasingly inaccessible, both personally and because of the ever-increasing complexity of his style, while his example had to a certain extent been falsified to them since they tended to look at him through Gauguin's eyes. As a subsidiary consideration we must remember that for the first time in many decades the primacy of Paris had been challenged by Brussels; and there are good grounds for supposing that in the 1890s it meant more to young painters to show in Brussels with Les Vingt and after 1893 with La Libre Esthétique, rather than in the constricted quarters of Le Barc de Boutteville or in the ever-widening chaos of the *Indépendants*. Perhaps this is one of the reasons why, when we think visually of the 1890s, we so often associate them with the decorative and applied arts on which the Belgians placed such emphasis rather than with mainline painting.

I believe that Fauvism shows a renewed apprehension of the fact that the work of the Post-Impressionists held the key to something completely new; and by focusing on individual elements in Post-Impressionist painting, however briefly, the Fauves were clearing the way for a reinvention of the vocabulary of art. But in the case of the painters of Chatou at least, they were still not entirely certain where the discoveries of Post-Impressionism might lead; and the precariousness of the balance in which they held a multiplicity of sources during the brief months of their fully mature Fauve style is demonstrated by the rapidity with which that balance was so conclusively destroyed. To this extent the Fauvism of Chatou can best be regarded as a final, marvellously youthful and vivid flowering of Post-Impressionist painting.

The Fauvism of Matisse was something different and ultimately something more completely personal and individual. Despite the fact that he was the movement's leader and undeniably its greatest artist, he was not the archetypal Fauve. If we want to catch the movement's urgency, its buoyancy and its impetuosity, it is to the work of Vlaminck and to Derain's Collioure and London periods that we must turn, while the movement's restlessness, uncertainty and intellectual doubts are most clearly mirrored in Derain's Fauve period seen as a whole.

It is quite obvious that any revolution effected by Fauvism was primarily colouristic. The statements made by the painters themselves on the subject are contradictory and confused; but all seem to have agreed that colour was to produce an immediate sensation of light that was to emanate directly and artificially forwards from the surface of the canvas, rather than to create an illusion or substitute for the changing effects of light observed in nature. This was something already implicit in Gauguin's painting lesson and it was achieved to a certain extent by himself, by Van Gogh and by the Neo-Impressionists and even in the late manners of some of the Impressionists themselves. But with Fauvism colour had reached a new degree of intensity and autonomy – there is a sense in which Fauvism marks the beginning of the advance of the picture towards the spectator, and to this extent at least it belongs very exclusively to the twentieth century.

But the fact that for the painters of Chatou the dilemma or the crisis of the late 1880s and the early 1890s still persisted in a very real form is underlined most vividly by comparing letters written by Sérusier and Derain to their respective friends Denis and Vlaminck. Writing in 1889 from Pont Aven Sérusier says: 'I find myself all at sea. What worries me above all is this: What part ought nature to play in a work of art? . . . Should one work from nature or only look at it and work from memory? Too much liberty frightens me, poor copyist that I am . . . yet nature seems to me poor and banal.'[21] Writing from L'Estaque in 1906 Derain says: 'I see no future except in composition, because working from nature I am the slave of things so stupid that my (deeper) feelings are shattered by them. I can't see what the future should be in order to conform to our tendencies; on one side we strive to disengage ourselves from objective things, and on the other hand we cling to them as both means and end.'[22] There is a subtle difference of emphasis. In Derain the dichotomy between two methods of work is more clearly seen and stated. Behind this statement there is furthermore the implication that heightened or transposed colour sensations are not enough. He seems to have realized that if colour had reached a new degree of autonomy within the general move towards a more conceptualized form of art and given to painting a new and luminous skin, its bones and sinews were still to be examined. And once again, in the summer of 1906, Derain is acting as a sounding-board of things to come.

So far little has been said about Cézanne's role in the evolution of Fauvism. Cézanne had been an early enthusiasm of Derain's; his influence had made itself felt when Derain resumed painting seriously after his release from the army, and one senses Cézanne's presence behind Derain's Fauvism from time to time during the next two years; indeed, there are echoes of Cézanne even in one of Derain's most strongly Gauguinesque works, in the hints or suggestions of a new planar spatial structure underlying and informing the more insistent surface arabesques. But it is in the months between the great Gauguin retrospective held at the *Salon d'Automne* in 1906 and Cézanne's own held at the same *Salon* the following year that the example of Cézanne becomes paramount for young painting. In certain respects it is made more dramatically manifest in the art of Vlaminck, who was resistant to outside influences, than in that of Derain, who, as we have seen, was if anything too receptive to every fresh aesthetic current that blew his way.

The influence of Cézanne on Vlaminck is sensed first in a general way in his works of late 1906 and early 1907, in which the ultramarines of Cézanne's last and most emotive manner predominate. Vlaminck is still marrying only certain superficial aspects of Cézanne to his previous work, so that the result is still fully Fauve in feeling. But with the great Cézanne display of the autumn all references to other artists were temporarily banished from his work; and it is now, at this moment, that Cézanne succeeded posthumously in convincing a large number of significant young artists of what he had so firmly believed in life: that the art of Gauguin was shallow and pernicious. And in a strange but very real way between

1906 and 1907 one does sense a posthumous clash or battle between these two gigantic artistic personalities.

Vlaminck's works of late 1907 show an intelligent way of looking at Cézanne. He seems to have realized that the rhythmic, parallel hatchings of Cézanne served to evoke naturalistic space and simultaneously to organize the surface of the canvas in terms of short thrusts and counter thrusts in and out of a more limited, very tactile and palpable pictorial depth. But it is characteristic of Vlaminck that he should have felt he could swallow Cézanne whole, in a way in which he had to a certain extent devoured Van Gogh, albeit after a prolonged period of gestation and at the sacrifice of much of the latter's subtlety and emotional depth. Cézanne was a painter of such infinite complexity that artists could look at him in an astonishing variety of ways, and get a series of totally different answers to the questions they put to him. Of all twentieth-century artists, possibly Matisse examined more different facets of Cézanne's art than any other, but he examined them one at a time and over a period of many years. The Cubists, on the other hand, tended each one to focus on a different aspect of his work, and in a sense it was by pooling the different results they obtained that they succeeded in producing an art that was totally new and different in kind from what had gone before. By attempting to come to grips with the multi-layered formal complexity of Cézanne's art in a single assault, Vlaminck had simply bitten off more than he could chew; and it could be argued that if Van Gogh invented him as an artist, Cézanne in certain respects was ultimately to destroy him (and hence, perhaps, his latter-day hatred and animosity towards the master of Aix), although between 1907 and 1909 Vlaminck produced some of his finest and to me most deeply moving canvases, precisely, I think, because Cézanne had forced on him, temporarily at least, an intuitive recognition of the indefinability and magnitude of great art. Discussing Cubism, Vlaminck said: 'Negro sculpture and the first tentative beginnings of the theory of reconstructing light (noticeable in the last canvases of Cézanne) were now united to meet the requirement of a new formula.'[23] This reference to Cézanne's light is in a sense odd because this is the aspect of Cézanne's art on which Vlaminck immediately turns his back. Light in Cézanne is the result of the orchestration of a personal but relatively full palette, deployed so skilfully that often quite heavily impasted hatchings of one colour blend into those of another with those effects of transparency so dear to the Cubists. Vlaminck on the other hand, while aiming at Cézanne's methods of planar construction, reverted quite simply to traditional landscape chiaroscuro, and, at a single throw of the dice, the colouristic ground he had won during the previous years was lost.

In Vlaminck's works of 1908 there is still a powerful feeling of light, but it is now that the Flemish and Lowlands heritage of which Vlaminck was so proud comes to the fore, and it is the light of the stormier Ruisdaels and of Van Coninxloo. Of his defection from Fauvism he later said: 'Working directly in this way, tube against canvas, one quickly arrives at an excessive facility. One ends in transposing mathematically. The emerald green becomes black, the pink flaming red etc. Winning numbers come up at every draw and immediate success becomes an impasse. Preoccupied with light I neglected the object ... either you think nature or you think light.'[24]

The history of Vlaminck's art during the following years was to be the abandonment of a search for style in favour of the cultivation of a manner. Shortly before his death in 1958 he remarked with pride that there was a Vlaminck manner in landscape painting just as there was a Corot manner or a Courbet manner.[25] But a manner is the unconscious result of a lifetime or at least of many years of labour – it is not something that can be willed into existence. I believe that in the years succeeding 1910–12 and his brief flirtation with Cubism, Vlaminck had become frightened of looking at other art. A failure of nerve resulted in a sense of guilt; and it is in this light that his remarks about visiting museums in the same spirit that he visited brothels take on a deeper and more damning significance.

The case of Derain is more complex and more interesting. He was one of the first artists to attempt to draw simplified conclusions from Cézanne's complex procedures of pictorial construction; this is apparent in some of his earliest extant landscapes at the turn of the century and is very obvious in the landscapes of 1908 when it still looked to many of his contemporaries as if he could have produced a viable alternative to the more experimental views of L'Estaque and La Rue des Bois produced by Braque and Picasso in the same year. This essay has limited itself to landscape because Chatou Fauvism was essentially a landscape style; but in his figure pieces of late 1906 Derain had looked at Cézanne in a deeply original way, and a single one of these would have earned him a significant position in the history of post-Fauve painting. In subsequent years he was prepared to explore the possibilities of a Cubist multiple viewpoint perspective, implicit in Cézanne's art, provided that it did not involve the shattering of the object and above all of the human body. This is something that is psychologically extremely hard to achieve, and Derain's inability or refusal to do so throws into relief the magnitude of the Cubist achievement.

In 1907, that epoch-making year, we find him writing to Vlaminck, not without a touch of nostalgia: 'The prospect of Chatou tempts me not at all.'[26] With his customary intelligence he seems to have realized that a chapter in the history of art was over. One of the defects of contemporary art-historical method (and this is particularly true of art history in the modern period) is that we tend to see history too exclusively in terms of successful revolution and sustained innovation. We stand to learn a lot about the nature of twentieth-century art by trying to understand sympathetically why one of the most naturally gifted artists of his age felt compelled to leave the field of battle.

3

Two New Views of Matisse: a Book and an Exhibition

VIRTUALLY all Matisse's important early patrons and collectors were foreigners: Americans, Russians, Scandinavians, Germans. It was not until 1922, when Matisse was in his fifties, that the French government purchased a work for the Musée du Luxembourg, choosing the somewhat conventional *Odalisque with Red Trousers*. But Matisse had still not had the critical attention he deserved. Apollinaire, who had done so much to keep Matisse's name before the public in the years before 1914, was dead. Breton, who was about to succeed Apollinaire as the most effective artistic impresario in France, had as a youth admired Matisse's work but was now coming to regard it with suspicion.[1] Reviewing a Matisse exhibition in 1919 Cocteau spoke of 'le fauve ensoleillé devenu un petit chat de Bonnard'.[2]

Matisse's popular reputation grew steadily throughout the 1920s, but Derain, his closest collaborator during the heroic years of Fauvism, and fourteen years his junior, was held in greater esteem by influential critics such as André Salmon and Roger Allard; the former saw Derain as the greatest French artist of his generation. In the early 1930s Ozenfant was writing of Matisse's art as 'a prolongation of the superficial painting of the Eighteenth Century'.[3] Most of the best writing on Matisse – and for that matter on French nineteenth- and twentieth-century art in general – has been in English. Roger Fry's short monograph of 1935 was the first attempt to demonstrate analytically why Matisse's achievement as a painter was unique.[4] And Matisse literature today is still indebted to Alfred Barr's *Matisse, his Art and his Public*, first published in 1951, which remains in many respects still the most satisfactory monograph on any major twentieth-century artist.

In 1984 Pierre Schneider, a French scholar who has dedicated much of his life to a study of Matisse's art, produced his own *Matisse*, the only book – if we leave aside Louis Aragon's imposing but somewhat idiosyncratic two-volume collection of essays of 1971 entitled *Henri Matisse, Roman* – to rival Barr's in importance.[5] The two books complement each other well, for while Barr's approach was detached and objective, Schneider produced a work that is, in the best Baudelairean tradition, 'partial, passionné, politique'. 'My work consists of steeping myself in things. And afterwards, it all comes out,' Matisse said to Père Couturier in 1949, and this is the approach that Schneider, after an immersion of fourteen years, adopted towards Matisse himself.

The result was large-scale in every way. Schneider had the cooperation of Marguerite Duthuit, Matisse's daughter and the principal guardian of his archives and reputation, and the book's 752 pages are packed with new information. Its ambitions match its length, for Schneider believes he has discovered the keys to a true understanding of Matisse's art. He is aware of the subtlety of Matisse's mind and of the complexities of the procedures that underlie the often seemingly effortless paintings and drawings. Again and again he stresses the duality of Matisse's art, the constant pull between the subjective and the objective, the fact that the work is so deeply rooted in the observation of things and yet so often highly abstract: that it is so sensuous and physical and yet so frequently ethereal and contemplative. But Schneider's own arguments, while they are embedded in truly impressive learning and scholarship, are basically simple. They are repeated with an urgency and enthusiasm that can be exhausting and irritating but that also give the book great momentum.

Schneider sees Matisse as standing simultaneously at the end of and apart from a tradition of Western art initiated by Giotto. Matisse detaches himself from this tradition primarily through his interest in, and ultimate identification with, the art of Islam and of 'all the Orients', and because in his *La Joie de Vivre*, 1905–6 (The Barnes Foundation, Merion) (also known as *Le Bonheur de Vivre*) his art became centred on the theme of the Golden Age, which put him in touch with the beginnings of things and with certain primal sources and principles of inspiration and creation. Linking these two cardinal aspects of Matisse's art, in Schneider's scheme of things, is the fact that around 1905 he became a religious artist or, at the very least, that his art has a religious quality to it and is best seen in a religious setting.

This view Schneider puts forward in his introduction and most specifically in his discussion of *The Conversation*, 1908–12 (The

Matisse, *The Conversation*, 1908–12

Hermitage Museum, St Petersburg), a pivotal work that is hard to date with precision but which had reached completion in 1913. It shows Matisse in his pyjamas confronting Madame Matisse in front of an open window of their suburban house at Issy. The theme is developed in the chapter 'The revelation of the Orient', where, for reasons that I cannot altogether understand, Schneider equates decorative art with the sacred: 'All true decorative art requires the presence of the sacred in the background: under different guises the sacred constitutes its unique meaning.' Further on in the book Schneider talks of Matisse as 'dreaming of a decorative – in other words religious – art'. Certainly much of the decorative quality of Islamic art is related to religious concepts, and Matisse was undoubtedly aware of this. Yet it is difficult to follow Schneider when he says of Matisse that, 'Religious faith was no more a part of his nature than instinct, but since the inner logic of his painting required it he became a religious painter.' Is he simply saying that Matisse put himself at the service of his art? In one of the central chapters of the book Schneider writes:

Matisse, *Le Bonheur de Vivre*, 1905–6

In elaborating a decorative style appropriate for images linked with mythical or religious themes, Matisse was after all conforming with what appears to be a basic rule in art history: abstract styles are characteristic of essentially religious artistic forms and themes, while realist styles are typical of periods of waning faith marked by secular themes and preoccupations.

Maybe it is a question of how you like your religion and your art.

It is in his discussion of *La Joie de Vivre* that Schneider comes closest, perhaps, to telling us in what way he sees Matisse's art as being religious. '*La Joie de Vivre*,' he writes, 'seeks to be the complete representation of the Golden Age, a sacred history of the origins, that is to say of happiness . . .' Matisse's religion is, then, one of happiness. This is much easier to accept, although Schneider's list of writers whose careers overlapped with Matisse's and who worshipped at that altar has about it, for someone trying to approach Matisse's art in this light, a somewhat uncomfortable ring: Nietzsche (not much room for the decorative there, one might have thought), Gide (whose desiccated attitude to pleasure has little in common with the genuine hedonism of Matisse's art), and Whitman (surely a strange companion for someone who was the archetype of the artist as an anti-Bohemian).

But it is true that as Matisse's aesthetic concerns evolved they seemed more and more to focus on pleasure, relaxation, idleness and luxury. In the celebrated *Notes of a Painter* of 1908 Matisse had spoken, in connection with his figure work, about his 'almost religous awe towards life'; approximately ninety-nine per cent of his figure pieces were of attractive young women, and this would seem to give credence to Schneider's view. Matisse's most forthright pronouncement on his religious beliefs came in his text to *Jazz*, written in 1946, when he asked the rhetorical question, 'Do I believe in God?' to which came back the answer, 'Yes, when I am at work.' From this it might be assumed that, like many other great artists, he recognized that his talent was something greater than himself.

In 1951, three years before his death, discussing his work in the Chapel of the Rosary at Vence, which had just been consecrated, Matisse said, 'All art worthy of the name is religious. Be it a creation of lines and colours if it is not religious it doesn't exist.' Interestingly enough it is in connection with the chapel that Schneider's attempts to divorce Matisse from post-medieval Christian or Judaic traditions of religious art seem most effective. There is more than a touch of the mosque about the chapel; of its tile panels, the Stations of the Cross gave Matisse the most trouble and they are the least successful aspect of the complex because in Matisse's art there was no room for guilt or for drama or for pain. Perhaps on the question of religion Schneider's simple statement in his introduction that 'for Matisse working means art and art is the sacred' comes closest to telling us the truth.

Each chapter of Schneider's book is devoted to a particular theme or aspect of Matisse's art, and this enables the author to range back and forth in time so that one is made aware, as never before, of the continuity and totality of Matisse's art; that every chapter can be read as an independent essay is an advantage in a book of this length, although it also inevitably leads to much repetition. Schneider, however, has also attempted to structure the book chronologically. He possibly distorts the true picture of Matisse's development by placing the section on 'The revelation of the Orient' before the one entitled 'Only by colour', which deals with Matisse's Fauvism and his emergence as a fully mature and independent artist. Matisse several times stressed the importance for him of his visit to Munich in 1910 to see the enormous Islamic exhibition, and it is surely after this that Islamic art became such an inspiration to him. He was almost certainly aware of Islamic art before this. Its influence is visible in some of the details of *La Joie de Vivre*, and it may well have encouraged him to clarify and heighten his palette. But in my view it did not play the all-important part in the colouristic revolution effected by Matisse in his Fauve canvases of 1905 and 1906 that Schneider would have us believe it did when he writes, 'Colour was the revelation of the Orient.'

Fauve pictures, and Matisse's in particular, achieved a new autonomy for colour, and they mark the beginning of the advance of the picture toward the spectator which has been a characteristic of so much twentieth-century art. Matisse had studied Redon's pastels, works of exceptional colouristic intensity, and one of his unique achievements was to attain the cloudlike and evanescent effects of this medium – the only one that incorporates no binding agent – in his oils. 'Divisionism' – Signac's name for the attempt to give Impressionism a more scientific bias and an even greater luminosity – and in particular the Divisionist sketch, initiated him into the discipline of the possibilities of using pure, prismatic colours. But it was Gauguin who was the final catalyst in liberating Matisse's colour, even though Matisse didn't always care for Gauguin's use of it. Schneider refers to Gauguin as frequently as he does to Matisse's revered Cézanne, and he is acutely aware of Gauguin's historical role. But he is bothered by him in relation to Matisse, and this is understandable because he has identified so completely with Matisse, and Matisse's own feelings towards Gauguin were so ambivalent.

So were those of a very large proportion of young artists who had come under Gauguin's sway. Cézanne ('Ce bon dieu de la peinture', as Matisse used to call him) was much easier to accept as a father figure because he was more sympathetic as a personality, and because his art seemed to open endless new paths of discovery in a way that Gauguin's did not. Schneider is absolutely right in stressing that Matisse distrusted Gauguin's art in many ways. Matisse seems to have found it too literary, too programmatic and *voulu* in its outlook. One senses that he was made uneasy by its underlying melancholy. Like most artists deeply influenced by their immediate predecessors he inevitably became interested in their personalities, and that of Gauguin he possibly felt too ruthless, too cold.

It may even be that Matisse sensed in Gauguin an aspect of himself that he was unconsciously anxious to conceal or disavow. I wonder if Matisse may even have been aware of that atmosphere of slight emotional chill which I for one sense beneath the surface splendours of *Luxe, Calme et Volupté* (1904), and even of *La Joie de Vivre*, the two works in which Schneider feels that Matisse sought and then found himself. 'La base de travail de Gauguin et celle de mon travail ne sont pas les mêmes,' Matisse said curtly in 1949. But in 1924 he had remarked to his friend, the painter Hans Purrmann, 'Only Gauguin could extricate me from Divisionism.' In 1950 he admitted that Gauguin was 'sur ma route'. And in one of his longest and most thoughtful reflections on colour, published in 1945, he said, 'From Delacroix and Van Gogh and principally through Gauguin . . . one can follow the rehabilitation of colour, and the restitution of its emotive powers.'

It was Matisse more than any other artist who saw through to its ultimate conclusion the greatest lesson that Gauguin had to teach – a lesson from which the Nabis and Matisse's fellow Fauves profited and subsequently retreated: that it was possible to be a decorative artist while remaining within the avant-garde; or, to put it more strongly and perhaps more appositely, that it was possible to be a decorative painter and simultaneously a high artist, even a revolutionary one. In this sense it was Gauguin who prepared Matisse for the revelation of the Orient which Schneider so rightly stresses and of which he writes with such eloquence.

Toward the end of his life Matisse said: 'From *La Joie de Vivre* – I was thirty-five then – to this cutout – I am eighty-two – I have not changed.' Schneider, having demonstrated that the true subject of the picture is the Golden Age, devotes much time and space to bringing in the greater part of Matisse's subsequent output under the same iconographic umbrella. Although there is, as far as I know, no proof that while Matisse was at work on the painting he was reading Longus and the other classical writers to whom Schneider refers, he would undoubtedly have been aware of them. With his move into a fully developed Fauve idiom Matisse had achieved what he came to think of as 'the return to the purity of means', which he defined in turn as 'the assertion of expression through colour'.

It is attractive to think that Matisse wished to apply these newly purified means to the depiction of a myth of man's beginnings. But if *La Joie de Vivre* is a revolutionary work it also kept alive a tradition of art that goes back to the Renaissance bacchanals of Bellini and Titian and in turn to the classical world. And if it marks a turning point in Matisse's art, despite its colouristic originality it is also an eclectic work. There are as many things that are un-Fauve about the painting as there are elements that speak for Fauvism as an ongoing, coherent style. Poussin, Agostino Carracci, Ingres and Puvis all seem as important to an understanding of it as do Cézanne, Van Gogh, Gauguin and the Neo-Impressionists.

Schneider's hypothesis is that although Matisse never again tackled the theme of the Golden Age so overtly or in its entirety – and perhaps the new purity of exclusively pictorial means was not after all suitable to a theme so deeply embedded in literature – it nevertheless is the key to an understanding of most of his subject matter and aesthetic. On the whole Schneider is remarkably persuasive and he undoubtedly provides new insights, although occasionally the reader may feel he pushes things too far (women, sleep, oranges and goldfish, for example, are among the Golden Age's attributes and can act as symbols for it).

Quite obviously many of the works that immediately succeed the pivotal painting are derived from components of its imagery. *La Danse* and *La Musique* of 1910 (The Hermitage Museum, St Petersburg), favourites of Schneider's, in fact owe stylistically most to the 1908 *Bathers with a Turtle* (St Louis Art Museum); and about this work Schneider is strangely reticent, possibly because it has an air of psychological tension that does not accord with the picture of Matisse's development that he means to paint. In the four great interiors of 1911 the theme of the Golden Age becomes more veiled, but it is now that the paradise of the Koran and that of our Western beginnings start to inform each other. Schneider is right in saying that *The Painter's Family* (The Hermitage Museum, St Petersburg) is among the most Islamic of all Matisse's canvases, and the other three are all in their different ways colouristic masterpieces that unquestionably have about them a euphoric and paradisiac air.

Schneider is particularly good on the first Nice period (1919–28). It helps to explain the charm and fascination of these paintings of young models dressed up in their party clothes, or as odalisques, and placed in over-decorated interiors if we view them as bourgeois

Matisse, *Bathers by a River*, 1909–16

metaphors for an Islamic Garden of Delights. The concept behind
the chapel at Vence is undoubtedly as much Utopian as religious,
and Matisse once remarked that he would like the nuns while they
were in it to feel that they were already inhabitants of the New
Jerusalem. The last great *papiers découpés*, moreover, are well
viewed as a final, spiritualized journey to Baudelaire's world of *luxe,
calme et volupté*.

It is the work executed by Matisse between late 1913 and 1917,
from *Portrait of Madame Matisse* (The Hermitage Museum, St
Petersburg) to the great Chicago *Bathers by a River*, 1909–16 (The
Art Institute of Chicago) – a period that includes the sombre,
magisterial canvases so superbly represented in the collections of
the Museum of Modern Art in New York – that can least well be
viewed under the light of the Golden Age, as Schneider recognizes.

The masterpieces executed during the First World War, on the
other hand, show Matisse at his most self-consciously modernistic.

55

Because of his complete fealty to Matisse, Schneider seems reluctant to acknowledge the extent of Matisse's reaction to the work of Picasso and other younger rivals and colleagues in French art. The *Bathers with a Turtle*, for a start, might with some justification be regarded as Matisse's answer to the pictorial bombshell that Picasso had dropped the previous year with *Les Demoiselles d'Avignon*.

I myself have never pressed Matisse 'summarily into the Cubist ranks', as Schneider claims. I have always seen him as a figure apart, both because of the magnitude of his gifts and because of their nature. But I would certainly contend that the impact of Cubism on Matisse was greater than Schneider would acknowledge. And one of the things that gives the totality of Matisse's art such resonance and depth is that having learned all he could from his immediate predecessors and mentors, from Courbet and Manet onward, he was then prepared to consult a style toward which he had originally felt alien and antagonistic, but which he eventually recognized as having something to offer the development of his own.

Matisse spoke of reworking his large *Still Life after de Heem* of 1915–16 (Museum of Modern Art, New York), the most Cubist of his pictures, 'according to modern methods of construction'. Many other of the greatest canvases of the period bear witness to Matisse's awareness of Cubist compositional procedures, although he put them to ends that were unmistakably his own. His use of large, upright, interacting but independent or self-contained compositional elements gave his work a new structural majesty. And the new compositional procedures also sharpened and clarified one of his supreme gifts as a painter: his ability to use pure unmodulated colour, frequently at maximum intensity or hue, in such a way that it defines the architectural breakdown of the picture plane, adhering to its two-dimensionality, while simultaneously playing its part in a naturalistic rendition of space.

In his introduction Schneider disclaims any attempt at writing a definitive book on Matisse. This is because he has preferred to put his unique knowledge of Matisse's life and output at the service of a view (one is tempted to say a vision) of the art which he believes to be the true one and which he is anxious to share with others. Given the fact that this is in a sense an 'official' book, in that the author was lent much support by the family, it might have been ponderous and cautious, and it is certainly neither. It is noteworthy, too, that while his book has an abundance of new material, Schneider never makes use of it gratuitously but always to enlarge our knowledge of aspects of Matisse's development, or to reinforce particular arguments. An astonishingly high proportion of works illustrated have never been reproduced before; not all of them show Matisse at his best, but their very unevenness helps to bring him to life as an artist. The drawings, often the most personal and revealing aspect of his talent, are scattered throughout the text. The book is full of splendid anecdotes. My favourite concerns the final stages of the chapel. Matisse had thanked the Mother Superior for allowing him to design it. When she understandably expressed surprise he insisted, 'I am doing it for myself.' Soeur Jacques-Marie, who had been Matisse's nurse and whom he loved, was also present and she exclaimed, 'But you told me you were doing it for God.' 'Yes,' said Matisse, 'but I am God.'

The display of Matisse's work during the last months of 1992 at the Museum of Modern Art, New York consisted of more than four hundred works and was not only the largest but also the greatest Matisse exhibition ever to have been mounted. Its like will not be seen again.

The exhibition held at the Grand Palais in 1970 in a sense acted as a prelude to the revelations in New York: it united for the first time many American Matisses with other masterpieces which had hitherto not been let out of Russia – although, oddly enough, France itself could not then compete with these two countries in terms of its own Matisse holdings. This situation has now to a large extent been rectified; and to take a single example, the second *Portrait of Auguste Pellerin* of 1917, arguably the greatest portrait to have been produced in this century and now in the Centre Pompidou, was one of the dominating features in the New York exhibition. The Matisses from the Barnes Collection are still held jealously under lock and key, although some of them were seen at the National Gallery in Washington in 1993 as part of a selection of works that were subsequently sent off on a fund-raising tour. The full-scale try-out for the Barnes mural *La Danse*, discovered only in 1992 in Matisse's old home at the Hotel Régina in Nice, was juxtaposed in Washington with the version eventually installed at the Foundation in Merion, Pennsylvania in 1933 (and to my knowledge never since dismantled) and the slightly earlier variant from the Musée de la Ville de Paris. (*La Danse I* and *II* will thus have to be renumbered, while to add to the confusion the version now in Paris was retouched substantially after Matisse returned to France from Merion in 1933.)

Apart from the absence of the Barnes pictures, and in particular *La Joie de Vivre* of 1905–6, New York found itself deprived at the last moment of two major works from Russia that were on view in Paris in 1970: *L'Atelier Rose* of 1911 (Pushkin Museum of Fine Art, Moscow) and more important still *La Musique* of 1910 (The Hermitage Museum, St Petersburg). This latter canvas was much revised while in progress and hence has a more fragile surface than its companion piece of the same year, the original *La Danse*. Despite the absence of these works the effect of the New York exhibition was quite literally stunning. And whereas the impact of the 1970 exhibition at the Grand Palais was blunted by eccentric and insensitive hanging, at MOMA the works were placed not in the usual temporary exhibition spaces but on the two main floors which normally house the Museum's permanent collections; and they were notably well and imaginatively arranged. The director of the exhibition was John Elderfield, and everywhere his years of immersion in Matisse's art and his love for it were unobtrusively in evidence.

The sculptures and drawings were interspersed between the paintings to particularly telling ends. The four enormous bas-relief versions of *The Back*, for example, were shown separately: the first of 1908–9 was placed next to the *Bathers with a Turtle* of early 1908, and its powerful, almost disturbing muscularity helped to explain how, as Matisse's figures came increasingly to resemble painted cut-outs, their contours simultaneously endow them with such a sense of physicality and bulk. The second *Back* of 1913, simplified and angular, rightly helped to introduce the most abstracted and experimental of all Matisse's canvases, while that of 1916, the most splayed out and monumental, informs the hieratic figures in *Bathers by a River*. *Back IV* (c. 1931), the most architectural and reductive, in a sense stood in for the *Danse* murals. The heavy brush-and-ink drawings of the 1940s which Matisse saw as surrogate paintings were placed among the canvases of the period rather than beside them and so on.

Whereas recent exhibitions and monographs have tended to focus on and to illuminate the works of Matisse's middle and late years, this exhibition raised questions about the early ones. Matisse was not the slow beginner he is often seen to be, although one does have the sensation of a young artist deliberately holding himself in check. The Dutch influences, patently obvious in the first still lifes and openly acknowledged in *La Desserte after de Heem* of 1893 (Musée Matisse, Nice-Cimiez), seem to persist through to the blonder works executed five to six years later; and it is almost as if Matisse were using the protection of earlier art, and in particular that of Chardin, to keep the more contemporary sources that were pressing in on him at bay. *La Desserte* of 1896–7 with which he made his mark at the Salon de la Société Nationale in 1897 is a work that acknowledges various aspects of Impressionism but also rejects much of what it stood for. Many of these very early works are marred by spatially awkward passages (these often occur in the lower corners); but the tonal values are astonishingly subtle and well-handled from the start.

The liberation of colour that informs the works executed in Corsica in 1898 with such startling if not always totally enjoyable results may possibly be explained in part at least by the fact that Matisse originally learnt about Neo-Impressionism through reading Signac's *D'Eugène Delacroix au Néo-Impressionisme*, serialised in *La Revue Blanche* that year; when he forced himself to confront canvases by the creators of the movement some six years later, again there is a feeling of both liberation and constraint – he did not like other painters coming up too close. The still lifes painted in Toulouse and Paris in 1889 are, on the other hand, totally original and they hint for the first time at his future stature. There was no 'dark period' at the turn of the century as so many of us were taught to believe, although the influence of Cézanne which makes itself overtly felt at this time did invoke a harsher, more sculptural response. Matisse once remarked that although Poussin informed Cézanne's art at the right distance, Courbet stood too near to him; and, in the same way, of his many mentors only Cézanne seems to have been allowed to look directly over Matisse's shoulder.

In view of Matisse's later assertion that 'if Fauvism is not everything . . . it is the beginning of everything',[6] it is perhaps surprising that the Fauve room in the New York exhibition should have been possibly the most restless and disjunctive. This has much to do with the nature of the movement itself; but, although Matisse was its undisputed leader, and despite the fact that he was prepared to learn from younger colleagues, again one senses that he was unhappy at being associated with any particular movement. John

Elderfield is surely right in saying that Fauvism is still misunderstood because it is too often seen only in the light of a single year, 1905, when it burst upon the public and when its stylistic eclecticism and disruptiveness seemed in themselves to constitute a new stylistic language. But if the movement subsequently burst its seams, so to speak, it was Matisse who undermined its coherence; and the works of 1906 and 1907 in this exhibition already seemed to breathe a freer air.

This brings us to a partial understanding of why Matisse is such an extremely hard artist to discuss, and, despite the constant visual delight and stimulus he affords, even at times to look at. He was incapable of producing a picture without seeing its counterpart or at least a variant of it printed on his internal retina. This is already apparent in two Brittany seascapes of 1896 (cat. nos. 10 and 11);[7] one is impacted, silvery and cold, the other expansive, pearly and rosy. The four views from Matisse's studio on the Quai Saint-Michel painted between 1900 and 1902 (nos. 39–42)[7] make a unified series; but this unity is the result of complementaries reinforcing each other rather than of the pictures flowing into each other or resembling each other. The precariousness of the balance in which Fauvism held its sources must have been unsettling to a man of Matisse's temperament and he set out to remedy the dilemma in *La Joie de Vivre* where the range of his sources was if anything wider than hitherto; but because they came from so many different ages and cultures they jostled him less and enabled him to find his own ideal and harmony. Simultaneously, and this is particularly obvious, for example, in *Still Life with a Red Rug* of 1906 (Musée de Grenoble), Matisse discovered that pattern could be used spatially rather than as a flattening device; and this provided him with the means of finding a totally personal counterpart to Cézanne's methods of planar construction.

If the works of 1906–7 which mark Matisse's detachment from his Fauve colleagues and the creation of several different Fauvisms of his own show the assertion of an artistic independence he was never again to surrender, the works of 1908–13 included in the section of the exhibition entitled 'Art and Decoration' revealed his emergence as a truly great artist. The *Bathers with a Turtle* of 1908 combines the graver aspects of the lessons learnt from Cézanne with the experience of Giotto and other artists of the Italian Trecento and Quattrocento encountered in Italy during the summer of 1907. As

Matisse,
Corner of the
Artist's Studio,
1912

one turned the corner into the largest room in the exhibition and confronted this work full on, one instantly sensed the depth of the impact of the Italian experience; Matisse had been among the first artists to 'discover' and collect tribal art, but it was on his discoveries of the 'primitives' of a European tradition that he was to rebuild the foundations of his art with such masterpieces as *Nymph and Satyr*, the *Game of Bowls* (both in The Hermitage Museum, St Petersburg) and the two versions of *La Danse*, all painted between 1908 and 1910, and which hung in the same space; this was one of only two rooms in the exhibition which contained any seating, and one needed it.

61

Matisse

The trip to Munich in October 1910 in the company of Marquet to visit the important exhibition of Islamic art confirmed Matisse's interest in achieving space through pattern, and a new spatial grandeur informs the decorative majesty of the studios and interiors of 1910 and 1911 (unfortunately the Musée du Grenoble *Interior with Aubergines*, like *L'Atelier Rose*, was unable to travel). These two main currents in Matisse's art, the monumentally reductive and the overtly decorative, were played off against each other in succeeding rooms at the Museum of Modern Art to dazzling effect. And they were epitomized by two of the greatest but least well-known paintings from Russia: *The Conversation*, begun probably late in 1908 and finished by 1913 (The Hermitage Museum, St Petersburg), and *Corner of the Artist's Studio*, 1912 (Pushkin Museum of Fine Art, Moscow), painted perhaps as *The Conversation* reached completion. *The Conversation* is a work of extraordinary *gravitas* and a colouristic *tour de force* in that two small rectangles of cobalt violet placed at the top of the canvas orchestrate the pervading deep blues and acid greens from stridency into hieratic sumptuousness. It is also a demonstration of the fact that however much Matisse may have insisted that he wanted his art to be 'like a good armchair', at its most challenging it is anything but: paintings like this need courage both to paint and to confront. *Corner of the Artist's Studio* is by contrast vaporous and thinly painted and shows simple things seen in complex if limited spatial settings and rendered apparently at great speed but with extraordinary virtuosity and complexity. The patterning here evokes a sense of almost mystic contemplation – like staring at a mandala.

Although the literature on Matisse is now so extensive, his relationship with Cubism has remained something of a sore point with Matisse scholars. The short introductory section in the catalogue[7] to Part IV of the exhibition, 'Abstraction and Experimentation', which covers the years 1913–17, says: 'The work of these years is said to reflect the influence of Cubism.' Well, yes, it does, although we know Matisse disapproved of many of Cubism's premises and manifestations. Here the contacts with Juan Gris seems particularly significant. In the autumn of 1914 they saw quite a lot of each other in Collioure; and subsequently Matisse, who was not a generous man, was kind to the young Spaniard. Maybe he felt freer to consult the work of an artist who was still not truly recognized and whose clear, somewhat expository mind must have seemed appealing. Gris's *Man in the Café* of 1912 (The Arensberg Collection, Philadelphia Museum of Art), for example, seems particularly relevant to Matisse's striking but problematic *Goldfish and Palette* of late 1914 (Museum of Modern Art, New York), although Matisse characteristically steers clear of many of Cubism's fundamental tenets.

To my eyes at least the hieratic grandeur of Picasso's *Harlequin* of 1915 (also in the Museum of Modern Art), which compelled Matisse's admiration, informs the figures of *Bathers by a River*, begun in 1909, abandoned in 1910 to be taken up again in 1913, and finally finished in 1916. And on purely visual grounds I would suggest that it was during his final phase of work on the canvas that Matisse began to make use of experiments with paper cut-outs to achieve his granite-like compositional effects and the extraordinary configurations of the bathers themselves who seem to wear their own contours like pictorial armour.

The rooms that led up to the climax of *Bathers by a River* were the most austere and demanding in the exhibition. The last area of the lower floor was challenging in quite a different way. Elderfield courageously decided to intersperse the last majestic and 'modernist' studio pieces of 1917 with new, markedly naturalistic works of the same period. The most ambitious of these was perhaps *Les Trois Sœurs* (now in the Musée de l'Orangerie). Auguste Pellerin, who originally owned the painting, presumably saw no inconsistency between the rigours of his own portrait and this new vision of domestic bourgeois decorum, and certainly recent Matisse scholarship has concentrated on showing that the themes in Matisse's art and the spirit that informs them do not alter as radically as one might have at first supposed. But, as presented in this particular exhibition, the schism looked raw and calls for further scholarly and critical reappraisal.

The upper floor of the exhibition began with 'The Early Years at Nice (1917–30)', and moved on very naturally to 'Themes and Variations (1930–43)', a reflective time in Matisse's art when he was occupied by his mural projects, some work in the theatre and his first great book illustrations. Matisse virtually stopped producing easel pictures between 1929 and 1934–5 and his approach to painting subsequently became in a sense more measured and spare. 'The Final Years (1943–54)', which saw the production of many of Matisse's greatest drawings, dealt with what he referred to as 'the eternal conflict of drawing and colour', a conflict resolved in the great *papiers découpés* initiated in the late 1940s.

This second half of the exhibition gave itself to one more easily and, although I visited it as often as I did the lower floor, it occupied much less of my time. Ideally it should have been visited on its own: after the rigours, skirmishes and successive victories charted below it took a while to adjust to the new enclosed world of hotel rooms and apartments transformed into artificial paradises. In a sense it might be fair to say that while in so many works up to 1917 Matisse transformed his surroundings into radical and audacious art, subsequently a protected and often artificially controlled environment shaped the art. Similarly Matisse now occasionally achieved his ends by reversing earlier strategies. To take the single issue of pattern: in *Harmony in Red* of 1908, for example, (The Hermitage Museum, St Petersburg) pattern is used with a boldness virtually unprecedented in Western art; and yet the way it is pulled, twisted and teased across the picture surface endows an apparently uncompromisingly flat painting with a sensation of convincingly naturalistic space and depth. The works of the early Nice period appear at first to be for the most part enclosed and spatially unambitious, while the richness of pattern in terms of wallpaper, screens and tiled floors is at times almost claustrophobic. But pattern is also now often used disjunctively and anti-perspectivally, so that seemingly relaxed visual idylls can be endowed with subliminal tensions. These pictures are not as uncomplicated as they might at first seem, and Matisse remained a radical artist to the end of his life. Because of their very artifice some of these pictures seem on reflection closer to the experimental canvases of the war years than does, for example, the straightforwardly naturalistic *Lorette Reclining* of 1916–17 (Private Collection). They are closer still, as John Elderfield remarks, to the earlier pre-war visions of Morocco, although once again these were visions of a paradise half experienced, half imagined and totally reinvented. The Nice interiors, as we know from photographs, were constantly being rearranged in terms of the theatrical props (the screens, textiles, objects and so forth) that had become a portable ingredient of Matisse's decorative repertoire.

There is no doubt at all that something had been lost. Not perhaps in terms of ambition, for Matisse always remained a 'high' artist, but in terms of heroism. And this loss of heroism involved not simply a repudiation of what was happening in contemporary art but also a feeling that the challenge of the art of the past no longer needed so urgently to be confronted. When the heroism asserts itself in the very late work it is of a different nature, something internalized and sublimated that picks up on earlier currents in his own work and that refers only indirectly to other forms of modernism (although it was to affect other artists so profoundly). As Matisse himself admitted, he now looked for confirmation not to the origins and traditions of Western art, but to a distillation of what he had learnt from the East.

The last two spaces of the exhibition were the only ones that brought with them, to me at least, a slight sense of disappointment. The large and remarkable interiors of the second half of the 1940s looked to my eyes all of a sudden awkward in scale, lacking both the intimacy of the small black and totally still pictures such as *The Silence Living in Houses* of 1947 (Private Collection), and the sense of breathing and expanding colour that informs both the great pre-1914 interiors and studio pictures and the final *papiers découpés*. Matisse was by now extremely fragile but one imagines he still felt comfortable handling the works of smaller dimensions. The final placing of the elements of the *papiers découpés* was done by remote control as he directed assistants from his wheel-chair or from his bed: hence their feeling of stopwatch precision. The interiors on an intermediate scale somehow call out to be larger – it is as if they are beating on the doors of other and as yet unimaginable pictures. The final room of *papiers découpés* did not bring the sense of total sublimation and release that it might have, partly, I suspect, because light levels had to be kept low to protect the gouache medium and partly because the works looked a little crowded.

But the totality of the exhibition, as well as the impact of a large proportion of individual works within it, was overwhelming. John Elderfield's introductory essay contains many new art-historical insights and suggestions. It deals primarily, however, with the way Matisse looked at things and at other art, and about how we look at Matisse, and is thus to a large extent about the psychology of visual perception as revealed by an investigation of the work of an individual artist. I suspect Elderfield's text will cause controversy among Matisse scholars; but it also opens the doors – or, since we are speaking of Matisse, the windows – on to a new wave of Matisse scholarship.

4

Pioneering Cubism

THE exhibition entitled 'Picasso and Braque: Pioneering Cubism', mounted at New York's Museum of Modern Art in 1989, brought together some 350 works by Picasso and Braque in one of the most magisterial of all Cubist exhibitions. Despite the legendary closeness of the collaboration between the two artists, most of the works on view had never been seen together before, and they never will be seen together in this way again. Many of the works were on the restricted lists of other museums and were thus in theory not free to travel; others were in the hands of private collectors who do not normally lend their pictures. The exhibition was conceived and organized by William Rubin, director emeritus of the department of painting and sculpture: seldom can a retiring museum official have achieved a comparable apotheosis.

Inevitably the exhibition was introduced by the *Demoiselles d'Avignon*, which continues to look completely different every time one confronts it. When the celebrated canvas served as the focal point of the exhibition dedicated to it some years ago, it looked simultaneously grave and apocalyptic; and for the first time, to my eyes at least, strangely benign, as if history had finally succeeded in embracing and taming it. Here it was displayed on its own and in such a way that spectators, after having looked at it, had to move around it in order to get into the rest of the exhibition beyond it. The picture once more looked menacing, and because of its isolation perhaps more aggressive than ever.

I approached the exhibition with a certain amount of trepidation, wondering whether with the passage of more than three quarters of a century pre-war Cubism might somehow have lost some of its challenge. I needn't have worried, for despite the extraordinary visual delight that it can offer, Cubism remains as baffling, as difficult as ever. When I published a book on the subject more than thirty years ago, I felt that I had to a certain extent at least come to terms with it. I continue to enjoy looking at Cubist pictures as much as I ever did, but I have come increasingly to realize that I do not really understand them, and I am not sure that anyone else does either. I have even come to believe that for the artists themselves many of their most significant and memorable achievements were begun as voyages of discovery, the final destinations of which were not known or appreciated until they had been reached.

The introductory section to the exhibition made one aware as never before of the disparity between Picasso and Braque's natural gifts. And one of the most moving aspects of the exhibition as a whole was that it told the story of how one of the most protean of all artists was prepared temporarily to accept the support and the stimulus offered to him by a fellow artist so much less talented than himself, and of how that artist accepted the challenge involved and in the process transformed himself into a major painter, who not only during the Cubist years, but at many other subsequent periods in his career, achieved true greatness. Virtually everything that Picasso touched is informed by his genius; Braque on the other hand remained throughout his life an uneven artist.

Another problem that faced Rubin and his colleagues was that Braque was so much less prolific than Picasso; even during the Cubist years when Picasso was working at what was for him a fairly measured pace, his output was between three to four times greater than that of Braque. The exhibition settled on a ratio of approximately two Picassos to every Braque. Periodically, in New York, individual works by each were brought into striking juxtaposition, but more often the artists were given alternating sections of wall space so that one became aware both of the collaborative aspect of their Cubism during its formative, early and subsequent high classical phases – from 1908 until the closing months of 1912 – and also of their individual trajectories.

The works by Picasso that follow the *Demoiselles* and reflect the first wave of his admiration for tribal art are among the most immediate and powerful that he ever produced. Many of them look as if they had been chiselled and carved rather than painted; contours of bodies and objects fuse and in the process bind the strongly volumetric forms to the surface. The bonding of objects and their immediate surroundings also induces dislocations of shapes, and these in turn often already carry with them implications of the multiple viewpoints of Cubist perspective. The Braques of these years by contrast look either weak and tentative or else somewhat schematic; outlines of objects arch over toward each other but seldom meet or touch, so that forms seem to float and flutter. It is very difficult to imagine exactly what it was that was beginning to draw these artists, so very different in temperament and approach, toward each other.

It was the attraction of opposites; the German dealer Wilhelm Uhde, who was among the first to buy Cubist pictures and who became a friend to both painters, wrote: 'Braque's temperament was limpid, precise and bourgeois; Picasso's sombre, excessive and revolutionary.'[1]

A shared interest in the art of Cézanne must have helped, although here again their attitude toward him was entirely different. The various landscapes done at L'Estaque, territory that Cézanne had made very much his own, show Braque submitting himself very candidly to Cézanne's example; the least arrogant of men, Braque nevertheless gives the impression of inheriting or assuming the mantle. The earliest of these works already have about them an analytic, reductive quality.

In the *Demoiselles* Picasso had approached Cézanne's canvases of bathers not so much in a spirit of enquiry as in a mood of aggression, even rivalry. Picasso's outlook was wider than that of Braque and his ambitions infinitely greater. If Cézanne had sought to reinterpret Poussin by way of nature, it might be fair to say that at certain moments in the creation of Cubism Picasso sought to reinvent certain great artists of the past – Raphael, El Greco, Ingres (as well as a host of anonymous tribal carvers) – by way of Cézanne. There can be little doubt that if Picasso encouraged Braque to draw more radical conclusions from his study of Cézanne and to confront his mentor less passively, Braque in turn persuaded Picasso to put more thoughtfully to Cézanne's art some of the questions it was waiting to be asked: questions about the implications of Cézanne's constant breaking and subsequent reaffirming of the contours of things, for example, the way in which the surfaces of his canvases seem to pulsate with life, while the subject itself remains so monolithic, so very still. In doing so Braque helped to bring Picasso more squarely into the mainstream of Post-Impressionist art, using the term in its broadest sense. In preceding years Picasso had already been recognized, along with Matisse, as one of the most important forces in young French art; but had it not been for his relationship with Braque he might have remained much more of an outsider on the contemporary Parisian scene, and his subsequent influence and dominance over it might have been of a different order and nature.

If Picasso was the more dynamic and unquestionably the more vivid personality in the partnership, at many key moments Braque's approach to Cubism was different from Picasso's. It was often he who solved the technical problems that inevitably arose in what ultimately became a reinvention of the vocabulary of painting. In doing so he often pointed the way ahead. Braque's major obsession, as he was to insist throughout his life, was with pictorial space. His first major contribution to Cubism was the creation of that 'tactile' or 'manual' space which he experienced or sensed in the natural and material world around him – 'tactile' in the sense that the space that surrounds and separates objects becomes as important, as palpable, as the objects themselves.[2] It was his desire to control and explore this space more rigorously that led him virtually to abandon landscape, and turned him into one of the archetypal painters of still life.

Picasso's approach to adopting the multi-viewpoint perspective that was central to Cubism was more incisive and daring than Braque's. But when in the latter part of 1909 the surfaces of Picasso's paintings began to breathe more freely, and when the figures and objects within them began to partake of their environments more openly, they were acknowledging a debt to Braque. Up until 1909 Picasso's career had been punctuated by large, ambitious canvases, in which are concentrated the distinctive characteristics of his various periods or manners. Subsequently, and as the collaboration with Braque intensified, he became increasingly concerned with the processes of painting, so that one painting seems imperceptibly to flow into the next.

A comparison of the works executed early in 1910 demonstrates how much more abstract Braque's vision was at the time. In the landscapes painted during the summer and in some of the subsequent still lifes he sometimes empties out the corners of his paintings and leaves them almost blank so that the internal relationships of forms become more fluid and precarious but also more self-sufficient in that they are not conditioned by the picture's outer edges; hence the subsequent fascination with the oval format. In other works the transparent planes by which objects and the spaces around them were now being rendered tend to align themselves on a subliminal vertical and horizontal framework.

Pioneering Cubism

If Picasso, with his bolder and more linear approach, was subsequently to give more explicit definition to the celebrated Cubist grids or scaffoldings, and characteristically to push these new methods of pictorial construction to more extreme conclusions, the general move toward greater abstraction was anticipated by Braque. Braque's work of 1910 is also informed by new sensations of light that reinforce the tactility of his space; in previous years and as he moved toward a more monochromatic palette his pictures had been bathed in a powdery, often cool light – even his siennas and ochres tend toward grey. Now the works themselves emit a silvery, poetic light. Picasso's use of light is more descriptive and factual; lights are juxtaposed to darks in a more traditional way, to engender a sensation of relief and to detach forms from their surroundings. It is now, too, that some of Braque's canvases begin to rival Picasso's in their accomplishment and presence.

Picasso's unfinished *Girl with a Mandolin (Fanny Tellier)* (Museum of Modern Art, New York) of the spring of 1910 reminds us that his engagement with the image was much stronger than Braque's and that his approach remained more volumetric. This is confirmed by the three portraits of his dealers, Vollard, Uhde and Kahnweiler. The idea of a Cubist portrait by Braque is virtually inconceivable (although it is possible that his *Girl with a Cross* of the spring of 1911 (in the Kimbell Art Museum, Fort Worth) may represent his wife Marcelle). And yet it is equally characteristic of Picasso that the works which he produced when he was working on his own at Cadaqués during the summer of 1910 were some of the most daring and abstract of all Cubist canvases.

Kahnweiler tells us that Picasso was dissatisfied with them,[3] and yet they are the prelude to what was in certain respects Cubism's highest period – the 'look-alike' years between the autumn of 1910 and the autumn of 1912, when the similarities between the work of Picasso and Braque are so great that even the trained and experienced eye has occasionally to pause and blink. This was a moment of intense visual excitement and experiment and yet also one of perfect poise and equilibrium, probably because it was also the moment of total harmony between the two painters, when the dialogue between them was one of trust and acknowledged equality. It must have been now that the painters had those private, secret conversations into which no third person could have possibly intruded, and to which both Picasso and Braque alluded in later life.

The works of this high, analytic, crystalline phase of Cubism are to me also the most mysterious; and I have come to believe that during their invention of a new pictorial language the two painters were now being carried along by forces beyond their own control. Invention involved restatement and consolidation, but simultaneously every new statement was a reinvention. The Surrealist critic Max Morise was to speak of these works as giving the painter 'the opportunity to photograph his thoughts'.[4] Of a particular one of them, Picasso's *Man with a Clarinette* of the summer of 1911 (Thyssen-Bornemisza Collection, Madrid), André Breton was to write that it 'remains a tangible proof of our unwavering proposition that the mind talks to us of a future continent and that everyone has the power to accompany an ever more beautiful Alice into Wonderland'.[5] These faceted, glinting, powerful and yet strangely insubstantial works were indeed the looking glass through which artists like Mondrian and Delaunay stepped into abstraction and Léger and the Futurists into a dynamic fragmented vision of a new mechanized world. These paintings, and the way they were displayed in New York, also remind one of how the highest moments of art are often held in precarious balance. The perfect poise and stability of the Italian High Renaissance was not all that long-lived either, and neither was Impressionism as a contained, cohesive moment.

During this, the most beautiful and hermetic phase of Cubism, it is in the figure pieces that the differences between the artists continue to reveal themselves, partly for the very simple reason that Picasso was above all else a painter of the human form and Braque was not. When Picasso had produced such startling, abstract and at times disturbing works at Cadaqués in 1910, it was because he was pushing new methods of work, new technical devices to extreme conclusions, just as he was to do again some two and a half years later. The figures of the intervening years, however abstract and homogeneous they might at first seem, are informed by a centralized, pyramidal weight and density that make one aware of them immediately as solid, bodily presences; despite their similarities many of these figures are strongly characterized.

The Accordionist (The Solomon R. Guggenheim Museum), executed at Céret in the summer of 1911, is seen by many as Picasso at his most Braque-like, but it has about it an incisiveness and a stylistic self-awareness that are very alien to Braque and that remind

Picasso,
The Accordionist, 1911

Braque,
Man with a Guitar, 1911

one of Picasso's passion for Ingres. A second, companion piece, *The Poet*, also done at Céret (Peggy Guggenheim Collection, Venice/the Solomon R. Guggenheim Museum, New York), has about it a decidedly reflective air, while a third of the series, *The Man with a Pipe* (Arensberg Collection, Philadelphia Museum of Art), has a more forthright quality than either of the others. Braque's *Man with a Guitar* (the Museum of Modern Art, New York) executed once again at Céret during this miraculous summer of artistic communion, was hung next to Picasso's *Accordionist* in New York and does indeed show Braque at his most solid and Picassoesque.

But in other contemporary and companion pieces of Braque's the centralized, triangular compositional areas tend to become pale or to fade, and the denser, more impacted passages of paint are drawn out to the painting's outer edges, so that eventually, in a work like *Man with a Violin* (Bührle Foundation, Zürich) of the spring of 1912, the figure becomes ghostlike and apparitional; in a sense we identify it through its absence. While Picasso's figures remain very much images, Braque's become presences. Although in all the works of this period, figure pieces and still lifes alike, the proportions of the things depicted remain more or less naturalistic, it is now in my view dangerous to try to reconstruct their subject matter too literally, doubly so in the case of Braque.

It is revealing within the history of Cubism that in the spring of 1912 Picasso should have invented collage, a technique that was to become so central to the visual products of Dada and Surrealism, while in September of that year Braque should have produced the first *papier collé*, in which pieces of wood-grained paper were incorporated into a picture, assuming a representational role yet remaining identifiable as pieces of paper. *Papier collé* is itself a form of collage but it is less adaptable to subversive effects, and more purely formalistic in its implications. It has long been recognized that with these new procedures there came about a change in the climate of Cubism and that now Picasso and Braque began increasingly to go their separate ways; and in the case of Picasso a great many separate ways. The geography of the exhibition spaces at the Museum of Modern Art, divided into two floors, with the later works gathered into the lower floor, made the break seem even more dramatic than in reality it was. Given the increasing diversity of Picasso's production, the ratio of the works necessary to document it increases over that of Braque's, whose path was not so much

73

narrower as more self-contained. Many felt that in these lower spaces Braque, as it were, went under, and at the official opening of the show members of the Picasso family were heard remarking in loud voices, 'But where is Braque?' meaning, of course, that he was nowhere at all.

I myself continued to feel that he was very present indeed. The wall displaying his works of the winter of 1912–13, was for me one of the most beautiful and exhilarating in the entire display. These particular Braques seemed to soar and float, not only creating their own internal spaces but opening out and informing the space around them; it must have been to this phase of his Cubism that Braque was referring when he said that before introducing objects into his paintings he had to create spatial complexes in which they could exist. By contrast many of the Picassos in this room looked once more increasingly dense and impacted; others were characterized by an almost aggressively graphic emphasis, as if to remind us once again that he was a natural draughtsman while Braque, on the other hand, was not.

It was in this gallery that I began to feel that something was missing; and then I realized that it was the presence of Juan Gris. Although Gris was some five years younger than Picasso and Braque and had begun his career very much as a devotee of Picasso, he had matured as a painter very rapidly and it was now, in 1913, that Picasso recognized that his erstwhile follower was a force to be taken into account. Gris seems to have encouraged Picasso to reaffirm the rigours of his draughtsmanship, and one also senses an awareness of Gris in the flat, brightly coloured areas that inform not only Picasso's *papiers collés* of the time but also many of the paintings. The extraordinary *Woman in an Armchair* (of the autumn of 1913, in a New York Private Collection), understandably so revered by the Surrealists, is, in a sense, Picasso's answer to Gris's challenge or emergence as a major force in Cubism.

Picasso and Braque's approaches and working methods were now analogous but in fact basically very different. Braque insisted that *papier collé* had been primarily a means of introducing colour into Cubist painting; and it is certainly true that although Picasso was at moments using colour more boldly, at times almost recklessly, Braque was ultimately more sensitive to its properties. But *papier collé* also allowed Braque to find new ways of manipulating pictorial space, building up his canvases with interacting, overlapping spatial elements, some of which were qualified in such a way that they become objects, or on to which a subject was superimposed.

Picasso's methods were much more physical and manipulative, largely as a result of his renewed interest in tribal art, and in particular his obsession with a recently acquired Grebo mask, an artefact that could with a certain amount of justification be described as primitive, but that was indirectly to condition an extraordinarily large percentage of twentieth-century art, much of it highly sophisticated and much of it technologically advanced. With Braque, representation and abstraction go hand in hand. Sometimes he begins with a recognizable subject, which is subsequently almost obliterated; at other moments he begins with an abstract spatial complex, which gives birth to the picture's iconography. With Picasso elements are welded, at times indeed simply willed, into representational entities. But what was now dividing the artists possibly even more fundamentally was that Picasso's new tribal sources, and the new methods and materials that accompanied them (several of which had been pioneered by Braque), were endowing his art with a strongly anti-aesthetic bias which was totally foreign to Braque's nature. Picasso now viewed tribal masks and figures not so much as works of art but rather as ritualistic objects, weapons for exorcism. Braque was an inventor, even a revolutionary, but not an iconoclast. Picasso, who was able to tap and rival the resources of the art of the past so much more fluently and directly, was all three of these.

A particular work by Braque, *The Pedestal Table*, (Collection Heinz Berggruen, Geneva), painted in Sorgues in the autumn of 1913, more than any other of Braque's pre-war Cubist canvases looks forward to his majestic canvases of the 1930s, in which decorative motifs and visual exhilaration unite with the metaphysical, and above all to the late studio paintings, in my view some of the greatest and most profoundly philosophical pictures to have been produced since the end of the Second World War.

The Pedestal Table identifies itself immediately as a still life: it contains a newspaper, a glass, a sheet of music. But other objects have begun to lose their individual identities: is the prominent palette shape just above the newspaper a bottle, a carafe or an out-of-scale musical instrument? Immediately to the side of it the decorative architectural scrolls that punctuate the upper areas of the picture suddenly seem to detach themselves from their context and to take on a life of their own – or are they the appendages of yet another object? Toward the end of his life Braque was to say:

> You see, I have made a great discovery. I no longer believe in anything. Objects don't exist for me except insofar as a rapport exists between them and myself.[6]

The first steps toward this particular state of consciousness which Braque described both as 'intellectual nonexistence' and 'perpetual revelation'[7] were taken here.

If in certain Cubist Braques and increasingly in much of his subsequent work, objects are themselves and yet not themselves, Picasso's images are themselves and yet simultaneously can evoke analogies with other things. Women's bodies are like guitars or violins, touchable and strokable; dots or pegs can represent eyes or nipples or navels, or in other contexts the appurtenances of bottles or musical instruments. Many aspects of the last phases of Picasso's pre-war Cubism point ahead directly toward Constructivism and Surrealism, whose visual manifestations would have been inconceivable without his example. Braque's work of the time opens up only into his own development; he was to consult Picasso's art from time to time, notably when he turned his attention to the human figure. But perhaps it is revealing that if by 1913 Braque was truly upon his individual path, two of the very last Picassos in the exhibition, *Wine Glass and Ace of Clubs (Homage to Max Jacob)*, (Collection Heinz Berggruen, Geneva) and *Pipe, Violin and Bottle of Bass* (A. E. Gallatin Collection, Philadelphia Museum of Art), both of the spring of 1914, show Picasso looking somewhat wistfully over his shoulder or out of the corner of his eye at Braque's most recent achievements. Picasso later told Kahnweiler that when, after the declaration of war, he had seen Braque off at the station at Avignon (together with Derain) he had never again been able to find him;[8] he was speaking, of course, metaphorically. But one of the most remarkable collaborations of all time had indeed come to an end, never again to be revived.

William Rubin's catalogue essay which he modestly entitled 'Picasso and Braque: an Introduction', is indeed relatively short; but it is also remarkably succinct; and, together with the lengthy footnotes, it gives one not only an account of the relationship between the two men, but also a picture of the state of Cubist scholarship today.

Braque,
The Pedestal Table, 1913

A truly fascinating appendix brought to light an important discovery. Archival material in the Musée Picasso, supplemented by that in the possession of the Laurens family (which inherited Braque's estate), reveals that in 1909 Picasso agreed to produce a 'decoration' for the Brooklyn library of an interesting but largely forgotten American painter, critic and collector, Hamilton Easter Field; the commission was negotiated by Frank Burty Haviland, a friend of Picasso's and an avid collector of tribal art. The project called for eleven pictures of very different shapes and dimensions, and, as Rubin suggests, Picasso undoubtedly saw the commission as an answer to the decorative triptych that Matisse had recently undertaken for the landings in the stairwell of the Moscow home of one of their greatest mutual patrons, Sergei Shchukin. (Only two of these three masterpieces, *La Danse* and *La Musique*, reached their Russian destination; the third, which Matisse reworked over succeeding years, is the great *Bathers in a River*, now in Chicago.)

The Picasso cycle never materialized; at least one of the largest of the projected panels was destroyed, others were repainted, although in at least two instances Picasso appears to have somewhat arbitrarily added to the dimensions of works that he had produced independently (without the commission in view), in the hope that they could be made to fit into the scheme.

This discovery raises and highlights some of the most basic and interesting questions raised by Cubism, questions which despite the wealth of literature on the subject have never been adequately addressed. Why in view of Picasso's and Braque's patently high aims did their Cubism limit itself to such simple and for the most part humble subject matter? Why was the scale on which they worked so unambitious? Why was the very concept of a decorative Cubist ensemble so inconceivable until Cubism had taken on a somewhat different and more accessible face after the war? In the winter of 1908–9 Picasso had reworked an ambitious multifigure composition, transforming it into a still life, the magnificent *Bread and Fruit Dish on a Table*, now in the Kunstmuseum, Basle. One of the reasons the Field project must have foundered is that it called for five pictures considerably larger than any that Picasso had produced in the years between executing this still life and the outbreak of war.

Presumably Picasso and Braque had to limit themselves to single-figure pieces – there is one exception, Picasso's *Soldier and Girl* of 1911 (Private Collection, Paris) – because the analytic complexities and rigours of a new method of representing solid forms and the spaces between them on a two-dimensional surface induced them to restrict their range of subject matter, just as it forced them temporarily to abandon colour. But the abandonment of colour also reinforces the militantly anti-decorative nature of almost all pre-war Cubism; these are paintings that can seduce the eye but that constantly challenge and sometimes trouble the mind, in a way that truly decorative art does not. When colour reasserts itself after 1912, and when decorative motifs (often architectural) begin to inform the paintings, they continue to be used in an intimate, private way.

In Picasso's case, his use of brighter colour and lively pointillist dotting or stippling is allied to his rejection of accepted or traditional canons of pictorial beauty and is related to his unorthodox use of materials, not only the cheap newspapers, simulated woodgraining, and wallpapers, used by Braque as well, but also Ripolin and enamel paint. The more truly decorative aspects of some of Picasso's work of 1914 – what Alfred Barr termed his 'rococo' Cubism – have about them in fact a popularizing, jocular down-to-earth quality. If Cubism of the previous years had been 'easel-sized', it was also informed by an anti-'easel' aesthetic, by the concept of what the painters themselves called *'le tableau objet'* – the picture as object. Despite the fact that during the years under discussion the Cubism of Picasso and Braque was on the whole unpunctuated by particular works that stand out strongly from the rest, each single picture works very much as an individual entity, a self-contained world. Possibly it was this as much as anything else that prevented Picasso from fulfilling Field's hopes.

5

Still-Life Lives

STILL LIFE as we now accept it emerged as a subject in its own right in Flanders and Holland in the sixteenth century; the English phrase derives from the Dutch *stilleven*. Still life never appealed to English patrons, who preferred pictures of their dogs and horses. The French, after toying with various alternatives – my own favourite is *vie coy* or *vie tranquille* – settled for the somewhat chilling *nature morte*, possibly in indirect acknowledgment of the fact that many of the earliest still lifes produced by France's neighbours had been *memento mori* or *vanitas* paintings, reflections on the finality of death and the transience of earthly pleasures. But the genre flourished in France, and in the eighteenth century Chardin endowed it with a totally new grace and humanity, even though still life continued to rank as the lowest order of painting.

A hundred years later Courbet, who had the ability to handle paint as if he were touching human flesh, broke fresh ground when he gave his depictions of fruit, flowers and dead game (the latter often lifted directly from Flemish prototypes) some of the physicality that he achieved in his female nudes. Significantly, in 1858 his contemporary Théodore Thoré (Wilhelm Bürger) in the first volume of his *Les Musées de la Hollande* protested about the generic use of *nature morte*: much Dutch still life, he pointed out, didn't look dead at all. Towards the end of the nineteenth century Van Gogh and Cézanne between them raised still life to a status it had never before enjoyed, the one on an emotional and psychological plane, the other through formal innovation and challenge. The Spanish expression for still life, *bodegón*, refers to simple domestic utensils and supplies from the kitchen cupboard and also to humble taverns and eating houses. Spanish painters eschewed the opulent displays in which northern artists came so to delight – Simon Schama's 'embarrassment of riches'[1] – and have tended to this very day to take a grimmer view of things, thus in a sense preserving some of still life's bleaker iconographic origins.

It was in the still lifes of the 1870s that the full force of Cézanne's genius first made itself felt. As time went on formal innovations first hinted at in the still lifes increasingly came to inform his landscapes while in return the still lifes became increasingly animate; objects seem to pulse, draperies become heavier and denser: they envelop and protect us. Early portraits and figure studies of family and friends, vigorous, clumsy, but always truthful, gave way to monolithic studies of sitters seen as still life. And it was through Cézanne more than through any other artist that in France in the early years of this century still life came to be recognized as the prime vehicle for formalist innovation and experiment. Two of the three creators of true Cubism, Braque and Gris, were essentially still-life painters. Although we think of Picasso primarily as a painter of the human body, during the years of his pre-war Cubism he produced approximately as many still lifes as he did figure pieces. The still lifes painted by Matisse in Toulouse and Paris in 1899 are the first works to hint at his future stature. His subsequent recognition that pattern could be used spatially in still life rather than as a flattening device provided him with the means of finding an independent counterpart to Cézanne's methods of planar construction. When Mondrian came to Paris he had already studied Cézanne's still lifes. Boccioni, the most gifted and also the most iconoclastic of the Italian Futurists, in some of his very last work executed before his death in 1916, paid implicit tribute to Cézanne's still lifes as a source of modernism.

Picasso had initially shown virtually no interest in still life; and it was only during his stay in Gosol in the summer of 1906, when his work acknowledged the new classicism that went hand-in-hand with a relaxed sensuality, that he turned to objects, endowing them invariably with playful erotic connotations. But in 1907 he produced his monumental *Still Life with Death's Head* (Hermitage Museum, St Petersburg), which with a certain amount of justification could be regarded as a postscript or even as a pendant to the *Demoiselles d'Avignon*. The picture, it has been suggested, may commemorate Cézanne's death the previous year.[2] It shows a skull, which is given an unmistakably masculine presence, partnered by an empty bowl; placed above the skull are the painter's attributes – a palette with its thumb-hole pierced by brushes; behind the bowl stands a painting of a female nude. Iconographically this is possibly the most prophetic and significant still life Picasso ever painted.

Picasso,
*Still Life with
Death's Head*, 1907

The second of Picasso's greatest pre-Cubist still lifes, *Table with Loaves and Bowl of Fruit* (Kunstmuseum, Basle), produced during the winter of 1908–9, began life as a four-figure composition and also as an indirect homage to both Cézanne and the Douanier Rousseau: their stylistic legacy remains, but the figures which were to have symbolized them have been replaced by the still-life objects.[3] At least one other still life of the period acknowledges the presence of a figure underneath it, and these transformations must have sharpened Picasso's feeling for pictorial metamorphosis and for metaphor itself. Picasso continued to explore Cézanne's figure pieces, and Cézanne's bathers in particular remained a source of constant fascination for him, although Picasso seems also to have recognized that in the latest and largest of them Cézanne had entered territory where he couldn't be followed. But he also saw that it was Cézanne's still life that could most squarely and profitably be confronted, and Picasso's own still lifes of 1908 and 1909 show him making the confrontation and striding down the road to Cubism.

Both of these early masterpieces were included in the exhibition somewhat eccentrically entitled *Picasso and Things* seen in 1992 in Cleveland and Philadelphia and then at the Grand Palais in Paris under a modified title: *Picasso et les Choses: Les Natures Mortes*. The modification was apt. In Cleveland and Philadelphia the exhibition was laid out in a straight chronological progression. The French curators were at the last moment deprived of a considerable part of their space and they decided to compensate for this by introducing a selection of later works at intervals throughout the first great display that the visitor saw. The results were startling and revealing. *Still Life with Death's Head*, for example, found itself placed opposite the sheep's-skull paintings executed in Royan in 1939. Picasso arrived there the day before the declaration of war and the agony of the times found expression in these tortured animal heads, teeth bared in pain and protest, eyes sightless but accusing. These images, reminiscent of Goya, are among the most savage and disturbing that Picasso ever produced.

Played off against the lurid reds and ochres of the Royan pictures the greens of the early Cubist paintings looked sombre and funereal, the greys marmoreal, the earth colours glowing but sullen. Flowers are metallic and looked as if they might have come straight off one of the monuments in the Père Lachaise cemetery. Seen in this context, even the beautifully balanced, glinting and translucent monochromatic Cubist pictures of 1910–12 looked severe and sombre and more Spanish than ever before. One of them contains the words *sol* and *sombra* (a reference to the seating arrangements in the bull-ring), reinforcing the impression that here, psychologically at least, there is more shade than light.

Later on the light is often fierce and unyielding, as though in the service of a pictorial Inquisition. Cézannesque knives no longer lead the eye back from the table edges into depth but plunge abruptly inward from the canvases' side edges. The food in the more relaxed and elaborate works of 1914–15, the only works in the exhibition which show a genuine sense of hedonistic abundance, is strangely inedible. Playing cards and dice read like wagers against fortune. The folded sheet metal *Guitar* of 1924 (Musée Picasso, Paris) looked like a gigantic fetish. Picasso's notorious superstition as well as his obsession with and fear of death permeated the atmosphere.

Skulls abounded and were the principal leitmotif of the exhibition, although human skulls can be replaced by those of sheep, bulls or steers, and also by classical sculpted heads that seem to hover between life and death; animal and human elements combine in detached heads of minotaurs. Skulls are accompanied mostly by bowls and jugs that can in their turn bring along fruit and flowers but are often left empty. Presiding over the second half of the exhibition was the larger than lifesize bronze and copper skull of 1943; two casts of it were placed by Picasso on the floor of his studio, near the door, so that visitors were likely to stumble on them. This sculpture was complemented by the skull and pitcher paintings executed between 1943 and 1945, Picasso's own dance of death. In many of them leeks placed below the skulls act as crossbones. If the food included in the later Cubist still lifes had seemed to defy consumption, during the paintings of the war years its unavailability underlines a pictorial message.

Picasso ate sparingly (and drank even less) but food is a major theme in his collected writings which were published relatively recently in a lavish volume invaluably edited by Marie-Laure Bernadac and Christine Piot.[4] The earliest of Picasso's surviving prose poems dates from 1935, the last from 1959; three-quarters of the text included here had never been published before. As early as 1926 in an interview with a Catalan journalist Picasso had threatened to write a book 'as thick as this', adding, 'and I will offer a prize of a dozen bottles of champagne to whoever can read more than three lines'.[5] The writings are indeed difficult, largely because – with the partial exception of the three plays – they are deliberately unstructured and also because of Picasso's rejection of punctuation, which he once described to Braque as 'a *cache-sexe* which hides the private parts of literature'.[6]

Picasso's writings have been claimed, by Tristan Tzara among others, for Surrealism, although André Breton and Paul Eluard (both admirers) in the *Dictionnaire Abrégé du Surréalisme* of 1938 allow only the recent poems into the canon.[7] And indeed the more one immerses oneself in Picasso's texts, the less surreal they seem, largely because, despite the astounding fantasy, his images are so obviously grounded in direct experience. Michel Leiris, in a short preface to the collected writings, sees them as being 'closer (on the whole) to Dadaist nihilism than to Surrealism' and goes on to compare them to James Joyce;[8] and opaque as they are many of these texts have a mesmeric, incantatory quality that eventually takes one over even when one isn't quite sure what is going on. The

Picasso,
Still Life with Jug and
Apples, **1919**

obsession with objects and their properties, particularly their colours and smells, makes the writings seem more relevant to Picasso's still life than to his figure work, as does the fact that the texts are for the most part surprisingly free of eroticism. As in the later still lifes there is an insistence on culinary matters: kitchens and dining rooms are frequent settings, and sideboards and pots and pans abound. Over much of the writings there hangs the smell of cooking: a text of 17 December 1935, for instance, ends with an image of anchovies frying in the heat of the sun. (A postcard sent by Picasso to Apollinaire from Cadaqués in 1910 which has recently come to light declares, 'Je suis le roy de la boullavaise.')[9]

On the other hand, sex does frequently find its way into the still lifes. The beautifully evocative *Still Life with Jug and Apples* of *c.* 1920, painted in elegant greys and fawns, more or less demands to be read as a configuration of body imagery and must surely still reflect his love of his wife Olga. When this love was seen to turn to hatred in the figures pieces executed between 1925 and 1932, the transformation finds no direct expression in the contemporary still lifes and those of the 1920s are the most colourful and sumptuously decorative Picasso ever produced, although in their exaggeration of scale and reckless use of colour and pattern there is perhaps an element of escapism.

These works reflect and draw on Picasso's contacts and collaborations with the world of the ballet and the theatre. Olga had come from this world and it was there that Picasso had found her; but she was a conventional, limited woman and it is hard to believe she would have found these works other than distasteful and vulgar. They speak of an exclusively male appetite, insatiable and in a sense cannibalistic. Picasso was to speak of his respect for objects which he saw as being charged with a life force of their own.[10] The objects with which he surrounded himself were simple and inexpensive, just as his taste in food was for the basic and unsophisticated; his dealer Kahnweiler claimed that Picasso was incapable of painting an object with which he did not have a familiar relationship.[11] And yet in a text of 1935 Picasso was to write of loving things and eating them alive:

> I can no longer bear this miracle that of knowing nothing of this world and to have learnt nothing but to love things and eat them alive and to listen to their farewells when the hours strike in the distance.[12]

And that was in a sense what he did to people too. It is, however, worth noting that if in his rendition of women Picasso often saw them as being grotesque, predatory and destructive, their counterparts in his still lifes are almost always fruitful and affirmative presences.

In so far as there is a heroine in the story of Picasso's still lifes she is Marie-Thérèse Walter, although in the Picasso literature she is invariably treated as the least interesting of his serious attachments. She was to remain in a sense his hidden partner, initially because she was under-age when he first seduced her, and her existence had to be kept secret from Olga, and latterly because he preferred it that way.

It was probably in 1925, when Marie-Thérèse was only sixteen, that the liaison was initiated; and in Picasso's work she first puts in an appearance, or a presence, in a vast *Still Life* of 1926 (Centro de Arte Reina Sofía, Madrid). Her finely etched Grecian profile is barely discernible, incised on the swelling body of a stringed instrument, while her extended legs are just visible between the table legs below.

Her corn-coloured hair informs the golden pitchers that appear in the works of 1931, and one of these, *Still Life on a Table*, painted on 11 March 1931 (Musée Picasso, Paris), was subsequently identified by Picasso himself as a symbolic portrait of his young mistress. The painting explodes with erotic energy, although the sheer scale of the canvas and its colouristic exuberance drain it of tenderness and render Marie-Thérèse a victim as well as muse and inspirer of the artist's passion. Gentleness does, however, break through in the smaller still lifes executed between 1939 and 1943 during weekends spent with Marie-Thérèse and their child Maya at the various accommodations arranged for them. These pictures depict ordinary kitchen accessories accompanied by humble foodstuffs and they show a touching concern with the apparatus of daily domestic life which he also recognized as being unsustainable and ultimately foreign to his nature.

Picasso's writings, too, confirm that however much he may have seen and used Marie-Thérèse as an erotic object, his love for her was genuine and opened up at least one aspect of his many-faceted character that he was probably unable to expose to anyone else. The written references to her are coded, but one of the more overt, recorded in a notebook entry of 20 November 1935, reads: 'Flower sweeter than honey – you are my flame and joy.'[13] The later Marie-Thérèse still lifes are complementary to the skull-and-pitcher series and are also the direct counterparts of the lonely wartime still lifes representing austere evening meals in the kitchen of the apartment in the rue des Grands Augustins, and of the pictures commemorating his visits to the restaurant Le Catalan, just down the street. Despite the fact that Le Catalan had access to black-market produce, the pictures inspired by it and related works of the time are among the saddest and grimmest of all still lifes.

After the war, when Picasso was spending an increasing amount of time in the South of France, his interest in still life to a certain extent waned, although trips to Paris and meals in his old kitchen provoked memories of harder times and some sober commemorative still lifes. In 1953 a series of *grisaille* paintings of dead cocks accompanied by sacrificial kitchen knives and bowls of blood signalled the final break with Françoise Gilot. It has been suggested that the striking *Still Life with a Bull's Head* of 1958 (Musée Picasso, Paris), painted in French tricolour colours and, according to Picasso, executed with 'four letter words', was a reaction against events in

Algeria that were to bring De Gaulle to power.[14] The bouquet of lilies of the valley placed next to the skull refers to the fragrance that had been brought into his life by Jacqueline Roque. The very last still lifes executed in the 1960s are colourful, but tortured and apocalyptic. The most important of these, *Cat and Lobster* of 1962 (Hakone Open Air Museum, Japan), shows a mangy tomcat attacking an array of seafood on a kitchen table in a black parody of Chardin's magnificent *The Ray Fish*, which Picasso had admired in the Louvre. And in this work one senses that Picasso is taking leave of the genre. As he came increasingly to equate the creative act with the sexual act, even the metaphoric properties of still life seemed inadequate to exorcise the decline of his body and the descent into dust. His *memento mori* had shown a fascination with death but certainly not an acceptance of it, and now he was looking for other purely carnal and historically referential subjects to keep death at bay.

When Gertrude Stein wrote that: 'Painting in the nineteenth century was done only in France by Frenchmen, apart from that painting did not exist, in the twentieth century it was done in France but by Spaniards,'[15] she was paying tribute to both Picasso and Juan Gris. She appears to have found Braque a bit boring and did not collect his work; and for reasons best known to herself she cherished the belief that Americans and Spaniards were brothers and sisters under the skin.

Despite a period of alienation during the war – itself brought about by Stein's abortive efforts to help him – she was a good friend to Gris. She bought three fine works of his in 1914 just before the outbreak of war, and as many again in the 1920s; by then her own taste in things visual was becoming less secure and Gris's own output was also becoming increasingly uneven. In 1925 Gris provided illustrations for Stein's *A Book Concluding With As A Wife Has A Cow A Love Story*, which like the text have a slightly folkloric quality to them. When Gris died prematurely in 1927 at the age of forty Stein appears to have been genuinely grief-stricken and described her essay *The Life and Death of Juan Gris* as 'the most moving thing' she had ever written.[16]

Picasso did not always behave wholly correctly toward Gris but he was one of the chief mourners at his funeral; Stein resented this. It is significant that although Picasso owned works by many of his contemporaries, he never exchanged works with Gris. Picasso liked to feel that he had exclusive rights to his friends and he may have resented Gris's friendship with Stein and the fact that after the war Gris became the painter whom the dealer Kahnweiler most cherished.

Gris was born in Madrid in 1887. As a student there he had worked, using his original name of José Victoriano Carmel Carlos Gonzáles Pérez, under the academic painter José Moreno Carbonero (who later also taught Salvador Dali). He preferred to emphasize the scientific basis of his studies at the Escuela de Artes e Industrias (afterwards called the Escuela Industrial). Gris began earning his living as a cartoonist, and appears to have been much in demand. Among the most distinguished periodicals to which he contributed was *Blanco y Negro*; he was still working for it in 1906 when he changed his name to Juan Gris, possibly as a pun. This same year he left for Paris where caricature was having a new vogue; Gris's arrival coincided, for example, with the publication of Paul Gaultier's serious study *Le Rire et la Caricature*. Gris was also avoiding military conscription in Spain, a move which cost him his passport and subsequently his freedom to travel. His cartoons show that he was a fluent, accomplished draughtsman in the conventional mode of the time; but there is no wit in his line, as there is for example in the commercial work of Bonnard and Lautrec. From the cartoons one might deduce that he had a sense of fun but very little sense of humour, and despite some good jokes a slight melancholy pervades many of them.

In Paris Gris quickly gravitated toward Picasso, as did every other expatriate Spanish artist, and soon Picasso had found him accommodation in the bowels of the Bateau-Lavoir. In 1909 Gris moved up to the studio just vacated by Van Dongen, on the ground floor and facing the Place Ravignan. (The ramshackle complex of studios fell away backward from the street level down the slopes of Montmartre.) In the Bateau-Lavoir Gris witnessed the birth of Picasso's Cubism. He began painting seriously in 1910, and in January 1912 *Paris Journal* announced his début as a painter with some fifteen oil paintings on show at Clovis Sagot's gallery.

But it was the *Homage to Picasso* (The Art Institute of Chicago), shown a couple of months later at the *Salon des Indépendants*, that first brought him to the attention of the public. The critic Louis Vauxcelles, one of Cubism's enemies, described the portrait as being of 'père Ubu/Kub',[17] a reference to Jarry's monstrous Ubu and to Gris's style, which was certainly more relentlessly cubifying than that of Picasso. It resembled the work of Jean Metzinger, seen by many as leader of the 'Salon' Cubists, who, unlike Picasso and Braque, showed in the public salons. A contemporary picture by Gris, *Portrait of the Artist's Mother* (Private Collection), looks like a bas-relief in plush, folded and buttoned back on to its canvas support, and bears a startling likeness to the late Douglas Cooper, who once owned the picture. Although too young to have known him Cooper was to be, togther with Kahnweiler, Gris's greatest champion, and his *catalogue raisonné* of Gris's work, which came out in 1977, with the collaboration of Margaret Potter, remains a model of its kind.

The exhibition of Gris's work at London's Whitechapel Art Gallery in 1992, which subsequently travelled to Holland and Germany, was not the most beautiful Gris exhibition there has ever been: there have been few as beautiful as that mounted by Cooper in Berne in 1955. But this was the most moving Gris exhibition I have ever seen, because the choice of works made one so strongly aware of the artistic personality behind them and of the workings of Gris's mind. The first pictures convey an extraordinary sense of loneliness and frugality, which are emphasized by Gris's adoption of a cool, restricted palette used to produce an effect of tinted *grisaille*.

Gris's studio still lifes have been carefully set up, but they also convey a sense of a life lived: plates and bowls are empty or scraped clean, foodstuffs are basic and limited, wine bottles are almost always not quite full, their contents rationed. The café tables often contain two or more glasses but there is none of the conviviality found in comparable works by Picasso and Braque. Cups of coffee (Gris's only form of self-indulgence) and other refreshments often denote not so much moments of relaxation as pauses for solitary communion. Gris's works are *bodegónes* in the true sense of the word in that they are humble pictures of humble objects. Picasso's still lifes have been compared to those of Zurbarán, and his admiration for his seventeenth-century predecessor is well known; but the relationship between Gris and the earlier work of Zurbarán is in a sense truer in that there is a shared asceticism.

Gris was originally viewed as a mere follower of Picasso, an impression he helped to foster, although in fact he soon came to prefer the work of Braque. In reality, apart from a few pieces of

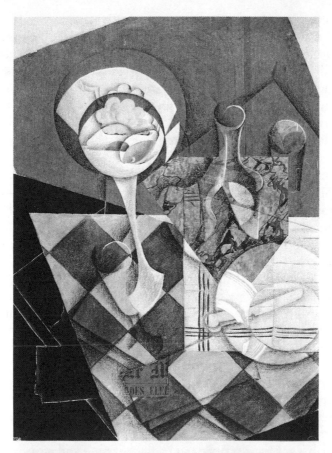

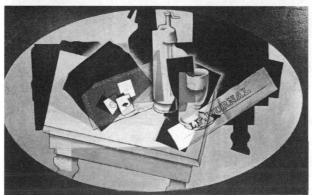

Gris, *Still Life with Fruit Dish*, 1914

Gris, *Still Life with Siphon*, 1916

apprenticeship, Gris's Cubism was wholly original, right from the start. In 1912 when Gris began to hit his stride Picasso and Braque were still making use of their celebrated Cubist grids, linear scaffoldings around which are suspended complexes of faceted translucent planes. These Gris immediately put to new purposes. In his hands they become like irregular geometric leaded windows; they organize compositions and form the point of departure for the analysis of objects: a jug is quartered and its sections seen from different angles – at eye level, from above, and in rotation from the side. Another group of paintings, initiated in the summer of 1913, are violently, almost garishly coloured. The intellectual rigours of Gris's art persist, but these canvases carry with them a whiff of the fairground and the cheap *cantina* and remind us that there was also a more popular side to his art. In later life Gris's greatest relaxation was dancing, and he loved folk and popular music.

The invention by Braque of *papier collé* in 1912, which involved incorporating into paintings and drawings strips of coloured or commercially decorated paper as well as other fragments of external reality – cigarette packages, theatre programmes and so on – in turn modified the appearance of Picasso's and Braque's paintings in that it led to simpler, more solid and less shadowy effects. These were noted by Gris and once again given a personal interpretation. Linear armatures now give way to compositions built up of sombrely coloured, upright rectangular slabs which, as with *papiers collés*, dislocate and modify the objects placed over them: for example the outline of a goblet inscribed over adjacent blue and white planes will be rendered by a white line over the blue plane and then again, seen from a different angle or viewpoint, by a blue line over the white plane.

Gris's own *papiers collés* of 1914 and the sombre, low-toned paintings of 1916 mark the summit of his achievement. His *papiers collés* are the most elaborate of all Cubist *papiers collés* and are in reality surrogate paintings. They have about them a feeling of tailor-made precision that distinguishes them from both Picasso's rougher, more spontaneous use of the medium and from Braque's more sparing and open effects: and although the layering and overlapping of pasted paper produces a sensation of depth it is an impacted depth as opposed to the freer, airy space achieved by Braque. Similarly, while Gris often juggles with the reading of things, using, for instance, wallpaper to represent a tablecloth, his *papiers collés* lack the alchemical properties of Picasso's. He used newspaper cuttings and other printed matter, often satirically or humorously, but always in a thoughtful way. These are works that make demands on the viewer at many levels. The paintings of 1916 are distinguished by a truly masterly use of blacks which are played off against greys and creamy off-whites to produce an astonishing sense of tonal nuance. These are the most quintessentially Spanish of all Gris's pictures. Despite their monastic severity they convey a sense of majesty and fullness, and with them one senses in an odd way that the odour of sanctity has descended on the artist.

Gris experienced great hardship during the war; money had always been a problem for him and was to remain one until the very final years of his life. But now with his dealer Kahnweiler in exile and unable to help, things were particularly bad. And yet the disruption of artistic life in Paris and the dispersal of its artists brought with it a sense of release, and, despite Gris's fundamental insecurities, a recognition of his own abilities and worth. Already Picasso had in his own work acknowledged that Gris was no longer a follower but a colleague and competitor. The Salon Cubists, and Metzinger and Diego Rivera in particular, were looking hard at him. Gris saw quite a lot of Matisse in Collioure immediately after the outbreak of war, and when Matisse eventually felt the need to come to terms with Cubism, a movement which he basically disliked, it was Gris's work that he first consulted. When Braque got back to work after being invalided out of the army, he turned to Gris's recent canvases at a time when Henri Laurens and Jacques Lipchitz were also doing so.

After the war Gris played an important if indirect role in the formation of Purism, a movement launched by Amédée Ozenfant and Charles-Edouard Jeanneret (Le Corbusier) in 1919. Purism acknowledged a debt to Cubism but felt that the intellectual clarity and formal innovations that had characterized it during its early, heroic years had subsequently been dissipated because the Cubists – and this is where the Purists made an exception of Gris – had failed to take into account the discoveries of science and the perfectibility of machine-made forms. Gris was now one of the most influential artists working in Europe, and at the time of his death he had become the acknowledged leader of what had come to be known as the 'second Cubism' or of Cubism as it was interpreted by artists in France during the 1920s.

Still-Life Lives

It was also during the war years that Gris's closest links with literature were made. His friendship with the poet Pierre Reverdy was cemented then, and despite odd moments of estrangement it was a friendship that bore many fruits. Reverdy was two years younger than Gris and came to see Cubism through Gris's eyes; and he was to become one of the most perceptive critics of Cubism's later phases. As a poet he was influenced by both Apollinaire and Max Jacob; and he was heir to both. His poems, like some of Apollinaire's and most of Jacob's, reflect a debt to Cubism in that they are beautifully constructed and coherent entities made up of overlaid, often seemingly fractured or dislocated parts. Reverdy shared some of Apollinaire's lyric gifts, although his voice is more hesitant and reticent; and he responded to the fantastic, proto-Surrealist side of Apollinaire's art. His work is more accessible than Jacob's but has some of the same underlying anguish that is the result of a simultaneous delight in and rejection of the sensory world.

Jacob had mystic proclivities and twice experienced visions of Christ (the second in a cinema); Reverdy was also of a religious bent but suffered from lifelong doubts. In 1917 Reverdy launched his lively and influential periodical *Nord-Sud* (a reference to the metro line that linked Montmartre and Montparnasse) which provided a forum for a new generation of poets, including two other writers close to Gris, Paul Dermée and the Chilean Vicente Huidobro. Picasso had always been drawn to poets and writers because he enjoyed their company: he picked up ideas from them and they saved him the trouble of having to read things for himself. In the case of Gris, the poets eased the underlying loneliness of his nature; he was an influence on them when he helped to inspire Reverdy's and Dermée's still-life poems written between 1915 and 1919, and his collaborations with Huidobro led to some literary experiments of his own.

Gris's work of the war years has often been compared to Reverdy's contemporary poetry, and in 1915–16 Gris produced the most beautiful of his book illustrations for Reverdy's *Au Soleil du Plafond* (not published until much later). These small exquisite works anticipate Picasso's miniature still lifes executed at the end of the decade. The comparison with Reverdy is rewarding but cannot be pushed too far. Reverdy was fascinated by the use of metaphor in Cubism and used it as the basis for his own aesthetic, most succinctly expressed in his essay *L'Image*, published in *Nord-Sud* in

94

March 1918. In it he defined the poetic image as the product of the 'coming together' of two or more 'distant realities'. Reverdy had observed the 'rhyming' shapes in Gris's work: the circle of a goblet seen from above picking up the sounding hole of a guitar, for instance – and strove to achieve similar effects in his poetry. But Reverdy's own confrontations did, as he suggested, bring together unexpected images, as when he talks of his own head being a lighted lamp. And it was the unlikeliness of his juxtapositions that made him an important figure for the Surrealists.

Gris by contrast stressed family likeliness and affinities of things. He remained bound to objects even though they became increasingly the products of his own imagination. But if Gris accepted the validity of visual experience, while Reverdy revelled in it and yet questioned and looked beyond it, they both became increasingly obsessed by abstracting and purifying the means by which they rendered their respective visions; and there is an underlying humility common to the art of both. But the art of the two men has a shared remoteness and purity as well.

It was in Gris's writings of the 1920s that the distinction between the 'analytic' and 'synthetic' method of approach was truly hammered out,[18] most notably in a lecture entitled *Sur les possibilités de la peinture*, which he delivered at the Société des Etudes Philosophiques et Scientifiques in the Sorbonne in April 1924. Ironically the lecture gained some of the publicity and prominence his art had hitherto failed to achieve. Within the context of Cubism, and put in its simplest form, an analytic approach involved working from representation towards highly abstract effects, whereas a synthetic approach meant working from abstraction toward a new kind of figuration or representation of objects. Gris's early Cubism had been in a sense more rigorously analytical than that of Picasso and Braque in that they were working conceptually and from memory and their images of objects are generalized, whereas Gris's still-life objects continue to belong to the real world and are subsequently dismembered, dissected and put together in what might be described as greater Cubist plenitude.

But already there were conceptual undercurrents in his art, and premonitions of what he would later call a synthetic procedure in that his compositions are almost from the start dictated by abstract geometric substructures: squares, golden sections and the diagonals which bisect them, and so on. By 1913 he was making preparatory drawings using rulers, templates, calipers and repeated geometric modules. These have been referred to as scientific, although in fact the calculations are sometimes random and arbitrary and conform to no consistent perspectival principles. On his deathbed Gris asked Kahnweiler and his wife, Josette, to destroy them. Earlier on Gris had gloried in his use of what he saw as verifiable compositional principles; now he was afraid of posterity viewing him as a cold and calculating artist. The loss of these drawings is great because one or two have survived and are truly beautiful.

In 1913–14 when Gris was making extensive use of *papier collé*, the manipulation of 'ready-made' compositional elements, even when they had been specifically tailored to the painting, must have sharpened his sense of achieving abstract compositional substructures on to which his imagery could be affixed. By 1915 he was able to write to Kahnweiler: 'My paintings are no longer those inventories which depress me so';[19] and the objects in his paintings had certainly become less literal. Six years later Gris was able to claim that he could produce to order a composition to suit any given size or format.[20]

In a sense Gris had moved from an initial Neo-Aristotelian position, concerned with the classification of objects and types of perception, to a Neo-Platonic belief in the perfectibility of form, a belief suggested in his writings, which have all the lucidity of his paintings. They make it clear that he had come to see painting as being made up of two interacting but completely independent elements. The first of them was 'architecture', by which he meant the abstract composition or sub-structure of a painting and which he conceived as flat, coloured shapes. This coloured architecture was the means or the vehicle of his art. The end, on the other hand, was the representational aspect of a canvas or its subject; this was sometimes suggested by the flat, coloured architecture itself or could on other occasions be imposed on to it. There is no doubt about which of the two aspects of Gris's painting now took primacy, not only in the sequence and construction of a painting but for its own sake. 'It is not picture X which manages to correspond with my subject,' he writes, 'but subject X which manages to correspond with my picture.'[21]

Kahnweiler saw Gris as working in a synthetic mode by 1916; in other words he felt that Gris's paintings now began as total abstractions and ended up with legible, representational subjects.

Christopher Green, who selected the Whitechapel exhibition and whose seven introductory essays made up a new and invaluable book on Gris, argues for a slightly later date. He suggests that it was towards the end of 1917, when Gris's collaboration with Reverdy was at its closest, that by the artist's own definition he achieved a truly synthetic procedure. Green believes that while Gris had previously used rhymed objects in his work, not only was Gris now marrying figurative subjects on to abstract pictorial sub-structures, he was also 'rhyming' some of these abstract shapes before qualifying them as objects.

Gris was later to confuse the issue because, like virtually every other painter, he was convinced that his most recent painting marked an advance on what had gone before, and, as the word 'synthetic' acquired talisman-like connotations in his mind he kept moving the goal posts, allowing only his most recent work through them. In any case, by 1921 he had made his position clear when he made his most famous pronouncement:

> Cézanne turns a bottle into a cylinder . . . I make a bottle, a particular bottle out of a cylinder. Cézanne works towards architecture, I tend away from it. For example I make a composition with a white and a black and make adjustments when the white has become a sheet of paper and the black a shadow.[22]

Gris then qualifies the statement by a revealing aside: 'What I mean is that I adjust the white so that it becomes paper and the black so that it becomes a shadow.' The countless 'adjustments' visible on close scrutiny in almost all of his paintings, from the very first to the very last, demonstrate that the instinctive balancing of forms and the modifying of their contours played as great a role in his picture-making as did his pictorial theory.

Green's view that in 1917 Gris moved into a new phase was reinforced by the installation at the Whitechapel Art Gallery, which broke the two sections of the exhibition at this point. And as one moved into the upstairs galleries, one did feel very strongly that a search for systems had been replaced by a sense of methods found and then disguised. The work of 1918 looks more architectural and in a sense more impersonal. The imagery remains the same; still life continues to reign supreme although the ratio of figure pieces to still life increases and there are a few somewhat awkward attempts at multifigure compositions. From a technical point of view the earlier pleating or overlapping of spatial effects is replaced by a feeling almost of bas-relief. And the incisive juxtaposition of lights and darks emphasizes the fact that Gris was not so much a draughtsman in his painting as a supreme manipulator of the painted edge. Gris's work retains its Spanish flavour but one also now gets the impression that he was perhaps unconsciously trying to integrate his work into a French tradition.

In 1916 and 1918 respectively Gris had produced his reinterpretations of works by Corot and Cézanne. Chardin was also much on his mind. Gris's great pictorial loves, Kahnweiler tells us, were almost all French and include Fouquet, Boucher and Ingres; the inclusion of Boucher is revealing. Some of Gris's work of the 1920s seeks to charm and in this it is not always successful. When he abandons his more traditional Spanish palette and moves into paler, softer hues, his colour sense becomes at times uncertain, and some of the more decorative, curvilinear pictures look either slack or self-conscious. In 1920 Gris suffered his first major illness, and although there were subsequently protracted periods of good health and good spirits, his physique had been undermined. From time to time the late work – and this is particularly true of the years 1922 to 1923 – shows signs of fatigue.

Throughout his career Gris's work is for the most part curiously unaccentuated, so that when we think of him we tend to get a composite picture of his works in our mind, increasingly so as his career moves to a close. The late horizontal window pictures executed at Bandol, however, do mark a high point and are infused by a new and totally unforced poetry and lyricism. The very late still lifes achieve something of what Braque subsequently used to refer to as '*le climat*', and which he described as 'arriving at a temperature which renders things malleable'.[23] The objects in the still lifes of 1925 and 1926 are self-contained, dreamlike and remote. Simultaneously they seem to buckle and bend, locking behind into a pictorial sub-structure which is, once again, both rigorous and deliquescent.

Gertrude Stein in what was in effect her obituary of Gris was at her best when she wrote, 'Four years partly illness much perfection and rejoining beauty and perfection and then at the end there was a definite creation of something... This is what is to be measured. He made something that is to be measured. And that is that something.' Yes, it is. To the end of his life Gris remained an isolated and in some respects a misunderstood and even somewhat tragic figure. He lacked self-confidence, yearned for it and never achieved it. But he had extraordinary self-knowledge and maybe this ultimately stood him in better stead. In 1915 he wrote to Kahnweiler:

I can't find room in my pictures for that more sensitive and sensuous side which I feel should always be there . . . Oh how I wish I could convey the ease and the charm of the unfinished. Well, it can't be helped. One must after all paint as one is oneself. My mind is too precise to muddy a blue or twist a straight line.[24]

Picasso, *Les Demoiselles d'Avignon*, 1907

6

Two Picasso Exhibitions,
Early and Late

WHEN the Museum of Modern Art mounted its huge Picasso exhibition in New York in 1980, it obtained the full support of the Picasso museums in Paris and Barcelona on condition that the *Demoiselles d'Avignon* (1907), in a sense the cornerstone of New York's collection, might be allowed to cross the Atlantic for a final time for display in these two cities. The New York exhibition was a triumph – the greatest Picasso exhibition there has ever been or ever will be, even though the late work was inadequately represented. Many of the great works seen together will never be reunited; *Guernica*, for example, was afterwards restored to Spain, according to the artist's ultimate wish, and is now, after an interval when it was shown in a dependency of the Prado under grotesque conditions, reigning supreme in the Reina Sofía, Madrid's own new museum of modern art. The relatively small *Demoiselles* exhibition shown in Paris in 1988 and Barcelona was a triumph of a different kind. It was accompanied by a two-volume catalogue,[1] which makes the *Demoiselles*, after *Guernica*, the most extensively documented twentieth-century painting.[2] In the catalogue, William Rubin writes at length about the picture with his customary thoroughness and incisiveness. It is now a moot point whether *Guernica* or the *Demoiselles* is the most famous image of the art of our age. *Guernica* has engaged the attention of specialists and commentators of every persuasion and has driven several of them insane. The *Demoiselles* remains more central to concepts of modernism and is ultimately the more important work – one of those rare individual works of art that have changed the course of visual history.

The *Demoiselles* was conceived and executed in a small, filthy studio in a ramshackle wooden building known as the Bateau-Lavoir, perched on the slopes of Montmartre. The picture can't have been seen by all that many people in the years after it was painted and, with one exception, almost nothing was written about it at the time, or even subsequently, by the people who must have seen it in its original studio setting while it was being painted or immediately afterwards. Fernande Olivier, who was living with Picasso at the time, does not mention it in either of her two memoirs.[3] Neither does Apollinaire, although he had written so poignantly on Picasso's earlier work and had already, and more than anyone else, helped to bring Picasso to early fame.

Max Jacob, who in the early years of the century shared with Picasso his top hat, his bed (they slept in it separately in relays), and indeed his very existence, and who at the time of the *Demoiselles* remained in many respects his *alter ego*, referred to the great painting only once, years later, and then casually, almost in passing.[4] Another of Picasso's writer friends, the poet, critic and journalist André Salmon, did however discuss the picture at some length in his *La Jeune Peinture Française*, which appeared in the autumn of 1912; and it was he who set the tone and formalistic approach in which the work was to be discussed for some fifty years to come.

Less surprisingly, we know about the reactions of Picasso's painter friends only through their work, or at second hand, through hearsay. Derain, possibly with Balzac's Frenhofer in mind, predicted that one day Picasso would be found hanged behind the painting.[5] In the event it was the picture that to a certain extent hanged Derain. An artist of great intelligence and enormous natural gifts, he now produced a large lifeless answer to the *Demoiselles*, a three-figure piece called *La Toilette*, which he subsequently destroyed; he recovered his balance but the direction of his art had been permanently altered.

Matisse was made angry by the *Demoiselles* and seems to have thought it was something of a bad joke,[6] although he reacted to it indirectly when in 1908 he produced his great *Bathers with a Turtle*, now in the St Louis Art Museum.[7] Braque, too, initially disliked the *Demoiselles*; but he studied the picture harder than any other artist, and indeed his subsequent friendship and collaboration with Picasso led to the Cubist revolution. Critics and collectors were similarly baffled. Gertrude Stein tells us that Shchukin, who had become an important patron of Picasso's, said: 'What a loss for French art.'[8] Leo Stein was derisive.[9] Vollard, always taciturn, said nothing.[10] Kahnweiler, who was about to become Picasso's dealer, subsequently became obsessed by the picture; but he was also made uneasy by it right until the end of his days.[11]

The *Demoiselles* was first shown publicly at the *Salon d'Antin* in 1916 in an exhibition organized by André Salmon. The picture, Picasso's only entry, became the centrepiece of the exhibition, which was extended by a couple of weeks – cultural events of a comparable importance (literary and musical sessions accompanied the show) were rare in wartime Paris. It was here that the painting, which was originally known to Picasso's intimates as *Le Bordel Philosophique*, acquired its present title. Picasso must surely have agreed to the way in which Salmon listed the work, but he came to dislike the title intensely, presumably because it seemed evasive and genteel; and he most often referred to the painting simply as 'mon bordel'. Although the Avignon of the title has been associated with a brothel in Barcelona's *carrer d'Avinyo*, near where Picasso's family lived, William Rubin is probably right in suggesting that Salmon chose the title because since the time of the papacy Avignon had carried overtones of sensuality and vice: the Abbé de Sade, Rubin reminds us, who was the uncle and tutor of the divine Marquis himself, quoted Petrarch on the subject.[12]

The *Demoiselles* was almost certainly seen at the *Salon d'Antin* by the great *couturier* and Maecenas Jacques Doucet, who was subsequently to acquire it. But it was André Breton, acting as Doucet's librarian, who urged his patron to make the purchase in a series of letters of such eloquence that we can only regret that he never wrote about the painting at greater length and independently, so to speak. (What a marvellous companion piece it would have made to that small masterpiece *Phare de la Mariée*, his essay on Duchamp's *Large Glass*.) In November 1923, when Doucet appears to have been still wavering, we find Breton writing: 'It is a work which for me goes beyond painting, it is the theatre of everything that has happened over the past fifty years, it is the wall before which have passed Rimbaud, Lautréamont, Jarry, Apollinaire and all those whom we continue to love.'[13] A year later, after the sale had been completed, we find him still reassuring Doucet: 'Here is the painting which one would parade, as was Cimabue's *Virgin*, through the streets of our capital.'[14]

Doucet paid 25,000 francs for the work, an astonishingly small sum even at that time, and Picasso probably agreed to the sale because Doucet had promised to bequeath it to the Louvre. (It never got there, but Doucet had almost certainly not acted in bad faith, and it is very likely that the Louvre may have verbally rejected the offer of such a controversial work.) Picasso never forgave Doucet for having got the work out of him so cheaply and he refused to come to see it when it was finally installed in the new mansion in Neuilly into which the Doucets moved in 1928. There it was given pride of place on the landing of an extraordinary staircase (the steps were of silver and red enamel under heavy glass and the newel posts took the form of exotic birds) conceived by Doucet himself and executed by the sculptor Csaky. Opposite the *Demoiselles* stood enormous double doors by Lalique (rescued from an earlier dwelling) that led into the 'studio' and beyond into the room where oriental antiques were displayed. The picture itself was encased in a forged metal frame, especially designed for it by Legrain, who had originally achieved fame as a bookbinder but had also come to be recognized as one of the greatest French craftsmen of his time. The Bateau-Lavoir was a world away.

In August 1929 A. Conger Goodyear, who was president of the trustees of New York's Museum of Modern Art, was taken to see the Doucet collection and was bowled over by it and its setting. Alfred Barr, then the museum's director, starred the *Demoiselles* in the list of paintings he wanted to put together for a Picasso show that was originally to have taken place in 1931, but for various reasons was not mounted until 1939. In the meantime, Doucet had died, the house had been demolished, and Madame Doucet had sold the collection of eleven Picassos (the eleventh turned out in fact to be by Braque) to the Seligmann Gallery, which had branches in Paris and New York. The *Demoiselles* was sold for six times what Picasso had received for it.

The picture sailed for New York in October 1937 on the *Normandie*, the Legrain frame travelling separately. In November it went on show at the Seligmann premises on East Fifty-first Street to the accompaniment of considerable publicity. On 9 November, Barr, who now described the picture as 'the most important painting of the twentieth century', urged the advisory committee to propose the picture to the museum's trustees.[15] In December the sale went through. (Things moved fast in those days.) The picture went on view on 10 May 1939 in an exhibition entitled 'Art in Our Time', which was designed to commemorate the tenth anniversary of the museum and its reopening in its present premises. Somewhere between Fifty-first and Fifty-third Streets the Legrain frame mysteriously disappeared.

The *Demoiselles* exhibition consisted of the great canvas itself, a handful of paintings that led up to it, and some five dozen oil paintings, watercolours and drawings that relate directly to it; equally revealing and exciting were the sixteen sketch-books that recorded the processes of Picasso's mind and eye at work over a period of some nine months from the autumn of 1906 through to the high summer of 1907. These he kept himself until his death, and until recently they were relatively unknown. The problems of sequence and date surrounding the sketch-books and the individual leaves within them have not been completely sorted out, and given Picasso's unmethodical working processes they probably never will be. But the sketch-books make it immediately obvious that this was by far the most elaborately plotted of all Picasso's masterpieces. Finally, there was what amounted to a small exhibition within an exhibition – a group of 'things seen': possible sources of inspiration. Many people expressed reservations about this section of the exhibition and saw it as being extraneous or didactic. I myself found it fascinating, demonstrating as it did that working from photographs and reproductions, the actual feel of works of art, the presence with which they confront us, becomes so completely lost.

The relevance of a particular El Greco, *The Vision of Saint John* (Metropolitan Museum, New York), known until recently as *The Seventh Seal* (and to Picasso himself, probably most importantly, as *Profane Love*), was first pointed out by Ron Johnson in 1980 and then elaborated upon, at the same time and entirely independently, by Rolf Laessoe and, in even greater depth, by John Richardson.[16] The affinities between this El Greco and the *Demoiselles* are so striking, not only on a multiplicity of visual levels, but also spiritually and psychologically, that it is hard not to believe that Picasso began the actual execution of the *Demoiselles* under its direct stimulus. Picasso had known and consulted El Greco's work for some time past, and he had almost certainly often seen this particular work, which belonged to the Spanish painter Zuloaga, then resident in Paris. But, as so often with Picasso, revelation seems to have struck at exactly the appropriate moment; and maybe this faculty is one of the attributes of true genius. It is hard to see much of El Greco in any of the surrounding studies. The presence of this singularly apocalyptic El Greco behind the *Demoiselles* helps to explain why Breton, for one, viewed the painting of the interior of a whorehouse as a mystical experience.

Picasso

Picasso must have seen Ingres's *Le Bain Turc* (Musée du Louvre, Paris) in the great Ingres retrospective at the *Salon d'Automne* of 1905. He certainly admired it and it was to obsess him in old age. It stands behind the *Demoiselles*, but at a distance. Cézanne's *Five Bathers* (Kunstmuseum, Basle), like the El Greco, strikes an instant chord of psychological rightness in relationship to the *Demoiselles*, and its sublimated but still uneasy sensuality seems infinitely closer to it than does the melting eroticism of the Ingres. Gauguin's *Oviri* (Musée d'Orsay) makes the point that for Picasso Gauguin's sculpture was more important than his painting. Matisse's *Blue Nude* (Baltimore Museum of Art) and Derain's *Bathers* (Museum of Modern Art, New York), both seen at the *Salon des Indépendants* of 1907 (it opened in March), are in different ways relevant to the *Demoiselles*, although they seem to exist in very different worlds from it; and great paintings though they are, the *Demoiselles* dominated and tamed them. The tribal art from Africa and the New Hebrides in the exhibition simply served to confirm what so many of us have always maintained: that while he was actually at work on the *Demoiselles* Picasso experienced its impact. As in the case of El Greco, Picasso must have already been aware of tribal art – his friends and colleagues had been talking about it and collecting it for at least a year – but it was at this moment that its implications struck home in the violence of the two *demoiselles* at the right-hand side of the composition.

Complementing the tribal art, and anticipating its impact on the *Demoiselles*, was a lifesize stone Iberian head of a man, dating from between the fifth and third centuries BC, and hence to a primitive period of the peninsula's indigenous art (now in the museum at St-Germain-en-Laye). This had been stolen from the Louvre in March 1907 and almost immediately entered Picasso's possession. An object of very little obvious aesthetic worth, it nevertheless has extraordinary presence. Half the head has been virtually obliterated by erosion; the other half displays an enormous scroll-shaped ear, a sharp wedge-shaped nose and a great bulging eye. These features are echoed in the heads of the two central *demoiselles*, and, as X-rays and preparatory studies show, underlie the heads of their companions.

Here we are confronted for the first time with one of the rawest and most profound aspects of Picasso's genius – his ability to take something that in itself comes pretty close to being nothing and to transform it into great and meaningful art. In his catalogue essay for the 'Late Picasso' exhibition, which by luck coincided in Paris with that of the *Demoiselles*, John Richardson writes evocatively of the Andalusian concept of the *'mirada fuerte'*, the way in which the Andalusian grasps a person or an object with his stare or steady gaze, possesses it, rapes it.[17] But if traditionally the *mirada fuerte* is a male prerogative, here it is given to the five naked women. The two outer figures stare past and through each other. The other three transfix us completely with their gaze, and it is only subsequently that we become aware of them as bodies. Eventually the painting stares us down.

Even before the richness of the sketch-books had been revealed to us, the basic iconography of the picture had been frequently rehearsed in the phase of the literature on the painting initiated by Alfred Barr in *Picasso: Forty Years of His Art*, which accompanied the Museum of Modern Art's 1939 exhibition. Two men were to have been included in the composition: a sailor seated among the women and a figure (later identified by Picasso as a medical student) who entered the composition at the left; he holds either a skull or a book, and on one occasion both. As the sketches evolved, the first to go was the medical student. Ultimately the sailor himself disappears. We, the spectators, are now seated at the inner table of the brothel (originally there had been two tables), opposite the *Demoiselles*, and we have by implication become their clients. The watercolour sketch from the Gallatin Collection in Philadelphia, which corresponds most closely to the *Demoiselles*, is, I suspect, not a final preparatory study for the painting but a subsequent footnote to it, a record of what the picture looked like before Picasso went back into it after his traumatic encounters with the tribal art displayed in the Trocadero (now the Musée de l'Homme). Thirty years later, recalling this revelation, Picasso spoke to Malraux of the *Demoiselles* as his first 'exorcism' picture: 'For me the masks were not simply sculptures, they were magical objects. They were weapons to keep people from being ruled by spirits, to help free themselves.'[18]

Leo Steinberg's essay of 1972 reads as persuasively as ever; and it now seems strange that for fifty years writers, including myself, should have written about the painting in almost entirely formalistic terms, and put to one side its erotic implications and thus denied the painting some of its supreme physicality. Rubin has repeatedly expressed his indebtedness to Steinberg. He now reaffirms it but wonders if Steinberg did not indeed go far enough in his 'psychosexual' analysis. Rubin can find no very direct links between the head of the squatting *demoiselle* (the most apocalyptic of all) and any tribal masks that Picasso might have seen. He now suggests that Picasso's imagination was fuelled by memories of the syphilitic patients he saw when he visited the hospital-prison of St-Lazare (and its morgue) in 1901; its female inmates were prostitutes contaminated by venereal disease.

In this connection Rubin reproduces some truly horrifying photographs from the turn of the century showing the heads of women suffering from tertiary syphilis. Picasso may well have been haunted by such nightmares; but the head of this *demoiselle* and the study for it have about them an hypnotic and barbaric beauty as well as an overpowering and corrosive vitality that make confrontation with the photographic images of pustular decay oddly gratuitous. These heads of Picasso still look deeply tribal and atavistic to me, and since he was ultimately interested simultaneously in the spirit that lay behind tribal art and in the formal visual principles that made that spirit manifest rather than in any particular example, I see no reason why he should not have manipulated these to his own psychological and expressive purposes. The squatting figure in the *Demoiselles* was undoubtedly the last to be executed and she remains the most enigmatic.

For that matter, and despite the wealth of research that has now been placed at our disposal, the picture itself remains something of an enigma. That Picasso should have felt compelled to make a major effort and statement at this moment in his career was only to be expected. He undoubtedly saw himself in rivalry with Matisse, and Matisse's *La Joie de Vivre*, shown at the *Salon des Indépendants* in 1905, had set the seal on his reputation as leader of advanced young French painting. In acknowledged and friendly rivalry Matisse and Derain had at the *Indépendants* just shown their two large 'blue' paintings. Prostitution and its dangerous consequences had been a major theme in Picasso's work in the early years of this century. But why should he have returned to the subject at this particular moment in his life, and why should he have chosen it to effect a major stylistic revolution? Although Picasso was still experiencing financial hardship, his work had begun to sell well to important dealers and collectors. The paintings done at Gosol during the summer of 1906, which in a sense represent him at his first full maturity, are classicizing and breathe an air of deep calm and content. Fernande Olivier had come to live with Picasso toward the end of 1905 and for the first time in his life he appeared to be enjoying a stable relationship with a beautiful woman whose physicality matched his own.

The choice of subject matter for his great new canvas may in part have been a deliberate and defiant answer to the hedonism of the work of Matisse and his fellow Fauves. Apollinaire, with his insatiable appetite for erotica, may well have been an influence; the original manuscript of his *Les Onze Mille Verges*, bearing the date of 1907, was one of Picasso's most treasured possessions. It is a pornographic *tour de force* and one of its set pieces is an orgy in a brothel. Rubin is almost certainly right in suggesting that it was Apollinaire who gave the painting its original title, *The Philosophical Brothel*. Several authors have suggested that Picasso himself had been attacked by venereal disease, and given his early way of life this is at least likely; if so, something may have happened to remind him of the episode. The years between 1898 and 1902 had seen the climax of the battle between those who wanted to abolish government control of prostitutes and those who wanted to regulate their activities, and the subject was still very much in the air.[19]

The second volume of Fernande Olivier's memoirs, which was posthumously published, makes it clear that when she met Picasso she was leading a promiscuous life, and this may account for some of the excessive possessiveness he showed toward her. Their 'adoption' of a thirteen-year-old orphan, Raymonde, seems to have introduced further complication into their communal life. In August 1907 Fernande wrote to Gertrude Stein in distress saying that she and Picasso were separating. By the end of the first week of September she had left. She was soon to return; but during the first half of 1907 there were tensions in the studios at the Bateau-Lavoir and these must have found their way into the general atmosphere of the building and into the *Demoiselles* itself.

But it is to the work of the autumn of 1906 that we must turn for premonitions of what was to come, and the tensions here are, or so it seems to me, purely visual and pictorial. They show massive female nudes whose girth is so abnormally distended that one can only convey an impression of them in words by describing them as pneumatic lay figures, pressed up against a glass surface and pumped fuller and fuller of air, so that they become increasingly swollen and monumental in appearance, while simultaneously flattening up against and across the surface that is immediately in front of them. An explosion was inevitable and this explosion was the *Demoiselles*.

The nudes that precede it, unique in the history of art for their distention, have been themselves discussed in psychosexual terms; but just as many of the figures of Cézanne's maturity assume the quality of still lifes, so these creations of Picasso seem to me to be primarily pregnant with purely formal and visual possibilities. The erotic implications of the *Demoiselles* are married to its formal innovations and are conveyed by them, as Leo Steinberg has so convincingly demonstrated.[20] But apart from a couple of expressionistic footnotes to the painting, it was succeeded, as it had been preceded, by what was on the whole a period of calm, of pictorial experiment and analysis. In the *Demoiselles* Picasso began to shatter the human figure and the pictorial conventions for rendering it. He spent the rest of his artistic life dissecting, reassembling and reinventing it.

At the time of the 'Hommage à Pablo Picasso' of 1966, which celebrated the artist's eighty-fifth birthday and which occupied both the Grand and the Petit Palais in Paris, I found myself spending a lot of time in the rooms devoted to the late work for the simple reason that they were completely empty, whereas the spaces that preceded them were intolerably crowded. The paintings worried me. Certainly it was almost universally felt at the time that since the early 1950s Picasso's work had fallen off. The two exhibitions of 1970 and 1973, held in the Palais des Papes at Avignon, showed only the most recent work (the 1973 exhibition, which opened a month after Picasso's death, contained 201 paintings chosen by the artist himself) and in retrospect appear protean, but they were then to a large extent ignored; and when they were noticed had an almost uniformly hostile reception. No less a figure than Douglas Cooper, a friend of Picasso's and a lifelong supporter, described the very last paintings as 'incoherent doodles done by a frenetic dotard in the anteroom of death'.[21]

My own conversion to the late work came when, together with my friends the late Roland Penrose and the late Dominique Bozo (then director of the still-to-be-opened Musée Picasso), I helped to choose the work for an exhibition entitled 'Picasso's Picassos', which took place at the Hayward Gallery in London in 1981. The exhibition was designed and hung in such a way that the last section came as one of its climaxes. That same year Christian Geelhard mounted an exhibition of the late work in Basle, and three years later Gert Schiff's 'Picasso: the Last Years' was put on at the Guggenheim Museum in New York; they saw the late period as beginning in 1964 and 1963 respectively. By now it was beginning to be obvious to many that Picasso had simply, as always, been light years ahead of the game.

If there are still any doubts about the originality and magnitude of the late achievement, they were dispelled by the exhibition in 1988 shared between Paris and London. The selectors cast their net wider and took as their starting point 1953, the year when Jacqueline Roque finally displaced Françoise Gilot as the principal figure in Picasso's life, and when he moved into the first of his final three dwellings and studios.[22] This enabled them to show Picasso carrying out his most intensive dialogue with the art of the past and in the process of doing so reassessing his own vast output, before moving in the second half of the 1960s into a new late style that bears comparison, in a very general way, with the late styles of, for example, Titian, Michelangelo, Rembrandt and Goya.

In other words, this exhibition allowed us to put the very late work in perspective. Far from decreasing in old age, Picasso's production was if anything accelerating (over one half of the twenty-three volumes of Zervos's *catalogue raisonné* are devoted to the last twenty years). The earliest painting in the exhibition, called *The Shadow* (Musée Picasso, Paris), showed a reclining nude who is in a sense present by her absence since she is conveyed mostly in terms of the bare white canvas; below her is a male silhouette or shadow. The picture is a farewell to Françoise Gilot.

Simultaneously, right at the end of 1954, Picasso had begun his variations on Delacroix's *The Women of Algiers* (Louvre), a painting that had long obsessed him. 'That bastard. He's really good,'[23] he once said to Françoise after having taken her to see the painting at the Louvre. These paintings cement the relationship with Jacqueline; Picasso identified her with the right-hand figure of Delacroix's masterpiece and once remarked, 'Delacroix had already met Jacqueline.'[24] *The Women of Algiers* also commemorates Matisse, who had just died. 'When Matisse died he left his odalisques to me as a legacy,' Picasso remarked to Penrose.[25]

Next came the interiors showing the new studio at La Californie, a large villa just above Cannes. These are imbued with a new feeling for space. Space is a concern in the first variant on Velázquez's *Meninas* (there were to be more than forty, all now in the Picasso Museum in Barcelona), begun in August 1957, and it has been suggested that the painting reflects some of the spatial concerns of Braque's late *Ateliers*.[26] Picasso had always been, and was to remain, primarily a painter of images, and for the most part space interested him only in so far as it gave his images room in which to exist physically and psychologically; in the years of their Cubist collaboration it was Braque who had invented a new kind of pictorial space in which Picasso's images could breathe more freely. Certainly the spatial complexities of the *Meninas* fascinated Picasso. In front of the first of his own *Meninas* he said to Penrose, 'Look at it and try to see where each of the figures is actually situated.'[27] If subsequently the figures in Picasso's work were once again to cannibalize the space around them, in devouring it they acquired a new breadth and monumentality.

The *Meninas* was important for Picasso at virtually every level. He had discovered its greatness in adolescence, and now in old age the questions that it raised concerning the relationship between art and illusion, between the artist and his subject, and between art and society must have permeated his consciousness more than ever before. Not only was the *Meninas* the archetypal studio painting, but its quality of pageantry – the diversity of its characters and the personal and public social rituals they perform – must have encouraged Picasso to begin to view both life and art as one great shifting kaleidoscope of visual revelations and sensations. The picture took him back directly to Spain's Golden Age, and not only to its art but to its literature.

In the same way Manet's *Déjeuner sur l'Herbe* (Musée d'Orsay, Paris) (over two and half years, from 1959 to 1962, Picasso, did more than a hundred variants of it), which itself reflected Manet's *hispagnolisme* and made overt references to masterpieces of the past, must have simultaneously led Picasso to reassess the origins of modern art as he had experienced it when he first settled in Paris in the early years of the century. Stimulus also came from the erotic implications of the painting that had so disturbed the critics of Manet's day. In 1929, on the back of an envelope, Picasso had jotted down: 'When I see Manet's *Déjeuner sur l'Herbe* I say to myself:

trouble for later on.'[28] Earlier, in 1924, the critic André Suarès wrote to a friend after seeing Picasso's own great canvas of 1907: 'These *Demoiselles* are Picasso's *Déjeuner sur l'Herbe*. He must secretly have thought so.'[29]

Picasso's motives for turning to artists of the past for inspiration have often been questioned. Was his own imagination exhausted, and did he need artificial stimulus, a ready-made subject? Was he challenging the art of the past, or did he want to exorcise the figures he was choosing as mentors by metaphorically taking possession of them? As his own painter friends disappeared or died and his own reputation went into decline, did he turn to the figures of the past for company and consolation? I believe he communed with artists of the past as painters have always communed with each other, out of a need for stimulus and in a spirit of both comradeship and competition. Picasso had always been fully aware of the art of the past, but now a sense of its totality came flooding through him. Raphael, Rembrandt, Goya, Ingres, Degas and countless others passed through his studio; and in his graphics he sometimes actually encounters them at the theatre or in a brothel. Occasionally he virtually lived inside the work of others. Slides of Poussin's paintings and of David's *Rape of the Sabines* and Rembrandt's *Night Watch* were projected in his studio so that they covered an entire large wall. In the case of Van Gogh, Picasso's ultimate great passion and obsession, one of the self-portraits was from time to time projected opposite him, from floor to ceiling; he was living in the Dutchman's mind.[30]

The theme of the artist and his model, like the studio interior, had preoccupied the painter from the 1920s onward. Now, centred as his art had become on the nature and mechanics of painting, the theme became increasingly dominant; during 1963 and 1964 Picasso painted virtually nothing else, and these pictures show his vision becoming increasingly internalized. He was working demo-niacally, harder than ever before. Virtually every writer who has ever written on Picasso has stressed the autobiographical aspect of his art, as he did himself: 'I paint the way some people write their autobiography,' he said to Gilot.[31] Picasso's debt to Jacqueline Roque is made abundantly clear. As one would expect she continuously makes her appearance in the art, although we sense her presence for the most part indirectly: many of the monumental female nudes in the first half of the exhibition have about them a tenderness that is rare in Picasso's art. It permeates in particular the paintings of 1964, some of which show the nude model playing with a cat; and these bear eloquent testimony to the central place Jacqueline occupied in his work and life.

The artist and model paintings, on the other hand, comment on the relationship not only between the painter and the naked model, but on the relationship between the act of love and the creative act. Again this had been a theme of Picasso's art since the 1920s, but it now became increasingly obsessive and explicit. In some of the first of the 1963–4 series the model is placed at a distance from the painter and her prime function seems to be that of furnishing the space around her. As the series progresses the painter moves up on her and eventually the model and the canvas on which he works become confounded. The painter's attributes – his brushes, the palette pierced by the thumb that grips it – become increasingly phallic. Finally it is the model and not her image that is being painted, that physically feels the painter's touch. Like the single nudes that flank them, many of these paintings have about them an almost elegiac quality. In many of them the paint quality itself has become sensuous, voluptuous, in a way it never had been before. The pictures depicting couples have a bucolic or pastoral air.

In November 1965 Picasso left the south precipitately for Paris, where, at the American Hospital, he underwent gall bladder and prostate surgery. Several writers have assumed that he was left impotent. Myself, I wouldn't be too sure, although he did remark to Brassai:

> Whenever I see you, my first impulse is to . . . offer you a cigarette, even though I know that neither of us smokes any longer. Age has forced us to give it up, but the desire remains. It is the same thing with making love. We don't do it any more, but the desire is still with us.[32]

But the operation marked a final milestone in his life. He was henceforth to become increasingly isolated, and more than ever his studio became his entire world. 'Painting,' he once said, 'that is actual lovemaking.'[33] And if he had previously used lovemaking as a metaphor for painting, now one senses increasingly that he was using painting as a metaphor or substitute for sexual intercourse; and this gives his art a new urgency and violence.

Already the elements of the late style had been present in his work. Matisse in old age had become increasingly preoccupied with

the concept of signs. 'Each thing has its own sign,' he said to Aragon, 'and the discovery of this marks the artist's progress in the knowledge and expression of the world, a saving of time, the briefest possible indication of the character of a thing.'[34] Picasso, much earlier, when he had been asked why the full-face heads in the *Demoiselles* had been given noses seen in profile, had replied that this was the surest way of 'saying' that they were noses. Now he confided to Hélène Parmelin, who with her painter husband Pignon was among the few people he saw regularly: 'I want to say the nude. I don't want to do the nude as a nude. I want only to say breast, say foot, say hand or belly. To find the ways to say it.'[35] Hitherto Picasso had 'said' things graphically, by the use of line. In his late manner, and in keeping with his increasingly painterly concerns, he was to 'say' things with great painterly sweeps and gestures and with increasing freedom and abandon, with that total disregard for any sense of stylistic conventions or unity that is in itself the hallmark of a late style.

Picasso had always drawn compulsively and continued to do so, but as an activity drawing had now become subsidiary to his painting, rather than pointing the way forward as it had so often done in the past; just as during certain periods of his career his paintings had been surrogate sculptures, the sculptures of old age become surrogate paintings. Printmaking, on the other hand, was fundamental to the art of his last decade, and it fed and complemented his work on canvas. His printmakers, the Crommelynck brothers, possibly the greatest living masters of their trade, were the last new friends he was to acquire. As his painting became simultaneously wilder and more emblematic, the etchings from the second half of the 1960s demonstrate that his hand was as steady as ever, his virtuosity undiminished, and his imaginative powers at a new and hitherto unequalled pitch of inventiveness; their style is broadly speaking classical, but their subject matter is not.

It is in the graphic work that the narrative aspect of Picasso's art finds it fullest expression. He said, 'I spend hour after hour while I draw, observing the characters and thinking about the mad things they are up to: basically it is my way of writing fiction.' In these late etchings the time barrier is exploded and the past meets the present. And in them the heritage of Spain's Golden Age surges most deeply through his work; the characters of its theatre and its literature meet figures that seem to come from nineteenth-century French painting and fiction, and together they stroll forward in time. The cast of characters multiplies and so do the quotations and references from the art of others; the artists of the past with whom he had conducted individual dialogues now move in and out of his studio simultaneously, freely and at will. Picasso spoke of the voyeuristic aspect of etching; more than in any other medium the artist is spectator at the birth of his own work, since he is never certain of the end result until the plate has been pulled. And the eroticism of these works, unmatched in the annals of the art of the West for its explicitness and inventiveness, has about it almost invariably a voyeuristic aspect. But it is also paraded before us in such a way that it transcends eroticism and becomes simply the focal point of some vast, constantly changing artistic theatre of life.

It is perhaps through the etchings that we can best approach the work of the final years. At one level, the very late paintings seem to flow into each other more insistently than at any other period in Picasso's career. At another, and increasingly as one stands back from them, they overwhelm us physically as individual images. This may in part be because the space the figures inhabit has become so dislocated, so dematerialized, that we lose our own spatial bearings in relation to them. (One has to stand quite far back from the late paintings to appreciate them fully, and it seems fairly obvious that late in the day Picasso was becoming progressively more farsighted.) Another characteristic of the late work is the enlarged eyes of all the figures. As with the *Demoiselles*, and even when the heads of the figures don't look directly at us, the pictures seem to stare at us and subdue us. New subjects include the kiss, works of an incredible ferocity in which heads seem to copulate, and what Picasso called his 'musketeers', figures in seventeenth-century dress, derived from his dialogues with Rembrandt.

Some of these 'musketeers' are in fact musicians or matadors, some hold pipes; their attributes are invariably phallic. They are not self-portraits (although these abound in the late work after an absence of decades), but they seem to be *alter egos* or in some odd way friends from the past; they are the flattest and most disjointed of the late single-figure pieces. A Spanish scholar, José L. Barrio Garay, has pointed out that the word '*mosquetero*' was also used for the non-paying spectators who stood at the back of the Spanish theatres in the Golden Age;[36] like the voyeurs in the etchings, maybe these musketeers are looking at the great *teatrum mundi* that Picasso's art had become.

Although the very late work is not autobiographical in the way that so much of Picasso's art had been, it is revealing at a different level of the condition of extreme old age. A work of 1971 (Collection Mr and Mrs Raymond D. Nasher) shows a naked couple; the man is not old but he appears to be infirm; it is hard to tell whether he is attempting to walk forward or whether he is squatting – in either case he appears to be collapsing. The young woman at his side attempts to support him but her hands are disproportionately small and inadequate to the task. The theme of childhood now recurs obsessively and we sense that the children held by the musketeers or on their mothers' laps are now the artist himself. The vaginal imagery takes on new connotations: great vertical gashes seem to invite penetration of a total sort; they are entries into primeval or preconscious worlds.

One of the very last paintings, called *Reclining Nude and Head* (Private Collection), is dated 25 May 1972 and appears to have been worked over several years. It is in some respects the most majestic and mysterious of all. The reclining figure at the bottom of the painting is angular and rigid, a human sarcophagus. The great dominating head above has been described as 'Jacqueline-like',[37] and has also been compared to the bicycle seat and handlebars that in 1943 Picasso had turned into the head of a bull,[38] a favourite image but one that in old age had virtually disappeared from his art. It also looks strikingly like the tribal Grebo masks that Picasso owned and that in 1912 and 1913 had helped him to make the transition from analytic to synthetic Cubism, from a new way of looking at things to a new way of making paintings. The last staring skull-like self-portraits resemble nothing so much as the eroded Iberian head that had been so crucial to the early stages of the *Demoiselles*.

7

Léger and the Heroism of Modern Life

The heroism of modern life surrounds and presses upon us . . . The painter, the true painter for whom we are looking, will be he who can snatch its epic quality from life today, and can make us see and understand . . . how great and poetic we are in our cravats and our patent-leather boots.

Baudelaire on the *Salon* of 1845[1]

IN a lecture delivered to a group of artists and students in 1914,[2] Léger described how some billowing, cloudlike plumes of smoke, seen from his studio window, had by contrast all of a sudden seemed to bring to life the dry, angular forms of the surrounding buildings. The incident is revealing in several ways. In the first place it is revealing of Léger's attitude towards life, of the way in which the changing urban scene was to be a source of constant fascination and stimulation; of his close friend the poet Blaise Cendrars, Léger once said: 'He is like me, he picks up everything that is going on around him. We were both geared to modern life, we plunged into it deeply.'[3] The incident is indicative, too, of the way in which a casual visual encounter can shape and develop an artist's life and vision. For the glance out of his window gave birth to an important series of paintings, *Les Fumées sur les Toits*, begun in 1910, in which Léger began to formulate his theory of contrasts. This theory lay at the basis of his first independent and original style, and the future developments in his art could with some justification be seen in terms of its steady development and reassessment. In succeeding years he was to strengthen and refine upon it until, in the heroic phases of the 1920s, he was able to infuse what had originally been a device for achieving pictorial movement and variety with a sense of classical repose and grandeur.

Léger came to his first artistic maturity in the years immediately preceding the outbreak of the First World War, when he emerged, together with Mondrian, Duchamp and Delaunay, as one of the four most original and gifted young artists attached peripherally to the Cubist movement. And it was the classical Cubism of Picasso and Braque that prepared the way for the revelation that he experienced when he saw the bonfire of leaves animating the city landscape into a new, dynamic life. Later in life he still remembered vividly the impact of their Cubist canvases, seen in Kahnweiler's gallery in the rue Vignon, paintings built up in terms of elaborate linear scaffoldings which supported subtle complexes of transparent and semi-transparent angled planes, out of which the subject eventually emerged, only to be absorbed once more into the pictorial flux in which it was suspended. The dialogue between abstraction and representation, which was so characteristic of the classical, hermetic years of Cubism, was one which was to absorb Léger, to a greater or lesser extent, for the rest of his life, and above all between the years 1918–28, the decade which saw, perhaps, the greatest of all his achievements.

Léger had known and admired the art of Cézanne for some time before he first came into contact with Cubist painting in 1910. But it was his second, renewed contact with a slightly later phase of Cubism that led him, in 1912, to reinterpret Cézanne in a more progressive and more truly revolutionary manner. For he now saw that if the subject in a painting by Cézanne conveyed an astonishing sense of solidity, at other moments it seemed to be completely absorbed into the overall spatial and colouristic harmonies of the pictorial complex. Braque, in his first Cubist canvases of 1908, had already shown himself sensitive to the totally new spatial sensations evoked by Cézanne; but Léger, with his more energetic, more outgoing outlook, saw Cézanne's art in more dynamic terms. Through a study of Cézanne his theory of contrasts became enormously enriched. In his first urban landscapes the curvilinear, flowing forms of smoke and cloud had been played off against the straight, unyielding outlines of the city's architecture. Now, in his figure pieces and still lifes executed between 1912 and 1914, the subject is generally static, while the space around it appears to throb and pulse; some forms are flat and thin, others markedly volumetric or three-dimensional; some shapes recede sharply into space, while others advance out of depth so forcefully that at times they appear to have an independent existence in front of the surface of the canvas; black is set off against white, while both in turn emphasize the brilliance of the primary colours blocked in around them.

Unlike almost every other figure in the Cubist world Léger was coming to see Impressionism, with its obvious enjoyment in the contemporary scene, as the starting point of the modern movement.

But when he said in 1913 that Cézanne was the only painter to come out of Impressionism who saw what was lacking in it[4] he meant, almost certainly, not only that Cézanne had reintroduced into painting a greater structural and three-dimensional sense of solidity, but that Cézanne's distortions of objects and natural forms gave his work a dimension of pictorial abstraction that made his art particularly significant for the twentieth century.

At the same time that Léger's art was flowering into maturity his attitude to life and its relationship to art was crystallizing into a coherent aesthetic. He had from the start rejected the static, pyramidal compositions of Cubism in favour of more dramatic, dynamic effects that often relied on the use of abrupt foreshortening; and in his subject matter, too, he cast his net far wider. If the true Cubists sang the poetry of the simple objects of daily life, Léger was to be the troubadour of life itself. He was fascinated by the throb of city life, and his almost Zola-esque appetite for it was wide enough to include its every aspect. He loved its bustle, its people, its architecture and its machines. It is not surprising that he found himself to a large extent in sympathy with the Italian Futurists, who since 1909 had bombarded Paris with their manifestos, and who had, towards the end of 1911, staged an invasion of the French capital prior to opening there a large exhibition of their paintings early in the following year.[5]

But from the start Léger's attitude towards modern life and its technology was shrewder, more objective, perhaps more mature than that of his visionary Italian friends. And he came to feel, in 1913, that the pulse and dynamism of contemporary life could best be conveyed by a move towards a more fragmented, more abstract idiom. During the course of this year he produced his revolutionary series of *Contrastes de Formes*, some of the first abstractions ever to be executed. When, in the following year, his subject matter reasserted itself, the still lifes, the landscapes and the figures seated, reclining or standing on staircases, were all now conceived of in terms of the same abstract, predominantly geometric and tubular forms that he was employing in his work of the previous year. In 1911 one critic had coined the term 'tubism' to describe Léger's particular brand of Cubism.[6] Now, in 1914, the forms in his art take on an almost metallic appearance; the way in which figures and their surroundings are rendered in terms of the same hard, unyielding forms suggests, for the first time in Léger's art, a vision of man as a machine, an integral part of an exciting new mechanical environment.

In so far as Cubism was never an art of pure abstraction the *Contrastes de Formes* of 1913 show Léger detaching himself from a Cubist aesthetic. His greatest achievements were yet to come, and in the post-war years his aesthetic was to be enriched and deepened through contact with a wide range of new sources. But an understanding of his pre-war production remains essential to an appreciation of the visual splendours which were to follow. And because he has been so frequently and loosely described as a Cubist painter, it is perhaps worth pausing to underline the factors that distinguished his art from that of his great contemporaries who had forged this deeply revolutionary style. In the first place, Léger's work was never truly analytical, in that he was fundamentally uninterested in an exploration of volumes and space in terms of their component parts. He had embraced the Cubists' dismissal of traditional perspective primarily as a means of fragmenting his subjects in an attempt to enliven and enrich the picture surface in a dynamic manner, rather than because he was interested in conveying a multiplicity of information within a single image; he was deeply aware of the necessity for preserving the integrity of the picture plane, but he retained until the end of his life the use of traditionally perspectival passages in his painting, as a means of pointing up the flatness of other, adjacent areas.

On the other hand, if we accept the terminology of Juan Gris, the purest and most theoretical of the Cubists, Léger's vision was never to become truly 'synthetic' either, although once again he was to produce his own highly independent version of this second major phase of the movement. In synthetic Cubism the Cubists were concerned with turning abstraction into representation, endowing abstract pictorial forms with the properties of material objects; Léger, in his works from 1912 onwards, was content to accept abstraction and representation as existing side by side within a single work without feeling the need to fuse the two, except in so far as they must work together to produce a dynamic sensation and a satisfactory composition. In the same way he practically never resorted to collage because he never felt the need to test the reality of his art in the face of the external world around him. For Léger the painting was not an autonomous object, as it was for the true Cubists, who saw their works as self-subsisting entities, not reflecting the outside world but recreating it in an independent fashion. Instead, he saw his paintings as reflections of, or confrontations with, the outside world, and he had come to feel, briefly, that totally abstract forms could most convincingly echo the dynamic pulse (what he called 'the fragmentation') of contemporary life.

Léger belonged to subsequent artistic movements peripherally, just as he had entered the Cubist orbit wholeheartedly but without ever becoming a true Cubist. No other major twentieth-century artist was to react to, and to reflect, such a wide range of artistic currents and movements. Fauvism, Cubism, Futurism, Purism, Neo-Plasticism, Surrealism, Neo-Classicism, Social Realism: his art experienced them all. And yet he was to remain supremely independent as an artistic personality. Never at any moment in his career could he be described as a follower; the very vigour and strength of his character would have in themselves rendered such a position inconceivable. But his originality lay basically in his ability to adapt the ideas and to a certain extent even the visual discoveries of others to his own ends. He was extraordinarily open-minded, but it is notable that he was attracted to successive movements only after their aesthetic had reached a very tangible and visually mature form of expression. He was an intelligent man, but he was also in some ways a simple man. And if the filters of his mind were translucent rather than totally transparent, this was to be in the last analysis an enormous source of strength to his art. Ideas percolated through to him at a measured pace, but the end products of his reflections were clear, beautifully distilled and crystalline, and in the process of their distillation they had become fully assimilated and subtly transformed to suit his tough, honest cast of mind. He never accepted an idea or an image until it seemed to him right and inevitable within the context of his own work. Because of this there are never transitional moments or passages in his art, only a series of successive phases, each of them conveying a complete statement of his position at the time. Picasso, in what is perhaps the most revealing statement about his art that he has ever made, remarked, 'I don't search, I find.'[7] Léger with equal justification might have said, 'I never travel, I simply arrive.'

For most French artists the war was a disruptive experience. Not so for Léger; indeed no other artist of his generation was to extract such positive conclusions from its squalor and horror. These years, when he was living and working with ordinary, working-class men, laid the foundations for his subsequent political commitment; and when he came to condemn much of his pre-war work as being too abstract, he meant almost certainly that it was lacking in social content. Then again, whereas he had already been deeply touched by Futurist ideas, it was the revelation of the sun glinting on the polished metal of artillery machinery that converted him totally to the idea of the artistic possibilities inherent in completely mechanized forms. The most immediate expression of his experiences (and perhaps the greatest war painting of the First World War) was his *Partie de Cartes* of 1917 (now in the Rijksmuseum Kroller-Muller, Otterlo), a latter-day interpretation of a theme dear to Cézanne, in which the robot-like figures of soldiers, their limbs of burnished steel, confront each other across a space that is both a table and a theatre of war. 'This was the first painting in which I deliberately drew my subject from the contemporary scene,' he later said.[8]

If Léger had emerged as a major artist in the years immediately before the war, it was with the great 'city' paintings executed in the years after 1917, when he had been wounded and invalided out of the army, that he established his claim to be considered as one of the greatest artists of the twentieth century. These years saw a steady flow of major masterpieces: the various versions of his *Eléments Mécaniques, Les Disques* of 1918 (Musée des Beaux Arts de la Ville de Paris), *Les Disques dans la Ville* of 1920–1 (Musée Fernand Léger, Biot), the *Tugboat* series, and most notable of all, *La Ville* of 1919 itself, the archetypal image of the modern metropolis, now one of the glories of the Philadelphia Museum of Art. In the pre-war years Léger had grafted his independent version of Futurism on to certain procedures of analytic Cubism. Now, at the height of his powers, he rendered architectural the compositional effects of synthetic Cubism to give definitive form to all that had been most positive, from a visual point of view, in the Futurist programme. The city's surge, its vitality, its pride in the new mechanical splendour of its machines and its architecture, all these qualities are captured in images that confront the spectator with a physical impact that is rare in any art, and which are made all the more powerful by the way in which the dynamic pictorial elements are bound together with the weight and inevitability of Cyclopean masonry.

From synthetic Cubism Léger adapted a form of composition that relied for its effects on a surface organization in terms of

Léger, *La Ville*, 1919

predominantly upright, vertical areas, often rendered now in unmodulated colour. Mechanical, tubular forms, like great shafts of metal, appear with frequency, but these are now tied into, and indeed made subsidiary to a flatter treatment of the picture surface; the coloured shapes tip and tilt, fanning out towards the edges of the canvas, only to meet opposing forces which tie them back again tightly into the overall, jazz-like rhythms of the composition. The bright raw colours call to each other across the surface of the canvas, pulling it taut like a drum. The vitality of the forms is such that at times they appear to advance towards us, so that we seem to share, palpably, in the painting's beat. Some areas become cells in space, in which we glimpse the life of the city's inhabitants; others are broken by letters, like fragments of giant billboards, while their harsh, dry imagery is thrown into relief by the contrasting, swirling, circular bands of colour. Never has the poetry of the first machine age been so grandly and proudly exalted.

After the hard day's work in the factories and the streets, the dignity of well-earned rest. In 1920 the human figure reasserts itself in Léger's work as a subject in its own right. The *Mechanic* (National Gallery of Ottawa, Canada) smokes his pipe against a background of bold geometric forms which might have been forged by the machine he has been wielding. The women, twentieth-century goddesses, odalisques of the Monoprix, stand or recline, surrounded by simple domestic equipment, products of the factory and of the labour of their men. They confront the spectators with an impassive gaze, their limbs massive and heavily rounded, not unsensuous, but composed of a substance suggestive of metal; their hair is like corrugated iron. In keeping with Léger's view of man as part of the vast machine of twentieth-century life, the smaller figure pieces of the period are called (or subtitled) *paysages animés*. The new industrial age is not inhuman: its machines are benevolent and confer on those who work with them a new status of grandeur.

It is indicative of the scope of Léger's talent that the new pictorial sources that were now informing his art and underlining his vision of life were, on the surface, contradictory and totally in opposition. His monumental figures can, to start with, be viewed as the quasi-mechanistic counterparts of Picasso's colossal Neo-Classical nudes. This phase in Picasso's art was initiated by his visit in 1917 to Rome and Naples where he studied their antiquities in an atmosphere which often evoked very potently the classical world, and where he was also able to see for the first time, in the original, the great fresco cycles of the High Renaissance. Picasso was drawn to adopt a Neo-Classical idiom for several reasons. In the first place he must have been aware of the fact that although his Cubist paintings were still richly inventive, they were becoming increasingly decorative in character; and the years immediately preceding his Italian trip had already witnessed a restless search for viable alternative styles. After a period of constant and revolutionary experiment, the massive grandeur of the classical past must have held out obvious charms. He may well have felt that in very recent years painting had to a certain extent got off the rails, and the fact that the Dadaists were making use of certain devices initiated by himself (his use of collage in particular) in order to give expression to their anarchistic gestures probably disturbed him. Finally, he was at a stage in his career when he felt the need to fuse his art on to the tradition of great art that had, in the last analysis, shaped his talent. He was one of those rare and fortunate artists who had never for a moment suffered an identity crisis, but he felt the need to pause and draw breath.

Léger, like Picasso, was an artist who had known from the start exactly who he was. But his attitude towards the past was much simpler; he never felt the need to question or to verify his art in relationship to it. He had always been attracted to art which had a high degree of formal content, and he did not see classical formal values as undermining the dynamic structure of his art. On the contrary, he recognized that the totally new sensations he was out to evoke could only be adequately conveyed if they were married to a very rigorous, formal discipline. And he was content, quite simply, to enjoy and be a part of the rationalist artistic climate (of which Neo-Classicism represented a major facet) that characterized much cultural life in Paris in the early 1920s, and which he felt to be sane and sympathetic. Of an earlier period of his development Malevich had written, 'We see that the sensation of metal brought Léger to metal itself, to the very elements of Futurism. His motor does not move nor do his screws move, as they would, entering another body, they may be said to flower, just as everything in his work flowers.'[9] So now Léger's art breathed the climate of Neo-Classicism, relaxed a little and expanded. This was the moment when the phrase *'le rappel à l'ordre'* was on everyone's lips (although Cocteau was to make it his own by using it as the title of a volume of essays which appeared in 1926).

In 1921 Severini, one of the first artists to try to effect a marriage between a modern idiom and one more deeply rooted in tradition, published his book *Du Cubisme au Classicisme*. Reproductions of works by Ingres papered the walls of progressive studios in Montparnasse. Renoir's last manner, which was classical in inspiration, and informed simultaneously by a quality of monumental distortion, looked for the first time startlingly relevant. Corot's art was re-evaluated and Ozenfant was no longer derided for his admiration for Puvis de Chavannes. Léger himself felt particularly drawn to David, a classicist who had shared, to a certain extent, his own social preoccupations. Indeed, Surrealism itself, a movement which stood at the opposite extreme from Neo-Classicism, could be viewed as part of the *rappel à l'ordre* in that it was consciously trying to fan the dying, nihilistic embers of Dada into a new, purposeful flame, and giving its programme for reforming life a much more intellectual and positive slant.

Léger's Neo-Classicism was, as might be expected, of a highly personal nature, or, to put it more accurately, it was remarkable for its high degree of impersonality. He avoided all the overtly classicizing attributes in which Picasso rejoiced; there are no flowing white draperies, no garlands of leaves and flowers, and his figures wear a garb that is strictly contemporary and yet timeless in its simplicity. The pitchers and the urns, which can transform a Picasso figure into a caryatid or a river goddess, become, in Léger's work, the implements of domestic, workaday life. The latent sensuality of Picasso's nudes, and the languor that characterizes the contemporary work of Neo-Classicizing artists such as Derain or La Fresnaye, these were qualities completely alien to Léger's art. He treats his figures, not without an underlying compassion, but with a detachment that was fundamental to his vision of the modern world; his figures are geared to contemporary life, and it is as part of the mechanism of life in general that they achieve significance. He lacked Picasso's historical sense, and he was able to admire the classical world and yet reject the art of the High Renaissance which he felt was too 'bourgeois' and too much concerned with problems of 'imitation'. But the affinities between the two painters are striking. Both adopt for their figures static, monolithic poses, and both make use of similar, heavy, generalized forms to render their limbs; the heads are composed of simple, almost geometrical shapes and the features are rendered in the same incisive, sculptural way. At times Léger's figures echo those of Picasso so closely that one cannot help suspecting him of consciously trying to inject a quality of contemporary slang in to Picasso's Neo-Classical vocabulary, and occasionally one senses that he is offering one more truly 'modern' alternatives to some of Picasso's canvases.

The other side of the coin, which at the time must have seemed the product of a totally different mint, was represented by Léger's interest in the work of the Dutch De Stijl group who had banded together in 1917, and in his increasing (if at times somewhat distrustful) admiration for Mondrian, the greatest and purest of its exponents. In the year of its foundation De Stijl launched a highly influential periodical of the same name, which maintained close contacts with French art, and in 1919 Mondrian returned to take up residence in Paris. In 1919 De Stijl published an important statement by Léger[10] – the first verbal attempt he had made to formulate his aesthetic since before the war – and in the same year it reproduced a fine drawing by him, related to his *Disques dans la Ville*.[11] The Dutch movement was characterized by a strong architectural bias, and its aesthetic showed, from the start, a considered appreciation of advanced technological procedures, culled from a wide range of sources, and an appreciation of the possibilities of the machine as a tool for social liberation, which Léger must have found particularly sympathetic. De Stijl also admired the machine for its beauty, but, unlike the Futurists, they refused to recognize it as a cult object or as an end in itself; Léger, who often stressed the point that he did not imitate the forms of specific machines but echoed them in imaginary forms that were exclusively pictorial, once again found himself in agreement.

On the subject of abstraction, however, he differed from them sharply. De Stijl stood for a more rigorously abstract art than any that had yet been produced. Léger, although he was later to modify his position during the years of his association with Le Corbusier, was opposed to abstraction as such. His aesthetic had been formed in the years before and during the war, by Cubism and Futurism, and while it was to be substantially modified by contacts with new ideas and art forms, it was never to alter radically. The basis of Mondrian's art was philosophical and metaphysical, and the path by which he had found his way into abstraction was more than slightly tinged with mysticism. He held a Platonic belief in the perfectibility of forms and viewed his total detachment from nature as a step towards a more spiritual way of life. Léger's mind was pragmatic, down to earth, and little given to abstract speculation; he felt, one suspects, that given the right social conditions and the right physical surroundings, the spirit would take care of itself. But he shared with De Stijl their belief in objective values, and saw that in this respect the movement was not incompatible with the spirit of Neo-Classicism. In 1920 Mondrian wrote: 'All the arts are striving to arrive at an aesthetic form (à la plastique esthétique) uniting the individual and the universal, the subjective and the objective, nature and spirit.'[12] A few years later Léger observed, 'Art is of course subjective, but a controlled subjectivity, based on objective primary materials.'[13] Mondrian's development was a battle to transcend emotionalism in art; Léger had rejected it out of hand from the start.

In the last analysis, he was attracted to De Stijl and to Mondrian for the same reason that he admired Picasso's Neo-Classicism, not so much because of its underlying aesthetic, but because he realized that they were producing important works, great art, which he could not afford to overlook. He was extraordinarily open and generous in his appreciation of the art of other painters, and it was his ability to express this admiration in his own work and yet to remain completely himself that was his greatest strength. His simplicity and openness of mind, above all his honesty, allowed him to get the best of every world without loss of integrity. It was in this respect that he scored most heavily and was able to compete on terms of equality with artists whose minds were deeper and whose talents were more profound. 'Léger sait faire du bon Léger de tout,' Ozenfant once remarked;[14] and he was right.

As early as 1918 Léger had begun to favour compositions in which the central areas of the canvas contained the most dynamic elements, tilting and fanning outwards or else revolving in a syncopated, centripetal rhythm, which were then stabilized by the more severe vertical and horizontal forms placed at the edges of the canvas, and which had the effect of containing the motion and tying the composition back on to the picture plane. At this time the device was probably an independent, intuitive invention, but the backgrounds of the figure paintings initiated in 1920 leave little doubt that Léger was by now studying the methods of De Stijl. If for a moment we mentally remove the figure from a painting like *Le Mécanicien*, for example, what we are left with resembles a more dynamic variant of a painting by van Doesburg. During the early 1920s De Stijl was, in fact, becoming increasingly international under the management of van Doesburg who had begun to proselytize for new recruits and who was extending some of the movement's original ideas to welcome certain developments in Russia and Germany, and he was in close touch with developments in Rosenberg's Paris gallery, *L'Effort Moderne*. Rosenberg was, at this time, Léger's dealer.

In a sense Léger used De Stijl (or Neo-Plasticism as Mondrian called his version of it) to develop his own all-important theory of contrasts a stage further, into a tighter discipline. He would never have dreamt of subscribing to Mondrian's and van Doesburg's exclusive use of the vertical and the horizontal, but the curving, circular forms in his art are now locked into a more classical, architectural framework; he realized that Mondrian's uncompromising insistence on the flatness of the picture plane was the culmination of a process that had been taking place for over a hundred years, and he felt that his own art must recognize the fact that a turning point in painting had been reached. The figures in his work are static, but composed of vigorous, rounded and elliptical shapes, strongly sculptural, and these in turn contrast with the vertical and horizontal bands that dominate and organize the space around them, forcing it right up on to the rigid, flat surface of the canvas; what is so baffling about these paintings, and what constitutes perhaps the greatest triumph of Léger's theory of contrasts, is the way in which the heavy, sculptural, Neo-Classical figures seem so convincingly at home against backgrounds executed in a fundamentally different idiom.

Of all the artistic movements to emerge in the post-war period, Purism was the one which took into consideration most (although by no means all) of Léger's aesthetic preoccupations. And although he never became a true Purist, and disagreed with its authors on several fundamental issues, he was nevertheless to produce the images which most strikingly and convincingly illustrated their highly ambitious programme. The Purists themselves gave visual expression to their ideas in paintings of great dignity and beauty, but in the last analysis, as in the case of Futurism, their manifestos and their theoretical writings were more exciting and visionary than the works which were inspired by them. Léger's avoidance and distrust of rigid theorizing gave him greater freedom than the Purists allowed themselves, and he enriched their doctrine, visually, by the use of sources which they would have considered 'impure'. The result was a richer, bolder brand of Purism.

Purism was the outcome of the meeting of the temperaments and the talents of Ozenfant and Jeanneret (Le Corbusier), who were introduced to each other in 1918 by the architect Perret.[15] Both were men of great intellectual gifts, although their minds worked in subtly different ways. Ozenfant was basically of a reflective and critical turn of mind. His magazine, L'Elan, launched in 1915, was one of the liveliest of the period, both in terms of its content and its presentation. Its list of contributors is impressive (these included Picasso, Matisse, Apollinaire, Jacob, Gleizes, Metzinger, Derain and de la Fresnay among others) and its bias became deeply Cubist, although there was already a slight tendency to theorize; the ninth issue, for example, published an extract from Plato's Philebus insisting on the beauty of geometry and geometrically inspired forms. Ozenfant was also already fascinated by the beauty of the machine, and together with his brother he had, in 1910, designed the body work of his own Hispano-Suiza (the Hispano-Ozenfant). Jeanneret, on the other hand, had undergone a rigorous apprenticeship in his training as an architect, and at the time of his meeting with Ozenfant he had behind him, as Reyner Banham puts it, 'a career rich in practically everything except painting as a pure art'.[16] His bent of mind was more truly scientific, and although he had a tendency to see things in a compartmentalized way, he was basically more imaginative and his intellect was more visionary. On 15 November 1918, to coincide with their first exhibition of Purist painting, the two men published *Après le Cubisme*, a text which outlined the ideas of the movement with great and exciting clarity. The year 1920 saw the publication of the first issue of the Purist periodical *L'Esprit Nouveau*, which ran through until 1927, and which expanded, in articles contributed by the two editors, the ideas expressed in *Après le Cubisme*; these were in turn given definitive form in *La Peinture Moderne*, which appeared in 1925.

Après le Cubisme was introduced by a quotation from Voltaire: 'la décadence est produit par la facilité de bien faire, par la satiété du bon et par le gout du bizarre'. Art, its authors felt, was in a decadent phase because it had followed a path of romantic disorder and above all because it had shown itself indifferent to modern life; this was an age of science, mechanism and industry, and art must reflect it. The Purists were aware of the Futurist revolt and they were deeply influenced by it, but they now dismissed it (with a certain amount of justification) as being undisciplined, romantic and bombastic. The new age was to be one of classical objectivity; not since Pericles, they said, had thought been so lucid, and it was the modern age that would realize the true aims and ambitions of the Greeks. In his highly influential book *L'Art*, published independently by Ozenfant in 1928 (the Purist partnership had begun to split in 1925), he stressed that Purism was not just a form of art but a 'super-aesthetic', an attitude of mind and a procedure; and it was a Neo-Classical form of life that was being advocated.

It was the discoveries of science and the power and possibilities of the machine that were to bring about this new golden age. Science and nature were basically in harmony, and art must move on paths parallel to them. Both art and science have 'generalization as their ideal', and both use 'analysis as a means of discovering invariables'; the ends of art and science are the same, for the search of science is for 'constants' while that of art is for 'invariables'. Beauty is governed by eternal laws and the principles that govern the construction of a classical temple are the same as those that underly the construction of a good automobile. 'A work of art should provoke a sensation of mathematical order,' they declared, 'and the means by which this mathematical order is achieved should be sought in universal means.' The emphasis on geometry is everywhere; for 'man is a geometric animal, animated by a geometric spirit.'[17]

The arguments employed by the Purists can be faulted. They harp on the laws of nature, for example, but they never really say what they are. They attack certain schools of art for trying to turn these laws into strict rules, when that is in fact often what they themselves are attempting to do. Like many ambitious young men they felt it was possible to be the Pope and St Francis at the same time. They advocate an ordered, rational and scientific art, but an art whose conclusions, for all their Platonic inevitability and perfection, must be reached intuitively. But for all their weaknesses, today, across a space of over half a century, the Purist writings still reflect an intense, bright light, like a piece of polished metal held up against a blue Mediterranean sky; and the best of their paintings contain some of the same controlled intensity.

As the title of their first manifesto suggests, the Purists saw themselves as heirs to the Cubists. They felt that Cubism was the only valid school of painting around, but they expressed grave reservations about the parent movement; its latter-day developments in particular they condemned almost completely, though not surprisingly (since they were so much closer to them in time), their own work often resembled most closely certain post-war Cubist works, rather than the products of its heroic, hermetic or classical phase which they most admired. They were drawn to analytical Cubism because of the way in which it subordinated the subject to formal, purely pictorial considerations, and they sought to emulate its austerity, its quality of anonymity, its sense of balance. They were prepared to admit certain early developments in the second, synthetic phase of the movement, but they felt that since 1914 Cubism, and the work of Picasso in particular, had tended to become decorative, frivolous and sensationalist.

In view of their strong intellectual and geometric bent it is not surprising that the Cubist to whom they were most drawn, and who was the most important single influence on the formation of their own style, should have been Juan Gris.[18] The Purists' choice of subject matter was basically a limited variant of that of the Cubists. They concentrated, in the period between 1918 and 1925, almost exclusively on still life, and they chose simple machine-made objects: bottles, cups, plates and jugs. At first they favoured austere arrangements of a few of these objects, but the number of objects in each individual canvas soon tends to proliferate and the compositions become correspondingly more elaborate. They chose their subjects partly because they were mechanically made and of simple, geometric design, but also because their very banality deprived them of any intrinsic interest and ensured an avoidance of any anecdotal quality, so that the aesthetic effect produced by the final painting was achieved through the artist's manipulation of his models and not because of their own beauty. They showed each object from whatever angle they felt was the most revealing of its formal properties, and they dismissed traditional perspective because it often gave a false idea as to the true structure of objects, so that their works often give the odd impression of being blueprints for objects that are already in existence.

It might perhaps not be unfair to say that Léger was attracted to the Purists because he saw them as objectifying and classicizing the ideas of Futurism. He never subscribed completely to their emphasis on mathematics and he was fundamentally indifferent to their mystique of number. Basically he was a popular artist, in the true sense of the word, and he sensed intuitively that theirs was an élitist position and that there was something a little cold and inhuman about their art: facts that they themselves came to admit. But he accepted many of their other assumptions and he probably enjoyed the way in which Purism forced him to rethink Cubism in the light of all his own subsequent discoveries. From 1923 onwards the object begins to play an increasingly important part in his art, at first in arrangements of still life and then more frequently in isolation, and as a subject in its own right. An enthusiasm for machine-made forms was in many ways the logical outcome of his love for the machine itself: in 1924 he declared, 'now a work of art must bear comparison with a manufactured object'.[19] But his choice of machine-made forms was much more daring, much more original and much more truly up-to-date than that of the Purists; modern, goosenecked reading lamps, typewriters, door handles and the plaques below them, all these and a wealth of other unlikely images make their appearance in his art alongside the more traditional subject matter inherited from Cubism. And although he was temperamentally at the opposite end of the pole from an artist like Gris, Léger reveals his

Léger,
Mouvements à Billes,
1926

Cubist heritage by the fact that every object in his paintings has been transformed by his imagination into a totally independent, original pictorial form. The object, he insisted, despite its import-ance was 'matière première', raw material to be manipulated by the painter, not an end but a means. He saw in orthodox Purism an element of 'imitation' which he condemned.

Colour, the Purists felt, was a secondary factor in painting, subservient to form or 'structure' (both that of individual objects and of the composition as a whole), which was all important. In the early phases of the movement both Ozenfant and Jeanneret restricted themselves to a severe, muted palette, reminiscent of that used by the Cubists some ten years earlier; and at the moments when his art was closest to theirs, Léger too tended to favour more sober effects, although even the most monochrome of his canvases are generally relieved by one or two bold, striking passages of colour. But he insisted that colour must play a cardinal role in contemporary painting, and he went so far as to suggest that the bright, strong colours so characteristic of modern machines (and which served no utilitarian purpose) transformed them into works of popular art.

Paradoxically, too (for the Purists shunned abstract art), his association with Jeanneret/Le Corbusier, at its closest in the mid-1920s, was to lead him to conceive the idea of a purely abstract mural art, which would emphasize the flatness of the wall, or, if the occasion demanded it, transform its two-dimensionality. His experiments with total abstraction form a minor part of his output and were confined to some ten canvases (usually strikingly vertical in format) executed between 1924 and 1926. But even in later years, when he was producing his own independent version of social realism, he never totally rejected the validity of abstract art as a decorative art of the wall, which could improve and transform the surroundings in which people worked and lived.

During the years of his contact with Purism, Léger made what he felt to be a major discovery and one which, at the time, he saw as his most important contribution to twentieth-century art. Earlier, in his immediately post-war work, the figures in his paintings, as well as some of the more abstract pictorial elements such as the letters, the target-like disc motives and so on, had often been sliced through the middle or cut off at the edges, so that they appear to pass behind the areas to their sides; the effect produced by this device had contributed to the sense of movement and dynamism for which he was striving, and, like so many of his other pictorial innovations, was related to his theory of contrasts. In some of the most Purist of his still lifes of the mid-1920s he readopted the device in a modified fashion; his aim was partly to give life to compositions that were becoming increasingly classical and static, but the juxtaposition of objects with fragments of objects also compels us to focus on them in a new way, and as a result of the confrontation both the partial objects and those left intact seem more vividly real and alive. At the same time he was coming to feel that whereas in the art of the past the objects depicted in paintings had always been enmeshed in the overall composition, now was the moment to reassert their right to an independent existence, to proclaim the advent of the object as subject. 'In 1923 and 1924,' he said, 'I produced paintings with as their main theme "objects" isolated from space and without anything in common between them. I felt the object which had been neglected, overlooked, could replace the subject.'[20] The concept was a simple one, but for Léger, who dealt in simple truths, it had the quality of a revelation, and it was to condition a large part of his subsequent work.

The concept of the object (soon to be extended to the concept of the figure as object/subject) arose, quite obviously, to a large extent from Léger's contact with Purist aesthetics. But as always with Léger, it had its roots even more deeply in simple, concrete visual experiences. His first practical contacts with the cinema date to 1921, the year in which he collaborated with Cendrars and Abel Gance on a film called *La Roue*. Perhaps the most important of his ventures into the medium, however, was *Ballet Mécanique*, the first film to be produced without a scenario or script, and which was photographed by Man Ray and Dudley Murphy from images assembled and selected by Léger; the musical score that accompanied it was by Georges Antheil. The film remains one of the pioneering cinematic experiments of the age. Objects and fragments of objects, buttons, phonograph discs, artificial limbs, an eye, a fingernail, pieces of twine and rope, all were photographed as images of absorbing interest and abstract beauty, brought into a new reality by their isolation, by the way in which the camera focused on them in close-ups, or by the unusual confrontations between them.

The sensation of the close-up view is very conspicuous in Léger's work of the mid-1920s, but in 1927 the results of his cinematic experiments were transferred even more directly to his paintings in that the objects now tend to float or revolve in an undefined space. The effect is to further emphasize the object as an independent entity, divorced from its ordinary physical surroundings and associational connotations, and the result might be described as the transformation of the '*nature morte*' into the '*nature vive*'. To the end of his life Léger was to be preoccupied with the problem of objects and figures revolving freely through space. The divers and acrobats of the 1930s, 1940s and 1950s, and the late paintings of workmen poised on scaffolding, can be seen as the result of Léger's new desire to paint the object/subject in 'free space'.

The juxtaposition of isolated objects in strange combinations inevitably raises the question of Léger's relationship to Surrealism. Léger knew the work of the Surrealist painters and many of the figures involved in the movement were his friends. He was touched by Surrealism (if only marginally) just as he had been touched, directly or indirectly, by every major European movement from Fauvism onwards. His art, however, stood for almost everything to which the Surrealists were most opposed. He was a rationalist with a strong classicizing bias to his art and thought. Surrealism, on the other hand, stood for certain romantic attitudes pushed to their most extreme conclusions. Since before the war Léger's vision had been irrevocably committed to a machine aesthetic, and it had gained in depth and sophistication as he encountered and assimilated other art with a similar bias. The Surrealists distrusted the machine profoundly and made direct use of it in their art and literature only in a humorous or satirical fashion.

And whereas the Surrealists were intent, to quote Ernst, on the 'coupling of two realities irreconcilable in appearance upon a plane which apparently does not suit them',[21] Léger's confrontations of unlikely images and objects in an undefined space is seldom disquieting, and indeed serves only to enhance their individual material existences. When the Surrealists quoted with reverence Lautréamont's famous remark, 'as beautiful as the chance encounter of an umbrella and a sewing machine upon a dissecting table', they were excited by the sexual implications of the imagery and by the fact that after their juxtaposition the objects involved could never be quite the same again. The Freudian implications of Léger's *Mona Lisa with a Ring of Keys* of 1930 would have brought joy to the heart of the simple Surrealist, and evoked (because of the obviousness of the erotic imagery) derision from the more sophisticated. But in Léger's painting the Joconda comes smiling through, chaste and intact, while the keys have become simply much more themselves, their physical existence sharpened into a new reality. Léger's relationship to Surrealism is perhaps the supreme example of his ability to partake of certain aspects of an artistic situation and yet to stand aside from it almost totally.

Between 1918 and 1928 Léger had been, perhaps, the most representative artist of his generation. The subsequent developments in his art lie outside the scope of this essay. These showed him taking a slightly different path, trying to adapt the discoveries of progressive, experimental European art to a more popular, more immediately accessible idiom. His political commitment became increasingly deep, but perhaps as a result of his years at the forefront of the avant-garde he never became a true Marxist in that, like many of the most gifted of his contemporaries who to a greater or lesser extent shared his views (Picasso is the most obvious example), he refused to admit that cultural values were dictated by or sprang from the masses. He felt that it was degrading to the nature of art to use it as propaganda. 'The work of art,' he said, 'ought not to participate in the battle, it ought to be, on the contrary, a repose after the combat of your daily struggles.'[22] As with Courbet, an artist whom he much admired, Léger's art at its strongest and best was always popular rather than partisan in its origins. He spoke out, in his art and in his occasional writings and statements, with the same rugged individualism that he always showed. And it was this individualism that allowed him to infuse his subjects, behind their detached, often strongly classical exteriors, with an underlying humanity and warmth. Despite the fact that his art continued to reflect and embody a large percentage of the artistic and stylistic dilemmas and achievements of the twentieth century, in the last analysis he remains, as Zola said of Courbet, 'simply a personality'. One of the strongest and most vivid of our age.

8

Ozenfant

A REAPPRAISAL of Ozenfant's work and of his position in twentieth-century art has been long overdue. Perhaps no other artistic reputation of comparable stature within the contemporary field has undergone, during the past decades, such an almost total eclipse. During the 1920s Ozenfant's position as a leading figure in the modern movement was universally acknowledged. In 1918, together with Charles-Edouard Jeanneret (Le Corbusier), he had launched Purism, a style which might with some justification be considered the first truly Post-Cubist idiom to be born in France. Between 1920 and 1925 he edited *L'Esprit Nouveau* (again for the most part in close collaboration with Le Corbusier), one of the most influential and intellectually challenging artistic periodicals of the time, and the counterpart in many ways of the contemporary, pioneering Surrealist reviews. The year 1928 saw the publication of his book *Art* (an English edition appeared in 1931 under the title *Foundations of Modern Art*), a work which was widely acclaimed and which was to affect deeply two generations of students. Then, at the end of the decade, his art underwent what at the time seemed a radical change. In his *Mémoires, 1886–1962* (published in Paris in 1968), Ozenfant was to recollect the dismay with which his 1930 exhibition of *La Belle Vie* series was greeted. Having come to terms with Purism, the public and the critics were unable to accept what in retrospect can be viewed, within the context of Ozenfant's art, as its logical and inevitable counterpart. The fact that he was unable, for intellectual and psychological reasons, to move into the sort of geometric abstraction that Purism had done so much to foster, and that he found himself at the same time basically unsympathetic to Surrealist ideology, threw him increasingly on to his personal resources.

Ozenfant was not to have another one-man show in France for twenty-three years. His reputation as an independent artist and his growing fame as a teacher insured that serious critics in France,

America and England followed his work with interest, but the kind of international acclaim that his friends and associates were by now receiving was still withheld. The climate of the 1950s and 1960s, which saw the emergence of hard-edge abstraction and a reversion to the objective, formalistically oriented values that Purism had championed some thirty years before, might have been expected to lead to a rediscovery of his early work and a re-evaluation of his position, but now other more intangible forces were militating against the long-delayed recognition of his true achievement. He left France in 1936 and did not return permanently until 1955, eleven years before his death. Inevitably he was now considered as something of an outsider and until the poet and dealer Katia Granoff discovered his plight and took him under her powerful wing his condition was precarious. For sixteen years, from 1939 to 1955, Ozenfant had lived and taught in the United States and he had become an American citizen. But for all his deep feeling for the country he remained essentially an alien (unlike Marcel Duchamp, Josef Albers and Hans Hofmann, to name only three contemporary emigrés); his school in New York kept alive a French tradition and played no active role in emergent revolutionary American art. And the months before his final departure for France were clouded by the fact that in the McCarthy era his passionately liberal sentiments had brought him into official disfavour. 'I am very happy with my urban New York life,' he wrote, 'where the pace ("*le tic tac*") is exactly geared to the needs of my work.'[1]

Ozenfant was born in 1886 of a prosperous, cultivated bourgeois family, at Saint-Quentin in Picardy. He was thus some five years younger than Picasso and Braque, the originators of Cubism. He was a year older than Juan Gris, the third great exponent of the style, and the painter to whom Ozenfant, during his creation of Purism, felt himself most deeply drawn. Ozenfant's evolution as an artist was, however, slower than that of his contemporaries, and it was not until the years immediately after the First World War that he emerged as a truly significant figure. This was partly because from the start the range of his interests was so remarkably wide; of all his colleagues in French art he was the intellectual *par excellence*. At the time that he was serving his artistic apprenticeship in Paris he was already delving into a wide range of disciplines. While most other artists were absorbing the teachings of the philosopher Henri Bergson at second hand, Ozenfant was reading his texts and actually attending lectures at the Collège de France where Bergson was the star attraction. At the Collège he was profoundly influenced by the mathematician and logician Henri Poincaré and enjoyed Romain Rolland's courses on the history of music. He had already begun to write and he had travelled a great deal. He frequented the museums and acquired a love for the art of the past that was to enable him to view contemporary developments in a wide context. At the Louvre his admiration already went to those upholders of the 'pure', formalist French tradition, to Poussin, Chardin and Ingres. He loved the Impressionists, and although it was only later that he came to a full appreciation of Cézanne's genius, he was already alert to the importance of Seurat, an artist who, like himself, was prepared to make use of the discoveries of science to enrich the visual arts. In the pre-war years he was aware of more up-to-date styles, but he moved slowly and he was not yet prepared to go down into battle himself.

It was the war that in an indirect but real way brought Ozenfant to maturity. From childhood he had been delicate and he was turned down by the army. He decided that the greatest contribution he could make to his country in a troubled time was to help to keep alive all that was best and most progressive in French art and culture. With this in mind in 1915 he launched at his own expense *L'Elan*, one of the liveliest, and certainly the most visually attractive, of the wartime periodicals. The magazine brought him into direct contact with all the leading artistic personalities of the day; 'the paper opened all doors to me,'[2] he later said. Among the contributors and other people who frequented his monthly 'Thursdays' were Picasso, Matisse, Jacques Lipchitz and the poets Guillaume Apollinaire and Max Jacob. Artists at the front and others who had fled abroad sent drawings and articles and eagerly awaited the next issue. The effects on Ozenfant's evolution were profound. In the first place he came to a deep belief that Cubism was the most serious and valid of recent developments in French painting and embodied the French virtues that he most esteemed: clarity, order, formal control and intellectual astringency. At a wider level he advocated the disciplines involved in the creation of a classically oriented, formalistic art as an antidote to the restless, desperate and occasionally cynical responses of many artists to a period of upheaval and strife. Perhaps more than any other mouthpiece of its time it was *L'Elan* that was responsible for launching that *rappel à l'ordre* that was to be the battle cry of so much progressive art in the post-war decade. Ozenfant's contribution to the climate which informed the Neo-Classicism of the 1920s has never been fully acknowledged.

It was in 1918 that Ozenfant was introduced to Jeanneret (Le Corbusier) by the distinguished architect Auguste Perret. The meeting was to have a decisive effect on the lives and careers of both men. Of the two, Ozenfant, at the time of their meeting, was the more sophisticated. He was one of the most widely read artists of his generation, and it was his appreciation of the literature of antiquity that was largely responsible for giving Purism its strongly Neo-Classical flavour; in *L'Elan* he had already published an extract from Plato's *Philebus*, insisting on the 'purity' and beauty of geometric forms. It is beyond doubt that it was he who initiated his new friend into the issues of modern painting. Jeanneret on the other hand had a wider technological background, and in 1916 had already produced a piece of architecture of real originality and distinction, his *Maison Schwob*. He brought to the partnership a tough, hard-hitting sense of professionalism. For seven years the two men worked together in much the same spirit of cooperation and mutual stimulation that had characterized the relationship of Picasso and Braque in the founding years of Cubism.

The first exhibition of Purist painting opened in November 1918, and to coincide with it Ozenfant and Jeanneret published *Après le Cubisme*, a text which is required reading for anyone interested in twentieth-century art. As the title suggests, the purpose of the book was to lay the foundations for a new Post-Cubist art. The authors express their admiration for the parent movement, and particularly for the classical phase of 1910–12, which Ozenfant was always to praise for its austere beauty and for the fact that it had cleansed the vocabulary of painting by its insistence on pure form – for its 'tendance vers le cristal'. At the same time they felt that even in the finest Cubist painting the balance between abstraction and representation was not always satisfactorily maintained, and they were particularly unhappy about the later manifestations of the movement, which had allowed for even greater freedom and decorative invention, and which they felt was all too often tinged by that 'romantic disorder' which the earlier phases had so rigorously eschewed. But above all they felt that Cubism was out of touch with modern life and that it had failed to take into account developments in recent science. The discoveries of science (which in turn were based on the laws inherent in nature) could help to restore to art those qualities of harmony, of balance and of inevitability, which had always characterized its highest manifestations. The war had brought with it an overwhelming recognition of the power and potentialities of the machine to influence everyday life. Many artists and intellectuals (the Dadaists and most of the future Surrealists in particular) viewed mechanization with distrust and saw the machine as potentially destructive to human and spiritual values. The Purists, on the other hand, were the supreme optimists of their age. They rejoiced in the purity and beauty of the machine and felt that modern man must take pride in its products which helped to reintroduce into daily life a sense of symmetry, proportion and utility. The art they advocated was a new, up-to-date, mechanized form of classicism. Throughout their writings there is an insistence on geometry, on number and proportion and on harmony. 'Man is a geometric animal,' they declared, 'animated by a geometric spirit.'[3]

The Cubist whom the Purists most admired and whose work most directly affected the appearance of their canvases was Juan Gris, the most rigorously intellectual of the Cubists, and the one who by Braque's own admission had pursued the more theoretical aspects of the movement through to their ultimate conclusions. Ozenfant was later to recall his long, stimulating arguments and discussions with Gris,[4] and the dialogue between Gris and the Purists, both verbal and visual, serves to underline very clearly both Purism's debt to Cubism and the originality of its premises. The Purists responded deeply to his 'geometric spirit', and they sought to emulate the lucidity and calm emanating from his canvases. They also learned from him how to give the objects in their paintings a sense of solidity by juxtaposing contrasts of light and dark, while at the same time forcing their forms to measure up to the rigidity of their two-dimensional support. However, the Purists found themselves unable to accept in Gris's work, and in all Cubism of the synthetic phase, the element of distortion, which, it seemed to them, falsified reality. Working 'deductively' or 'synthetically' (the terms are Gris's own), from abstraction to representation, Gris endowed the forms in his paintings with the attributes of objects in the external world, but he took pride in the fact that the objects that he evoked could exist only in his mind and in the context of each individual painting; his pipes, goblets and musical instruments correspond to their mundane prototypes, but they always exist simultaneously as abstract forms. The idea of a square goblet or a triangular pipe outraged Purist sensibilities because they saw machine-made forms as beautiful in themselves, as being sane and healthy. And to this extent the objects in their paintings are symbols of the products of man's mastery over science and of his ability to control his environment – in a quite different sense from Gris's they are 'products of the mind'. The Purists condemned slavish imitation but they felt that the very ordinariness of the objects they depicted served to heighten the emotional impact of their harmonious compositional arrangements and the architectural substructures of their pictures. The Cubists had invented the concept of the 'tableau objet', of the painting as an object which did not echo reality, but which recreated it in an independent form. In keeping with the new age they were proclaiming, the Purists talked of the painting as a 'machine à émouvoir', of the work of art as an aesthetic mechanism which could enhance the quality of contemporary life.

Purism came to maturity in 1920. By now both Ozenfant and Jeanneret were producing canvases of a sober, ordered grandeur that reflected the clarity and originality of the ideas they had formulated two years earlier. The canvases of these years show simple arrangements of bottles, glasses and pipes, most often in the company of a musical instrument – in short the subject matter was that of the Cubists. The objects in Purist painting, however, are kept intact and look smoothly polished. They are always shown in their most generalized or informative aspect; in some cases there is an attempt to combine various views of an object into a single image, but contours are retained unbroken, and Ozenfant in particular soon came to prefer a pure profile view, which he felt conveyed the maximum information about an object's formal properties without resorting to distortion. Tactile sensations, which had been so important for the Cubists, are deliberately avoided – the musical instruments in particular look like pieces of sculpture or architecture rather than like objects to be handled and plucked. The paint is applied evenly and impersonally and the simple subject matter is given an hieratic dignity. But if these paintings are remote there is nothing inhuman about them; they reflect rather man's need to order his surroundings. Their geometry comes across not as an empty theoretical exercise but rather as a *presence*, calm and reassuring.

Ozenfant,
Nacres I, 1926

Soon the objects in Purist still lifes began to multiply, partly from a natural desire for compositional enrichment, but also under the influence of commercial photographs of *'verrerie du commerce'*, which showed groups of mass-produced plates, cups, carafes and so forth – mechanically produced images of machine-made forms. At the same time significant differences in the two men's work started to appear. The objects in Le Corbusier's work tend to conform more rigidly to a vertical and horizontal framework, and they overlap in such a way as to suggest very real spatial relationships, while he increasingly favoured a palette of bright, often rather harsh colour. Ozenfant, on the other hand, made a much more calculated use of contour. During those years he was to become, and to remain throughout his life, a master of the simple, expressive silhouette. He piled objects up on top of each other, dovetailing one contour into another and often welding forms together into a single compact mass which he then placed against a neutral ground, so that all depth is negated. This is very evident, for example, in *Nacres No. 2* of

1922 (Philadelphia Museum of Art), one of the most beautiful works of the period. Characteristic, too, is the soft, pearly colour, which introduces a new and very personal note of elegance and refinement. It is in keeping with the lucidity of Ozenfant's mind and art that he should have been attracted, all through his life, by objects made of glass. At the same time he was evolving a very individual technique, building up his canvases by means of innumerable small strokes laid on with a soft, heavily loaded brush. This method of work was aimed partly at achieving permanence, but it gives his paintings a sense of enormous solidity, and it helps to counteract the sensation of extreme flatness which his compositional effects often produce. From this time on his paintings frequently give the impression almost of being painted bas-reliefs.

From the start *L'Esprit Nouveau* had shown a lively interest in architecture, and its columns did much to revive an interest in a discipline that had fallen sadly behind developments in the other visual arts; Ozenfant was never to forget the excitement that he experienced, around 1918, when his writer-friend Henri-Pierre Roché showed him photographs of American grain silos. And the geometric substructure of much Purist painting had helped to give its products a strongly architectural feel. In 1926 Ozenfant produced his *Grande Composition Puriste*, 1926 (Estate of Katia Granoff), a work which marked a reversion to the austerity of early Purist principles, and one which represents in many ways the culmination of his Purist style. Three monolithic elements stand grouped together against a white background: a jug, with diagonal fluting; an enormous bottle which repeats the flutes, now vertical; and, behind and to the left, the same fluted motif now unmistakably transformed into an architectural, classical colonnade. The same configuration of elements appears in a major work of the following year, placed squarely at the centre of the composition and surrounded by a strongly architectonic arrangement of soberly coloured forms, a reminder of the fact that, like Le Corbusier and Léger, Ozenfant had in the mid-1920s been preoccupied with the idea of a revival of mural art (in 1926 he was to produce some remarkable essays in this field). To the right and above the still life appear the silhouettes of a mother and child, echoing its contours and rendered in the same sober but rich terracottas. To the left is a palm tree which picks up the green tonalities of the architectural surround. It is as if Ozenfant were saying visually what he had so often declared in print: the forms of nature, human life and the products of man are interdependent and are governed by the same universal laws.

The Purists had placed the human form at the top of the hierarchy of subject matter for painting, but they had been prepared to let man appear in their paintings at several removes, as the initiator and controller of the machine-made objects which form the furniture and condition the mechanics of everyday life. For ten years, between 1916 and 1926, the human figure had been absent from Ozenfant's art. During the following years it was to be a dominant, an almost obsessional concern. At this time Ozenfant experienced a new revelation. In *Foundations of Modern Art* he records how his five-horse-power motor car broke down while he was travelling in the Dordogne.[5] By chance he found himself within walking distance of the prehistoric caves at Les Eyzies. The discovery of the art they contained was to be of the same importance to him as his recognition of the significance of Cubism and of the impact of the monumental simplicity of the mid-western grain silos. For a long time Ozenfant had believed that art was a manifestation of universal, unchanging laws; for him the present was our momentary apprehension of what would almost at once become a strand in the tapestry of history. The Purists had not on the whole been sympathetic to so-called 'primitive' art although they recognized that its forms had been important in forming the new artistic vocabulary of twentieth-century art. Now, in the caves at Les Eyzies, Ozenfant suddenly felt himself almost mystically in harmony with *all* art, with a great flux of forms and images that constituted, for him, the continuing proof of man's highest aspirations and endeavours. The simple imprints of hands laid on the rocky walls of the cave many thousands of year before became, almost literally, the laying on of hands.

It is perhaps not too difficult to see why the figure style evolved by Ozenfant in the late 1920s and early 1930s baffled and distressed his contemporaries; the canvases of these years belong very clearly to the age in which they were conceived, and they still defy categorization. The first paintings of groups of bathers, executed for the most part in a narrow range of warm, earthy colours and with the figures often isolated against a virtually monochromatic background, have about them a quality of pictographic immediacy that owes much to Ozenfant's apprehension of neolithic art. And to this extent they relate, albeit at a considerable distance, to certain Mirós and to some of Picasso's contemporary Surrealistic works, which often share a similar inspiration. At another level Ozenfant's bathers, so diverse in pose and so freely grouped, anticipate Léger's acrobats and divers of the 1940s and 1950s, a fact of which Ozenfant was justifiably proud. And yet Ozenfant's work has about it a pondered, rational and calculated quality that divorces it from Surrealism and its affinities, while he lacked Léger's facility for using the most up-to-date artistic idioms to render immediate the predicament of modern man. The canvases of embracing couples and of mothers and children lack the vitality of the first multifigure compositions, and they sometimes look both overworked and a little clumsy, although at their best they have a quality of solemn timelessness. The importance of Purism as a dynamic, progressive aesthetic had lent even the most casual of its products a quality of distinction and interest. From now on Ozenfant was to be an artist very much on his own; but if his work henceforward was to be somewhat uneven in quality one senses nevertheless in everything he did an underlying conviction and determination, a dedication to the cause of art that lends to his finest works that air of calm assurance that is peculiarly his own.

Already in the late 1920s, when he was still executing works that were in a Purist idiom, Ozenfant was engaged on others which give the impression of being concerned with unearthly or superhuman cosmic dramas. In some ways these relate to his early, youthful pre-war landscapes which preceded his all-important encounter with Cubism; and the sense of awe which as a young man he had experienced in the face of nature, and which returned with a deeper force with his discovery of the art of the caves, was to condition and underly much of his subsequent production and to lend to even his most classical visions a suggestion of underlying, hidden elemental forces. Some of the later landscapes, many of which include a prominent architectural motif, hark back to certain early Purist works, but they have about them a submerged intensity, a new feeling of weight. They are less immediately ambitious than the large figure pieces but they are among the most successful and imposing of his works.

In retrospect Ozenfant became deeply aware of a dichotomy in his character and art. On the one hand he was by instinct a classicist, a devotee of the art of the South, an art of clear sunlight and unchanging forms. On the other he was a Northerner, an inheritor of the Gothic, romantic tradition of dreams, of abstraction and of mystery. From the late 1920s onward these streams alternate in his work, often informing and reinforcing each other. But to my mind there is no doubt where his affinities truly lay and where his talents spoke most eloquently. The best work of his latter years shows a reversion to the values and principles which had transformed him into a significant figure of the avant-garde. The yachts at rest in a Mediterranean blue, the classical aqueducts and the solemn sea and landscapes stretching out toward infinity, perhaps above all the bare corners of empty rooms, with windows open on to empty skies, these are Purist in every sense of the word. It is the feeling for continuity in art, for its constants, that gives his work its particular flavour and that ultimately constitutes its importance. From the start he had been too deeply steeped in the art of the past and in modern life to distinguish between the two. In his *Mémoires* he was to write: 'I have often been criticized for my two apparently irreconcilable drives: the obsession with permanence and my all-absorbing interest in the present (*l'obsession de la permanence et mon énergique intérêt pour l'actuel*). Can't people realize that the present is our own moment of eternity?'[6]

9

Futurism in Venice

IT IS ironic that the grandest exhibition of Futurism ever to be mounted should have been mounted in Venice, for the Futurists held Venice in particular contempt. On the evening of 8 July 1910, Marinetti, the movement's commander-in-chief, together with a group of Futurist painters, placed themselves in a strategic position on the Clock Tower overlooking the Piazza San Marco, armed with eighty thousand copies of their manifesto *Contro Venezia Passatista*.[1] These they hurled at a crowd of astonished Venetians who had just alighted from the ferry from the Lido and were crossing the square on their way home to supper. The manifesto accused Venice, among other things, of being a 'jewelled hip-bath for cosmopolitan courtesans' and 'a great sewer of traditionalism'. 'Let us fill the stinking little canals with the rubble of the tottering infected old palaces. Let us burn the gondolas, rocking chairs for idiots, and raise to the sky the majestic geometry of metal bridges and smoke-crowned factories, abolishing the sagging curves of ancient buildings.'

Timing was all-important, and Marinetti's sense of timing was one of his greatest assets. One Sunday in that same year, as the faithful were leaving the Basilica after mass, trumpets blared from the summit of the Campanile, and there was Marinetti, megaphone in hand, to deliver a torrent of anti-Venetian and anti-clerical abuse. His lecture at the Teatro La Fenice on 7 May caused a splendid scandal and was punctuated by the 'resounding slaps' administered to the audience by the painters Boccioni, Russolo and Carrà.[2]

On the other hand it is entirely appropriate that Fiat should have chosen in 1986 to inaugurate its new centre at the Palazzo Grassi with an exhibition entitled *Futurismo e Futurismi* because the Futurists worshipped machines and in particular 'the racing automobile . . . more beautiful than the Victory of Samothrace'.[3] In the atrium of the palace, and visible from the Grand Canal, were placed a Fiat Model 1 car of 1908–10, identical to the one owned by

Marinetti and in which it so pleased him to be photographed, and a Bugatti 13 of 1910–23. The latter looked brave but vulnerable – a toy for adults. In the light well of the vast central hall were suspended two airplanes, a Blériot X and a Spad VII. Like the automobile the 'gliding flight of airplanes with propeller sounds like the flapping of a flag' had been celebrated in the first and founding manifesto of Futurism, which appeared on 20 February 1909.

Automobiles and flight inspired two of Marinetti's most famous poems, '*A l'Automobile*' of 1905,[4] which was published three years later as '*A mon Pégase*',[5] and '*L'Aviatore Futurista parla con suo Padre, il Vulcano*', which came out in *L'Aeroplano del Papa* in 1914.[6] Aeroplanes figure in contemporary poems by his friends, Libero Altomare, Paolo Buzzi and Enrico Cavacchioli. The Futurist painters, who formed a more cohesive group than the Futurist poets, on the whole preferred their machines earthbound. And the entire movement itself was rather like a machine put together by inspired amateurs, at times showing great form and originality, at others collapsing in a shower of flying rivets and exploding mufflers.

Futurism proper occupied the *piano nobile* of the Palazzo and it did not seem inappropriate to see these works on pristine white panels suspended under heavy, coffered and painted nineteenth-century ceiling decorations; for although the Futurists flaunted the concept of modernity, their own modernism was at times little more than a veneer laid over their Symbolist origins. They sought to reject the past out of hand, but their attitude to the nineteenth century in particular was ambiguous: they could never make up their minds what, in the interest of the modern, they wanted to keep and what they wanted to reject.

The Futurists sought publicity obsessively; they would have been delighted by the fact that the Italian press treated the exhibition as the cultural event of the decade, and they would certainly have enjoyed the fanfares which accompanied the opening. The day before the opening Venice awoke to find a brand-new, enormous white boat anchored by the Doge's Palace. That night on board the presidents of Fiat and United Technologies (who co-sponsored this particular exhibition) entertained a thousand luminaries from the worlds of politics, society, finance, technology and the arts; the lagoon was aswarm with security forces disguised as human frogs.

The following morning, in a gigantic and beautiful tentlike structure erected in the Arsenale, the activities of the new Palazzo

Grassi were inaugurated by the president of the republic. After the official opening itself there was a gala evening at the Fenice with snippets of Futurist and other modernist dance, music and mime. Earlier in the day there had been a private presidential visit to the show. Simultaneously, in the nearby Campo San Stefano, the Comitativo per Il Dritto alla Casa staged a demonstration against what was happening. People gathered around a black coffin which bore the name of the president of Fiat, Agnelli, sang socialist songs and waved banners declaring that Italy had no need of new museums while Italians were homeless or inadequately housed.

About this the Futurists would have had more complicated feelings. They wouldn't have been too bothered about the plight of the homeless; they had strong feelings about how society should be organized but very little social consciousness. However, section ten of the founding manifesto of 1909 *had* declared, 'We want to demolish museums and libraries.' Still, the movement flourished on paradox and was not averse to bending facts when circumstances called for it; and exposure was all-important. Similarly, while art critics were condemned as useless or dangerous, the Futurists adored to be chronicled. There was a mountain of documentary material in this exhibition, some of it new. Every room had at least one case of it, and much of it was absorbing.

The literature on Futurism, and most of the publicity surrounding this exhibition, make much of the fact that Futurism was the first cultural movement of the twentieth century that sought to change not only art but life itself. It is perhaps doubtful if, during the early stages of the movement at least, anyone other than Marinetti saw things in quite this way; many of the artists involved viewed it rather as a platform from which to launch their own talents and careers. Even Marinetti was less interested in reforming life than in dominating and possessing it completely.

In this he was on the whole surprisingly successful. He had great personal charm which he used to considerable effect, but which he was also prepared to sacrifice to a deliberately offensive public persona. He had a quick but coarse and buccaneering mind. He had limitless vitality and his appearances as a lecturer, orator and performer were galvanizing. He was born in Alexandria in Egypt (in 1876) and liked to hint that he had absorbed strange powers through being suckled at the breast of a Sudanese wet-nurse. In fact the Alexandrian background was important because, given the family circumstances, it ensured that he grew up bilingual in French, and even more so because it was there that his father, a prominent lawyer, consolidated the family fortune that Marinetti inherited and that enabled him to be not only Furturism's leader and impresario but also its Maecenas: theatres and galleries could be rented, manifestos and books published, trips taken and excursions arranged. One of the most interesting exhibits in the show was a recreation of the study in the Milanese flat where Marinetti wrote the first manifesto, surrounded by furnishings from the family home in Alexandria. It told a tale with its extraordinary profusion of oriental carpets and ceramics and its Islamic lamps and furniture, all clearly expensive but of no aesthetic worth. The effect was opulent but shoddy.

After he had been expelled from his Jesuit school in Alexandria (for reading Zola) Marinetti took his *baccalauréat* in France before going on to study at the university in Pavia and then in Genoa. Until 1911 most of his writing was in French. His first book, a florid epic poem of Hugoesque pretensions, called *La Conquête des Etoiles*, went straight over the top; and there he was to remain. A play, *Le Roi Bombance*, performed at Lugné-Poë's Théatre de l'Oeuvre in 1909, had both Rabelaisian and social pretensions, but is little more than a feeble pastiche of Jarry's *Ubu Roi*, which had been seen at the same theatre ten years earlier.

Mafarka le Futuriste, a novel of 1909, is regarded by some as his finest prose work and by others, including myself, as almost unreadable. It is set in a mythical Africa – a counterpart and answer to D'Annunzio's vision of the continent – and is a tale of high adventure and violent physical passion. Mafarka, a supermacho if ever there was one, is one of the most objectionable creations in all fiction. Apart from his general awfulness, Mafarka's most notable and presumably most noticeable characteristic was his eleven-metre-long penis which he wrapped around himself while asleep; I picture him in this condition as a sort of recumbent Michelin man – but of course less benign.

Mafarka was the subject of three trials for obscenity, much welcomed by the author for the publicity they brought. In the meantime Marinetti had also been getting on with what he was best at: advertising and promoting himself. Sarah Bernhardt had been persuaded to declaim his verse in her salon; a book on his work had been published, presumably commissioned and paid for by himself.

Celebrities such as Rachilde, Apollinaire, Jarry and Verhaeren, to name but a few, had been bombarded with cajoling and flattering letters. In one of the cases of the exhibition a letter from Bergson, written in 1903, showed the philosopher trying patiently to answer a Marinettian questionnaire. It was placed, suggestively, next to some of Marinetti's notes for a lecture on Nietzsche; for Nietzsche and Bergson were to be the two most important intellectual influences on the founding manifesto of Futurism.

The way in which this first manifesto was launched illustrates Marinetti's genius as a showman; he simply rented the front page of a leading Paris newspaper, *Le Figaro*. The Italians were naturally enormously impressed, and the French curious, irritated and outraged. There were already undertones of the fierce nationalism that was to characterize the movement, but in its initial stages it was directed towards and against France. Some years later Marinetti was to say to the musician Francesco Balilla Pratella:

To conquer Paris and appear in the eyes of all as an absolute innovator...
I advise you with all my heart to set to work to be the most daring, most advanced, most unexpected and most eccentric emanation of all that has represented music to date. I advise you to make a real nuisance of yourself and not to stop until all around you have declared you to be mad, incomprehensible, grotesque and so forth.[7]

The initial manifesto must be accounted Marinetti's most important single work. Its aim was to shock and arrest – it ends, 'Erect on the summit of the world we hurl our defiance once more at the stars!' – and it still makes exciting and compulsive reading. Marinetti's writing had hitherto been derivative, and the intellectual content of the manifesto is in turn eclectic. The campaign for the destruction of the past is Nietzschean and the exaltation of violence owes much to Sorel.

Contemporary commentators were quick to point out that there were plenty of different nineteenth-century prototypes for the idea of introducing urban and even mechanistic iconography into the arts. Bergson had for some time been lecturing and writing on the need to understand the properties of speed and motion if man was to evaluate and understand his sensory perceptions and his relationship with the world around him.

What is new is the tone of the manifesto. The previous bombast and hyperbole are still present, but they are now harnessed, even disciplined, and put to the service of a new spirit of urgency and vitality. And by saying what they said more noisily and insistently than anyone else the Futurists were able to persuade not only themselves but also a lot of other people of the novelty of their premises. The manifesto was the literary form that enabled Marinetti to find his true voice. By 1916 over fifty manifestos, on every aspect of art and life, from architecture and theatre to lust and politics, had been published, and Marinetti wrote or had a hand in most of them. The manifesto was to be the Futurists' ideal vehicle of communication: it could be short, it was cheap and quick to publish and to disseminate, and its adoption marked the movement's essentially popular aspirations.

The concision and pace of the manifesto style also helped to effect the most important literary innovation of the movement. This involved a move from *vers libre* to the Futurist *parole in libertá*, which by 1913–14 had become a lingua franca of all the movement's various manifestations. *Parole in libertá* basically involved taking Mallarmé's and Bergson's principle of analogy several stages further: as Marinetti observed, 'Analogy is no more than the deep love that unites distant, diverse and seemingly hostile things.' The Technical Manifesto of Futurist Literature, which appeared on 11 May 1912, sought to free words from the corset of Latin syntax. Nouns were to explode at random and were more potent when doubled (man-torpedoboat/woman-gulf); the static, bland indicative was to be replaced by the more evocative infinitive; adverbs and adjectives weakened verbal impact and were out. The ideal was Marinetti's *immaginazione senza fili* ('wireless imagination') proclaimed in a manifesto of 1913, which now also abolished syntax and advocated a state of imaginative intoxication in which the original element of an analogy could be suppressed in favour of the second, which could then be linked to an indefinite succession of further dizzying images. 'It is not necessary to be understood,' the Futurists declared.

Marinetti's greatest achievement in this style was his 'Zang Tumb Tumb', a description of the siege of Adrianople in the Balkan war of 1912, published in 1914, though passages from it were already being declaimed by him a year earlier.[8] Fragments caught on an old recording are still spellbinding, although the voice is surprisingly light and tenorlike and one misses the rolling of the famous white eyeballs. Only the Neapolitan poet Cangiullo, a slightly later recruit to the movement, could match Marinetti's versatility in *parole in libertá*, and his *Piédigrotta* of 1916 is a masterpiece of the genre.[9] Hand in hand with the verbal pyrotechnics came the most daring typographic inventions, some of Futurism's most influential and enduring contributions to the ethos of our century, although these had been anticipated in Apollinaire's *L'Antitradition Futuriste*.

Not the least remarkable feature of the Futurists' manifestos was that they were not written to support or explain existing attitudes or bodies of work, rather they were blueprints for experiments and experiences that were still to come. In the founding manifesto Marinetti had spoken of 'we', but it was a royal 'we', and the document was a challenge and an invitation to others. The first to accept were the painters. The *Manifesto of the Futurist Painters* came out on 11 February 1910. In his autobiography Carrà tells us that it was drawn up by himself, Boccioni and Russolo, but it bears Marinetti's imprint. It was signed by five painters, two of whom (Bonzagni and Romani) withdrew hastily when they realized what they were letting themselves in for; their names were replaced by those of Severini and Balla. A second, technical manifesto of painting came out two months later and this was almost certainly the work of Boccioni, who for the next three years was to dominate the visual side of the movement.

Boccioni was the most gifted of the Futurists, except possibly for the architect Sant' Elia, who is anyway in many respects a special case. He was also the most ambitious, which is saying a lot. As Marinetti identified increasingly with Futurism as a whole, he transferred his personal aspirations to its larger interests; not so Boccioni. He had his first major one-man show at the Ca' Pesaro in the summer of 1910, already under the aegis of Marinetti, whom he had met at the beginning of that year. It was while the Ca' Pesaro exhibition was being shown that Boccioni moved into his first Futurist phase.

By 1908 Boccioni was working in his fully developed Divisionist manner, or rather in the Italian variant of the style; for while he applied pure colour in short, broken touches, there is very little optical science in their separation. Already he was interested not so much in the properties of light observed in nature as in the overall activation of the picture surface through very physical, vigorous, choppy brush strokes. Many of the canvases were views of the

Milanese suburb at Porta Romana where Boccioni had gone to live late in 1907, a suitable home for a young painter who had just written of his desire 'to paint the new, the fruit of our industrial age'.[10] Oddly enough these are not optimistic paintings and have about them an Antonioni-like air of loneliness and displacement. A residue of this tinges even the most assured of his Futurist pieces; maybe the rejection of the past was not so exhilarating after all. Soon, in pictures that were still identical in style, he turned to scenes of night life and violence, as in the *Rissa in Galleria* (Pinacoteca di Brera), which shows a crowd gathering around two fighting prostitutes in a city arcade flooded by garish electric lights.

The largest and most important work of Boccioni's first Futurist phase, *La Città Sale* 1910–11 (The Museum of Modern Art, New York), begun during his Ca' Pesaro show, was given pride of place in the largest of the rooms in the Palazzo Grassi. It looked impressive but it also served to underline some of the contradictions inherent in Futurism. It shows an emergent suburb under construction not by men with machines but by pygmy figures trying to control giant workhorses whose enormous blue halters give them unmistakable Pegasus-like qualities. Next to the painting stood the original plaster of Boccioni's most important sculpture, *Unique Forms of Continuity in Space*, a striding figure which seems to combine the men and the beasts in the painting into a single image, although there are also suggestions of mechanistic imagery in the straight lines of the head. The armless sculpture, with its rippling muscular dislocations, also conjures up vivid associations with the fluttering wet draperies of the much despised classical Hellenistic past: the speeding automobile and the *Victory of Samothrace* have come together in unholy wedlock.

Boccioni's work is of the utmost importance for an understanding of the nature of the earlier and in many respects most weighty phases of Futurism. His most ambitious pictorial cycle, the *States of Mind* of 1911, demonstrated how Futurism was 'modernized' through its contacts with Parisian Cubism, and, to a lesser extent, through its adaptation of certain aspects of chronophotography. In May 1911, *La Città Sale* had been shown at the Esposizione Libera in Milan. The exhibition was savaged in *La Voce* by the Florentine critic Ardengo Soffici.[11] Boccioni and his Milanese friends rushed off to Florence to confront their detractor who in turn rallied supporters of his own; two physical battles ensued.

But Soffici soon became a friend (and a Futurist) and he showed Boccioni an article he had written on the French Cubists and photographs of their work.[12] Severini, who was living in Paris, also visited the Esposizione Libera. He had by now put his name to the painters' manifesto and he was appalled to find that the work of his co-signers was shamefully *passatista*. He persuaded Marinetti to finance a jaunt to Paris for the painters as a prelude to the exhibition they were planning to launch there. Together with their mentor, Boccioni, Carrà and Russolo arrived in the French capital in November. Then, in an astonishingly short space of time, they reworked earlier canvases and produced new ones for their exhibition at the Bernheim Jeune gallery in February 1912.

The *States of Mind*, a title derived from Bergson, whose thought Boccioni was coming to see as increasingly exploitable for his own ends, was conceived as a triptych set in a railway station and designed to show the physical and psychological sensations of the people who say their goodbyes, depart or are left behind. Some early versions at the Palazzo Grassi showed the influence of Edvard Munch and even, in the caricatural treatment of the heads in some of the preliminary drawings, of Romani, one of the artists who had almost immediately asked to be disassociated from Futurism. Except for a certain roughness of handling, these works could have been executed in the 1890s. In the final post-Parisian version the linear grids of Analytic Cubism have been borrowed as the basis for a rigorous formal organization of the picture surface and played off against the earlier, swirling Munchean rhythms to create a series of spatial elements or cells into which are fitted the protagonists – the humans and the machine that is to be the instrument of their separation. In the central panel the locomotive, seen in Cubist multiple viewpoint simultaneously from in front and from the side, presides like a malevolent deity, while the numbers boldly stencilled across it (again derived from Cubist procedures) defiantly proclaim the painting's true modernity.

An essential element of the most famous Futurist images is the painters' attitudes to various forms of motion, coupled with the nature and range of their iconography. Many of the pictures such as Carrà's most ambitious and truly Futurist canvas *The Funeral of the Anarchist Galli* (Museum of Modern Art, New York), Boccioni's *La Città Sale* or Severini's steely and powerful depictions of mechanized war still look powerfully contemporary and put one in mind of the Neo-Expressionism of recent years. The 1986 exhibition made it possible to reconstruct most of the 1912 exhibition which travelled on from Paris to Britain, Germany, Belgium and Holland. It created enormous interest and was accompanied by various lectures, performances and demonstrations; at the end of the tour Marinetti had a scrapbook of 350 newspaper clippings to commemorate it.

Few of the paintings were of the quality of *States of Mind*; but it was the exhibition as a whole that caused such a stir. It is an example of the way in which indifferent art can be extremely influential. And I wonder if there are any conclusions to be drawn from the fact that among works which contain so much commotion and violence two of the most dominating images at the Palazzo Grassi were of Boccioni's mother: the somewhat repellent but commanding *Materia* (Mattioli Collection, Milan), a painting of 1912, and the sculptured head *Antigrazioso* of 1912–13 (Galleria Nazionale d'Arte Moderna, Rome). In any case she was clearly a formidable woman; and when Boccioni left for the front in 1915, she followed the train in an open carriage shouting 'Long live the Futurists, long live Italy, long live the volunteers!'[13]

Boccioni was killed in an accident in July 1916 when he was thrown from his horse. Already he had turned his back on Futurism, though he would probably have denied this. In 1912 he had accompanied the exhibition to Munich where he had seen and admired Kandinsky's work; and under Kandinsky's influence he became, briefly, a genuinely original colourist and produced some of his most exciting and liberated work. But it is proof of his intelligence that he seems to have realized that even if he had used Picasso's first fully mature Cubism of 1909–11 to organize and modernize his own work, he didn't completely understand it. His pictorial development now showed him going backwards in time to investigate Picasso's 'Negroid' or pre-Cubist work and then further back to a study of Cézanne. None of these works were completely Futurist or possibly not even Futurist at all. But they tell us much about the dilemmas that plagued and vexed the movement.

Giacomo Balla (born in 1871) was some ten years older than the other painters involved in the movement. Both Boccioni and Severini had studied with him briefly in Rome at a time when Balla was producing thoughtful, socially conscious canvases bathed in a calm, almost surreal light, the result of his very personal approach to Divisionist theories. He seems to have been a father figure to his

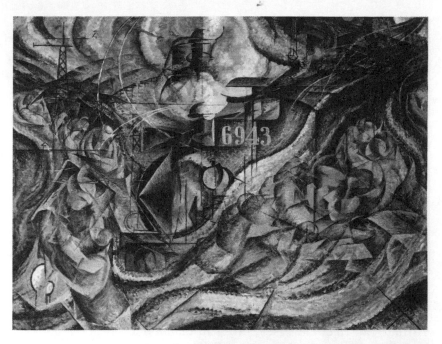

Boccioni,
*States of Mind:
The Farewells*, 1911

Boccioni,
Matéria, 1912

younger colleagues; and he was the most sympathetic of the painters: strong, gentle and, in the early phases of his career, wise.

He had been persuaded to sign the manifestos, and he was to have been included in the Bernheim Jeune exhibition although his single entry *Street Light* of 1909 (Museum of Modern Art, New York), was in the event not shown, possibly because it didn't look sufficiently modern. It was only in 1912 that he began to be completely absorbed into the movement, producing some delightful paintings of figures and animals in motion, based on the photographs and diagrams of Etienne-Jules Marey. Of his early Futurist years he was to write:

> Little by little acquaintances vanished, the same thing happened to his income, and the public labelled him mad. At home his mother begged the Madonna for help, his wife was in despair, his children perplexed . . . but without further ado he put all his *passéiste* works up for auction, writing on a sign between two black crosses: FOR SALE – THE WORKS OF THE LATE BALLA.[14]

As Balla in turn became more familiar with Cubist procedures his work grew in sophistication. In 1913 he produced a large series of virtually abstract canvases, often in black and white or monochrome, composed of tightly controlled linear rhythms around which are suspended complexes of transparent interacting planes: these bear titles like *Speeding Automobiles and Lights*, *Abstract Speed*, and so forth. Between 1911 and 1914 he also executed some extraordinary colouristic abstractions which, if I interpret them correctly, are to do with the diagrammatic movement of light, and which almost look as if they might have been done in the 1960s.

But changes were taking place within him. In 1914, as part of his contribution to the cause of Italian intervention in the war, he published a remarkably silly manifesto on clothing called *Il Vestito Anti-neutrale*: 'Futurist shoes will be dynamic, different one from the other in shape and colour, ready joyfully to kick all the neutralists.' It was around this time that he shaved off his patriarchal beard. Next, with a much younger colleague, Fortunato Depero, in 1915 he published *La Ricostruzione Futurista dell'Universo*. His own painting was going seriously off the rails, but he seems not to have noticed or minded. He began to decorate everything in sight in bright and often tasteless colour schemes. He just couldn't stop himself. From shoes, handbags, plates and teacups he turned to trays, chairs, letter racks, wastepaper baskets. On and on he went. Finally he was reduced to producing wooden Futurist

Balla, *Speeding Car and Light*, 1913

flowers, some angular and spiky, some lumpy and curvaceous. For
the rest of their lives his two elderly daughters, suitably named Luce
and Elica (Light and Propeller) preserved the Futurist wonderland
that was his Roman home. Many of its contents were on show at the
Palazzo Grassi.

From the start the Futurists had glorified war; and the period
when they were campaigning in favour of Italian intervention in the
First World War was an exciting one for them and produced some
good art. Then the war took its toll. Other members of the movement besides Boccioni, including the visionary Sant' Elia, were
killed. Many were wounded including Marinetti, whose old enemy
and rival D'Annunzio sent red roses to his hospital bed. But even
before they were separated by the war, the artists had begun to drift
apart and the movement had begun to lose much of its bite and
momentum. Although throughout the war years and well into the
1920s Futurism continued to gain new recruits, their activity
became increasingly diversified and diffuse; many of the figures
involved in the movement devoted a considerable part of their
energy to furthering the Fascist cause.

Yet for those of a Futurist persuasion there was certainly much to
enjoy. There were Balla's own sets for Stravinsky's *Fireworks*

(1917), in which the movement of coloured lights over and inside the décor replaced human performers in a genuinely imaginative and inventive way. There were Prampolini's mechanistic theatrical spectacles and Depero's puppets performing in his *Balli Plastici* to music by Alfredo Casella. In Rome there was dancing at the Tic Tac, décor by Balla, and drinking in Depero's Cabaret del Diavolo (his two important restaurants in New York, created between 1929 and 1931, have unfortunately vanished). There was Virgilio Montari's *Fox Trot Sorpresa* and Aldo Giuntini's fox trot, *The India Rubber Man*.

With the exception of Sant' Elia, whose bearing was aristocratic and who was a dandy (he was provided with free clothes by the grandest Milanese tailor, so good a clotheshorse and advertisement was he), the Futurists were inexorably bourgeois in appearance, but there was nothing like a waistcoat or a necktie from Depero's thriving workshop in Rovereto to enliven habitual attire. And then there was Futurist food. Already in the early 1920s there was talk of reforming the Italian diet, but it was not until the end of 1930 that Marinetti got around to issuing a manifesto on the subject, with all the authority of someone who was now a member of the Italian Academy and secretary of the Fascist Writers' Union.

The biggest Futurist banquet took place at the Taverna Futurista Santolopato in Turin on 8 March 1931: fourteen dishes were dreamed up by five artists and the two resident cooks, and although few of the guests got beyond the first course, it was clearly a *serata* to be remembered. Marinetti's *Cucina Futurista*, written in collaboration with the painter and writer Fillia, which came out in 1932, makes entertaining reading and should be reissued and translated. Basically the book is an extension of what came to be known as 'tactilism', a concept which preoccupied Marinetti throughout the 1920s and which involved combining contradictory or opposed sensations and experiences. In cookery pasta was out, but there were many exciting innovations such as salami in a hot sauce of coffee flavoured with eau de Cologne. Futurist diners were also asked to stroke samples of velvet, silk or emery paper with their left hands, depending on what was being forked up with the right, while warmed perfume was sprayed over the heads of the bald. Bliss was it . . . yes, indeed.

Many writers about Futurism, like the organizers of the 1986 exhibition, choose to take a wholly optimistic view of the movement, playing down its place in the incipient climate of Fascism, inextricably linked as this was with some of the darker, more shadowy sides of Futurism, and the Venice exhibition gave perhaps excessive prominence to the decorative and often somewhat childish paintings of Balla and his artistic grandchildren. Inevitably the *Futurismi*, the vast display of international art on the top floor of the Palazzo Grassi, chosen if only unconsciously to assert Italian dominance and supremacy in the field of twentieth-century modernism – works from sixteen countries were shown – gave rise to the question of Futurism's influence abroad.

Pride of place was given to the Russians, because many Russian artists called themselves Futurist (or Cubo-Futurist) and there was a genuine and fruitful dialogue between Russia and Italy. Marinetti's visit to Russia in 1914 was not the success he made it out to be; he offended some people while there and subsequently many more when he airily took the entire Russian Revolution and its art under his wing by proclaiming, 'I am delighted to learn that the Russian Futurists are all Bolsheviks and that for a while Futurism was the official Russian art.'

But in many ways the Russians were the Italian Futurists' true heirs. During the war years and in the period immediately succeeding 1917, theirs was the most genuinely experimental art in the world; they put their faith wholeheartedly in a technological revolution which the Italians had proclaimed but with which they had rather toyed and flirted; the Russians produced art that was environmental in a wider sense and on a larger scale than the Italians had envisaged. For a while at least the Russians truly lived their art in a way in which ultimately the Italians did not. And yet although the Russians quite understandably came to resent Marinetti's claims to primacy, the Italian movement had undoubtedly been for them an example and a catalyst. The Russian manifesto *A Slap in the Face of Public Taste* of 1912, for example, signed by Mayakovsky, Burliuk, Khlebnikov and Kruchenykh, bears the unmistakable imprint of its Italian forerunners. Rayonism, the pictorial movement launched by Larionov in 1913 with a manifesto that borrows ideas and terminology from the Italians, admitted that 'Rayonism is a synthesis of Cubism, Futurism and Orphism.'

The first Russian room at the Palazzo Grassi assembled work by Larionov, Goncharova and others, which demonstrates that for a while advanced Russian painters had much in common with their

Italian counterparts. The succeeding rooms, however, failed to make a central point: whereas the Italian Futurists were genuine revolutionaries for a relatively short time (Boccioni, the most brilliant of them, executed a virtual short circuit in less than five years), the Russian avant-garde was only just getting going when the Italians had passed their peak. It was at The Futurist Exhibition Tramway V held in Petrograd in February 1915 that Kazimir Malevich and Vladimir Tatlin emerged as the two rival personalities and artistic forces who were to change the face of Russian art. Both had reached their artistic conclusions through their experience of Cubism and most particularly through a study of the Synthetic Cubism achieved by Picasso and Braque during 1912 and 1913. The first major 'analytic' phase of Cubism involved, and was the result of, its initiators looking at the external world in a completely new way. So to a certain extent did the Futurists, and they adapted certain features of Cubism to express this vision more forcefully and dynamically.

Although Synthetic Cubism did not in any way turn its back on the original premises, it was above all now concerned with new ways of making art, assembling abstract forms and shapes into mean-ingful configurations which did not resemble objects in the external world but rather paralleled or recreated them in an independent pictorial or sculptural form. Having analysed and fragmented their subjects almost to the point of complete dissolution, they now proceeded to put them back together in a totally new form. This the Russians realized and seized upon at once (in a way the Italians failed or refused to do), although they undoubtedly saw Cubism as being more abstract than in fact it was; and it was this that enabled them to start drawing startling and unexpected conclusions of their own.

Russian artists had had the advantage of following the evolution of Cubism at first hand and from its earliest formative stages. Many of Picasso's finest works, influenced by tribal art, had found their way to Russia and they struck a chord in the eyes and hearts of artists like Goncharova and Malevich, partly at least because there was in Russia a strong indigenous tradition of popular folk art. Subse-quently, through exhibitions but above all through the collection of Sergei Shchukin, they were able to follow the evolution of Cubism (Tatlin also visited Picasso's studio in Paris in 1914) and by doing so they evolved their own independent languages.

The Italian Futurists encountered Cubism at a moment when it had reached a first climax of complexity and sophistication. It was this sophistication that so excited them; but they were also in a hurry. Until Boccioni's later investigations, they showed virtually no knowledge of the movement's father, Cézanne (the Russians did). And Boccioni, at least, despised primitive art, so that when in his own sculpture the devices and principles of modernism failed him, he was forced ultimately to look for help and prototypes in a despised Renaissance and classical past. Italian Futurism was one of the very few modern movements to turn its back on what tribal and ethnic art had to offer and teach, and these lessons were as important for the second major phase of Cubism as they had been for the first.

Severini, resident in Paris, produced Synthetic Cubist works, but the Italians, although they used the term 'synthetic' (as in their 'Synthetic Theatre') never produced their variant of Synthetic Cubism, although in an indirect way it touched the decorative creations of artists such as Balla, Depero and Prampolini. Collage and *papier collé*, so inextricably bound up in the formulation of Synthetic Cubism, were used by the Italians in a purely literary way, as a means of incorporating words and typography into painting. Boccioni's use of collage in the *Charge of the Lancers* of 1915 (Jucker Collection, Pinacoteca di Brera, Milan) shows a total misunderstanding of the principles Picasso and others had been following. Only in his *Dynamism of a Racing Horse + House* (1914–15) (Peggy Guggenheim Collection, Venice, Solomon R. Guggenheim Foundation), a multimedia construction unlike any other sculpture he executed, does he seem to have felt the necessity of facing the challenge of looking at some of Cubism's later manifestations and the artist probably saw his piece as unfinished.

The works in the last Russian rooms didn't look all that different from the ones in the first and gave very little indication that deep changes had taken place in Russian art. Many of these works had very little to do with what Futurism stood for. They appeared to have been chosen simply because they resembled in a very superficial way some of the paintings on the floor below in that they were fragmented, made use of transparent planes, had implications of movement, and were for the most part brightly coloured. And this is true of a large proportion of the works in the sections that followed. Many of them could have existed without any knowledge of Futurism (although it is certainly true that as a movement it had been well advertised) and simply with a second- or third-hand appreciation of some of the properties of Cubism that the Futurists themselves had found so useful and stimulating. As a friend with whom I visited the *Futurismi* observed, 'Futurism is everything that is bright and goes zigzag.'

In the *Futurismi* rooms there was a certain amount of good art on view, much that was indifferent and some that was bad. A tiny Cubist section contained a couple of beautiful pictures; these were tucked in after a room given to Belgium, and were chronologically out of sequence. One could, however, appreciate that the organizers faced a dilemma. To have placed the Cubists among the Futurists' antecedents would have implied a closer connection than the purely visual one which so clearly existed. It is certainly true that the works on the *piano nobile* felt closer to the Symbolist works on the ground floor than to the handful of Cubist paintings above them. Of all the Cubists, Léger was the most attracted to Futurism; he felt its impact and in his city pieces executed immediately after the war many aspects of Futurism's visual programme of incorporating the dynamics of the machine age into art found their finest and most exhilarating expression. A work by Léger of 1912–13, admittedly one much admired by Marinetti, was on view, but nothing later.

Of the various other *Futurismi*, the one that made the greatest impact was British Vorticism, partly because the intellectual astringency of Pound and Wyndham Lewis seemed to permeate all the works on view, and partly because Vorticist artists became interested more or less simultaneously in Futurism and both major phases of Cubism; so that their art, together with many Russian works, appeared more forward-looking than much of what surrounded it. Of the Americans Joseph Stella shone forth as one of nature's Futurists because he obviously found the modern urban scene so full of wonder, and so to a certain extent did John Marin and Max Weber. From here one was led on to the final sections of the Palazzo Grassi exhibition dedicated to the decorative arts, which were dominated by Balla but which were sufficiently catholic to include a couple of very un-Futurist pieces from the Bloomsbury group's Omega Workshops.

Still, this enormous, restless and febrile exhibition generated great energy and excitement, as did Futurism itself, and it continues to vibrate in memory.

10

Supreme Suprematist
(Malevich)

ALTHOUGH Kazimir Malevich became a legend in Russia during his lifetime and is considered by many to be the greatest Russian painter of the century, he is much less well-known than his two contemporaries and peers in the creation of abstract art, Kandinsky and Mondrian. When in 1919–20 the Visual Arts Section of the People's Commissariat of Enlightenment selected works by 143 artists for distribution to various Soviet museums, Malevich's name took precedence over all others; Kandinsky himself, who had returned to Russia from Munich in 1914 and subsequently joined in the revolutionary excitement, chaired the purchasing committee; his own painting was by now acknowledging a debt to Malevich's, to its detriment. But within a couple of years the forces of reaction were already set in motion, and in 1929 the director of the Tretiakov Gallery in Moscow, Fedor Kumpan, was given a lengthy prison sentence for having organized an exhibition of Malevich's work. It took Malevich two and a half years to retrieve his pictures, and although many of them eventually passed into state collections they were not seen again until relatively recently. In 1930 Malevich was himself interned for questioning. He died in 1935 at the age of fifty-seven, in great poverty.

Malevich travelled abroad only once, in 1927, when he accompanied a large selection of his work for exhibition in Warsaw and subsequently in Berlin. In Germany he also visited the Bauhaus in Dessau, where Moholy-Nagy oversaw the publication of his essay 'Suprematism and the Additional Element in Art', which appeared under the title of 'The Non-Objective World' (*Die Gegenstandslose Welt*); for forty years this remained the only one of Malevich's voluminous texts available in the West, and it had been tampered with in translation. On Malevich's return to Russia he felt that the political situation had worsened for him and he issued instructions that the pictures he had left behind in Germany, together with a packet of theoretical texts and a series of explanatory charts, should

169

not be returned to him: maybe he hoped that the works might be shown in other Western cities, and he may even have considered escaping to the West.

In 1935 Alfred Barr, prescient as ever, managed to smuggle a group of Malevich's paintings out of Germany, where they were in danger of being destroyed as part of the campaign against 'degenerate art'. Barr had come to Germany looking for works to include in his 'Cubism and Abstract Art' exhibition at the Museum of Modern Art in 1936. (Two of the canvases he brought out rolled up in his umbrella – fortunately it wasn't raining when he crossed the frontier.) Seven of the fifty-five Malevich oils known to have been exhibited in Berlin eventually found their way into the Museum of Modern Art's collections. A few others were dispersed in public and private collections and many appear to have been irretrievably lost. But in 1958 the remaining thirty-one paintings entered the Stedelijk Museum in Amsterdam, complementing its unique holdings of works by Mondrian and making it the mecca for students and lovers of early geometric abstraction.

In 1988, thanks to perestroika, the Russians and the Dutch pooled their resources and the State Russian Museum in Leningrad, the Tretiakov Gallery in Moscow and the Stedelijk Museum in Amsterdam mounted the largest Malevich exhibition yet to have been seen. The Malevich exhibition which was subsequently mounted at the National Gallery of Art in Washington was slightly smaller but undoubtedly stronger; it brought together for the first time carefully chosen pictures from a wide range of American, Russian and Dutch collections to produce the most thoughtful and revealing survey of Malevich's art to date.[1]

Armand Hammer, long known for his promotion of Soviet-American commercial collaboration, had originally envisaged reconstructing the 1988–9 exhibition in America, and it was he who made the initial contacts with Soviet officials. He subsequently played no role in the final conception of the revised Washington version of the exhibition, which, shortly before he died on 11 December, went on view at his own still uncompleted Armand Hammer Museum of Art and Cultural Center in Los Angeles but in a reduced form. In view of the congratulatory letters from George and Barbara Bush, Mikhail and Raisa Gorbachev, and Hammer himself, published in the catalogue, it is ironic that every single one of the American Maleviches had been removed from the California showing. Presumably American curators were reluctant to lend on the ground that the new Hammer buildings (by Edward Larrabee Barnes) had not been tested for climatic and security conditions. One cannot help wondering why the Russians and the Dutch could in that case have been less particular and possibly Hammer's capricious attitude toward American museums may have played a role in the story. The American paintings played an integral part in this particular presentation of Malevich's art, and their loss was deeply felt.

Despite the many recent new insights into Malevich he remains an enigmatic figure. He clearly had great charisma, and photographs of him taken in his youth and in his prime generate a feeling of exceptional intensity. We know that he was an inspired teacher. He corresponded and collaborated closely with many of the most celebrated Russian artists of his generation, including Mayakovsky and Eisenstein, but few of them appear to have known him really well, although he developed a lifelong friendship with the composer and painter Mikhail Matiushin. He was a prolific writer and a voracious reader, but he had received only a rudimentary education. He grew up in various rural communities in and around Kiev and Kursk and was largely self-taught; even those fluent in Russian (I myself am not among them) find his writings difficult.[2] And yet in 1919, the year in which he completed one of the most important of his texts, 'On the New Systems in Art: Statics and Speed', he also produced an essay on poetry, and the previous year the poet Kruchenykh in his eulogy on 'zaum' – transrational language – praised Malevich as one of its most effective practitioners.

The first major turning point in Malevich's career came in 1907, when he moved permanently to Moscow. His arrival there coincided with the first independent exhibition of a new group of Symbolist artists, Blue Rose, held in the house of the painter Pavel Kuznetsov. Kuznetsov's influence can be seen in a revealing group of studies for frescoes, dating from this year, which Malevich showed in Moscow in 1908 and then again in 1911 as *The Yellow Series*, but which subsequently disappeared from view until their inclusion in the American exhibitions. In them the pantheism that characterized the work of so many of the Blue Rose artists takes on a genuinely mystical dimension, and the naked figures which appear in all of them do not so much commune with their landscape surroundings as become literally absorbed into nature. The pictures are also totally devoid of the submerged eroticism that pervades so much other contemporary Russian Symbolist art: and they radiate some of the innocent spirituality that characterizes so many anonymous provincial Russian icons.

The Yellow Series, taken in conjunction with the superb large gouaches of 1911–12, depicting different aspects of labour and society – chiropodists, floor polishers, gardeners and so forth – reveal for the first time Malevich's full potential as an artist. These later works are explosive, raw, deliberately clumsy and totally unself-conscious. By now he had come into contact with Larionov and Goncharova, who were at the time trying to give certain forms of French Post-Impressionism a specifically Russian flavour by injecting into it aspects of icon painting and local folk and peasant art; the Neo-Primitivism which they sought struck a natural chord in Malevich's makeup and they helped him to hear it within himself. Malevich himself was also aware of the most recent developments in French art, and it is possible to find echoes of Cézanne, Matisse and Braque in his figures; but these references seem irrelevant: Malevich's creations remain archetypically Russian – like characters out of Gorky or Kuprin – and supremely themselves.

The question of sources, however, becomes a prime concern in discussing the next phases of Malevich's development, for it was to a large extent through his creative misunderstanding of them that he was able to reach such startlingly original visual conclusions of his own, just as his thought was the result of a sort of collage of the most disparate and often most unlikely intellectual influences. By 1912 Italian Futurist manifestos had already been widely distributed in Russia. But whereas many outside France tended to approach Cubism through the type of Italian pictures that owed most to it, for the simple reason that Futurism was more accessible and fundamentally popular in its appeal, Russian artists, and Malevich in particular, tended to look at Cubism through a Futurist aesthetic or programme. The results were for the most part striking; and if there has been a tendency to underplay the influence of the Italians upon the Russians, the reason may be that in Russia the achievements of the parent movement were superseded at virtually every level.

Malevich's immersion in Cubism, although it was to have its most far-reaching results in the 'alogical' work of 1913–14, had a splendidly logical start in that he began by investigating and identifying with the work of Léger who, more than any other artist associated with Parisian Cubism, was able to retain a French sensibility to purely formal values and yet to subscribe to Futurism's vision of the modern mechanized scene and to its insistence on the dynamic fragmentation of matter. Léger was also the French artist with whom Malevich had temperamentally most in common. (The two men never met, but Léger's second wife, Nadia, claimed to have been a pupil of Malevich. In moments of emotion she also claimed that she and she alone held the secret to an understanding of Malevich's art, which she would one day divulge; unfortunately, to my knowledge she never got around to doing so.) Léger's *Essai pour Trois Portraits* of 1911 (now in the Milwaukee Art Center) was shown at the second 'Knave of Diamonds' exhibition in Moscow in 1912 in which Malevich also participated. The Léger was to inspire a poem by Benedict Livshits that appeared in *A Slap in the Face of Public Taste* published in December 1912, a document that can in some respects be regarded as the first fully integrated product of Russian Futurism. Léger was a frequent visitor at the painting studio known as the Académie Russe, run in Paris by Marie Vasiliev; during 1913 and 1914 he was to deliver there two important lectures which were subsequently published and certainly read in Russia.[3]

Another link was the gifted Russian painter Alexandra Exter, in certain respects a pupil of Léger's, who divided her time between Paris, Kiev and Moscow, carrying back and forth with her photographs of the artist's work. Léger's particular brand of Cubism had early on been dubbed 'Tubism', and the geometric metallic configuration of his figures and compositions find an echo in, for example, Malevich's *Taking in the Rye* and *The Woodcutter*, both of 1912 (and both in the Stedelijk Museum, Amsterdam), works which Malevich himself classified as Cubo-Futurist.

Other slightly later Cubo-Futurist works, like the arresting *Face of a Peasant Girl* (also in the Stedelijk), show an awareness of the early and hermetic phases of Picasso's Cubism, a moment in art that Malevich was subsequently to recognize as a turning point in twentieth-century painting; here it looks as if the Picassian prototype (in the Sergei Shchukin collection)[4] had been transposed into metal and subsequently bent and twisted by a powerful fist. The element of abstraction and fragmentation or dislocation in the earlier phases of Cubism was at the service of an attempt to analyse

Malevich, *Taking in the Rye*, 1912

forms in such a way as to present them to the spectator in greater fullness or completeness. Malevich, on the other hand, saw this analysis as an attempt to shatter the subject: 'The Cubists, thanks to the pulverization of the object, left the field of subjectivity'[5] he was to declare. Cubism was in many respects a classically slanted art in its search for balance and poise, and both Picasso and Braque tended to favour the classical pyramid in their compositions. Malevich, even at a later date when he was distinguishing more clearly between the aims of Cubism and Futurism, continued to see Cubism as being explosive. Cubism had taken objects apart but an appreciation of its aims involves the spectator's ability to put them back again. Malevich on the contrary believed, according to Futurist principles, that 'All matter disintegrates into a large number of component parts which are fully independent.'[6]

Even odder was the way in which Malevich interpreted the later, Synthetic Cubist works which Shchukin added to his collection in 1913 and 1914. By now the subject matter in Picasso's work had once again become more immediately legible and he undoubtedly saw the abstract pictorial substructure of his works as reinforcing the realism, the materiality of his subjects, and as helping to lend them weight and substance. Malevich, on the other hand, seems to have viewed the areas of *papier collé* in Cubist works, and flat slab-like planes derived from them, as new configurations working *against* the subject, challenging its importance and supremacy. Although many of Malevich's canvases of 1914 have at first glance a very Cubist look about them, in all of them the subject defies a logical visual and intellectual reconstruction, the kind of reconstruction that is fundamental to the mechanics of Cubism, and the paintings are essentially medleys of disconnected fragments buried in an abstract pictorial architecture. From the start the Cubists had sought an art that was anti-naturalistic but simultaneously representational in a non-imitative fashion. Malevich, when he first saw Synthetic Cubist works, seems to have felt that their creators were in search of some super-reality of a transcendental nature which challenged the subject's existence. In his own last Alogic and Cubo-Futurist works the subjects' identities become menaced rather than reinforced by the large oblongs and quadrilaterals that surround them or that are superimposed over them. And when Malevich subsequently achieved abstraction he saw the geometric forms in his pictures as being dynamically charged with all the wealth of visual material that he had absorbed in his formation as an artist, just as he felt that they could in turn be split or broken apart to form a whole new pictorial vocabulary.

All of Malevich's interests and worlds – his belief in Futurism, his absorption in Cubism, his love of poetry and sound, his fascination with his own Russianness – came together in 1913 when he agreed to collaborate on an opera for the Saint Petersburg Union of Youth. *Victory over the Sun*, which had two rapturously received performances at the Luna Park Theatre, had a prologue by Khlebnikov and a nonsense libretto by Kruchenykh; the plot, in so far as there was one, involved the stabbing of the sun and its enclosure in a square container for Futurist but somewhat obscure ends.

Khlebnikov and Kruchenykh were in some respects complementary characters, the one a dreamer who nevertheless produced verbal experiments as daring as Mayakovsky's own, the other an extrovert whose verse invited performance in staccato platform style; Malevich learned from both of them. Music for the opera was composed by Matiushin and combined 'ready-made' sound effects with pianistic dissonances and odd passages of thin, wistful melody.

Malevich

A trick photograph taken at the time of the production shows Matiushin, Kruchenykh and Malevich with a grand piano upside-down over their heads, and it catches some of the flavour of the enterprise.

It was at this time that Matiushin introduced Malevich to Howard Hinton's book on *The Fourth Dimension*,[7] a concept that intrigued artists throughout Europe. Malevich seems to have found Hinton's diagrams helpful; and the row of squares in *Portrait of the Composer M. V. Matiushin* of 1913, a work to which Malevich was particularly attached, may be a reference to the 'higher cubes' belonging to a 'higher space' discussed by Hinton, and possibly also a reference to the quarter tones which were among the most daring aspects of Matiushin's operatic score.

Malevich's sets for *Victory over the Sun* were executed in black and white for economic reasons, but the costumes were decorated with brightly coloured and often jagged abstract shapes and motifs. The general effect was Cubo-Futurist, but the curtain for Act II, Scene 5, consisted of a simple square against a white background; and it is possible that when Malevich saw this geometric emblem hanging motionless in the theatrical arc lights it appeared to him all of a sudden strangely numinous, filled with some breathless, expectant hidden truth. Certainly Malevich saw the opera as a landmark in his career; and the importance he attached to it is surely relevant to his subsequent insistence that Suprematism had originated in 1913. The lighting of *Victory over the Sun* was one of its most avant-garde features, and the costumes were designed in such a way that often only parts of the performers, their heads or their legs for instance, were visible. The players must have presented an appearance not unlike the configurations of coloured forms that were soon to appear in Malevich's paintings.

At the 'Tramway V' exhibition mounted in Petrograd in February 1915, Malevich was represented by works of his Cubo-Futurist and Alogic styles; it was at this exhibition that it became obvious that Tatlin and Malevich together were to form the spearhead for future developments in revolutionary Russian art. At the end of this same year at '0.10. The Last Exhibition of Futurist Painting', also in Petrograd, Malevich launched the Suprematist movement. It was accompanied by the obligatory manifesto, although friends had tried to persuade Malevich not to publish one, on the grounds that there were all too many of them around. In fact it is one of the grandest of all the Russian manifestos of the period; it betrays a debt to Italian Futurist prototypes but it has about it a dignity and almost biblical resonance that the Italians never achieved. Toward the beginning of it Malevich declared, 'I have turned myself into the zero of form.'[8]

He had indeed. Visitors to the exhibition must have been stunned to be confronted with thirty-six totally abstract works, the first of their kind. Hung across the corner of Malevich's space was *The Black Square*, which was to become his own emblem and that of the movement. '*The Black Square*,' Malevich proclaimed, 'is the face of the new art. The Square is a living, royal infant. It is the first step of pure creation in art.'[9] Recent X-rays of the first *Black Square* (now in the Tretiakov Gallery, Moscow) have revealed a more elaborate abstract composition underneath it; and if *The Black Square* is a static form and certainly the most minimal image yet to have been produced, Malevich himself saw it as being charged with energy and dynamic power. In one sense, it was Futurism's ultimate revenge on Cubism.

Although with hindsight we can to a certain extent come to an understanding of early Suprematist works by exploring the visual and intellectual avenues that led to them, nevertheless there is a sense in which Suprematism sprang ready-formed from the brow of its creator. And this distinguished Malevich's approach very sharply from that of Kandinsky and Mondrian, who had inched their way into abstraction over a period of many years. His art differed from theirs in other fundamental ways as well. Once Kandinsky had moved into abstraction, to a large extent he turned his back on the natural phenomena that had originally inspired and moved him, and Mondrian did so completely. Malevich's attitude toward nature was much more receptive and sympathetic. He sought through Suprematism, 'a world in which man experiences totality with nature', although he also stressed that simultaneously, 'Forms must be made which have nothing in common with nature.'[10] And there remains in Malevich's writings, underlying his exaltation of modern technology and urban life, an undercurrent of nostalgia for the green pastures and meadows of his youth; at his own request his ashes were buried in an open field next to his dacha in Nemchinovka.

Ultimately Mondrian's art is more contemplative and more profoundly philosophical than Malevich's, and it gives more enduring pleasure and sustenance to the eye. Kandinsky's early abstractions are exhilarating because, apart from their sheer physical beauty, the apocalyptic fervour and drama of the subjects underlying them have epic implications. To be confronted by Malevich's work is like travelling in uncharted territory.

Already in his first Suprematist paintings Malevich had found what over the next few years was to be the true subject of his art. It was to be an art about flight, about man's ascent into the ether and into the planetary world of the future. On the page showing 'the Environment that stimulates the Suprematist' in 'The Non-Objective World', Malevich illustrates photographs of airplanes in formation and aerial views, and these patterns of flight and overviews of townscapes clearly formed the basis for many of the compositions of tipping, tilting planes and shapes that appear almost at once in his Suprematism.

The concept of flight was one that was obsessive in Russia before 1917, and it became, in a sense, one of the leitmotifs of the great revolution itself; in so far as there is a hero in *Victory over the Sun*, it is the aviator who flies in at the end of it. In his tantalizingly brief fragments of autobiography[11] Malevich tells us how as a child he had sacrificed to flight, tethering chickens on the thatched roof of the cowshed in order to watch at closer range the arcs described by the wings of hawks as they closed in on their prey. Perhaps, too, flight was a motif that allowed him unconsciously to fuse his love of nature with the most daring products of a new, mechanized world. If *The Black Square* can be viewed as the collision of planes in space to fuse into a new entity, the idea of a journey through space is also the theme that unifies the three different phases of Suprematism that Malevich came to distinguish.

The first of these was black and corresponds, Malevich tells us, to economy. Malevich's use of the word is baffling until one realizes that it is derived from the nineteenth-century German philosopher Richard Avenarius, whose *Philosophy as a Reflection on the World, According to the Minimal Waste of Energies*, originally published in 1876, came out in Russian translation in 1913. Avenarius rejected all processes of deductive reasoning and claimed that truth could be apprehended through direct perception; if the truths so perceived appeared to be unconnected or contradictory, 'economy' of thought could be produced by formulating a compromise or synthesis of the two: 'for two different and to our perception different groups of ideas have been reduced to one'. He goes on to say, 'A system (of ideas) through its real or assumed completeness is useful in giving us calm

Malevich,
Suprematist Painting,
Eight Red Rectangles,
1915

in the face of every possible special problem and, through its real or assumed inner consistency, preserves the advantage of a feeling of security in which every consequence arising from the basic central idea serves the purpose of confirming it retrospectively; everything is connected with everything else, everything supports and reinforces everything else.'[12] This engaging concept must have reinforced Malevich's own vision of shapes as representing ideas coming together to form new ones.

The second phase of Suprematism (which seems to have been initiated almost immediately after the black) was the red or coloured phase, corresponding to revolution. The titles later ascribed by Malevich to the forms of earlier phases are relatively straightforward and formalistically descriptive: *Suprematist Painting, Eight Red Rectangles*, 1915, and *Suprematist Painting, Black Rectangle, Blue Triangle*, also 1915 (both in the Stedelijk Museum, Amsterdam), for example. It is hard to establish a sequence for the works, but stylistically the movement seems to have been away from relatively simple compositions with a few bold elements towards works of greater complexity, where the shapes are more varied and deliberately contrasted. Next perhaps are works where the smaller shapes tend to drift off towards the edges of the canvas as if in an attempt to wing their way out into the space outside the pictorial arena. These were succeeded by a number of paler paintings where the centre of the canvas tends to empty out and the larger forms now also brush the edges of the canvas or are cut off by them. Related titles of these become symbolic: *Composition of Suprematist Elements, Expressing the Sensation of Metallic Sounds – Dynamic (Pale, Metallic Colours)*, 1917 (Museum of Modern Art, New York). There then occurs a sharp break with the 'fading away' paintings, which appears to be an attempt to release form from the flat, two-dimensional picture plane.

The final phase of Suprematism is the white which corresponds to 'pure action'. Now the beam, diagram for the path of matter and light into space, replaces the plane, and now the terminology is frankly mystical: *Suprematist Composition Conveying the Feeling of a Mystic 'Wave' from Outer Space*, 1917 (Stedlijk Museum, Amsterdam), and so on. The series reaches a climax in the *White Square on White* (Museum of Modern Art, New York). And it would be nice to think that the *Black Square* had split apart, forming new configurations that had taken on bright colour, and that as these wheeled and drifted to the edges of the canvas they had paled and faded, and that as they revolved through an infinite space they had regrouped or reassembled to form the purified white square. As a small boy, when his father was employed as overseer in a series of sugar factories, Malevich had been fascinated by the miracle that occurred when the dark, raw molasses was fed into the machines to emerge as a white crystalline substance. In 1919 he was able to declare: 'The blue colour of the sky has been defeated by the Suprematist system, has been broken through and entered white as the real concept of infinity.'[13] And a year later:

> What in fact is the canvas? What do we see represented on it? . . . a window through which we discover life . . . blue does not give a true impression of the infinite. The rays of vision are caught in a cupola and cannot penetrate the infinite. The Suprematist, infinite white allows the beam to pass on without encountering any limit.[14]

During the years immediately following the launching of the Suprematist manifesto, Malevich's thought evolved considerably, largely under the influence of his reading of Hegel, whom he interpreted in a characteristically wilful fashion. His view of the cosmos, always on a considerable scale, became if anything more expansive, and certainly increasingly eccentric. And in Hegelian manner Malevich at least implicitly constructed a tripartite system to investigate the history of art. In Hegel's exposition of the evolution of world spirit he divides history into three periods. The first is a period of total unselfconsciousness in which man intuitively begins to identify with nature. Malevich equated this period with primitive art, which he saw (somewhat surprisingly) as aspiring to imitate nature, or to copy her slavishly. Hegel's second phase shows the slow turn towards a state of consciousness in which man seeks to separate himself from nature, although the separation remains only partial or imperfect. Malevich connected this period with Classical and Renaissance art, which he seems to have felt lacked a certain dimension of pictorial truth because of an excessive concern with imitation or 'skilful reproduction', which in the case of painting often resulted in an insufficient emphasis or recognition of the integrity of the flat pictorial support. The third and final stage of Hegel's view of evolution is that in which spirit detaches itself from nature and achieves total freedom, thus becoming 'pure universal form . . . in which the spiritual essence attains the consciousness and feeling of itself'. It was this move towards an advanced inward spirituality that Malevich felt had been initiated by 'the Realists, Impressionists, Cubism, Futurism and Suprematism', and brought to conclusion, presumably, by himself.

The most significant document for understanding his new position is perhaps *God Is Not Cast Down*, published in 1922, a crucial period for Malevich when he was reconsidering the whole future of art. It soon becomes obvious that God, as viewed by Malevich, is an embodiment of the super-artist, and he suggests that man (the artist) can reach perfection 'through all that he produces' so that he can achieve 'a state of rest' and act 'no longer as man but as God'. Already in 1920 Malevich had announced the death of easel painting. 'There can be no question of painting in Suprematism,' he declared. 'Painting was done for long ago.' In his essay *On Poetry* (1919) he had already condemned craftmanship out of hand: 'The poet is not a craftsman, craftsmanship is nonsense.' At the same time, in *On New Systems of Art* he had given a hint of how he had come to see his Suprematism when he had written: 'The important thing in art is signs flowing from the creative brain.'

One of the peculiarities of Malevich's writings is the recurrence, in his discussions of creativity, of the image of the human skull. And

Malevich

Malevich's latter-day Suprematist paintings are no longer paintings in the traditional sense at all. Rather they are signs, messages, pictorial planets, emanating from the artist's skull – in itself white, spherical, translucent – and directed out through infinite space toward some ultimate unknowable Godhead, seat of perfection, purity and infinite repose.

Lissitzky, the most gifted of Malevich's disciples, and a more educated and hence more accessible writer, was to clarify his master's position in a lecture entitled 'New Russian Art', delivered in 1922. In it he distinguishes between two kinds of signs. One type, he posits, is derived from our knowledge of the world and natural phenomena and can be easily read and identified, since the idea exists before the pictorial sign for it is identified.

> Now the second possibility: a sign is designed, much later it is given its name, and later still its meaning becomes clear. So we do not understand the sign, the shape, which the artist created, because man's brain has not yet reached the corresponding state of development.[15]

After the Suprematist *Whites* Malevich painted less and less, and during succeeding years gave himself over increasingly to teaching and writing. A moving photograph shows members of Malevich's UNOVIS ('affirmation of life') team departing from Moscow to their new headquarters in Vitebsk around 1920. His students, many of them little more than children, wore black squares stitched on to their sleeves, and they adopted as their slogan 'Art into Life'. On the anniversary of the Revolution in 1920 they transformed the grimy town into a pageant of coloured signs. Eisenstein was to write:

> All the main streets are covered with white paint splashed over the red brick walls, and against this white background are green circles, reddish-orange squares, blue rectangles. This is Vitebsk 1920. Kazimir Malevich's brushes have passed over its walls. 'The squares of the town are our palettes' is the messages which the walls convey.[16]

Long before the doctrine of Social Realism was even imminent Malevich had fallen out with avant-garde Constructivist colleagues because he felt that the role of art could never be utilitarian. But he was a prophet and a reformer and given his own social concerns it was inevitable that he should have turned his attention to architecture. And together with his students in Vitebsk and subsequently Petrograd (renamed Leningrad in 1924), he executed a large number of architectural designs and three-dimensional models in plaster of Paris. One original model survives, while others have been reconstructed from casts taken in part from surviving original elements. Although they are all beautiful and continue to look visionary, the original continues to shine forth among them.

Everything that Malevich produced is informed by his extraordinary sense of touch – the sense of his hand remains almost uncannily alive and present. The architectural constructions (with one or two possibly later exceptions) were never practical or functional; and once again they may best be seen as messages, designs, blueprints for the builders of the future. Malevich called his constructions 'blind architecture' and also referred to them as 'planits'. Even in these solid, three-dimensional structures there persists the obsession with the white purity of flight. A note attached to one of the drawings touchingly reads:

> Thanks to its construction the planit is easy to clean. It can be washed daily . . . the material is matt white glass . . . the planit will be accessible from all sides for the earth dwellers who will be able to be in it and on top of it.[17]

The year 1922, in which Malevich publicly voiced his reservations about the Constructivists grouped around Rodchenko, also saw the formation of the Association of Artists of Revolutionary Russia, designed to counter the dominant role played by the avant-garde in the arts since the inception of the Revolution; forces were by now rapidly polarizing. Malevich's own activities continued to proliferate. In 1923, for example, he became involved in the proposal to convert the Petrograd Museum of Artistic Culture (MKhK) into a scholarly institute for research on the culture of modern art; his teaching activities multiplied and diversified and he participated in various exhibitions and helped in the organization of others. But he was in fact becoming an increasingly isolated figure and there are indications that more and more he found himself in disagreement with colleagues of both the left and the right; certainly the Russian authorities were viewing his concerns with mounting suspicion. In 1926 he was dismissed as director of GINKhUK (a revised form of MKhK) after an attack on the institute, 'A Cloister at the Expense of the State', had been published in *Pravda*. Subsequently it became extremely difficult for him to get new theoretical texts published. By the end of 1930 Malevich was registered at the Union of Art Workers as unemployed. In 1932 he was given a small working space in the basement of the State Russian Museum, but even there his tenure was insecure.

An important recently discovered letter from Malevich to Meyerhold written in 1932 makes it clear that his attitude toward Constructivism was if anything more negative than before, and he seems to have seen it as betraying the achievements of his own non-objective art and the ideal society it had envisaged. It is hard to tell whether his references to the new figurative Soviet art, whose necessity he acknowledges, are involuntary or even possibly deeply ironical. And against the ambiguity of his intellectual position the problems posed by his own late paintings become increasingly complex and baffling. In his own 1929 retrospective at the Tretiakov Gallery he was already recapitulating subjects and compositions he had first broached in 1912 and 1913, and these reprises, though incisive and commanding, are cold and a little empty compared with their earlier counterparts. Other works, like the large *Sportsmen* of *c.* 1928–9 (State Russian Museum), which shows faceless athletes in latter-day Suprematist costumes, are colouristically original and have about them a sort of submerged optimism that is invigorating but also somehow strangely heart-breaking. One of these works in particular, *Suprematism, Female Figure* of *c.* 1928–32 (also in the State Russian Museum), has some of the same mystic intensity that informs the *Whites* of 1918.

Many somewhat impressionistic canvases that have hitherto been thought to be early (and some of them bear early dates in the artist's own hand) were in fact executed at the very end of his career; desperately pressed for funds as Malevich was, he probably felt that works such as these might more easily attract a market. Malevich was a tireless correspondent and it is likely that other letters will come to light which may make it possible for us to come to an understanding of how he saw the problems he was facing. The last three paintings in the American exhibition (all of 1933, two years before his death), paintings of himself, his wife and the critic N. N. Punin (an early supporter who later became seriously antagonistic to much in Malevich's art), are disquieting essays in an archaizing Renaissance style; they are signed with tiny Suprematist squares. Subversive whispers?

11

White Magic: Brancusi

IN many respects Brancusi is the art historian's dream. He and Picasso, in very different ways, are the two artists who did most to change the face of sculpture in the first half of this century – white magic, black magic, as a critic once observed.[1] Many see him as the greatest sculptor of our time. Yet although he lived to be eighty-one he produced relatively little: some 220 works all told, if we exclude the original works in plaster that were subsequently transformed into marble or wood or cast in bronze. Most of the early, more conventional, pieces have been lost. There was only one sharp break in his work, which occurred in 1907, the year of the *Demoiselles d'Avignon*, which marks the most important single turning point in twentieth-century art. After that his work evolved with beautiful symmetry and inevitability.

By the mid-1920s Brancusi had produced well over half his entire output and introduced virtually all his major themes: 'All my sculptures have been done during the last fifteen years,' he said to Ezra Pound.[2] After that it was a process of reflection, refinement and distillation. The totality of his mature achievement seems marvellously self-contained, as does each individual work. The sculptures give themselves to use easily, seem on the surface of things to pose no problems and make few demands. Almost more than any other works of art they appear to be simply and splendidly themselves.

And then the man and his history are fascinating. He became a legend in his lifetime, and although this may have originally worried him a little, he came to enjoy it and certainly to play up to it. In later years he claimed to have come down from 'beyond the mountains and beyond the stars'.[3] He also took to talking about himself in the third person: 'After seven years of Herculean labour, and having fled the town, running in every direction without finding his place, he went to another, bigger town, where, while carrying out the hardest tasks, he mastered the sciences and the arts.'[4] He was in fact born in the Romanian village of Hobitza in 1876, of well-to-do peasant stock. His father was severe and remote and his elder step-brothers used to beat him. At the age of eleven, after several trial attempts, he ran away, encouraged by his wise old granny. In nearby Tirgu Jiu he worked in the dyeing vats that produced the fibre for the beautiful traditional Romanian carpets, and also in a dram shop.

From there Brancusi moved on to Craiova, making his living as a waiter: because he was so small his employers used to insert him into the wine casks to scrub and clean them; he told cards and read coffee grounds for the café's customers. He loved music and it was at this time that from old disused casks he constructed a violin, instinctively using Stradivarius's principles. This caused, understandably, something of a stir and led indirectly to his being admitted to the local school of arts and crafts. He had hitherto had virtually no formal education; throughout his life he wrote French phonetically. He was recognized as an outstanding student and completed the five-year course in four, after which he was admitted to the Ecole des Beaux-Arts in Bucharest, where he won several honours. A photograph of the head of Laocoön, done from a plaster cast, demonstrates astonishing facility (the Laocoön itself would eventually be placed in his 'bifsteck' category of art). Most extraordinary of all was his *Ecorché*, an anatomical figure (without skin, displaying the muscles) that he executed in collaboration with a distinguished physician, Dr Dimitrie Gerota, using a plaster cast of the Antinoüs as a starting point. This was bought by the state and four casts of it were made that can still be seen in art schools and academies in Romania.

In 1904 Brancusi set off for Paris, sack on his back, flute in hand. Needless to say he encountered many adventures on the way. He was fond of telling how on the road he thought he tasted fame for the first time; however a cow, apparently rapt and dewy-eyed at his piping, was simply urinating on the other side of the hedge: 'I asked myself, What is fame? As you see, cow piddle, that's all.'[5] In Lunéville, on his way to Paris in 1904, he suffered a nearly fatal attack of pleural pneumonia. While recovering in a hospital a fellow patient lent him Madame Blavatsky's *Isis Unveiled* in its French translation; since he was trying to teach himself French by reading it, one can't help wondering how much of it he understood, although, given the nature of the book, understanding is perhaps not what is needed to appreciate it best. At any rate his friend the writer Peter Neagoe, who sought to immortalize Brancusi in his novel

The Saint of Montparnasse, tells us that 'Gradually *Isis Unveiled* changed his entire way of thought, even his way of life.'[6]

Brancusi arrived in Paris on 14 July 1904. Again he was forced to support himself, this time as a dishwasher at the Brasserie Chartier. But again he demonstrated his capacity for survival. He obtained a Romanian government scholarship which enabled him to enrol at the Ecole des Beaux-Arts as a student of the academician Antonin Mercié. He also worked as a chorister and beadle at the Romanian church; despite his poverty he was something of a dandy and he enjoyed the dressing up. Brancusi almost certainly worked briefly under Rodin, although he also denied having done so.[7] Latterly he said that he was taken to lunch with Rodin by two Romanian ladies resident in Paris, one of whom had sat for the great man. Questioned about what he had made of the occasion he said that he had enjoyed himself and particularly like the champagne; but when it was suggested that Rodin might take him on as an apprentice, he was outraged. In any case it was *à propos* of Rodin that he made his famous remark about nothing growing under the shadow of great trees.

But there is little doubt that Rodin set the standards against which Brancusi felt that he must subsequently measure himself; many of the themes he dealt with and even the titles of several of his works were those used by Rodin. In 1952 he wrote a *'Hommage à Rodin'* and stated that Rodin's *Balzac* was 'indisputably the starting point of modern sculpture'. Rodin was kind about the works that Brancusi showed at the *Salon d'Automne* of 1906, which featured a vast Gauguin retrospective, including a large number of Gauguin's primitivizing sculptures in wood and clay; these must surely have had a determining effect on Brancusi's subsequent evolution.

Two photographic self-portraits help to tell much of the subsequent tale.[8] The first, taken probably in 1915, shows Brancusi perched on the *Doorway* (now in Philadelphia), which was part of a simple architectural doorway or shrine in which he used to place work in progress. Brancusi hated to be photographed by others, probably because he was vain and self-conscious about his shortness. He was in fact of great physical beauty and in his own photographs he did himself proud, generally placing the camera low down so that he appeared to be taller than he was. Here he seems to be on top of things from every respect, bristling with energy and self-confidence. His reputation was steadily growing. More important from a practical point of view, five of his sculptures had been prominently displayed at the Armory Show in New York in 1913, and John Quinn, whom Alfred Barr described as 'the greatest American collector of the art of his time', had become interested in his work. Quinn was to become Brancusi's greatest single patron, building up by far the largest collection of Brancusi's works in either private or public hands. In 1914 Brancusi had his first one-man show at the Photo-Secession Gallery in New York; and it was his contacts with America and American collectors that absolved him from financial worries and enabled him to live his life as he wished and to fashion his career as he thought it should be fashioned.

The second photograph of himself Brancusi took possibly in 1955, two years before his death. We see him seated in the portal he had sculpted in 1929 to separate the studio where he displayed his works from the areas in which he worked and lived. In 1916 he had rented a studio at No. 8 Impasse Ronsin and had clearly fallen in love with it. Subsequently in 1927, he moved a few doors down into a new studio at No. 11; eventually he took over four others and some were made to interconnect. As he produced less and less, his studios became not simply working and living spaces but works of art in their own right. He quickly got rid of all conventional furniture and furnished them with stools, tables, fireplaces and stoves of his own making. His tools, which he loved and to which he spoke and sang, were prominently displayed.

He became increasingly reluctant to part with his sculptures and he spent much of his time moving them about, making different arrangements of them, photographing them in their studio settings as other people might photograph their family and their friends. But in this late photograph it is Brancusi himself who has become the work of art. For a long time he had been obsessed with the concept of whiteness – in 1920 Blaise Cendrars wrote to him from the Alps, 'I am alone in the snows as you are in your white studio,'[9] – and in the photograph Brancusi wears what had become his accustomed white peasant costume; on his head is a strangely shaped cap, a bit like a Phrygian bonnet. Whitest of all is his beard, through which he claimed to absorb wisdom. But even wisdom, he seems to say, is now superfluous. As in his earlier photograph he smiles his peasant smile, but he has obviously gone beyond. He said, 'I am no longer of this world. I am far from myself, detached from my body. I am among essential things.'[10]

The literature on Brancusi continues to mount and has tended to polarize between Romanian writers, who rightly stress his ethnic origins, and American and European critics, who have sought to emphasize his modernism and universality. Barbu Brezianu has written beautifully on the early years.[11] Sidney Geist, more than anyone else, has cast light on the evolution and meaning of his work, although by his own admission his approach has been primarily formalist.[12] And yet Brancusi somehow still evades us, and I suspect he always will. This is partly because, as Romanian commentators insist, his background is so different from that of his contemporaries and peers with whom he linked up in Paris. What has perhaps been insufficiently underlined is that because of the provincialism and the relative isolation of the Romanian artistic climate he was more thoroughly indoctrinated in a nineteenth-century academic tradition of art than any of his contemporaries working in Paris or even in Spain or Italy. Although he broke with this tradition, I believe it affected him deeply; even after he was fully launched on the modernist stream, he continued to draw inspiration, as Sidney Geist has shown, from such fundamentally conservative artists as Ernest Dubois and Emile Derré.

Brancusi partook of the primitivist spirit that touched such a large proportion of the Parisian avant-garde, but in a very different way. Indebted to Gauguin, he nevertheless rejected him, partly, I suspect, because he must have thought that Gauguin's sculpture, as opposed to his painting, had about it a somewhat amateur, homespun air; the concept of finish remained fundamental to Brancusi's art. Paradoxically, when his contemporaries were first reacting to the exciting discovery of tribal art, he turned first to many of Gauguin's own 'primitivizing' sources. He loved the Egyptian and the early classical art he studied in the Louvre and the early medieval pieces in the Musée de Cluny; he enthused to his friends about what he saw in the Musée Guimet, rich in Indian, Javanese and other oriental art. And for all the importance of the impact of tribal art upon early-twentieth-century modernists, the recent tendency to equate modern artists' fascination with 'primitive' art with their discovery of tribal sculpture and artefacts has fatally distorted the situation at the time, for to artists of Brancusi's generation 'primitive art' was a nebulous concept that could accommodate examples of almost any art that did not visibly and immediately stem from a Greek classical or Renaissance tradition.

Brancusi

When Brancusi turned to 'art nègre', he looked at it from a different point of view. Virtually alone among his contemporaries in Paris he had grown up in a community that still enjoyed a thriving tradition of folk and peasant art, and he was unimpressed by the exoticism, the strangeness and the magical properties of tribal art; these were the very qualities that led him subsequently to reject it. He responded to its formal inventiveness and under its stimulus produced some of his boldest, most direct sculptures; he responded, too, to the strong element of craft in tribal art, to its reductiveness, to the way in which it made basic simple forms expressive and meaningful.

The simplicity and reductiveness of Brancusi's own work, which are among his greatest legacies to subsequent modern art, are quite obviously hard won and to a large extent deceptive. They had a lot to do with Brancusi's conviction about the value of direct carving and fidelity to materials: concepts he shared with many of his contemporaries but that he pushed to more extreme conclusions. Rodin had been essentially a modeller, with all that that implies for the process of building things up additively, slapping and pressing clay into clay, twisting, bending, manipulating, gouging. Brancusi turned himself into the archetypal carver, slowly working inward, reducing and compressing, removing layer after layer until he had released his material's hidden inner life; even his obsessive polishing of his bronzes can be seen as an extension of the carving process. Yet the perfection of the end results poses certain problems. Quite clearly the works are charged with meaning; they are about themselves but they are about something else, too. Of one of the simplest of his works he said, 'Through this form I could change the cosmos, make it to move otherwise.'[13] If the works are self-contained, they also contain secrets. This makes them hard, not to look at, but to talk about.

Another problem in assessing Brancusi's achievement is that although his work stands at the core of the modernist movement, and although during the first quarter of the century he himself was so obviously at the centre of things, as an artist he somehow always managed to stand somewhat apart. When he was presented with a chart of 'isms' drawn up by Alfred Barr and published in Michel Seuphor's *Art Abstrait* in 1949 and saw that he didn't fit into any of them, he was delighted.[14] In the years before the First World War he came to know *le tout Paris*, and after the war it increasingly sought him out. He was a genuine Bohemian and he liked to reminisce, for example, about his drunken escapades before the First World War with Modigliani, to whom he was in many ways a mentor. Later, in 1922, on an impulse, he and Raymond Radiguet jumped on a train to the Côte d'Azur; in Nice, on another impulse, they boarded a boat to Corsica and had to be reprimanded by the captain for obstreperous behaviour. Cocteau, who saw himself as Radiguet's protector, was not amused and behaved insultingly to Brancusi, although the next day he wrote a note of apology.

Brancusi was not an intellectual but he was perhaps most loved by those who were. His closest friendships were with Marcel Duchamp, who when he was away from Paris wrote to him almost weekly, and with Erik Satie, whom he saw with increasing frequency till the latter's death in 1925. Pound was fascinated by him and so was James Joyce, who in 1929 chose an abstract diagrammatic portrait sketch of himself as the frontispiece for his *Tales Told of Shem and Shaun*. (When Joyce's father saw it he said, 'My God, how the boy has changed!') He was peripherally involved with the activities of the Dadaists in Paris and was more attracted to the intellectual anarchy of Tzara and Picabia than to the more doctrinaire stance of the Surrealists; Breton was something of an enemy. But as the 1920s progressed Brancusi became increasingly solitary; and maybe in a sense he always had been – as early as 1919 he had written, 'We see life only in reflections.'[15] On the other hand he continued to enjoy cooking unorthodox studio meals for friends from time to time, and even in old age made the occasional sortie into the *beau monde*. There is even something equivocal about his modernity. In 1912 he had visited the Aeronautic Exhibition at Le Bourget with Léger and Duchamp and was struck by the beauty of the machines. Asked what most characterized the modern world, he replied, 'Speed!' But for his own symbol of flight he chose a mythical bird. He deplored contemporary fashion and in old age spoke nostalgically of the destruction of Romanian rural society by urban values.

Brancusi was obsessively secretive about his private life, and although this helped to foster his legend, the growth of the legend in turn helped to make his work seem isolated, a thing apart. He was attractive to women and there seem to have been several in his life; but the only overt relationship he enjoyed was with his white Samoyed bitch Polaire, whom he acquired in 1921. She accompa-

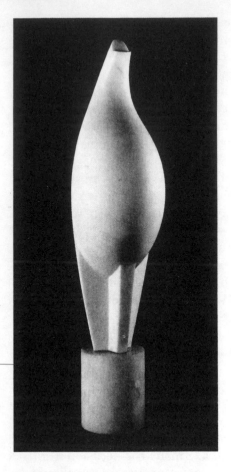

Brancusi, *Maiastra*, 1915

nied him everywhere, even to the cinema; she would accept food
from no one but himself and menaced female visitors to the studio.
She became, in her own way, a celebrated Parisian beauty and
friends would ask after her in their letters. When she was killed by
an automobile in 1925 Brancusi was desolated, although characteristically he also remarked that her disappearance would enable him
to concentrate harder on his sculpture. She was buried in the canine
cemetery at Asnières. It is significant that in the latter part of
Brancusi's career depictions of animals far outnumber those of
people. The most thumbed of the small assortment of books placed
on a shelf above his bed to help relieve his escalating insomnia was
La Fontaine's *Fables*, which characterizes human frailty in terms of
animal behaviour.

The publishers of two recent books on Brancusi both claim them to be definitive.[16] In the case of Radu Varia's it might be found to be so by those who share his particular cast of mind. He has an excitable intelligence, is very much into matters spiritual, cosmic and occult, and he is convinced that he has discovered the keys to an understanding of Brancusi's art. He leaps in at the deep end, so to speak, by seizing upon Brancusi's latter-day fixation on the life and work of the eleventh-century Tibetan ascetic Milarepa. *Le Poète Tibetan Milarepa: ses Crimes, ses Epreuves, son Nirvane*, as recounted by his disciple Ras chung pas (Rechung), translated from the Tibetan and with a good introduction by Jacques Bacot, was published in Paris in 1925.

Brancusi may have come across it soon afterwards; it was a time of great enthusiasm for oriental thought among French artists and intellectuals. Milarepa was an extremely sympathetic character, whose saintliness was tempered by a healthy streak of cynicism. His father died when he was very young and a wicked uncle and aunt cheated him out of his patrimony and forced him, together with his mother and sister, to perform the most backbreaking and menial tasks. Being a lad of spirit he ran away and very sensibly took a crash course in black magic. He caused his uncle's crops to be devastated in a hailstorm and brought down the roof of the ancestral home during the wedding celebrations of his cousin, killing all the assembled guests. His uncle and aunt were out of the building seeing to things, and were hence spared, largely, one suspects, so that they could subsequently be confronted with Milarepa's sanctity; by then Milarepa had developed what must have been the maddening habit of meeting abuse and adverse criticism by breaking into song – but of course it inevitably won him the day. (Brancusi's acts of black magic were relatively harmless: he once got so angry at the rudeness of a Parisian taxi driver that he willed the taxi to break down; on another occasion he stopped a torrential storm by playing a record of African chants on his homemade phonograph at top volume.)

Milarepa repented his early acts of vengeance and set out in quest of truth. He placed himself at the feet of the great teacher Marpa, who for seven years subjected him to savage penance and discipline. Marpa had studied at the Indian university of Nalanda; he was a Sanskrit scholar, translated Buddhist texts, and was largely responsible for introducing Buddhism into Tibet, where it fell on fertile soil. He came from a school that had to undergo not only prolonged intellectual indoctrination but also severe courses in yogic exercises, which eventually led to the production of the inner heat that enabled the initiate to withstand the icy Himalayan cold clad only in a white loincloth. Milarepa, although he was designated Marpa's successor, disdained Buddhist texts; maybe, like Brancusi, he wasn't a true intellectual. In any case he was a marvellous poet and his outpourings have been compared to those of Saint Francis, although the one learnt compassion through wisdom, the other wisdom through love. Not the least of Milarepa's talents, and one that fascinated Brancusi, was his ability to fly: at first Milarepa was not sure if the sensation of being airborne was simply a state of spiritual ecstasy, but soon he was into the real thing, and after that there was no holding him down. He died after being poisoned by a jealous lama at a beer fest; he knew in any case that his time had come.

Varia writes: 'Brancusi knew the meaning of *Jetsun Kahbum* [Milarepa] long before he knew the book itself.'[17] And further on, 'It is extraordinary that, a thousand years apart, the lives of Jetsun Milarepa and Constantin Brancusi, with the happiness of childhoods turned to despair, would appear interchangeable.'[18] Well, yes and no. Brancusi unquestionably identified with Milarepa, and, according to some, believed himself to be Milarepa's reincarnation. Brancusi was in certain respects an ascetic, and he strove for purity in his work; Milarepa's vision of a blissful world 'delivered from the shadows' finds an echo in Brancusi's claim to have eliminated shadows in his sculpture. But Brancusi was no saint. He was basically a kind man, but he had his selfish and ruthless side (and so, it could be argued, did many saints); as he got older he tended to become a little cranky, possibly to drink a bit too much, and from time to time he enjoyed being rude to people. He was horrible to the painter Wols, who had begged for an audience, and he sent Montale away although he had come with a letter of introduction from Pound. In his fellow Romanian Ionesco, however, he met his match.

The second major theme that informs Varia's book is his obsession with Romania as 'the repository of ancient European civilizations redolent with Celtic mythology', a background that enabled Brancusi to reassert 'the presence of a monumental, solar, cosmological dream mythology that had disappeared from the earth's surface thousands of years ago'.[19] If Varia, as can be seen, enjoys taking on major issues, the book is also full of shrewd insights, as for example when he speculates on the parts that Marie Bonaparte and the beautiful Irish girl Eileen Lane might have played in Brancusi's life, although the prose in which he renders them is often a little hard to take: 'One of these women dramatically filled the vault of his inner heaven with darkest shadows; the other with the sparkling dawn of midsummer days.'[20] Some of the chapters that deal with the work itself are somewhat perfunctory.

It is in his discussion of the great environmental ensemble at Tirgu Jiu near his birthplace in Romania that Varia's approach is perhaps most illuminating. The complex that Brancusi worked on during the 1930s consists of three structures. The *Endless Column*, or the *Column of the Infinite*, was commissioned to commemorate the deaths of the heroes from the district of Gorj who fell on the banks of the river Jiu in a significant battle during the First World War. The second element to be finished was the *Gate of the Kiss*, and the third the mysterious *Table of Silence*, which stands at the river's edge. To these elements Varia adds a fourth: the space they create and encompass. The ensemble was inaugurated on 27 October 1938. I myself have not been to Tirgu Jiu, but Varia is surely right in insisting that the elements must be approached in the reverse order to that in which they were conceived and executed; and if Brancusi may not have consciously related the parts to each other in the way Varia sees them, I suspect he would not have rejected Varia's interpretation.

The *Table of Silence* is surrounded by twelve massive stone stools, which Varia sees as symbolizing the signs of the Zodiac. He also relates the table and the stools to Celtic myth – he reminds us, for example, of the ceremonies of the twelve Knights of the Round Table. The *Table* is for contemplation and communion, the beginning of a spiritual journey or odyssey. 'The *Gate of the Kiss* represents the rite of passage across the threshold of another world, existential access to a higher reality, impenetrable to anyone who has not experienced the altered consciousness brought about by the *Table of Silence*.' The *Endless Column* beyond it – the works are arranged along a single axis – he interprets as 'representing empyrean flight to the hidden heart of cosmic space'.

In an entry to the catalogue of his 1933 exhibition at the Brummer Gallery in New York Brancusi described one of the Column's numerous antecedents as '*Column without End* – a project for a column which when enlarged will support the vault of the sky'.[21] Varia's comparisons and analogies with Egyptian architectural complexes and the spatial principles they embody are also stimulting. Brancusi considered Tirgu Jiu his masterpiece, and it is a tragedy that the even more gigantic *Endless Column* he had first envisaged on the shores of Lake Michigan during his visit to Chicago in 1939 as a sort of tribute to the country that had done most to support him was never realized. The idea of it was still preoccupying him in the year of his death.

The second book, *Brancusi* (1988)[22] is of a very different nature. In 1947 two young Romanian art students, Natalia Dumitresco and Alexandre Istrati, arrived in Paris to study painting on a French government grant. That same year they were taken to see Brancusi by one of his neighbours, the sculptor George Theodorescu. Brancusi took to them and asked them to come again. They were able to rent the studio opposite his own and by the following year he was helping them to make it habitable as well as workable. He gave them a much-prized old wooden press which had been one of the sources for the *Endless Column*, saying, '*Voici l'esprit de votre atelier.*'[23] The Istratis in turn became indispensable to him and in a very real sense his family. When Brancusi died, he left the contents of his studio to the French nation, but otherwise they became his sole heirs. Many of Brancusi's devotees have spoken of them with bitterness, claiming that they were obstructing Brancusi studies by denying scholars access to important documentary material. If this was so they have now made amends by using the material in their possession to produce an episodic but completely absorbing biography of Brancusi, tracing his life and career from year to year.

The book contains so much new information of various kinds that it is hard to know how best to describe it all. The authors reproduce his Romanian art school certificates. Brancusi reminisced to them endlessly and dictated fragments of autobiography to them. There are quotations from unpublished notebooks and reproductions of hitherto unknown aphorisms, drawings and sketches. Brancusi gave them insights, which they pass on, into the genesis of several of his sculptures. There are many quotations out of letters from friends, and sometimes the letters are reproduced in full. Those from Duchamp (he and Brancusi addressed and wrote to each other as 'Morice') demonstrate the depth and gentleness of his devotion to an artist whose aesthetic represented in many respects the antithesis of his own. The notes from Satie are affectionate, witty

Brancusi, *Endless Column*, 1920

and strangely touching too. Here is a single extract from a letter of 26 January 1923, when an exhibition entitled *Pou qui Grimpe* (*The Clambering Louse*) was about to open at the premises of La Belle Edition in the rue des Saints-Pères: 'The much maligned louse is no more filthy than any other animal. So it is a banal prejudice to be afraid of lice. A parasite? The louse? No more so than a horse, and a thousand times cheaper to feed and bring up than the illustrious steed.'[24]

The letters to and from collectors demonstrate that although Brancusi handled his affairs shrewdly he was also candid about them, and that as a result many of his patrons felt protective toward him. Sculptors will be intrigued by the lists of materials ordered and these may eventually help to solve problems of dating that still surround some of the works. The Dumitresco-Istrati cornucopia is not, however, without its difficulties. It is not always clear when they are quoting from unpublished writings of Brancusi, or from notes they took after talking to him, or simply remembering what he once said to them. It would have been good to have had reproductions of entire pages of his texts and aphorisms rather than the fragments that are interspersed as vignettes; the fact that they are partial and disjointed and not dated makes it hard to follow them and to chart the evolution of his thought. The authors are as reticent about Brancusi's private life as he could have wished. They do, however, tell us that in 1924 he became engaged to a young blonde dancer, presumably the woman named Marthe, whom they subsequently refer to a couple of times and who appears to have occupied for a while a central position in his life; it would have been interesting to know a little more about how she and Brancusi's other women friends fitted into his scheme of things.

Almost the only thing that these two books have in common, other than their subject, is that they both cast new light on the intriguing matter of Brancusi's unrealized project for a shrine or temple for Yeshwant Holkar, maharajah of Indore. The commission was engineered by the writer and impresario H. P. Roché, who together with Duchamp did most to promote Brancusi's work and reputation after the death of Quinn in 1924. (Between them they bought the Brancusi holdings in Quinn's collection, thus saving the sculptor from the disastrous effects of the Quinn sales.) The Temple of Indore, referred to variously as the *Temple of Deliverance*, the *Temple of Meditation* and the *Temple of Love*, was to have been erected on the maharajah's estate near his palace. Dumitresco and Istrati tell us that Brancusi was already thinking about the project in 1930, the year of the maharajah's accession. In 1933 Roché brought the maharajah to Brancusi's studio and the maharajah bought the great bronze *Bird in Space* (now in the Norton Simon Museum) and later, in 1936, two others, in white and black marble (now in the Australian National Gallery in Canberra). These were to be the presiding spirits of the temple.

Dumitresco and Istrati publish documents and sketches showing that originally the temple was to have been open to the air, with the birds and a fourth sculpture in niches at the sides of a rectangular pool of reflecting water; the fourth sculpture became, in Brancusi's mind, the work known as the *Spirit of Buddha* and also as *King of Kings*, although it is unclear whether it was produced with the temple in view or whether (as is more likely) it was already in existence. As Brancusi's ideas evolved the temple became a small pantheon-like structure, lit by a single open aperture in a vault or dome; at certain times of year direct sunlight was to pierce through this opening and strike the bronze bird. Another sketch reproduced by Dumitresco and Istrati shows that at one point Brancusi conceived of the monument as a small stupalike building, very Indian in feeling. He once talked of the entrance as a very narrow low door that would have forced each visitor to stoop on entering; Roché tells us the entrance was to have been through a subterranean passage.[25]

Brancusi planned to take with him to India a triumvirate of Romanian collaborators: the engineer Georgescu-Gorjan and the stonecutter Ion Alexandrescu, both of whom had worked with him at Tirgu Jiu, and the architect Octav Doicescu. Georgescu-Gorjan has written that by the time Brancusi sought to recruit him, the sculptor saw the internal space of the temple as egg-shaped. Varia quotes from a statement made to him in 1966 by Doicescu to the effect that the temple was to be in the form of 'a large apple, thick, firm, and self-contained, hewn in a single block of marble'. He also declared that the monument was to be a mausoleum for the maharanee: 'Inside, at the place of the apple core, would lie the funeral urn of the departed maharanee.'[26] Varia says that she died and was cremated in Paris in 1937, and he argues that the maharajah's desire to turn the temple into a small, latter-day kind of Taj Mahal fundamentally altered the nature of the undertaking and

Brancusi's thinking about it. In a later unpublished letter to Varia, Doicescu reaffirms that the monument was to have been apple-shaped inside and that the outer contour might have been bird-shaped. Alexandrescu also talked of 'the apple-shaped tomb'.[27]

Clearly Brancusi talked to all three men in vague or generalized imaginative terms and probably never decided on a final form for what had obviously become for him a piece of architecture-cum-sculpture. Varia, who in 1978 delivered a paper on the unfathomable Celtic mystery of the apple to the first International Symposium of Celtic Civilization, held in Toronto, naturally favours the apple theory. Brancusi was in India for most of January 1938 as the maharajah's guest, but he never saw his host. Some reports say the maharajah was ill, some that he was away on a tiger hunt, some that he was threatened by financial ruin and was reluctant to lose face with Brancusi by telling him that the deal was off. (A footnote in Varia's book states that in 1937–8 the maharajah still enjoyed an annual revenue of $70 million.) Whatever the reason, it is sad that the twentieth century lost what would have clearly been one of its most beautiful and remarkable monuments.

12

Picasso's *Góngora*

ALTHOUGH Picasso enjoyed his excursions into the theatre, and in particular his collaborations with the Diaghilev ballet, for the most part he disliked working to order and shunned commissions of all kinds. He did, nevertheless, illustrate some fifty books and was peripherally involved in the production of twice as many again, contributing frontispieces (often in the form of a portrait sketch of the author), dust jackets, vignettes and so forth. Even in cases where his images figure prominently, most of them bear no relation to the text and were simply selected from existing material that seemed not inappropriate; such was the prestige of his name that authors and publishers were happy to settle for what was offered to them.

In approximately twenty cases, however, the illustrations do relate to, or at least parallel, the texts even if they weren't especially created for the purpose. At least six of these achieve the status of *livres d'artiste*, works of art or precious objects in their own right. And his *Góngora*, which came out in 1948, was possibly the one closest to his heart. *Góngora* was to affect the future development of Picasso's art in a way that his other literary collaborations did not. In 1905 Apollinaire was already stressing Picasso's heritage from the Spanish seventeenth-century baroque. But it was in old age that it informed his art most fully and poignantly, and the work on *Góngora* must have helped to set the stage for the extraordinary visual pageant – and much of the late work can only be described in terms of theatre – that was still to come.

The question of Picasso's relationship to literature is fascinating and complex. During his formative years as a painter he had been attracted to art that had a literary flavour: to the Pre-Raphaelites, Munch, Lautrec and the lithographer Steinlen. Impressionism and anything else that smacked of *peinture pure* he eschewed. Throughout his life he preferred the company of writers, particularly poets, to that of other painters and sculptors. His own literary output was considerable and has never received the attention it deserves.[1] From the mid-1930s onward he produced poetry and semi-automatic, stream-of-consciousness texts in both Spanish and French; one of the last and most significant of these, *El Entierro del Conde de Orgaz*, pays tribute, in its title at least, to Góngora's contemporary and friend El Greco. Picasso also produced two plays and *The Dream and Lie of Franco* (1937), a unique fusion of words and visual imagery (based on the popular Spanish *aleluyas*, or strip cartoons) and perhaps the most effective artistic political broadsheet of this century.

And yet several people who knew Picasso well claimed that he read very little. The photographer Brassaï, a close friend, claimed no one had ever seen Picasso with a book in his hand.[2] His library was selective and quirky, including French and Spanish classics, the *Série Noire* and works by Swift. It also contained some valuable first editions, among them a volume of Góngora's *Obras* published in Lisbon in 1667; these may well have been brought as propitiatory offerings by those fortunate enough to visit the Minotaur in his lair. All his friends were united, however, in agreeing that he was remarkably well-informed on literature both past and present. He talked about his own work in relation to Molière and Shakespeare. He could quote from Kierkegaard and Heraclitus and Valéry, and he could hold his own in conversations about recent developments in the thought of Lévi-Strauss and Barthes. Potential mistresses were urged to read Sade, although at least one of them was advised to make simultaneous incursions into St John of the Cross. A sexually voracious man, he claimed to have been deeply moved and influenced by Tolstoy's *The Kreutzer Sonata*.

Opinions on how he acquired his literary knowledge varied. His Surrealist friends claimed he had X-ray eyes and could devour the contents of a book by looking at its cover. Some who were close to him said that he read in bed late at night. I myself suspect he didn't open many of the books he talked about and that he absorbed information through listening to the conversation of his writer friends and other intellectuals. Once, after an eloquent analysis of Bergson in relationship to his own *Portrait of Kahnweiler*, he admitted to never having read him and to have picked it all up from his sitter.[3]

Picasso's name was first linked to Góngora's in 1901 on the occasion of his first Paris one-man show when the critic Félicien

Fagus commented on his ability to absorb everything into his art including popular imagery and, somewhat obscurely, what Fagus calls 'Góngorism, that other form of slang'.[4] But Picasso would have been aware of Góngora since childhood if only because after Góngora's death his name had become synonymous throughout Spanish society with everything that was dark and difficult and unfathomable; Spanish peasants are reputed to have referred to particularly overcast and menacing days as 'Góngoras'. After centuries of neglect, in 1898, Góngora's poety began to be revived, succeeding and in certain respects paralleling the rehabilitation of El Greco, whose art was to affect Picasso's own so deeply. The revival reached a climax in 1927, when the tercentenary of Góngora's death produced a spate of learned articles and tributes; including many by the Spanish 'poets of 1927': Lorca, Alberti, Diego and Guillén. The Góngora revival was followed in France; and indeed it was a Frenchman, R. Foulché-Delbosc, who in 1900 was largely responsible for sorting out the canon of his work according to date and authenticity.

By the second decade of this century critics in both France and Spain were comparing Góngora to Mallarmé because of the deliberate hermeticism of the work of both poets, and because of their extended and elaborate use of metaphor. In 1927 the critic Petriconi called Mallarmé 'the Góngora of the nineteenth century'. In 1922, Z. Milner, who was to do the French translations for Picasso's *Góngora*, published an essay on Góngora and Mallarmé in *L'Esprit Nouveau*.[5] In retrospect the comparison is not particularly fruitful (and Mallarmé almost certainly knew nothing of Góngora's work). For whereas Mallarmé's avowed intention was to describe not the object but the psychological effect it produces, Góngora achieves his abstraction by substituting the attributes of people and things for the objects themselves (hence his habit of using adjectives as nouns), so that his images become simultaneously distanced and evanescent and yet intensely physical, at times voluptuous. But the comparisons must have helped French intellectuals to view Góngora from the perspective of the avant-garde. Góngora and Mallarmé, Kahnweiler once told me, were Juan Gris's two great poetic obsessions.

Picasso's own interest in Góngora was probably quickened through his contacts with Gris and their mutual friend Pierre Reverdy and the circle of writers publishing in his *Nord-Sud*, one of the liveliest and intellectually most challenging of the reviews which kept young French literature alive during the First World War; the first issue came out in the spring of 1917. Contributors included the future Surrealists and the Chilean poet Vicente Huidobro, a passionate 'Góngorista'. Many of Huidobro's poems were translated into French by Gris (some actually appear to have become collaborative efforts), and Gris's comments and criticism of them in letters to Huidobro centre on the use of metaphor; a recently published fragment of manuscript in Gris's hand shows how in transcribing Huidobro's *Arc Voltaire* he at one point crosses out the word '*comme*'. Reverdy had defined his own aesthetic in the first issue of *Nord-Sud* when he wrote, 'The more the affinities between the two contrasted realities are remote yet accurate, the stronger the image will be – it will have more emotive strength and poetic reality.' In one of his most important critical texts, *Self-Defense: Critique Esthétique*, published in 1919, Reverdy condemns the use of '*comme*'; metaphor, he suggests, is always more potent than simile.[6]

The Surrealists in turn were to declare: '*Nous avons supprimé le mot comme*'; a tomato is no longer 'like' a child's balloon, rather a tomato *is* also a child's balloon.[7] It is hard to believe that they would not have venerated a poet whose use of metaphor remains unrivalled for its richness and complexity, and one whose work, moreover, so often has about it a dreamlike quality, an almost painful vividness that is also somehow remote and intangible. And yet the literature of and about Surrealism makes almost no mention of Góngora. The reason for this may be that very little Góngora existed in French translation, although the *Fabula de Polifemo y Galatea* (together with the *Soledades*, the most difficult and 'Góngoristic', and also in many respects the most *surréalisant*, of his works) had been translated into French (by Marius André) in 1920. One writer deeply involved with Surrealism did, however, proclaim allegiance to Góngora, and I believe that it was through him that Picasso came increasingly under the poet's spell.

Robert Desnos had been the star of the Surrealists' *époque des sommeils* (1922–4), when his ability to put himself into a trancelike state anywhere and at any time compelled universal admiration and envy. Subsequently he was to drift away from orthodox Surrealism and into the orbit of Georges Bataille, who in the late 1920s appeared for a moment to offer an alternative to Breton's vision of the movement which Bataille considered to be insufficiently 'black'. Desnos himself was the most difficult of the poets to have been associated with Surrealism. His literary heroes besides Góngora were Villon and Nerval, who could, like the Spaniard, raise the language of popular culture to 'an indescribable atmosphere, to an acute imagery',[8] a phrase which could well be used to describe Picasso's Góngora illustratons. Desnos had been writing about Picasso since 1925. The two men subsequently became friends, and Desnos was to be an influence when Picasso began his literary experiments.

Although Picasso had done so much to invent Surrealism and was then in turn to be so deeply touched by it, his art during the 1920s and 1930s stands apart from orthodox Surrealism precisely because he refused to eliminate the word or the concept 'like'. Magritte's female torso surrounded by a head of hair is both face and body, and Miró can use a literal depiction of a fruit to represent a woman's breast. But Picasso's great sculpted heads of Marie-Thérèse Walter are heads that are *like* phalluses, and the breasts of his *Girl in Front of a Mirror* (Museum of Modern Art, New York) are breasts that are *like* apples. Picasso was undoubtedly more drawn to the Surrealist writers and to Surrealist literature than toward visual Surrealism, which he tended to view with a certain amount of distrust. And he was closest to true Surrealism in those of his writings where he makes use not so much of metaphor as of a kind of dense, coded system of linguistic allusions which recalls Góngora's use of metaphor, although, as Breton was to remark, Picasso's writing still takes its departure in immediate reality and not in the world of the dream.[9]

The codes in Picasso's texts are occasionally impossible to break, just as it is sometimes impossible to fathom Góngora's true meaning. But when in a Picasso poem bells and trees and planks of wood bleed, and when flowers moan and pots and pans take on animate qualities, we sense that they are standing in for something else. I believe that Góngora's name should be placed high on the list of writers who shaped Picasso's literary style and vision, a list which includes Saint Teresa, the Saints John of the Apocalypse and of the Cross, Alfred Jarry (Picasso owned the original manuscript of *Ubu Cocu*), Reverdy and Desnos.

Góngora's world is essentially Virgilian and melancholy; but nature for him is also rich and sumptuous and full of jewelled nuance. Picasso's vision is apocalyptic, full of violence and pain, brutality and blackness. But the texture of Picasso's writing, matted, dense and physical, wordy but also intensely visual and palpable, proclaims Góngora's influence and heritage. Here is a passage from the *Soledades* in an admittedly slightly flat translation by Gerald Brenan:

> [A pine tree] treading clumsily underfoot a stream which, like a trodden snake, spitting liquid pearl instead of venom, hides in its twists (which are not complete circles) flowers which the fertile breeze gave in exuberant birth to the variegated bosom of the garden, among whose stems it leaves behind the silver scales it had put on.[10]

And here is a recently published entry which Picasso made in his journal on Christmas Day 1939, transcribed by Lydia Gasman:

> ball of wax for the touch void of the sky's night empty of caresses and laughter the house's torn skin purrs its stench in a corner the coal dust folds the sheet the unhinged shutter on the window flees the eagle till you barely tell them apart.[11]

When, after the war, Picasso was approached by the publisher Colonna to collaborate on the first of a new series to be entitled *Les Grands Peintres Modernes et le Livre*, Góngora must have seemed an obvious choice, although it is unclear (to me at least) whether he was proposed by Colonna or by Picasso himself. Sabartés may have had a hand in the project; for more than ten years Picasso had been making portraits of him as a scholar dressed in the clothes of Góngora's day, and the two men's talk was often of things Spanish. His old friend Desnos had died tragically in 1945; he must have been very much in Picasso's thoughts for a text by him was used to introduce a book on Picasso's recent paintings which came out in 1946. It might at first seem strange that Picasso didn't elect to illustrate the *Letrillas*, the most accessible and catchy and lilting of Góngora's works, which incorporated and commented on refrains from popular songs, and which would have reminded Picasso of a tradition of Spanish culture he enjoyed in his youth. The *Fabula de Polifemo y Galatea*, with its rich vein of eroticism, must also have been tempting; throughout his life, but particularly from the 1930s onward, Picasso was fascinated by ringing the changes on the theme of beauty and the beast.

Instead he chose to illustrate twenty of Góngora's sonnets, in some respects the most nearly perfect of all Góngora's works in their formalized inventiveness and in the precision of their rhyme schemes. They are the works that show the poet at his most traditional and urbane. Of the twenty sonnets, eight are love poems, and Picasso's work on them is an indirect tribute to Françoise Gilot and to a new phase of family life they were beginning together. The quality of splendour that characterizes all twenty, and the choice of the classical sonnet form itself, may also reflect a reaction to the austerities of life endured in wartime Paris.

Picasso set to work at the end of December 1946 or very early in 1947, and the project occupied him, off and on, for almost two years. *Góngora* is unique among the books illustrated by Picasso in that the poems were copied out in Picasso's own handwriting. After being transferred to copper plates by the master printer Lacourière these were returned to Picasso for him to embellish the margins. Some of the borders comment on the texts, others are purely decorative; this was also the time of Picasso's greatest involvement with the Madoura pottery in Vallauris, so that ornamental motifs flowed freely from his hand. The first sonnet, 'The Poet: To An Excellent Foreign Painter Doing His Portrait', which comments implicitly on the relationship between painting and poetry, is preceded by a portrait of Góngora, after El Greco. Before all the other nineteen sonnets are placed full-page illustrations of young women's heads. Obviously these relate to the poetry only in a generalized way. But it is at the same time astonishing how the heads are characterized so that they catch the flavour of the poem that follows from each of them. The head preceding 'On the Death of Henry IV' is the most regal; in front of 'The Poet Reproaches the Sun for Obliging Him to Leave His Lady' we see a wedge of a profile, reminiscent of Gilot's, vanishing behind a cloud of dark hair; the girl who introduces 'To Lycius, On the Brevity of Life' is the most thoughtful and she holds a breviary, while the image that corresponds to 'On the Death of Doña Guiomar de Sá' has the chiselled fragility of a medieval *gisant*. The seventh sonnet, 'On the Tomb of Dominico Greco, an Excellent Painter', is the only one in which the text is left to speak entirely for itself without the use of *remarques* (marginal embellishments). The volume ends, resonantly, with 'The Poet Decides to Sing of Tombs'.

In 1985 Baziller reissued *Góngora* in an approximate facsimile – approximate in that although the scale and format of the original are retained, the superb quality of the paper that was especially manufactured for the original could not be duplicated for economic reasons and, inevitably, subtlety is lost. John Russell's elegant short introduction catches perfectly the spirit of the time in which this and other French *livres d'artiste* were executed and received. It is perhaps a pity that the publishers didn't ask, say, the translator, Alan S. Trueblood, professor of Spanish and comparative literature at Brown University, to tell us something about the sonnets (they come in fact from all periods of Góngora's working life) or that John Russell did not include a word about the unusual technical processes Picasso used: possibly they wanted to keep new textual matter to a minimum in order to recreate as closely as possible the appearance of the original edition.

The technique Picasso employed involved a lot of sugarlift aquatint, which Lacourière taught him. This was much used for commercial work in the nineteenth century, particularly for fashion prints, but had subsequently been little explored. Basically it differs from ordinary aquatint in that the artist works on the plate as he would on paper, in darks on to a light ground, rather than in lights on to the dark ground of the prepared plate, as is normal in other etching techniques. Sugarlift aquatint thus allows for direct painterly and brushy effects as well as for a particularly broad and bold use of line. Picasso's use of the technique in this volume is absolutely direct, very quick and improvisatory: for example, the plates were not immersed in an acid bath, and the acid was simply dabbed on with swabs. With the greys being bitten into in this way, some of the true blacks were achieved by painting on to the plate with brushes dipped in full-strength acid. Picasso also at times used his fingers to smear on the sugarlift solution and he used sandpaper and muslin to achieve some of the halftone textural effects. Throughout he combined the sugarlift technique with direct, traditional dry point etching.

Professor Trueblood quite rightly did not attempt to find an equivalent for Góngora's rhyme schemes, but he did keep the fourteen-line sonnet form, as did Z. Milner in the original French edition. The translations are dignified and eloquent and score by virtue of their clarity, although one of the sonnets at least, 'To Licitus, a Very Stupid and Very Rich Gentleman', defeated him. I must admit that it foxes me too, and maybe it also foxed Picasso – the young woman who introduces the poem has a distinctly quizzical look about her. If the translations lack some of the slightly sardonic, self-mocking quality of the originals and much of their underlying melancholy – to borrow a phrase of Picasso's own, 'the black light of the looking glass' – maybe these are particularly Spanish qualities and nuances that cannot be caught in English.

The fact that the poems are identical in length and format gives the book a beautiful, measured feeling. And having the texts well-reproduced in Picasso's own script lends them a sense of immediacy and provides us with insights into the workings of his mind. On several occasions he has skipped a line and then gone back and inserted it in haste and irritation. It is a source of endless fascination to observe the way in which he varies the rendition of individual letters according to the word which contains them and the configuration of other letters surrounding them. Some of the *remarques* look a little casual and the illustrations as a whole lack the linear perfection of the two works illustrated by Picasso in variants of his Neo-Classical style, Ovid's *Metamorphoses* of 1931 and Aristophanes's *Lysistrata*, which appeared three years later. *Góngora* doesn't have the extraordinary iconographic and stylistic variety of the illustrations to Balzac's *Le Chef-d'oeuvre Inconnu* (1931) but then neither does any other book illustrated by a single artist. The plates for Buffon's *Histoire Naturelle*, which appeared in 1942, employed a more complicated and sophisticated use of sugarlift aquatint and are technically superior.

Perhaps the most striking of all Picasso's illustrated books is Reverdy's *Le Chant des Morts*, which Picasso was working on at the same time as *Góngora*, and in which he used a kind of invented pictorial script of his own to complement the poems reproduced in Reverdy's own fine handwriting. But *Góngora* nevertheless ranks with these other masterpieces and has about it a quality which is all its own. It is – together with the earthy and bawdy illustrations of *La Celestina*, published in 1971 – the most Spanish of all Picasso's books, not only for the obvious reason that the poetry is by a Spanish genius and the greatest of all Spanish sonnet writers, but because the illustrations themselves have that quality of nobility tinged with sadness, of gallantry tempered with arrogance, which is so particular to the character and art of the Spanish people.

13

Picasso and Surrealism

He always in his life is tempted, as a saint can be tempted, to see things as he does not see them. Again and again it has happened to him in his life and the strongest temptation was between 1925 and 1935.

Gertrude Stein, *Picasso*, 1938

EVERYBODY knows by now,' wrote Pierre Naville in April 1925, in the third issue of *La Révolution Surréaliste*, 'that there is no Surrealist painting.' Two months later the same review published André Breton's brilliant article, 'Le Surréalisme et la Peinture',[1] in which he set out to refute Naville's statement. It was the work of Picasso, Breton claimed, that held the most rewarding answers to the problems involved in the creation of a truly Surrealist visual idiom. 'A single failure of will-power on his part would be sufficient for everything we are concerned with to be at least put back, if not wholly lost,' Breton declared. And in one of the key passages of the article the leader of the Surrealist movement went on to say, 'We proudly claim him as one of ourselves, even though it would be impossible and would besides be impudent to bring to bear on his means the critical standards we propose to apply elsewhere. Surrealism, if it is to adopt a line of conduct, has only to pass where Picasso has already passed and where he will pass again.'

Subsequently Breton was to modify his views; even Picasso was unable to escape totally unscathed from the endless series of pogroms which characterize the most fanatical and least sympathetic aspect of the Surrealist world. But towards the end of his life, striking a more objective and factual tone than was his wont, Breton wrote, 'The attitude of Surrealism to Picasso has always been one of great deference on the artistic plane, and many times his new propositions and discoveries have renewed the attraction which drew us to him . . . [but] what constantly created an obstacle to a more complete unification between his views and ours is his unswerving attachment to the exterior world [to the 'object'] and the blindness which this tendency entails in the realm of the dream and the imagination.'[2]

This was to be Breton's final pronouncement on the subject, and it was in many ways a fair one. Picasso never became a true Surrealist because he was unable, as William Rubin succintly remarks, to approach external reality 'with the eyes closed',[3] Surrealism's ideal way of facing the material world. As early as 1930, at a time when to many observers Picasso might with some justification have seemed very much a part of the Surrealist world, Michel Leiris wrote with great perception, 'In most of Picasso's painting one can see that the subject is almost always completely down to earth (terre à terre), in any case never borrowed from the hazy world of the dream, nor immediately susceptible to being converted into a symbol, that is to say never remotely "Surrealist".'[4] And in a statement made to André Warnod in 1945, Picasso himself remarked, 'I attempt to observe nature, always. I am intent on resemblance, a resemblance more real than the real, attaining the surreal. It was in this way that I thought of Surrealism.'[5]

But if time has shed a cooler light on the vexed problem of Picasso's relationship to Surrealism, Breton's panegyric of 1925 contains an equal proportion of historical truth. Together with de Chirico and Duchamp, Picasso was one of the three major influences on the development of visual Surrealism, and within this trinity it was undoubtedly to the Spaniard that Surrealism, during the heroic years of the movement, gave pride of place. For its painters and writers he was a figure apart, a prophet who had pointed the way forward and whose miraculous powers of invention continued to be a source of inspiration even at the moments when they recognized that his path was not their own. In return, the admiration of a group of young artists unique in the annals of history for the intensity with which they sought to free the creative imagination provided Picasso with renewed stimulus; he enjoyed their company, particularly that of the poets, allowed his work to be shown in the first major exhibition of Surrealist art,[6] and agreed to the reproduction of his paintings in various Surrealist publications. His contacts with Surrealism released in his art a fund of new imagery that was to result, in the second half of the 1920s and the early 1930s, in works of extraordinary strength and originality: not since the creation of Cubism had his powers of imagination been so concentrated, his vision so revolutionary and intense.

Around 1921 *Les Demoiselles d'Avignon* had passed into the collection of Jacques Doucet, through Breton's offices, and it was reproduced in the 15 July issue of *La Révolution Surréaliste*. It was a work that had to a large extent provoked the Cubist revolution, but its impact had been so great, so stunning, that artists (including Picasso himself) had tended to concentrate on the many formal problems raised by the painting rather than on the work as an emotive whole. Sometime early in 1925 Picasso set to work on another canvas, comparable in dimensions, that was to mark a turning point in his career almost as great as that initiated by the *Demoiselles* eighteen years earlier.[7] The *Three Dancers* (Tate Gallery), like the *Demoiselles*, was worked on over a space of several months, and the rough, uneven quality of paint (particularly in certain passages in the left-hand side) testifies to the way in which Picasso's original concept of the subject was modified and revised as the work progressed. The finished painting was reproduced in the same issue of *La Révolution Surréaliste* as the *Demoiselles* and there can be little doubt that the two works are intimately connected – not so much on a visual level as on a deeper psychological and emotional plane. Picasso's work during the previous years had been occupied with the decorative possibilities of latter-day Cubism (and also, to a lesser extent, with a simplification of its formal, architectural properties) and simultaneously with the evolution of a Neo-Classical idiom, which for all its beauty had brought him as close to conformity as was possible for an artist of his temperament. It was not surprising that a reappraisal of the *Demoiselles*, the most significant work of his first artistic maturity, should have forced him to reassess his position as the most important single force in contemporary art.

The *Three Dancers* is not a Surrealist work, but the quality of obsessive neuroticism that radiates from the canvas and the sense of unease and displacement which it produces in the spectator serve to place Picasso's art in a Surrealist context. The *Demoiselles*, for all the violence of the heads at the right-hand side, is disturbing primarily because of its stylistic inconsistencies. The problems that it posed were mostly formal, pictorial ones.[8] Originally it had been conceived of as a moral allegory, but the physical implications of the subject matter had been slowly and deliberately suppressed as the work progressed, and in the final product only the title hints at any hidden layers of meaning. In the *Three Dancers* the process was reversed. The title suggests nothing that the viewer's eye cannot apprehend for itself, and what had in all probability begun as a

Picasso,
***Three Dancers*, 1925**

simple restatement of a theme that had occupied Picasso since his encounter with the Diaghilev ballet eight years earlier, acquired, as the painting developed, a multitude of hidden references and a wealth of meanings.

The author and painter, John Graham, writing of Picasso's art in 1937, compares it to that of primitive artists who 'on the road to the elucidation of their plastic problems, reached deep into their primordial memories',[9] and there is certainly about the *Three Dancers* a strong air of ritual. The painting's rhythms progress from the frozen balance of the central figure to the stately *passacaglia* executed at the right, to the frenzied, possessed convolutions of the dancer at the left. The dancers are clearly all women, but as we study the work we become aware of a brooding male presence in the form of a great black profile, half shadow, half substance, situated behind and linked to the figure on the right. Like some mysterious atavistic dignitary this presiding genius seems to control and direct the activities of the three initiates.[10] While he was working on the painting Picasso had received the news of the death of a close friend of his youth, the Catalan painter Raymond Pichot, and he remarked to Roland Penrose that the painting should really be called 'The Death of Pichot'; he added that 'the tall black figure behind the dancer on the right is the presence of Pichot'.[11]

The untimely loss of an old friend must certainly account for some of the element of anguish and emotional distress which the painting so powerfully conveys. And Pichot's death must in turn have reminded Picasso of the tragic end of another friend from his Barcelona days, Carlos Casagemas; indeed the lives and deaths of these two men were curiously interrelated.[12] Casagemas's suicide had induced Picasso to produce, in the autumn of 1901, a strange painting called *Evocation* (Picasso Museum, Barcelona), a work with strong allegorical overtones ranging from the mystic and religious to the profane and quasi-blasphemous, and rich, like the *Three Dancers*, in iconographic complexity. Casagemas's death is also commemorated, in a more indirect fashion, in *La Vie* of 1903 (The Cleveland Museum of Art), a canvas of deep philosophical significance that appears to be primarily concerned with death, rejuvenation, love, loneliness and betrayal. Originally the male protagonist was to have borne Picasso's own features, but the melancholy countenance of Casagemas was eventually substituted: as the sombre meaning of the painting had revealed itself to the artist, memories of his friend's unhappy life must have returned to haunt his imagination.

When the great psychiatrist C. G. Jung came to write on Picasso's art he did so with little sympathy and with a strange lack of historical perception.[13] Picasso's work is viewed by Jung in terms of a progressive detachment from exterior reality and a move into more 'interior', 'unconscious' or 'subconscious' realms. The early Blue Period is seen as evidence of the first stages of schizophrenia and as the symbol of 'Nekya', a descent into hell and darkness. Picasso's subsequent evolution, Jung felt, was an ever more desperate effort to shelter behind a barrage of unintelligible symbols, leading the painter inexorably into the murky gloom of a neolithic night. Jung's analysis of Picasso's Cubism and of his Neo-Classicism reveal a totally negative appreciation of the problems facing contemporary art, but if he had been able to appreciate Picasso's achievement at its true historical worth he might with justification have remarked that in the *Three Dancers* and much of his immediately subsequent work Picasso had embarked on the journey inwards and downwards that was the ultimate destination and aim of all the true Surrealists. Picasso's journey, it is true, was undertaken for very different purposes. He never shared in Surrealism's programmatic (or even in its semi-programmatic) approach to the problems of the subconscious, and he rejected the supremacy of the dream world over the stimulus of the waking, visual world. Basically he was driven in on himself for personal reasons and in a totally intuitive fashion; he had come, too, to a stage in his career when he felt the need to examine his position in relationship to his earlier art and to the sources of his creativity. The conclusions which he reached when he had explored the labyrinths of his psyche were not those of his Surrealist friends; but for some ten years their paths were parallel, and it was in part at least the Surrealist experience which endowed his work of the period with its depths of psychological meaning and its emotional intensity.

If Jung was insensitive to the beauties of Cubism and to the currents of experimental formalist art that sprang to so large an extent from it, he was nevertheless to be an influence on the Surrealists, and the strong Neo-Romantic flavour of his thought was in many ways more congenial to the Surrealist climate than that of his master, Freud, to whom the Surrealists paid greater honour. Ironically enough, Jung's contribution to Surrealism was one which served to underline the links that it had with Picasso's art. It was at least in part through their appreciation of Jung's writings that the Surrealists became so deeply absorbed by the interrelations of myths, of patterns of thought and behaviour – by the symbol behind the symbol. Their interest in primitive ritual and in the art to which it gave expression was to be one of the movement's principal characteristics, and in the 1920s when the painters were working in a wide variety of individual styles, it was their common fascination with primitive sources that was to be one of the most consistently unifying factors in their art. Picasso, who had already explored the possibilities of tribal art in great depth, and whose influence on the younger Surrealists was another factor that bound them together, was now in return stimulated to a new interest in the primitive forms that obsessed them.

In terms of its composition achieved through the interlocking of flat, upright shapes of unmodulated colour, the *Three Dancers* is still basically a Synthetic Cubist work. A comparison with the two versions of the *Three Muscians* (Philadelphia Museum of Art and Museum of Modern Art, New York), executed four years previously, and generally acknowledged to represent the climax of Picasso's post-war Cubism, reveals a complete similarity of procedure. but whereas the faces of the *Three Musicians* are masklike (indeed they appear to be wearing masks) and slightly sinister, they lack the expressive force of the heads of the *Three Dancers*. Ultimately it is tribal art that accounts for the facial conventions employed in the two great canvases of 1921, for the devices Picasso uses are an extension or clarification of certain techniques he had evolved between 1911 and 1914, years when a second wave of interest in tribal art had affected the appearance of his work;[14] but in the musicians' heads the conventions of tribal art have been simplified and to a large extent made more decorative. And they certainly convey little or nothing of the *Three Dancers'* atavistic intensity. It was while he was at work on the *Demoiselles* that Picasso had first become aware of the formal and expressive properties of tribal masks, and in the *Three Dancers* he appears to have once again consulted the art forms that had been one of his major sources in the creation of Cubism. The head of the central dancer is primitivizing only in its angular simplicity, but the pointed black skull of Pichot's profile, with its knotty projections caused by the gaps between the fingers of the hands that touch each other above, has a strongly African flavour, while the sharp contrasts in light and dark (to become a prominent feature in Picasso's figures in the succeeding year), the predatory mouth and the treatment of the hair in the figure to the left suggest that Picasso had returned to a study of the masks he had so avidly collected when he made his first dramatic break with the conventions that had governed Western art for five hundred years. One mask from his collection (from Papua New Guinea), of which Picasso had executed a painting in 1907, seems particularly relevant in relationship to the frenzied dancer.[15]

Underpaintings clearly reveal that it was this figure which underwent the most drastic revisions in pose, and the distortions in anatomy and facial expression are the most drastic and extreme – in a sense she is the direct descendant of the squatting figure in the *Demoiselles*, the last section of the painting to be executed as well as the most daring and prophetic. Elizabeth Cowling has suggested that while he was at work on the *Three Dancers* Picasso may have been looking at Eskimo art, which was much in vogue in Surrealist circles, and she remarks on the way in which certain Eskimo masks divide the face into two contrasting parts which fuse together to produce a single Night–Day or Tragedy–Comedy image.[16] Eskimo art may also account for the strange, contorted anatomy of this figure and the way in which the various members of the body are hinged together rather than organically connected. Similarly Eskimo figures sometimes have holes punched through the body, just as Picasso has done: the circular form between lower arm and breast can be read as a negative space, and yet the addition of a striped red disc in the centre forces the shape up on to the picture plane and makes it suggestive of the breast above (itself rendered like an Eskimo eye), while the blue lozenge between the legs, bisected by an upright black stripe, seems to belong to the plane and imagery of the metal railing of the balcony beyond the window, and yet to act simultaneously as the figure's sex.

If Picasso's reawakened interest in primitive art accounts for some of the expressive distortion that is so much a feature of the *Three Dancers*, the painting was simultaneously being informed by other, very different iconographical references. The fluted or pleated shift which clothes the upper part of the left-hand dancer (falling away from one of her breasts and reappearing below in corrugated stripes of green, red, black and white) recalls Picasso's earlier interest in classical drapery, and Lawrence Gowing in his brilliant analysis of the painting has drawn a parallel between this possessed dancer and the 'Weeping Maenad at the Cross' from one of Donatello's San Lorenzo pulpits, a figure directly inspired by classical prototypes;[17] only an artist of Picasso's stature could have recreated an image from the most sophisticated period of classical art in forms derived from primitive sources. Then again, while it is unlikely that any Christian imagery was in Picasso's mind when he began the *Three Dancers*, he can hardly have been unaware that as the painting progressed the composition took on strong similarities to traditional Crucifixion scenes. The way in which the suspended central dancer, with her raised arms fixed to a line corresponding to the top of the window, is flanked on one side by a comparatively calm male presence and on the other by a frenzied woman is reminiscent in particular of Grünewald's *Crucifixion* panel from the Isenheim Altarpiece, in which the figure of St John acts as moral commentator while the Magdalen on Christ's right is contorted with grief; Picasso's admiration for Grünewald led him in 1932 to execute a series of variations on the Isenheim *Crucifixion*, and it is possible that Grünewald's great masterpiece was already at the back of his mind in the finishing stages of the *Three Dancers*. Not until he executed his own more strongly Surrealist *Crucifixion* in 1930 was Picasso to produce a work so multi-layered in meaning, so richly complex in its iconography.

The sense of structure that underlies and governs the emotive properties of the *Three Dancers*, the pictorial sophistication involved in the manipulation of the composition's planar architecture, and indeed Picasso's whole method of work, building up to a final statement through a long succession of related works (in this case the groups of dancing figures that had greatly preoccupied him since 1917), all these are qualities which serve to place the canvas to one side of true Surrealism. But if it is the Cubist heritage that underlies the formal properties of the *Three Dancers*, paradoxically it was a reassessment of his pre-war Cubism that was to lead Picasso to adopt in the succeeding years an approach that was to bring his art considerably closer in feeling and appearance to the Surrealist works executed by his younger colleagues in the automatic techniques which represented the Surrealist ideal in the early and middle years of the 1920s.

Breton pinpointed what was perhaps most fundamental to Surrealist visual techniques when he wrote, quite simply, that Surrealism had suppressed the word 'like'; a tomato is no longer 'like' a child's balloon, rather for anyone with the slightest appreciation of 'the marvellous', a tomato *is* also a child's balloon.[18] It has never been sufficiently stressed that the question of the interchangeability of images had been posed, within the context of twentieth-century art, by Synthetic Cubism, and most markedly by that of Picasso. Indeed, Breton himself appears to have been to a certain extent aware of this when, in *Le Surréalisme et la Peinture*, he mentioned that the principles involved in Picasso's and Braque's use of collage had analogies with certain Surrealist procedures; and later in life he was to reaffirm that it was Picasso's constructions of the Synthetic period that remained, from the Surrealist point of view, his most significant achievement.[19] Picasso in fact was subsequently to come closer to Surrealism than Breton in old age was prepared to admit, but Breton was right in underlining the importance of Picasso's immediately pre-war works.

During the second major or Synthetic phase of Cubism, initiated by the discovery of the techniques of collage and *papier collé* during the course of 1912, the Cubists had evolved a method of work by which they now built up towards a representational subject matter by the manipulation of abstract pictorial elements, rather than, as in their previous work, beginning with a clearly legible subject which was subsequently fragmented and abstracted in the light of the new Cubist concepts of form and space. In the case of Picasso's Synthetic Cubism, the process of qualifying the highly abstract shapes he was employing in such a way as to give them a representational coefficient, or in order to relate them to recognizable phenomena in the material world, was given a certain quality of ambiguity and paradox. During the preceding years of Analytical Cubism he had been working with a relatively limited range of subject matter: almost exclusively the human head or three-quarter-length figure and still lifes comprising musical instruments and a few ordinary objects of daily domestic usage. As his Cubism became increasingly abstract in appearance he had evolved a kind of sign language, a form of pictorial shorthand, to represent the ever-recurrent themes; this pictorial sign language could, with very slight modification, be used to render objects which in the external, material world are very disparate in their formal properties. For example a simple double curve could be used to represent the side and back of a human head, drawn up on to the surface in simultaneous or multi-viewpoint perspective. The identical double curve could be used to render the outline of a guitar, or even on occasion the contour of a bottle. Now, with his adoption of a 'synthetic' method of work, working from abstraction towards representation and beginning more or less at random with forms that had become an almost automatic part of his vocabulary, Picasso could, in the next stage, qualify them in such a way that they become the representations of particular objects with analogies to the other objects which they *might* have become. To pursue the example of the head and guitar: by drawing symbols of the human physiognomy (eyes, nose, mouth) to the side of a double curve, this basic pictorial substructure can be made to read as a man's head, while by sketching in a circular sounding hole and the neck of a guitar over an identical double-curve form Picasso presents us with the pictorial equivalent of a kind of musical instrument.

What distinguishes Picasso's approach from that of the Surrealists, not only in his Cubism but in his works of the 1920s, is that he always tells the spectator how his images are to be read: his heads are heads, his guitars are guitars, however comparable or interchangeable their basic pictorial forms. And even at his most Surrealist he avoids the total ambiguity of imagery that the Surrealists courted as an ideal. Yet there is about much of his Synthetic Cubist work a strong element of alchemy, a sensation of the very physical manipulation of forms to produce unexpected images, which distinguishes his procedures from those of his Cubist colleagues, Braque and Gris. Apollinaire in his lecture *L'Esprit Nouveau et Les Poètes*, delivered in 1917 and eagerly discussed by the future Surrealists, constantly stresses the importance of 'the effect of surprise' on emergent art forms. 'Surprise,' he writes, 'is the greatest source for what is new,' and he would almost certainly have agreed, as Breton did, that this was a characteristic of much of Picasso's immediately pre-war Cubism. In a sense it was the element of 'surprise' that was to a certain extent already detaching Picasso in those years from a purely Cubist aesthetic. Perhaps this is what Breton sought to convey when he wrote in his 1925 article, 'O Picasso, you who have carried the spirit, no longer of contradiction, but of evasion to its furthest point.'

Erotic imagery, all-important to Surrealism, played a very minor role in Cubist iconography. But in a series of drawings executed in Avignon during the summer of 1914, works so markedly fantastic as to make them genuinely proto-Surrealist, Picasso makes use of what might be called his 'procedure by analogy' to produce effects that are disquietingly physical in their impact. In *Nude with Guitar Player* (Musée Picasso, Paris), a typical example, the right-hand section of the torso of the reclining female nude is rendered by a simplified version of the ubiquitous double curve, while exactly the same linear convention is used to convey the outline of the guitar which rests on the musician's lap and across which he runs his hand, with the result that an undercurrent of erotic tension communicates itself to the spectator. The breasts of the reclining woman, rendered twice (thus giving an erotic twist to Cubist multi-viewpoint perspective) are derived from a slightly earlier work, *La Femme en Chemise* (Collection Mrs Victor Ganz, New York),[20] a canvas that was understandably much venerated by the Surrealists. Here the upper breasts with their peg-like nipples, strongly reminiscent of certain conventions employed in tribal art, appear to nail into place the oversized, pendulous projections below, while the relatively

Picasso,
La Femme en Chemise,
1913

naturalistic flesh tones and the insistent modelling (which do not appear in any other Picassos of the period) underline the figure's physicality. As in many of the Avignon drawings of 1914, a surrealistic sense of displacement is produced by the way in which the features of the head, traditionally the seat of intelligence and spirituality, are reduced to a few insignificant dots and dashes while the breasts, stomach and even the hair underneath the woman's raised arm are given exaggerated emphasis. The depiction of the features of the face by a series of abstract forms (dots or circles for the eyes, a single or double straight line for the nose, and in the case of the Avignon drawings discussed above a curved comma for the mouth) are recurrent devices in Picasso's Synthetic Cubism and derive from a study of Grebo masks of which he owned an example. In these masks, as in Synthetic Cubist painting, very disparate forms, abstract and meaningless when seen out of context, are assembled in such a way that they take on a symbolic representational significance: two circles placed at either side of an upright linear form become eyes, the curved gash below a mouth, and so on.

The idea of painting as a sign language was one which was to fascinate the Surrealists[21] who, particularly during the early years of the movement, appear to have seen the visual arts as aspiring to the condition of literature rather than, as in the case of so many of their predecessors, to that of music, an art form which Breton despised for its formalism and its inability, in his view, to disorient conventional thought patterns and modes of perception. The imagery of the Avignon drawings and the idea of painting and drawing as ideogram seems to have been very much in Picasso's mind when he was working on the ballet *Mercure*, mounted in the summer of 1924 by Count Etienne de Beaumont's *Soirées de Paris*, with music by Eric Satie and choreography by Léonid Massine. One of the original sketches for the night scene shows a reclining figure on a sort of bed or table, and rendered as in the Avignon series in terms of simple linear means, although the line has here taken on a more spontaneous, free-flowing almost quasi-automatic quality. The Surrealists, who despised ballet as a form of corrupt bourgeois entertainment, had originally been hostile to the idea of *Mercure*, but after seeing it had been forced to change their minds. Breton was drawn to it for its visual simplicity and above all for the way in which it helped to project the spectator back into a state of childhood and hence on to the psychoanalytical path inwards. In his 1925 article on painting he wrote:

> When we were children we had toys that would make us weep with pity and anger today. One day, perhaps, we shall see the toys of our whole life, like those of our childhood, once more. It was Picasso who gave me this idea . . . I never received this impression so strongly as on the occasion of the ballet *Mercure*

and he specifically (and rightly) links the ballet in this respect with *La Femme en Chemise*.[22] The critic Max Morise, writing in the first issue of *La Révolution Surréaliste* (December 1924), discusses *Mercure* in connection with the possibility of achieving an automatic visual procedure that would parallel automatic techniques in literature. Morise must have been familiar with the first sketches for the night scene as well as with the final spectacle, for he dwells admiringly on Picasso's contemplated use of the word 'étoile', scattered across the background, to replace the painted or drawn image of a star – a device which he felt could convey to the spectator equally pungently the atmosphere of a constellated night sky. Gertrude Stein in one of her remarkable flashes of insight wrote, 'Calligraphy as I understand it in him had perhaps its most intense moment in the *décor* of *Mercure*. That was written, so simply written; no painting, pure calligraphy.'[23]

Picasso's collaboration on *Mercure*, the most progressive and inventive of his excursions into the theatre since *Parade* of 1917, and the Surrealists' enthusiasm for it, appear to have brought him closer into the movement's orbit; he was at the time seeing Breton with some frequency and had in the previous years executed two line portraits of him. In 1924 he produced a remarkable series of drawings, composed of large dots of varying sizes in seemingly arbitrary arrangements, linked by curved and straight lines, and several of these were reproduced prominently in the January 1925 issue of *La Révolution Surréaliste*. Virtually all of these drawings can in fact be 'read' as musical instruments and occasionally in terms of body imagery, but the Surrealists undoubtedly saw them as essays in pure 'automatic' drawing, and the starting point for some of them may indeed have consisted of a random sprinkling of dots over the white paper surface. At the time Ernst was independently executing comparable works, possibly inspired by astrological charts, in an attempt to evolve a technique more truly in keeping with the Surrealist writers' contemporary insistence on the supreme validity of automatic, stream-of-consciousness procedures.[24]

The extent to which Picasso was now prepared to submit his art to new and revolutionary technical experiments is vividly emphasized by comparing two large, important works of 1926, identical in size: *L'Atelier de la Modiste* and *The Painter and his Model* (in the Musée National d'Art Moderne and the Musée Picasso, respectively). The first of these could with some justification still be classified as a latter-day Cubist work; there is a strong insistence on undulating forms, but these are superimposed on to an angular compositional substructure and basically the painting is constructed on the same principles as those underlying the two versions of the *Three Musicians* of 1921. The proportions of the figures are naturalistic and the use of a multi-viewpoint perspective is emphasized only in the treatment of the heads. In *The Painter and his Model* the subject is conveyed by a meandering, 'automatic' line applied over a background broken down into simple shapes slightly differentiated in tone. The head of the reclining model is reduced to a tiny calligraphic mask, while her hands, crossed behind her head, differ wildly in scale; a giant foot projecting at the bottom centre of the composition introduces a sensation of violent foreshortening. The anatomy of the painter, who occupies the right-hand side of the composition, is treated with the same somewhat baffling anatomical freedom and the features of his head, his eyes and mouth, have been reversed on their axes with disquieting effect. The inclusion of a naturalistically rendered thumb, clutching a palette, adds further to the sense of fantasy and displacement. Subsequently Picasso was to revert frequently to the theme of artist and model to ring very consciously the changes on different stylistic procedures, rendering the model, her depiction on the canvas at which the painter works, and the painter himself in different idioms. Here, however, the effect is one of a totally intuitive work, executed at great speed. The imagery and exuberant fantasy recall the Avignon drawings, and the fact that Picasso was now exploring their possibilities on a large scale is suggested not only by the similarities between some of them and the *Mercure* sketches, but also by the fact that four of them were reproduced as full-page illustrations in Waldemar George's *Picasso: Dessins*, published in 1926, the year in which *The Painter and his Model* was produced.

Picasso's Avignon drawings and the paintings of the mid-1920s that represent in many ways a continuance and development of them after a lapse of some ten years, were to have a considerable impact on the art of Ernst, Miró and Masson, the three painters who illustrate, in different ways, the various tendencies that characterize visual Surrealism during the middle years of the decade. In Ernst's *One Night of Love* of 1927 (Private Collection), the linear skeins of paint (achieved in part by throwing string dipped in paint at the canvas, but subsequently somewhat 'doctored') take on configurations reminiscent of those in *The Painter and his Model*, while the conventions used to represent the head of the upper, dominant presence owe much to Picasso's heads of 1926. Miró, who had looked up Picasso immediately upon his arrival in Paris in 1919 and who later willingly acknowledged his debt to him, studied his work year by year and with particular attention in the early 1930s. Picasso by his own admission was in turn influenced by the discoveries of the younger men, particularly by those of his Spanish compatriot.[25] Breton in *Genèse et Perspective Artistique du Surréalisme*, published in 1941, wrote that 'the tumultuous entrance upon the scene of Miró in 1924 marked an important stage in the development of Surrealist art', and he goes so far as to add, 'It might be fair to suggest that his influence on Picasso, who joined Surrealism two years later, was to a large extent a determining factor.'[26]

Breton's claims for Miró are exaggerated, but it was partly at least through Miró's example that Picasso began to explore a range of new primitive sources which were to bring his art closer to true Surrealism, and it was through these sources and Miró's interpretation of them that a rich vein of erotic imagery was released in his art. The iconography of Surrealism was charged with a high degree of sexuality and sexual symbolism, and the eroticism so much a feature of Picasso's work in the years following 1925 was to ally his art still further to that of his Surrealist colleagues.

Miró appears to have discovered neolithic cave art while he was working on *The Tilled Field* of 1923–4 (The Solomon R. Guggenheim Museum, New York) a work which more than any other marks his entry into Surrealism. The importance of neolithic art for Miró was incalculable; its impact upon him was comparable to that of tribal art on Picasso in the years between 1907 and 1909, and it was to condition his subsequent development at an equally deep level. A comparison between a chart of neolithic tracings compiled from various sources to illustrate motifs that also appear in Miró's work and almost any of his drawings of the 1930s or 1940s shows how completely he had identified himself with an art for which he felt an admiration of an almost mystic intensity.[27] One of the features of neolithic art that seems to have interested Miró from the start is the way in which frequently the various limbs of the human body and the genital organs are rendered in exactly the same way so that all the parts of the body appear to be interchangeable and each is endowed with phallic significance. Sometimes the sex is so highly exaggerated in proportion that it becomes the largest member of the body, and at times it appears to be deliberately confounded with or equated to the whole figure, while in other instances the organs of both sexes seem to combine within a single figure. All these become characteristic features of Miró's work after 1924, and particularly over the succeeding fifteen years when his work is often so notably characterized by the aggressiveness and invention of its erotic imagery.

Neolithic art also provides the key to some of Picasso's stylistic innovations during the second half of the 1920s and, like Miró, he exploits its sexual symbolism; it seems likely that the frankness and spontaneity of the younger man's handling of erotic imagery may have acted as a challenge to Picasso's own powers of invention. Through tribal art he had become interested in the evolution of a pictorial sign language and now the ideographs of man's earliest ancestors must have had for him some of the same fascination that they held for the Surrealists who yearned, so to speak, to put themselves in a state of primitive grace and innocence, free from prudery and restraint. (The taboos of primitive people they found more sympathetic than those of their own age, and although they were interested in ethnography and anthropology, at the same time they found it easy to ignore the conclusions of these sciences when they contradicted their own highly romantic approach to cultures of the past.) Picasso seems to have been particularly drawn to Easter Island hieroglyphs, and *Woman in an Armchair*, executed in January 1927 (Private Collection, New York), for example, is like a gigantic, scaled-up version of one of these lively little images.[28] Once again in the Easter Island symbols the limbs are stylized and distorted and virtually interchangeable. The same is true of Picasso's sleeping figure: the forms of her right arm and her left leg are almost identical and the curvilinear rendering of the limbs retains a strong calligraphic flavour. The way in which arms and legs seem to swell and expand until they become virtually the whole figure is a characteristic of much of Picasso's work in succeeding years and reaches a climax in the Acrobats and Swimmers of 1929 and 1930. In one instance, the *Minotaur* of 1928 (Musée National d'Art Moderne, Centre Georges Pompidou, Paris), Picasso actually reduced the figure simply to head and legs, which support an enormous phallus, a kind of configuration anticipated by Miró several years earlier.

A comparison between the 1926 *Painter and Model* (Private Collection) and a reworking of the same theme the following year illustrates how quickly Picasso had assimilated the language of neolithic art. The figure of the model has many of the properties of the Easter Island hieroglyphs, while the painter is rendered in a simple, stiff, stick-like style found in certain neolithic ethnographic groups; the dichotomy between soft, swelling, pendulous forms used in one figure and the stiff, angular forms of the other was one which was to fascinate Picasso in the following years, and often paintings which employ only one of these conventions are immediately

226

succeeded by others using a contrasting or complementary technique. Here, the strongly sexual flavour of *Woman in an Armchair*
has been further exaggerated and to a certain extent bestialized by
the way in which the enormous breasts of the model hang down
from the head in a single continuous line, while the limbs,
particularly the right leg, assume phallic overtones. The disturbing
reversal of the axes of mouth and sex suggest analogies between the
different organs of the head and body, and in the series of heads
begun in 1927 the features of the face are frequently charged with
erotic implications.[29] This is particularly true, for example, of
Woman Sleeping in a Chair (Private Collection) where the metamorphosis of the features into sexual organs in a sleeping figure suggests,
as Robert Rosenblum remarks, that the relaxation of consciousness
has released the sitter's repressed sexuality.[30] Particularly disquieting is *Study for a Monument* of 1929 (present location unknown),
where the mouth, reversed on its axis and open to expose two rows
of sharp, barbed teeth, acts as a symbol of sexual menace to the small
male figures below. The displacement of the different parts of the
human body and in particular of the genitals to the head was a device
fundamental to much Surrealist painting. As early as 1912
Duchamp had suspended the 'sex cylinder', his symbol for the
female organs, in front of the face of *The Bride* (Philadelphia
Museum of Art). Miró constantly equates the pubic areas of the body
to the head, and Magritte was to give the device its most explicit
treatment in his *Rape* of 1934 (Menil Collection, Houston).

In keeping with the climate of Surrealist taste Picasso's art in the
years immediately after 1925 was being informed not only by
neolithic sources but by a wide variety of other primitive art. The
1920s witnessed the climax of the Parisian intelligentsia's passion
for primitive art, and the Surrealist writers and painters were, like
Picasso himself, compulsive collectors. However, as the decade
progressed there was a pronounced shift in emphasis away from the
tribal art of Africa; the Surrealists now condemned it for its
formalism, for its occasional realism and above all they felt that it
had too often been tainted by contacts with the West – the classical
African civilizations of Ife and Benin in particular were shunned.
On the other hand Eskimo and American Indian pieces were much
in demand and Oceanic art in particular was admired for the
qualities which they had come to feel were lacking in much African
art. They saw it with some justification as being more lyrical, more

imaginative, more grotesque and fantastic. Most of all they loved what they felt to be its childish innocence, its flashes of humour, and they delighted in its characteristic element of metamorphosis which so often carried with it an enrichment of sexual imagery. 'Oceanic art,' Breton was to write, 'expresses the greatest immemorial effort to take into account the interpenetration of the physical and the mental, to triumph over the dualism of perception and representation.'[31]

Picasso never turned his back on African art, but he seems to have shared to a large extent in the Surrealists' new enthusiasms. It has already been suggested that Eskimo art, which was also influencing Miró at the time, may have been in part responsible for the most startling deformations of the *Three Dancers*. The elongated, flattened heads of the *Artist and Model* of 1928 (Museum of Modern Art, New York) (to take one example among dozens), with their strongly incised, linear features, may owe something to Oceanic shields, although the realignment of the features of the head of the model is reminiscent, too, of certain African masks. The new primitive sources are always fully assimilated before they are allowed into his canvases, so that it is harder to make specific confrontations. And just as in the formation of Cubism Picasso was ultimately more interested in the principles behind tribal art than in its visual appearance, so now he approached Oceanic and other primitive art at a deeper level than many of his younger colleagues. He was alive to its linear beauties and to its strong decorative appeal, and its fantasy undoubtedly encouraged him in taking the extreme liberties with natural appearances that are so fundamental a characteristic of his art during the years of his association with Surrealism. But it was above all his understanding of the techniques by which Oceanic artists endowed their work with its deep sexuality that allowed him to achieve such disquietingly surreal effects of his own, and to achieve them with a force all the greater for its subtlety – a subtlety that sometimes evaded artists more orthodoxly Surrealist in their orientation.

The interchangeability or confounding of the different members of the human body, so characteristic of neolithic art, tends to resolve itself in much Oceanic art into an equation between the features of the human face and the sexual members of its body. In a characteristic type of Sepic Valley statuette, for example, the nose and the penis are joined in a single, unbroken form, and hence unequivocally equated. Picasso's interest in introducing sexual imagery into the treatment of the human head had been a feature of his art since 1924.[32] The fact that he was conscious of the implications of what he was doing is confirmed by a series of drawings of naked women executed in 1929, in which the heads are bent over backwards until the features become confounded with the pubic areas of the body and in the process acquire unmistakably phallic properties. In certain works by Picasso, his *Head* of 1929 is a good example, the entire female head appears to stand proxy for the male genitals; and this painting and similar works evoke comparison with certain New Guinea masks. A related sculpture, *Woman's Head*, executed three years later, makes the same point even more forcefully in its three-dimensionality. This *Head* relates in turn very directly to another sculpture of the same year, Picasso's *Cock* (the original plaster of the *Head* is in the Musée Picasso, Paris, while that of the *Cock* remains in the Picasso family), a powerful depiction of the sexually aggressive bird which from some of the earliest manifestations of art had been used to symbolize the erect male organ. Yet another powerfully disturbing piece of sexual imagery may be derived from a study of Oceanic art. The sharp, pointed, stabbing tongues, which appear first in the *Sleeping Woman* of 1927 (Collection Betty Barman, Brussels), and are later used in more aggressively physical encounters, appear to derive from the conventions used in much New Guinea sculpture to depict the male phallus. In this type of Oceanic art the curved or pronged shapes that protect the sex give it an air of mystery and magic; in Picasso's work variations of the same encircling motifs endow the same form, transferred to the human head, with a quality of menace and aggression. *The Kiss* of 1931 (Musée Picasso, Paris), uses the devices of Oceanic art to produce an atmosphere of sexual violence paralleled only in certain esoteric forms of Oriental art. Perhaps it is Picasso's ability to incorporate into a single form the elements of both male and female sexuality, and yet to leave each image so unequivocably itself, that both separates Picasso's vision from that of the Surrealists and yet enables him to achieve some of their aims so powerfully and independently.

Premonitions of some of the disturbing violence to come, and of the assault upon the human head and body in terms of extreme and at times sadistic distortion, can be sensed in certain works of 1924 and in the *Three Dancers* of 1925. But it is in the years between

1927 and 1932 that Picasso makes his most concentrated attack on the female form. In a series of Bathers, initiated in the summer of 1927, the human head is often reduced to a grotesque pinpoint, while the enormous breasts, sex and limbs (particularly the legs) are inflated almost out of recognition and appear to be composed of tumescent substance, half pulp, half bone. Often their sexuality is symbolically underlined by the way in which they insert a key into the door of a beach cabin; sometimes their arms can be read as phalluses and occasionally head and neck too acquire a thrusting, masculine urgency; parallels can be made with the biomorphic idiom developed by Arp in previous years, but although the heavy, swelling forms used by both artists have a certain similarity, the confrontation serves to underline the witty but grotesque sexuality of Picasso's work. When the theme of the Bathers is tackled again over the following years the forms of the bathing women either become flatter and more angular, or else harder, rounder and more flinty, more purely bone-like. This is true, for example, of a series of brooding pen-and-ink drawings executed during the summer of 1928, where the human form is conveyed by configurations of forms reminiscent of weather-worn stones and bones, propped and piled on to each other in arrangements that are precarious and yet have a quality of static balance reminiscent of ancient dolmens. In their extreme distortion and abstraction of body imagery and in their composite quality, the way in which the figures are built up of various formally independent elements, these 'bone' drawings of 1928 look forward to the more orthodoxly Surreal drawings of *An Anatomy*, reproduced in 1933 in the first issue of *Minotaure*, a publication with strong Surrealist leanings, and for which Picasso also designed the first cover. *An Anatomy* consists of thirty small images in which the human anatomy is reinvented with every imaginable permutation: a chair becomes a torso, sporting two cups for breasts, a circular cushion with a serrated wheel dropping from it stands for loins and sex, a door and a form reminiscent of a coat-hanger are transformed into trunk and arms, and so on. Basically all the figures are female, but each one carries within herself a powerful symbol of her male partner: one dangles a second pair of circular breasts between her legs, while another balances a cylindrical cup in a triangular tray, situated between her thighs. In a unique series of drawings executed a few months later depicting copulating couples, and which ranges in mood from the idyllic to the bestial, or to the wittily obscene, Picasso's flights of anatomical fantasies reach an almost science fiction level.

The image of woman as a predatory monster reaches its ultimate expression in Picasso's work in two complementary images of 1930 and 1932 (both in the Museum of Modern Art, New York). The first of these, *Seated Bather*, appears to have her face and limbs chiselled out of stone, and she relates, once again, to the 'bone' drawings of 1928, although in contrast to their megalithic simplicity the balancing of the head, breasts and limbs on the spinal column involves a more elaborate feat of balance; in keeping with his sculptural experiments of the time, much use is made of negative spaces or volumes: the stomach, for instance, is present by its absence. The air of menace about the figure is intensified by the fact that it is placed against a calm blue background of sea and sky. Her pincer-like arms and jaws and her expressionless, sub-human eyes give her the air of an enormous praying mantis, carved in granite. The praying mantis was an insect which held a morbid fascination for the Surrealists because of its unconventional mating habits; that the image is one which interested Picasso is suggested by a group of drawings of 1932 in which bathing figures are rendered by leaf-like forms suggestive of the mantis's camouflage wings.[33] The *Seated Bather's* pictorial counterpart is *Bather with a Ball*, executed two years later. Here the rubbery, swelling forms of head and limbs refer back to the first works of the Bathers series, the drawings of 1927. The gay colour and an air of wilful absurdity only partially disguise the bather's true nature: her mouth, eyes, nose and hair take on the configuration of a giant squid, and her limbs, though grotesque, are sinister and tentacular.[34]

In keeping with Surrealist concerns, or paralleling them, the element of sexual drama in Picasso's art is sometimes placed within the wider context of its relationship to the creative act. In *Figure and Profile* for example (present location unknown), probably a work of early 1928, the male presence makes itself felt in the form of a simple black profile to the right, rendered with classical economy, its mouth slightly parted as though in pain. The female figure has been reduced to an obscene diagrammatic polyp. She appears as a painting within a painting, and it is as if the male (the painter) has sought to exorcize her powers of destruction by depicting her as twice removed from reality. Sometimes the relationship is reversed. In a work of the following year it is Picasso, the male profile, who appears as a painted effigy, hanging on the wall behind the female fury (Private Collection). Head thrown back, hair bristling and teeth and tongue bared, she seems to menace not only the painter's manhood but his creative powers as well. In another work of the series the male presence has disappeared leaving behind as his symbol the blank, dark canvas, now totally at the mercy of the sawlike teeth and the dagger tongue.

Picasso's final separation from his wife Olga did not take place until the mid-1930s, but the paintings of the late 1920s bear eloquent testimony to the way in which the social habits imposed upon him by an increasingly unhappy marriage had come to seem a threat to the well-springs of his creativity. Olga had entered his life at a crucial moment; already in the months before the outbreak of war in 1914 his ever-increasing celebrity, and the fact that alone among his Cubist colleagues Picasso was entering a phase of real economic prosperity, were serving to detach him from the life of communal Bohemian existence that was in many ways fundamental to the Cubist aesthetic. His loneliness and isolation during the war years, when Paris was abandoned as the home of the avant-garde, must have been great, and a certain lack of artistic direction is visible in the style-searching to which his wartime work bears witness. His first working contacts with the Diaghilev Ballet in the winter of 1916–17 (he went to Rome with Jean Cocteau to design costumes and scenery) must have given him the sense of belonging once again to a particular aesthetic and intellectual world, and he undoubtedly enjoyed the element of teamwork involved in working as guest designer for one of the most progressive theatrical ventures of its time; even the odd moments of friction between the various collaborators on *Parade* carried with them an element of excitement. Olga was a dancer with the company. The fact that he met this beautiful woman, with her fine, symmetrical features and her sense of style, in Rome (from whence he travelled to Naples), that is to say in surroundings that evoked for him very vividly the sensation of the classical past, probably encouraged him to believe that a reassertion of classical values could solve the artistic dilemma that faced him. His first portraits of Olga testify to the calm, contained nature of his love. The magnificent Maternities which followed the birth of his son Paul in 1921 reflect perhaps the summit of his love for his young Russian wife, although the element of heavy, almost elephantine distortion that begins to inform many of these canvases would suggest that the implications of conventional family life were already producing an undercurrent of unease.

Olga was a woman of a certain natural distinction, but she was on the whole conservative by nature and not the ideal wife for someone of Picasso's extreme, passionate, elemental nature. Olga's ideal world was that which marked the boundary line between high Bohemia and high society; Picasso, though obviously happier in the former, belonged to neither. The theme of the dance, so intimately related to memories of his first encounters with Olga, was given a cataclysmic change of mood in the great canvas of 1925, a work in which Picasso re-examined his artistic conscience and returned to some of the sources that had helped to transform him into a symbol of pictorial revolution. There can be little doubt that subsequently he came to see married life with Olga as incompatible with the total freedom necessary to him as an artist. The sense of conflict and claustrophobia produced by his desire to fulfil the obligations of his marriage and yet retain the emotional and moral independence demanded of him by his art resulted in a series of works of compelling if disturbing power and originality; but the tensions were too great to be maintained.

Not only the sources behind Picasso's imagery, but the sensation of unease, of displacement and of occasional violence which are conveyed by so many of the canvases executed between 1925 and 1932 serve to relate Picasso's work, at a distance, to that of the Surrealists. On the other hand the fact that these qualities were the result of undercurrents in his personal life, and not part of an intellectually conceived programme to dislocate conventional modes of morality and perception, forcefully underlines the differences between his own and the Surrealist approach. And it is characteristic of him as an artist that when further developments in his private life were to channel the main currents of his art through fresh territory, he should have felt free to acknowledge more overtly his links with the Surrealist world.

Picasso's brief adherence to orthodox Surrealism is presaged in a handful of works executed between 1929 and 1930. It was a time when he was subjecting the human body to a series of violent deformations and dislocations, but these, as he was to stress, were invented as a means of rendering his art more physically real than the real. On the other hand a work such as *The Open Window* of 1929 (Private Collection) does appear to show a genuine interest in

233

'the marvellous', and in the deliberately ambiguous effects that were so much the province of true Surrealism. The painting is obviously basically a still life, but its imagery remains obscure. Two feet, one upside down above the other, are joined together at the calf to form a single unit, which is then transfixed by an arrow; this sort of anatomical operation, of the most disquieting implications, might well have delighted Dali, Magritte or Belmer. (In Picasso's play *Le Désir Attrapé par la Queue*, Act Two, Scene I is set in 'A corridor in Sordid's Hotel. The two feet of each guest are in front of the door of his room, writhing in pain.') On the other side of the canvas a bodyless head (a plaster cast?) is fused to a hand, fingers outstretched, which acts as a base or support, a device reminiscent of those employed on occasion by Miró. In *The Painter* of 1930 (Moderna Museet, Stockholm), a 'soft' version of the mannequin head so dear to de Chirico and the Surrealists reaches out an enormous hand; a body, the size of the hand and apparently female sits under the head, its members taking on the configuration of an Egyptian cat. The painter at the extreme right is in Picasso's by now familiar 'stick' style, while two 'neolithic' acrobats disport themselves on the canvas within the canvas.[35] This latter work could with justification be seen as a latter-day version of the great *Painter and Model* of 1926, one of the most Surrealist of the canvases of the 1920s, although the even more extreme switches in scale and the obscurity of the body imagery (as opposed to the curvilinear confusion of the earlier work) place it, like *The Window* slightly to one side of the main developments in Picasso's art.[36]

Picasso's collaboration with *Minotaure*, the Surrealist periodical, in 1933 served to strengthen his contacts with the Surrealist writers, many of whom he had known for some time. To the first issue Breton contributed an important essay, 'Picasso dans son Elément', and other collaborators included Reverdy (an old friend of Picasso's and in many ways a father figure to the Surrealist poets), Eluard (to whom Picasso was drawing ever closer), Michel Leiris, Tériade (the magazine's publisher) and Dali, by now one of the movement's stars, who was represented by a spirited essay on Millet's *Angelus*. The magazine was not exclusively Surrealist in its policies (the first issue also included an essay by Raynal, another friend of Picasso's of long standing whom the Surrealists distrusted) and this in itself may have made Picasso happy to be so closely associated with its inception.

Picasso himself admitted to being influenced by Surrealism only in 1933, 'at the moment when he was suffering from matrimonial difficulties which were soon to culminate in a separation from his wife Olga', and he added that this was mostly in his drawings.[37] This was the year that saw the cover for *Minotaure, An Anatomy*, and the erotic drawings, all works of the late winter and spring, and all showing marked affinities with Surrealism, although the cover design was linked to the movement only iconographically and was rendered in a pure, linear, Neo-Classical style. During the summer, while staying at Cannes, Picasso executed yet another series of drawings which are more immediately recognizable as Surrealism than anything he had hitherto produced. The most characteristic drawings of the series consist of two upright, composite images, which suggest human presences; usually these have specifically male and female attributes, although this is not always the case. The drawings have obvious affinities with the personages of *An Anatomy*, but whereas these had a certain iconographic unity, despite their fantasy, and were still related to the 'bone' drawings of 1928, the Cannes figures or presences are characterized by the apparently gratuitous assembly of totally unrelated objects which achieve a semblance of coherence only because each element is rendered by the same quick, nervous line. In *Minotaure*, a characteristic work of the series, the presence to the left consists of a flowering armchair which sports a human arm, and which supports, precariously, a chequered board. From the chair and the board rise forms suggestive of a young tree trunk and a rough-hewn wooden plank. To the former is pinned a piece of paper corresponding to the position of a human head. Opposite this presence, passive and presumably feminine, is raised a formidable male counterpart, standing on a low base or plinth. A straightbacked chair is surmounted by a naturalistic arm and shoulder, while the shoulder in turn balances a bull's head. Opposite this head and pointed towards the presence opposite is a dagger, apparently fixed by wire to the back of the chair. The drawing which appears to have been executed at great speed in a state of semi-trance contains, as one might expect, familiar Picassian imagery. The woman/armchair, for example, recalls *La Femme en Chemise*, while the flowering plants which it sprouts are echoed in the backgrounds of contemporary nudes. The bull's head and dagger relate to the cover of *Minotaure* and to the series of works which were to lead up to *Guernica*. Much of the imagery in these drawings (the fragments of furniture used in *An Anatomy*, for example, and which John Richardson has suggested may be symbolic of the breaking up of the painter's household)[38] can be paralleled in drawings and paintings by wholly Surrealist artists; other works of the series make use of an architectural setting, and sometimes an architectural element, a column for example, is made to stand as a substitute for the human figure. Ultimately, however, Picasso's excursion into official Surrealist territory would seem to owe most to the Surrealist 'Exquisite Corpse', a game practised avidly not only by the movement's painters but also by its writers. In this game each player draws an element to the human body, attaching it blindly to that which the previous player has folded over out of sight. Played by a single artist it is not surprising that the imagery in the component parts would relate to his work, past, present and future.

There can be little doubt that in the last analysis Picasso was more deeply drawn to the Surrealist writers and to Surrealist literature than towards visual Surrealism which, for the most part, he regarded with a certain element of mistrust. Since his Cubist days he had been fascinated by the interrelationship between the written word and the painted image, and like the Surrealists he was interested in the idea of painting as sign language. The years 1935 and 1936 were in many ways distressing for Picasso, from a personal point of view, witnessing as they did the legal complications of his final separation from his wife, and his normally prodigious output was much reduced. It was perhaps only natural that he should have turned to the written word as an alternative to paint and canvas. His poetry and his prose poems were to occupy him some eighteen months, until the outbreak of the Spanish Civil War brought on a renewed frenzy of pictorial activity; the winter months of 1935–6 witnessed the most concentrated phase of literary activity. Picasso's Surrealist friends were needless to say delighted, although at first Picasso seems to have been diffident about exposing his ventures into a new territory to the public. Early in 1936, however, *Cahiers d'Art* brought out a special Picasso number (it was classified by the magazine as the last of their 1935 publications) built around extracts of his recent writings.[39] Breton, who despite the fact that he was often irritated by Picasso's total independence, was constantly looking for ways of grafting his genius on to official Surrealism, wrote a eulogistic and perceptive introduction, *Picasso Poète*, and the same issue contained a beautiful essay on Picasso by Eluard and sympathetic texts by Christian Zervos (the periodical's editor), Dali, Man Ray and Georges Hugnet. Benjamin Péret, one of the original members of the movement, contributed a long poem which bore Picasso's name as its title. Surrealism had originated as a literary movement and Picasso's writings helped place him, more squarely than anything he ever produced in the visual field, in a Surrealist context. They gave the impression of having been written quickly in a stream-of-consciousness technique (although we know they were much revised), and to this extent they relate more closely to Surrealist texts produced in the early 1920s during the *Saison des Sommeils* than to the more selfconscious and pondered literary products of the late 1920s and 1930s. In common with these early Surrealist texts, Picasso's writings are fantastic, often hard to follow, and lacking in any conventional literary structure: originally dashes were used as punctuation but in accordance with technical procedures laid down in the first Surrealist manifesto, these were subsequently suppressed. But even in these most wholehearted excursions into orthodox Surrealism Picasso's fantasy is ultimately not of a Surrealist brand. What distinguishes his work from that of his poet friends of the movement is its extraordinary physicality, its earthiness and directness. These qualities are achieved, technically, primarily by the way in which he tends to group and concentrate types of words; noun is piled upon noun, adjectives are strung together one after another, verbs follow each other rapidly. Every image calls up another which serves to reinforce it rather than to dislocate it from everyday reality. The chain reaction from image to image often works around in a circular fashion to its starting point.

It is interesting to note that although as a painter Picasso had never been primarily a colourist, in his poetry colour is all important, and his insistence on it helps to reinforce the tangibility of the visual imagery which is obsessively physical. There is for example an insistence on food and kitchen utensils which looks forward to his still lifes of succeeding years. Breton, searching for leitmotifs in the poems, comes up with a series of images relating to the bullfight, and these, while they relate simultaneously to concerns in Picasso's contemporary paintings and drawings, seem to project him back in time to his Spanish boyhood and adolescence; he talks of Barcelona and in the passages which relate to his childhood the recurrent colours are, significantly, the varying shades of blue of his Blue period. The Surrealists who constantly sought to project themselves back into a state of childhood seldom succeeded in doing so, other than in a selfconsciously analytic way, and their art is by and large characterized by its extreme adult sophistication. Picasso, on the other hand, can evoke a feeling of awakening sensibility with a feeling of almost anguished poignancy.

The poems have about them an hallucinatory intensity. Here, for example is a passage which evokes the atmosphere of an empty room:

> the wing twists corrupts and eternalizes the cup of coffee of which the harmonium in its timidity caresses the whiteness the window covers the shoulder of the room with thrusts of goldfinches which die in the air.

And at its best, as in the passage which Breton rightly exalts, Picasso's writings have a quality of apocalyptic grandeur worthy of the writings of those visionary saints for which Spanish literature is so rightly famed:

> give tear twist and kill I cross light and burn caress and lick embrace and watch I strike at full peal the bells until they bleed terrify the pigeons until they fall to earth already dead of fatigue and bar all the windows and the doors with earth and with your hair I shall hand all the birds which sing and cut all the flowers I shall cradle in my arms the lamb and I shall offer him to devour my breast I will wash him with my tears of joy and grief and I shall lull him with the song of my solitude by Soleares and engrave the etching the fields of wheat and oats.[40]

The year 1932 saw a marked change in Picasso's art, not so much stylistic as in terms of mood and of sexual imagery. The exact date of his meeting with Marie-Thérèse Walter is not certain but the visual evidence of the paintings of 1932, which radiate so strong an air of erotic fulfilment and relaxation, would suggest that their love was then at its height. Marie-Thérèse's full, passive, golden beauty was to preside over Picasso's art for the next four years; most typically she is seen in what appears to be a dreamless sleep. Her firm, pliant limbs are rendered by the same undulating forms that had characterized much of Picasso's work since 1925, but whereas before these had so often seemed predatory or tentacular, their rhythms now become slower, softer, more welcoming and more organic. The Marie-Thérèse paintings tend to be more lyrical in their colouring and often the backgrounds are highly patterned. Everywhere there are symbols of growth and fertility. In *The Mirror*

(Gustav Stern Foundation, New York), a work dated 12 March 1932 and one of the most beautiful of the first Marie-Thérèse series, the forms used to render the sleeper's yellow hair resemble silky seed pods, while the same shapes repeated in the mirror, directly above, and which spill out from the supple buttocks, are rendered in green, the colour of nature's renewal;[41] and indeed at this time Picasso makes constant if intuitive use of colour symbolism. In the works which followed from the *Three Dancers* Picasso had adapted the devices of Cubist multi-viewpoint perspective to include in each figure the maximum amount of sexual imagery; here the mirror reflects not the woman's shoulder and back but the lower part of her body, so that we experience a sense of physical totality although the painting is basically a study of a half-length figure. In *Reclining Nude* (Private Collection), a work of the summer, the sleeper has become a sort of Persephone figure, garlanded and recumbent on a carpet of flowers, while out of her loins there issues forth a surge of flowers and foliage. *Girl in Front of a Mirror*, executed a couple of days after *The Mirror* and perhaps the most famous painting of the series (Museum of Modern Art, New York), introduces a note of psychological complexity. The girl confronts her own sexuality calmly and with a certain reverence; the tender lilacs of her face and body have become in the reflected image deeper, more mature, and the breasts have ripened into fruit, while the wallpaper behind echoes their circular forms discretely but insistently. Just as in the work of the second half of the 1920s the single female figure generally carried within herself the symbols of her male counterpart, so here the girl's breasts and forward arm raised in a gesture of embrace and acceptance form a giant phallus which reaches forward and up towards the reflection which suggests the girl's prospective maturity.

In the works of the late 1920s the brutalized female form had been presented as a threat to creativity. *The Painter* of 1934 shows the sleeping model giving herself up to the painter's art, like an offering of fruit and foliage. She has become simultaneously mistress, model and muse, and in a sense it is she who has now become the victim, in that her sexuality has so clearly been laid out as a sacrifice to the artist's gifts.

The image of woman as a predatory monster, the theme which had endowed Picasso's art with the 'convulsive' drama so dear to Surrealist aesthetics, was one which was to recur in his art sporadically during the succeeding years. Some drawings of the summer of 1934, for example, show a female fury (descended from the tumescent bathers of 1926) holding a dagger to the throat of her gentler, flower-like sister. Earlier in this same year the recumbent Nudes of 1932 had been reinterpreted in disquieting, highly Surrealist imagery. And throughout the 1930s Picasso continued to produce periodically works which, like the best Surrealism of the period, had the power to shock the spectator out of his habitual modes of perception; many of the works of 1938 in particular, which take up again the themes of the late 1920s and early 1930s, have about them an obsessive, somewhat horrific and shocking quality. Generally speaking, however, the symbolic quality of the eroticism and the violence that had been so characteristic of the work of the late 1920s and early 1930s and which had owed so much to a reappraisal of primitive art, is replaced as the 1930s progressed by an increasingly overt physicality and by an explicitness and forthrightness that was removing Picasso's art ever further from the world of Surrealism.

Picasso's most completely Surrealist works date, it is true, from the years between 1933 and 1935. But these excursions into a world that was not fundamentally his own, although they were of great importance to his development as an artist, stand aside from the mainstream of his talent. The paintings which celebrate his relationship to Marie-Thérèse are already at a further remove from Surrealism than those which had recorded his increasingly desperate and negative feelings towards Olga. The techniques he employed in *The Mirror* of 1932 are not fundamentally different from those of *Woman in an Armchair* of 1926: there is the same use of a free, metamorphic line, capable of describing an arm, a leg, a nose or a plant in terms of the same basic repertory of forms. And yet there is a feeling of contentment, an extrovert enjoyment of the healthily physical that removes the later work from almost everything that Surrealism aimed for. It is true that the Surrealists extolled the value of love 'in its broadest sense', but basically they were, in the words of Aragon, 'the mind's agitators',[42] and on the whole their use of the erotic in their art was placed at the service of jolting the spectator out of an unthinking acceptance of conventional and traditional patterns of behaviour and moral standards. Picasso's previous work had produced much of the same sense of shock, not it is true so much because of its subject matter (which by Surrealist standards was for the most part conservative), but by virtue of the extraordinary distortions to which the human body had been submitted and because of the savagery of the erotic imagery which these distortions so often suggested.

It was his fascination with a new range of primitive sources and their use of metamorphic, erotically charged imagery that had related Picasso's concerns most closely to those of his younger Surrealist colleagues in the years before he was prepared to overtly acknowledge the movement's influence. The series of sleeping nudes initiated in 1932 were still to a large extent being informed by primitive sources or at least have strong affiliations with certain forms of primitive art; it has been suggested, for example, that Picasso may have been influenced by the much reproduced Hal Saflieni *Reclining Woman*, one of the most ancient renditions of the female form, and the Venuses of Lespugue and Willendorf, which with their heavy, ripe, bulging forms can be viewed as ancestresses of Picasso's images of female fecundity.[43] But it is significant that these art forms of the remote past were precisely those which over long centuries were to be transformed into the classical figures of Greece and Rome. In a sense the Venus of Lespugue is closer to the Venus of Milo (and hence to Titian, Rubens and Renoir) than the work of a Sepic Valley craftsman of the nineteenth century is to a contemporary sculpture by Rodin. Picasso's Neo-Classicism had to a large extent gone underground during the second half of the 1920s but it had never been totally suppressed and during the 1930s classical values and imagery were once more to assert themselves strongly (if sporadically) in his art. Classical mythology, in a Freudianized form, began to interest the Surrealists in the latter stages of the movement,[44] and to this extent Picasso was once again a pioneering figure in its history. But basically it was in large part against the classical heritage of the West that the Surrealists were in revolt.[45] The tradition to which they belonged was that of northern mysticism and northern romanticism; the cultures of the past which they admired were those remote in spirit from the world of antiquity or so primitive in their evolution as to seem to have little to do with its products. Their love of Oceanic, Eskimo and North American Indian art and of neolithic cave painting was perfectly in keeping with their romantic impulse towards the irrational and the intuitive. It was all part of what might be called the journey downward. This was a path which from time to time fascinated

Picasso, but he refused to see it as leading only in one direction, and he continually felt the need to fuse his art on to the great traditional sources from which in the last analysis it had sprung. An etching of 1933, *Model and Fantastic Sculpture*, shows a young woman directly descended from the nudes of antiquity confronting her Surrealist counterpart, a fantastic composite image simultaneously comic and frighteningly grotesque – as strongly as any other single work the etching illustrates Picasso's recognition of the two worlds to which his art at the time owed allegiance.

The classicizing not only of the outward forms of Picasso's art but of its imagery and symbolism can be seen most clearly by comparing his *Crucifixion* of 1930 (Musée Picasso, Paris) to the mythologizing works which succeeded to it and to which it in many respects forms a prelude. The *Crucifixion*, despite its small scale, was the most complex painting, both formally and iconographically, that Picasso had produced since the *Three Dancers* on which he had been at work five years earlier. Virtually every figure in the crowded composition is treated in a different idiom and the painting as a whole reads like a dictionary of the different manners of distortion to which Picasso had subjected the human form during the years before and immediately after its execution. The sources involved, both stylistic and iconographic, are legion. To those already discussed could be added Cycladic sculpture, Australian aboriginal art, and, as scholars have pointed out, the apocalyptic imagery of the eleventh-century commentaries of Beatus of Liebana or the *Apocalypse of Saint Sever*, a work Picasso certainly knew.[46] The preparatory sketches show not only an obvious interest in Christian iconography and a strongly primitivizing strain but also an interest in classical art. The Mithraic references stressed by Ruth Kaufmann in her analysis of the painting[47] are overlaid (particularly in the figure of the horseman with a lance) with suggestions of the ceremony of the bull-ring. The work is deeply irreligious in spirit and it evokes the sensation of some primitive atavistic ritual, cruel and compulsive. In all these ways the *Crucifixion* can be considered a product of Surrealism, and its affiliations with the movement are further strengthened by the fact that some of the related sketches appear to be indebted to the work of Miró – one of the rare instances of Picasso borrowing directly from a Surrealist colleague.[48]

The importance of the *Crucifixion* for an understanding of *Guernica*, the crowning achievement of the 1930s, has been often and justifiably stressed. But a comparison between the *Crucifixion* and the large etching entitled *Minotauromachia*, perhaps the most important single work produced by Picasso in 1935, and highly relevant in its iconography to the great mural, illustrates the extent to which Picasso was prepared to sever his connections with the world of visual Surrealism. The stylistic differences between the two works speak for themselves: the primitivizing has given way to the classicizing. And although some of the motives in *Minotauromachia* are not unrelated to the earlier work, its iconography has undergone the same classicizing process, the same movement upwards into the realm of traditional, identifiable moral allegory. The imagery is deeply personal and much of the symbolism defies analysis; indeed, it is doubtful if Picasso himself had any very explicit programme in mind when preparations for the work were begun. But whereas in the *Crucifixion* a traditional theme had been drained of its religious connotations and imbued with a quality of primeval brutality and darkness, many of the motives of *Minotauromachia* are readily identifiable within the context of traditional Western art. The doves, the young girl and the flowers she clutches are all obviously symbols of innocence and peace, while the candle she holds, and against which the monster shields his face, surely stands for truth and light. The Minotaur was a creature who had interested the Surrealists because of the sexual irregularity of his conception and because he could be taken to represent the unbridled forces of the Freudian id. For Picasso he was a more human and more complex creature, more man than beast even at his most savage, and embodying in his multiple guises much of the human predicament. In *Minotauromachia* he appears at his most rapacious and destructive and the work can be viewed as a symbolic depiction of the battle between unreason and truth, between darkness and light, with the forces of good challenging those of evil. These were exactly the traditional moral distinctions which the Surrealists had sought to destroy; the words which one is forced to use in an attempt to interpret Picasso's allegory have no validity and indeed no place in their vocabulary.[49] The symbolic depiction of moral and ethical conflicts and concepts was obviously not one that was exclusive to classical and traditional Western art but it is noteworthy that when Picasso introduces into the Minotaur series elements borrowed from more distant or esoteric traditions (the winged, birdheaded figure which appears in the sketch for the drop curtain for Romain

Rolland's *Le 14 Juliet*, for example), the effect is immediately markedly more Surrealist.

It was soon after finishing *Minotauromachia* that Picasso plunged into his most intensive phase of literary activity. Some twelve months later, in January 1937, he embarked on another work to be intimately bound up with his conception of *Guernica*, and one which represented an almost unique fusion between visual imagery and the written word. This was *The Dream and Lie of Franco*, a folder consisting of two etchings each divided into nine sections treated in the manner of a strip cartoon or a Spanish *alleluia*, and accompanied by a short, wild and violent poem. The first stages of the work, etched in pure line (the aquatint shading was added subsequently), and consisting of only fourteen scenes, appear to have been executed at white heat, as does the poem; the quality of the line is hectic, compulsive and conveys a sense of overriding urgency. Much of the imagery is also highly surrealistic: the figure of Franco, 'an evil-omened polyp', is rendered as a cluster of obscene, hairy, root-like forms with strongly phallic connotations, which in one of the scenes become metamorphosed into the horse's head. The sequence of images appears to be unimportant although it is perhaps significant that the first compartment shows the polyp attacking a beautiful classical head with a pickaxe. The riot of imaginative fantasy which spills out without regard to the unities of time and space, the blasphemy and iconoclasm, the erotic exaggerations, the way in which the pictorial idiom is so completely at the service of the artist's obsessed and frenzied vision, all these factors ally the work to Surrealism; and perhaps more than any other work by Picasso *The Dream and Lie of Franco* breaks down, as the Surrealists so passionately longed to do, distinctions between thought, writing and visual imagery.

Guernica, the great mural to which the last four episodes of the *Dream and Lie* so concretely relate, detaches itself once again from the world of Surrealism. A large public statement, inspired by a particular event in contemporary history, it militates against much that Surrealism stood for. Its imagery, though in some ways baffling, is once again susceptible to the kind of analysis that is customarily applied to great mythological works of the past, and its sources, as has often been stressed, are also embedded in the traditions of classical Western art. And yet the debt of *Guernica* to Surrealism has perhaps never been sufficiently emphasized. The expressive distortions, the ability to render states of emotion by the use of a few calligraphic markings, the conventions used to evoke grief and horror: these were features of Picasso's art that had been developed during the years of his association with the movement; in the last analysis the work owes as much to the primitive sources of Surrealism as it does to a knowledge of the traditions of classical art. And Picasso's method of work, his ability to think aloud in images, to contradict himself and change his mind in mid-stream, to fuse such a multitude of widely diverse iconographic material in a single work, speak eloquently of the Surrealist experience.

In the second Surrealist manifesto, which appeared early in 1930, Breton declared:

> Surrealism's dearest aim now and in the future must be the artificial reproduction of the ideal moment in which man is a prey to a particular emotion, is suddenly caught up by the 'stronger than himself', and thrust, despite his bodily inertia into immortality. If he were then lucid and awake he would issue from that predicament in terror. The great thing is that he should not be free to come out, that he should go on talking all the time the mysterious ringing is going on.

Nothing could better underline both the surreality of Picasso's achievement and the differences between his position and that of the members of the movement than an attempt to relate Breton's words to Picasso's art of the period between the *Three Dancers* and *Guernica*. Like the Surrealists, Picasso had experienced 'the stronger than himself'; but it was not a condition he had, or could have, induced artificially and it arose from certain inevitable circumstances in his private life and, in 1937, from the recognition of a world tragedy. He continued to be 'lucid and awake' and he issued forth from 'that predicament' not 'in terror' but with a combined sense of relief and anguish. It would never for a moment have crossed his mind that he might not be free 'to come out'. He had simply, as always, obeyed the dictates of his art.

14

The Blind Mirror:
André Breton and Painting

THE FIRST issue of *La Révolution Surréaliste*, the official mouthpiece of the Surrealist movement during the second half of the 1920s, appeared in December 1924. The back page consisted of an advertisement for the First Surrealist Manifesto which had been issued two to three months earlier. Its author was André Breton, and the manifesto had established him, at the age of twenty-eight, as the undisputed leader of the most controversial and influential artistic movement of the decade, although the Surrealists themselves would at this point have claimed that it was no such thing. The importance of the manifesto can hardly be over-emphasized, but it appears to have caused relatively little stir at the time of its publication and it was through the rapidly widening circulation of the periodical that Surrealism began to effect the change of consciousness which was its avowed intent.

The lead article in the first issue was on dreams, that all-important Surrealist concern, and it contained towards the beginning the sentence: 'The dream allows man all his rights to liberty.' Embedded in it was a photograph of an extraordinary object by Man Ray, *The Riddle of Isidore Ducasse*, of 1920, subsequently destroyed. Ducasse was the real name of a young poet who had died in 1870 and who wrote under the pseudonym of Lautréamont. Breton had discovered Lautréamont in the spring of 1919 and a reading of *Les Chants de Maldoror* had converted him more than any other single work or intellectual source, to the idea of a completely new visionary literature which would reveal to man his own true self. The phrase from Maldoror which was to echo like a leitmotif through Surrealist literature is: 'as beautiful as the chance meeting of an umbrella and a sewing machine upon a dissecting table', and the mysterious object enveloped in sacking in Man Ray's photo is a sewing machine – redolent with female connotations.

The most immediate prototype for this kind of proto-Surrealist object is to be found in the work of Marcel Duchamp, a hero for the youthful Breton. Duchamp's *Why Not Sneeze* of 1921 (Philadelphia Museum of Art) Breton continued throughout his life to regard as one of the most magical of twentieth-century icons – a view he had already put forward in a lecture delivered in 1922 in which he had related it in spirit to Lautréamont's verse. As a very young man, just before the outbreak of war, Breton had fallen under the spell of Valéry and his art, and he was later to say that for him only Duchamp was bathed in the same peculiar intellectual lustre.

Breton was undoubtedly the animating figure behind the foundation of *La Révolution Surréaliste*, but the first three issues were edited by two of his friends, Pierre Naville and Benjamin Péret. However, Breton almost certainly chose the Man Ray for illustration (we know that he helped to supervise the layout of the first issue) and must also have produced the second major image it contained, a Picasso *Guitar* of 1924. Throughout his life he maintained that Picasso's Cubist constructions, begun in 1912, were among his most significant works. He saw them as precursors of Surrealism because he was struck by their anti-aesthetic bias (many of them were constructed out of material classifiable as rubbish). As a correlative to this they represented to him supreme examples of visual alchemy – something visually charged with meaning out of nothing. Breton had first discovered Picasso's constructions in the November 1913 issue of Apollinaire's *Soirées de Paris* and it was through the reproductions in the pages of this review that Breton was introduced and converted to modernism in the visual arts. Subsequently he was to search out Apollinaire, who was to replace Valéry as his poetic mentor, in part at least because of Apollinaire's love of contemporary painting (a love definitely not felt by Valéry); it was Apollinaire who prepared Breton for his immersion in the work of Rimbaud, to be followed in turn by the all-important, blinding revelation of Lautréamont.

There had been little reference to things visual in the first manifesto, although three artists – Picasso, Duchamp and Picabia – are invited to share in the hospitality dispensed at Breton's imaginary, half-ruined château outside Paris. But in the first issue of the periodical, in an article entitled *Les Yeux Enchantés*, the critic Max Morise was to expose the problem adherent in creating a valid form of visual Surrealism that would conform to the automatic procedures, pronounced in the manifesto to be all important as a method of attaining the surreal. Morise points out that literary surrealism at the time depended for its most successful results on the rapid succession of images and flow of ideas, whereas painting is by nature a static art. He takes the case of de Chirico who produces dream-like images but who conveys them by conventional means which inevitably allow for the intervention of memory and the conscious processes: 'The images are surrealist but their expression is not.' And here he is pinpointing the wider dilemma that continued to haunt Surrealist painting, most particularly during the 1920s. Was the dream life, to the Surrealists in many ways the ideal state and superior to the waking, conscious life, a reality to be expressed or a mystery to be explored? Does a painting by de Chirico have the same validity as the sort of automatic drawings first produced by Masson in 1923 and which pervade the magazine throughout almost its entire run? Morise comes down on the side of the more automatic and abstract processes as the means of fixing dream imagery and he clearly feels strongly for Masson's drawings which he describes as 'unexpected appearances witnessing the most imperceptible waves in the flux of thought'. The third issue of the periodical contained the terse and famous statement by Pierre Naville who rebuts both alternatives and proclaimed, 'There is no longer anyone unaware of the fact that there is no such thing as Surrealist painting.'

In the meantime Breton was becoming unhappy about what he felt to be the incipient anarchism and pessimism of the second and third issues of the magazine, a tone which was largely the result of the intellectual ascendance that Antonin Artaud was exercising over the editors. Artaud was one of the most unpredictable and most extreme personalities to be associated with the movement, and although in the first manifesto Breton had more or less proclaimed that no holds were to be barred in the creation of a new consciousness and the destruction of the existing moral order, he was, oddly enough, a man who disliked excess. He was intellectually fearless and a genuine radical, but there was also a strong streak of conservatism in his makeup. Like a lot of imaginative people similarly endowed, he was attracted to recklessness in others, to those who were 'capable de tout'; but understandably enough he often felt more comfortable in their company if they happened to be dead or distant.

Breton now acted quickly. He took over the editorship of the fourth issue, and in an editorial explaining why he had done so he sought to place Surrealism more squarely within the social issues of the day, a process that was to lead to his own turbulent and unhappy involvement with the Communist Party to which he officially adhered in 1927. But subsequently he acknowledged that another reason for his takeover was that he was unhappy with the treatment the visual arts were receiving in the publication. The images reproduced in numbers two and three had been of works which were mostly small in scale and predominantly graphic in emphasis and had almost certainly been selected by Masson, the artist who was closest to the editors and to Artaud. The pages of issue number four and of all the subsequent issues through to the final one of December 1929 were to be enriched by an astonishing diversity of visual material, including reproductions of many of the works now acknowledged to be the movement's masterpieces. Breton accompanied the exposé of his takeover with a drawing by a seventy-nine-year-old medium – a reaffirmation of his belief in the power of the subconscious and its potential for revelation and a call to artists and intellectuals to allow their own voices to come through. The first issue under Breton's editorship also carried the first installment of his most important statement on the visual arts – his *Le Surréalisme et la Peinture* – which came out in book form, slightly expanded, in 1928.[1] In the first installment he makes the point that visual language is no more artificial than spoken language and indeed he goes on to say: 'Auditive images are inferior to visual images, not only in clarity but also in strictness . . . and are not destined (unlike visual ones) to strengthen the idea of human greatness.'

Breton's essay (or book) begins with the sentence, 'The eye exists in a primitive stage.' And it seems probable that Breton may already have been familiar with Lucien Lévy-Bruhl's *La Mentalité Primitive* of 1922, which was followed in 1927 by *L'Ame Primitive*. Lévy-Bruhl's work was, we know, discussed by the Surrealists in the early 1930s. Where Lévy-Bruhl differed from fellow proto-anthropologists such as Fraser, whose *Golden Bough* was at this precise moment being avidly read in a recent translation by French intellectual circles, and for that matter from Freud himself, was that he felt the primitive mentality was not, in Freud's terminology, simply a social and cultural 'childhood', a prelude to more sophisticated thought processes, but was rather a state apart. Breton argued that a study of it could be revealing because through primitive eyes things could be seen as both natural appearances and as numinous phenomena – as themselves and simultaneously as something else and hence as potentially reconciling contradictions between the rational and the irrational. Breton seems to imply that the eye (and hence the image it records) has an innocence denied to other modes of apprehension and that painters are, potentially at least, in a state of grace.

Le Surréalisme et la Peinture is an extraordinary document. Breton himself was to rank it with the literary products of Surrealism he most admired and he was to equate it in importance, by implication at least, with his semi-documentary novel *Nadja*, also of 1928, a minor masterpiece. The richness of imagery in *Le Surréalisme et la Peinture*, the sense of urgency, the dense and brilliant quality of the prose are to be matched in Breton's work perhaps only by *L'Amour Fou* of 1937, his headiest statement on this obsessive Surrealist concern, which contains a veritable torrent of verbal marvels, and which celebrates his relationship with his second wife Jacqueline Lamba, and then again in *Arcane 17*, composed during the war though not published till 1947, a work inspired by his love for Eliza Bindhoff (to become his third wife). This was the densest and most symbolist of his prose works, in which woman is seen as virtually the sole key to the surreal and the redeeming principle of the universe. And there is a very real sense in which *Le Surréalisme et la Peinture* also commemorates one of the great love affairs of the twentieth century: Breton's love of painting. It was a love that was to last him all his life, but it was at its most intense between 1925 and 1928.

One might expect to see in *Le Surréalisme et la Peinture* the influence of Apollinaire, that other great impresario of twentieth-century French art, and it is there, particularly in the passages on Picasso. But a comparison of the two men's art criticism serves rather to throw the uniqueness of Breton's achievement into relief. In the first place much of Apollinaire's criticism was journalism produced for financial gain, and hence in Breton's view impure. Then again, Apollinaire's visual sense was uncertain; and yet although he very seldom describes works of art he could occasionally write of a painting in such a way that we get a clear impression of what it might look like. Like Apollinaire, Breton rigorously avoids describing the appearance of individual works; but he ultimately achieved something much more difficult: he contrives to excite the reader into an awareness of what a painter's work might feel like; and he accomplishes this by the way in which the images and texture of his prose mirror what he feels to be the individual artist's special qualities. Thus the cadences in the passages on de Chirico are the slowest and most haunting; those which deal with Ernst are the most urgent, reflecting the astonishing cornucopia of visual images pouring forth from his studio. The images in the section on Miró are the most whimsical, the most constellated and magical; those relating to Tanguy the most exotic and jewelled, those on Arp the most philosophical and so on. Then again, whereas Apollinaire had an uncanny gift of conjuring up an artist's outward personality, of giving one, almost, a feeling of what he might have been like to meet, Breton gives one an insight into the more secret mental processes by which the work might have been produced. And here surely Breton has learnt much from that unique document about the creative process: Valéry's *La Soirée avec Monsieur Teste* – a work dedicated metaphorically to Degas – Breton's favourite text by Valéry and a work he claimed to know by heart. Breton lacks, it is true, Valéry's extreme subtlety of analysis and control of nuance, but he was working on a broader canvas and his aims were different. Finally, Apollinaire was a man whose love of painters was ultimately stronger than his love of painting, and he became a champion of Cubism largely because of his passion for what was most modern and up-to-date but also out of affection for its creators. Breton put his far greater feeling for painting at the service of promoting a movement which meant more to him than the individual talents of personalities to which he felt drawn. His prose he holds up to painting as a mirror, not in which it might see itself reflected, but through which it might pass.

And yet despite its originality there is, I believe, a very direct prototype for Breton's art criticism. The clue comes in the very moral line Breton takes on the responsibilities of the painter who, he feels, is under pressures (largely commercial and financial) not experienced so acutely by writers and because he recognizes an immediacy in painters' means of expression which can convince and transform consciousness even more directly than the written word. The question of art and morality inevitably raises the shade of Baudelaire, and we remember that in the first manifesto Breton tells us that Baudelaire is Surrealist in his morality. Breton was acutely aware of Surrealism as a latter-day form of romanticism, and he inherited from Baudelaire the idea of art as something heroic and profound which could carry man forward but which must simultaneously reflect the immediate requirements of its age, although there is a difference of emphasis in that while Baudelaire insisted on the moral obligation of artists he is really using the fine arts as a support, a vehicle, even an investigation into his own morality, whereas Breton is in fact encouraging artists to invent a totally new morality.

But at a purely visual level Breton would have undoubtedly concurred with what Baudelaire called, 'la culte des images (ma grande, mon unique, ma primitive passion)'. If ever there was criticism that was, again in Baudelaire's words 'partial, passioné et politique' it was Breton's. Both men saw themselves in their critical roles not just as commentators but as artists in their own right; and if in this respect Breton does not begin to rival Baudelaire's stature as a poet, as a writer on art he possessed certain advantages over his mentor. He had an innate sense of history which Baudelaire did not; witness the extraordinary coup he achieved in the first of the issues of *La Révolution Surréaliste*, edited by himself, in juxtaposing *Les Demoiselles d'Avignon* of 1907, a work then still unknown to the general public although it had to a certain extent at least provoked the Cubist revolution, with the second major turning point in Picasso's career, the *Three Dancers* of 1925 which shows him reassessing his relationship to the new Surrealist avant-garde. Baudelaire did not in fact *look* very hard; Breton did. And this brings us to a recognition of one of his greatest gifts: he had a superb eye. And what renders him unique among writers on art, both past and present, is that he tells us even more about what *he* is thinking about his artists through what he chooses to reproduce and by the sequence in which he presents us with images in reproduction than through his complementary prose.

I believe that, whether consciously or not, the structure of *Le Surréalisme et la Peinture* is modelled on the grandest of all Baudelaire's Salon pieces, that of 1846. In both cases substantial general passages lead up to the discussion of a favoured genius – Delacroix in Baudelaire's case, Picasso for Breton – to be followed by shorter passages of generalities weaving in and out of discussion of other artists. Breton's lyrical, more general passages on Picasso are in many respects among the least satisfactory in the book, partly because the tone is one of total adulation, something that did not come naturally to Breton, so that the note struck is somewhat artificial, and partly because at this time Breton tends to equate the dream and the subconscious too exclusively. His knowledge of Freud was still considerably more rudimentary than he would have had us believe. He still saw automatism as a means of communicating with the dream life, and his attempt to discuss Picasso's art in terms of dream imagery is unconvincing for obvious reasons, as he himself was soon to admit. In his text, however, he again shows his historical insight when he pinpoints the end of 1909, after Picasso's return to Paris following the summer spent at Horta del Ebro, as a key period in Picasso's art in that it marked the emergence of a new idiom, concerned still with visual phenomena yet 'strongly anti-naturalistic in appearance'. As a very young man he had been bowled over by the *Man with a Clarinet* of 1911 (Thyssen-Bornemisza Foundation, Madrid) of which he now writes: '[This picture] remains a tangible proof of our unwavering proposition that the mind talks to us of a future continent and everyone has the power to accompany an ever more beautiful Alice into Wonderland.'

It is certainly true that in their reinvention of the vocabulary of painting in the years between 1909 and 1913 the Cubists had produced works that looked marvellously open-ended and mysterious. It had seemed an art of infinite possibilities, as its effect on other artists was to demonstrate. But subsequent developments had gone on to underline the fact that the revolution effected by Cubism had been primarily formalistic; or, to put it differently, whereas early and high Analytic Cubism involved a new way of looking at the external world, fully formed Synthetic Cubism was involved with new ways of making pictures. Breton was obsessed by Cubism and particularly by its earlier phases which he recognized as a turning point in twentieth-century art; but he was a realist and recognized that the clock could not be turned back. And his talents as an impresario told him that he must exploit and promote his artists' most recent products. What he would have liked to work with was the mysterious crystalline Cubism of 1910–12: what he was faced with was the more style-conscious works of its recent products.

Breton does his best to explore the possibilities of adapting latter-day Cubism to Surrealist ends, and his attempts to do so are truly fascinating and instructive to watch. In his choice of illustrations he picks unerringly on Picasso's more ironic and subversive Cubist pictures. He also makes a brave attempt to explore the Surrealistic possibilities of the most grotesquely distorted products of Picasso's

de Chirico,
The Child's Brain, 1914

Neo-Classical style. In the illustrations to the book – as opposed to the original articles which appeared in *La Révolution Surréaliste* – he tacitly admits defeat by dropping Neo-Classicism completely; and he ends up, most skilfully, by underlining the visual links between Picasso's extraordinary *La Femme en Chemise* of 1913 (Collection Mrs Victor Ganz, New York) and his most recent biomorphic works of 1927–8.

Towards de Chirico, Breton adopted a more constant stance than he was to show to any of his other artists. The works of 1910–17 he hailed as immutable points of orientation, comparable to Lautréamont's achievements; and he says, 'These works we will go on consulting for the rest of our lives.' The passages related to de Chirico's paintings (for once again he doesn't describe them) are among the most haunting in the book, partly because they are thrown into relief by the violence of the denunciations which follow them, and which express so potently Breton's rage and despair at what he saw as the betrayal of a great talent which subsequently, in Breton's words, failed 'to live out the most beautiful poem in the world; so much the worse for him,' he goes on to say, 'if he suddenly imagined he was master of his dreams'. *The Child's Brain* of 1914 (National Museum, Stockholm), which belonged to Breton and which he cherished all his life, remained for him the most magical of all twentieth-century canvases; and he pays tribute to the impact of de Chirico on the movement as a whole when he says, 'It was in the squares of de Chirico more than anywhere else that we held our secret meetings.' Indeed, we know that the Surrealists often helped to put themselves into trances by staring at de Chirico's depictions of urban landscapes.

Both Picasso and de Chirico had been brought to fame in a measure at least by Apollinaire's journalism. Now Breton was to perform a similar function for a new generation of painters, although while Apollinaire was always ready and anxious to promote new talent for its own sake, Breton was out to recruit for what he had come to see as the greater scheme of things. Masson was easy enough to press into service. Like Breton and all the other Surrealists, Masson was fascinated by alchemy, and Breton had bought Masson's alchemically inspired canvas *The Four Elements* (Private Collection, Paris) out of Masson's first one-man show. Masson's automatic drawings had been known to readers of *La Révolution Surréaliste* since its first issue. But it is revealing of Breton's ambitions for the movement that he should have chosen to reproduce in *Le Surréalisme et La Peinture* (the passages on Masson were the last to appear in serialized form) a large, historically important work, *Woman* of 1925 (Private Collection, Montreal), which attempts to marry a quasi-automatic use of line to a Cubist substructure. Breton was particularly drawn to Masson because of what he saw as the anti-aesthetic element of his work: 'Masson is perfectly right to be distrustful of art.' The fact that Masson's view of the dream had more in common with Nietzsche's than with Freud's, Breton, who disliked the German philosopher with an almost personal hatred, chose to ignore.

The last installment of *Le Surréalisme et la Peinture* also introduced through images two new stars, Ernst and Miró. With his extraordinary feeling for quality and his sense of the visually significant, Breton went straight to major works by both artists, although here his omissions, what he chose to ignore or reject, tell us as much about how he hoped to see Surrealism develop as do his inclusions. He reproduced Ernst's *Pietà*, *Révolution la Nuit* of 1923 and his *Two Children Threatened by a Nightingale* of 1924 (in the

255

Tate Gallery, London and the Museum of Modern Art, New York respectively), both of which have autobiographical connotations of which he was undoubtedly aware and both of which are susceptible to the kind of Freudian interpretation that he and his friends enjoyed applying to painting. The first I believe to be a painting about suicide, an obsessional subject at the time for Breton and his circle – the debt to *The Child's Brain* is obvious – the second about rape or seduction; the space here is very Chiriquesque but there is also a reference to the medieval 'hortus conclusus', although here significantly the gate has been swung open and virginity has flown. But Ernst's paintings of 1921–4 which are pervaded by a more general sense of myth and a quality of dark atavism, and which are hence more Jungian in feeling, these Breton avoids. Breton distrusted the thought of Jung, although the strongly Neo-Romantic flavour of the latter's work parallels in many respects the concerns of some of the Surrealists often more comfortably than do the more truly scientific aims of Breton's idol Freud (who, understandably enough, came to view the movement with extreme distrust and ultimately with hostility). Recent research has confirmed the importance of Jung for an understanding of Ernst's work of the early 1920s.[2] It was only in the 1930s that Breton's interest in myth strengthened steadily, and although he approached it from a Freudian point of view, by 1945, when *Le Surréalisme et la Peinture* was reissued in book form, he had been touched at least indirectly by the intellectual currents he was resisting in the 1920s; it is only now, at this late date, that he reproduces an all-important work of Ernst's *The Elephant of the Celebes* of 1921 (Tate Gallery) which might with justification be called the first Surrealist painting and which is deeply Jungian in its orientation, according it the status of a full-colour plate.

The section on Ernst is the longest in the book, a recognition of the vastness and diversity of Ernst's iconographic range, a fact which Breton acknowledges and praises in his text and also by reproducing more of his work both in *La Révolution Surréaliste* and subsequently than of any other artist. This iconographic richness was the result, although Breton doesn't say so, of Ernst's use of collage procedures and the subsequent techniques of *frottage* and *grattage* which came out of Ernst's collages of 1919–20. These were the first works by Ernst that Breton encountered; he wrote a preface when they were exhibited at the Galerie Sans Pareil in 1920 and he was subsequently to see them, quite rightly, as the first products of visual Surrealism. Breton mentions these early collages in *Le Surréalisme et la Peinture* in the second installment and immediately after a passage in which he says, 'The day of the pipe . . . the newspaper and the guitar (of Cubism) is almost over.' And yet Breton reproduces none of these remarkable early works in the periodical, although when the articles appeared in book form his historical sense impelled him to include a single one. Perhaps because these early collages are small (often minute) in scale, their magic and subversive humour tend to work slowly, and despite his anti-aesthetic bias, Breton was still trying to promote visual Surrealism in terms of large, imposing works which individually challenged the art of the past. His choice of images for illustration in his articles of 1926 and 1927 demonstrated the fact that he was exploring the possibility of promoting a metamorphic, biomorphic idiom which by virtue of its bias towards organic but highly abstract forms represented a patently modern and up-to-date idiom which might suit Surrealist ends where Cubism had failed.

Breton introduced Miró to the public in his takeover issue with two major works of which the *Catalan Landscape, The Hunter,* 1923–4 (Museum of Modern Art, New York) was the most historically significant. This was a work which had recently entered Breton's possession and whose subsequent loss from his collection he was to mourn. Breton certainly could never have been described as an innocent character; but when circumstances forced him to part with this picture he recognized that some of his youthful idealism and optimism had also left him. To the extent that the images are conveyed in a hieroglyphic, script-like idiom, it is the work which makes a bridge between the sort of thing reproduced in previous issues and the new, grander pantheon of images presented by Breton; its imagery also finds analogies in some of Breton's own contemporary poetry which searches in an unsentimental way to capture the landscape of childhood. The next phase of Miró's art, the works of late 1924, 1925 and early 1926, which are mystically oriented and at least superficially the most automatic in appearance of any contained in the Surrealist canon – these Breton eschews rigorously, partly, I suspect, because he saw them as paralleling visually that intellectual void or abyss to which he had seen the two previous issues of the magazine heading. He was aware of Miró's enormous natural gifts, as he makes clear in his text of 1928, and he was also aware of the fact that to the public Miró's work must represent the apogee of automatism, although he mistrusted Miró's use of it; and despite their unbridled fantasy and their dream-like poignancy many of these works were in fact rigorously and even meticulously planned.

Miró is in many ways the test case for Breton, and he is the artist (apart from the later de Chirico) whom Breton treats most severely in his book. He attacks him for his 'petit bourgeois' spirit and his absorption in painting at the expense of wider social issues. In a passage, fragments of which have all too often been quoted out of context, and which more than any other in his entire text expresses a premonition of events to come, he writes: 'In place of the innumerable problems which do not concern him in the least, despite the fact that the human character is moulded from them, Joan Miró cherishes a single desire – to give himself up utterly to painting and to painting alone . . . to that pure automatism which . . . I have never ceased to value . . . but whose true worth and signifi-cance Miró unaided has, I suspect, verified in a very summary manner. It is true that may be the reason why he could perhaps pass for the most Surrealist of us all. But how far are we from this "chemistry of the intellect" that we have just discussed?' If in the periodical Breton ignores the pivotal work of 1925–6, although in the book his sense of justice prompted him to include one of the circus pictures of 1925 (now in a Private Collection), he chooses one of the least extreme and reductive. But he picks him up again in 1927 with the important *Personage Throwing a Stone at a Bird* of 1926 (Museum of Modern Art, New York), in which forms are once more clearly delineated and in which the dominant image is rendered in swelling biomorphic forms.

The new biomorphic, sinuous idiom which had by now touched Miró was pioneered by Arp in Zürich during the war years in works which Breton was subsequently to classify as embodying all that was 'most liberated and new'. Arp, whom Breton admired as a fellow poet, is an artist treated particularly gently by Breton; and Breton seems to have sensed that the biomorphic approach that could make one form represent simultaneously or flow into another (by the simple expedient, for example, of turning it upside down), and which involved duality of imagery, could lead to that reconciliation of opposites which was to be the avowed programme of the second manifesto of 1929. Perhaps the simple fluidity and apparent effortlessness of so much of Arp's contemporary work made Breton think of a line from his own volume of poems, *Clair de Terre* of 1923 in which he speaks of 'the white curve on the black ground which we call thought'. What is certainly true is that it is in connection with Arp's work that he first uses the phrase 'communicating vessels' which he was to adopt for the title of that all-important essay of 1932 in which he attempts to invalidate the traditional antithesis between dreams and action. The biomorphic idiom shared by Arp and Miró was to touch both Ernst and Masson, and Picasso had already invented his independent variant of it. Biomorphism was a viable Surrealist style, in that it was capable of, in their own words, following 'the dictates of thought'; it could be a flexible tool for the revelation of the marvellous and the poetic, and it was singularly adaptable when put at the service of the erotic, always a prime concern of the Surrealists, but one which as the 1920s progressed was to be increasingly confounded with their obsession with the marvellous. If Breton had patiently nurtured it, it might have proved adaptable even to his own changing demands. One of the most notable features of Breton's later writings and recorded interviews and conversations was his sense of wonder at Miró's art both past and present, his feeling almost of nostalgia for a visual paradise he himself had inhabited briefly and then lost. But in 1928 it was Miró's work more than that of any of his contemporaries which illustrates why for Breton this biomorphic idiom with its abstract bias was already becoming suspect in his eyes. It was quite simply too easily allied to visual beauty, too prone to aestheticism in its orientation, too – for want of a better word – stylish; and yet, paradoxically, too productive of results that were, from Breton's point of view, personally capricious and idiosyncratic.

The image of the mirror is a recurrent one in Breton's work, and, as one reads and rereads *Le Surréalisme et la Peinture*, it increasingly conveys the impression that Breton was trying to hold up to painting a mirror which would not so much reflect its achievements but through which it was to pass collectively into a new Surrealist wonderland. It has never been sufficiently stressed that whereas in the book Breton talks once or twice in a general way of 'Surrealist painters' and 'Surrealist painting', and by implication the painters he reproduces represent certain aspirations of the movement, he only ever refers to one of the painters as actually being Surrealist – and this is Miró (in the passage quoted above), whom he censures;

while in the bridge passage which leads out of a discussion of de Chirico (the most obviously Surrealist of the movement's precursors) and which leads in turn to Ernst, the artist whom Breton, implicitly at least, was forced to recognize as being the Surrealist *par excellence*, he says 'in terms of literature and art we do not exist' – a point he had already implied and one at which he often hints.

There is a sense in which the Surrealist painters did pass through the mirror held up to them, in that their work had more in common from a stylistic point of view between 1926 and 1929 than it had in previous years, and Breton was subsequently able to say that the later years of the 1920s were a particularly brilliant period for the movement, especially with reference to the visual arts. And yet the mirror was, for Breton at least, blind. His increasing political involvement was making him feel the need for greater communal action; yet greater stylistic unity among his artists was proving to be self-defeating in his eyes in that it emphasized a growing aesthetic bias.

Surrealism had begun as an idealistic movement using developments in late nineteenth- and early twentieth-century thought to carry further the Romantic quest for self-discovery. But it was also a movement about communication; if it sought to reveal to man his own deeper, truer self, it also in the process sought to reveal man to man. And yet as each artist examined his individual psyche, and as he was encouraged by the Surrealist ethos to embark on what might be called the voyage inwards and downwards, it is not surprising that each artist was finding his identity in his role as artist and was becoming increasingly committed to communication through purely artistic means. Breton had seen this as Miró's position all along and had chastised him for it. And now the case of Ernst all of a sudden became even more revealing. Of all the painters, he was the most intellectually committed to Surrealism. He undertook his technical experiments in order to discover fresh imagery, new Surrealist iconography. Yet one has only to compare his early large manifesto piece *The Circle of Friends* of 1932 with *The Friends become Flowers* of 1928 (in the Wallraf-Richartz Museum, Cologne, and the E. J. Power Collection, London, respectively) to see that whatever the initial impetus for experiment, it was resulting in a greater interest in paint for paint's sake, in the beauty of its effects.

Throughout 1926 and 1927 Breton had been keeping his visual options open. In the same issue of *La Révolution Surréaliste*, June

1926, in which Jean Arp had put in a visual appearance with *Table, Mountain, Anchors and Navel* (Museum of Modern Art, New York), he had reproduced his first Tanguy, a very recent work, *The Invisible Ring* (present location unknown) and the juxtaposition of these two works on opposite sides of a double-page spread is revealing and in a sense symbolic of things to come. They are the last two painters to be discussed in *Le Surréalisme et la Peinture*. Breton, significantly enough, talks about Tanguy in relationship to spiritualist mediums; and the strange, mysterious diagrammatic images of Tanguy do indeed look as if they had surfaced from the unconscious. They have been marvellously resistant to art-historical source-spotting although the title makes references to an occult legend (the story of Gyges), and the composite imagery of this and other contemporary works is drawn from a wide variety of sources: astrological charts, alchemical treatises, diagrams of the psychic and nervous centres, scientific and spiritualist journals and so forth. Quite clearly Tanguy's work was alive with that 'chemistry of the intellect' (the phrase is Edgar Allan Poe's) that Breton missed in Miró. And the fact that his work was still somewhat raw and clumsy was possibly an advantage in Breton's eyes: here was a vision that could be shaped. Tanguy was to become the artist possibly closest to Breton on a personal level, and despite the relatively few years that separated them in age, he was to be his pictorial Benjamin. In one of the introductory paragraphs to the first installment of what was to become the book, Breton had written: 'It is impossible for me to envisage a picture as being other than a window, and . . . my first concern is then to know what it looks out on . . . nothing appeals to me so much as a vista stretching away before me out of sight.' It was these vistas which Tanguy set out to produce for Breton in a vision that was intensely personal but in a style that was not.

In the meantime, Breton's stormy and complicated relations with the Communist Party were being re-enacted, with a reversal of roles, within the Surrealist movement itself. Breton was prepared to put Surrealism at the service of the revolution, but only on condition that it kept its independence and its right to comment, criticize and protest. Towards his own cohorts, on the other hand, he took an authoritarian stance. In February 1929 a letter was drafted, modelled on Communist questionnaires, and sent out to some eighty names inviting them to choose between individual and collective action, an act which precipitated an instant break with

Masson, who found it offensive. The last issue of *La Révolution Surréaliste* came out on 15 December 1929 and it contained the Second Surrealist Manifesto. There had been excommunications previously within the party movement. Now they were carried out on a grand scale, and there is a sense in which things had come full circle because the strongest attack was on Georges Bataille who had become the presiding genius of what had once been known as the rue Blomet group – the writer closest to Masson all along and to Miró in the for him critical years 1924–5 – and the writer who had also helped to influence the tone of the second and third issues, whose direction had prompted Breton to take control of the magazine.

This last issue showed a pronounced visual reorientation. Of the sixteen major illustrations, only two have any connection with the biomorphic or automatist tendencies of previous issues. Breton reproduces for the first time in the magazine, and very prominently, two recent Ernst collages, although significantly they are works in which the collage elements are culled from visually consistent sources (steel-point engravings from nineteenth-century magazines), so that the results, though iconographically startling, lack the poetic, magical, very hallucinated Rhenish medieval quality of the earlier series. Two new visual talents are introduced: Dali, with three important works, including *The Accommodations of Desire* of 1929 just acquired by Breton (Collection Jacques and Natasha Gelman, New York), and Magritte, presented at less than full strength by a page of his word-and-image drawings (an indication perhaps that Breton was about to reaffirm his belief in the power of the alchemy of the word over that of the painted image). On the final page was the famous montage which showed a small Magritte nude surrounded by the surviving painters and the new recruits to the movement in a state of simulated or waking dream. The Magritte nude for a long time had been thought to be lost but was later discovered in the possessions left behind by Breton at his death (and now in a Private Collection). Did he secretly cherish it as a souvenir of the end of his most passionate involvement with the visual arts?

Breton had discovered Dali's work too late for inclusion in *Le Surréalisme et la Peinture*, but he wrote the preface to Dali's first one-man Paris show at the Galerie Goemans which opened on 20 November 1929. Again it is a remarkable document. The only individual work of art he mentions is *The Lugubrious Game* of 1929 (Private Collection), which, as Dawn Ades has remarked, is really

Dali's Surrealist 'pièce d'acceptance'.[3] Dali had begun to make his mark on the Paris scene largely under the auspices of Bataille, who was briefly challenging Breton's supremacy. Dali at the last moment refused to allow Bataille to reproduce *The Lugubrious Game* in his periodical *Documents*, forcing him to substitute a linear diagram of it instead. Breton's attitude to Dali mirrors, on a visual level, the combination of commitment and resentment he evinces towards politics in the Second Manifesto. He acknowledges the element of sensationalism in Dali's work, and he even hints that it has within it the seeds of corruption. He was a pure and in some respects a prudish man and Dali's subject matter in these feverish panegyrics to auto-eroticism he must have found hard to take, though even after the final break between the two men Breton continued to support the early work. Breton never felt for Dali's work what he had felt as a youth for Matisse and Derain and then subsequently for de Chirico and Picasso and for the younger men whose reputations he helped to make. The way in which he embraced Dali's cause has about it something of that cold ferocity experienced by a lover when out of intellectual or moral conviction he decides to end a great affair.

By 1929 Breton was arguing from a much closer knowledge of Freud and he was now interested in Freud's concept of the artist as a successful neurotic. He quoted from Freud in the Second Manifesto: 'If he [the neurotic] possesses the artistic gift, psychologically so mysterious, he can, in place of symptoms, transform his dreams in artistic creations.' Obviously Dali was Breton's man; and in this connection it is worth mentioning that Dali was the only Surrealist painter for whom Freud evinced respect. Breton was now accepting, in part at least, Freud's methods of observation and dream interpretation, although, unlike Freud he still felt that dreams in themselves actually help solve problems as opposed to explaining them. And briefly at least he seems to believe that the dream has a space and time of its own and therefore an almost material existence. In the latter respect again Dali's work comes to mind. Breton ends his 1929 piece on Dali: 'The art of Dali, the most hallucinatory to date ever to be known, constitutes a veritable menace. Absolutely new beings, visibly evil in intent, have been put on the march. And it is a sombre pleasure to see how nothing can stop their passage except they themselves, and to recognize in the way in which they multiply and blend, that they are predatory beings.'[4] It sounds like a malediction on the visual optimism of the 1920s.

Le Surréalisme au Service de la Révolution, successor to *La Révolution Surréaliste*, Breton felt to be the most glittering of the Surrealist periodicals and it generates a feeling of neurotic if at times somewhat glacial excitement. The illustrations, mostly by Dali, Tanguy and Ernst, are now no longer interspersed through the various texts but rather are contained in a separate section at the back of each issue. Although this was almost certainly done for financial reasons, it is somehow symptomatic of Breton's altered attitude to the visual arts. He was later to say: 'Surrealism at that time reminds me of a demasted ship, which could from one moment to the next either have gone to the bottom or have triumphally reached the land of which Rimbaud spoke, where he would at last have known the true life.' And indeed there was a sense at least in which painting had previously been the movement's sails, catching the intellectual winds, twisting and spinning in its polemical squalls, helping to propel the movement forwards, never, it is true, on a single course, and certainly to unknown destinations, but with a sense of zest and adventure Surrealism was never to recapture.

15

Duchamp: *The Large Glass**

I N 1926 *The Bride Stripped Bare by her Bachelors, Even* (perhaps
already known to its familiars as the *Large Glass*) was shattered
while in transit following its first public appearance at the
International Exhibition of Modern Art at the Brooklyn Museum.[1] It
is a work that today still holds a substantial claim to be the most
complex and elaborately pondered art object that the twentieth
century has yet produced. It had occupied its author's physical
energies, intermittently, over a period of eight years, between 1915
and 1923, when it was abandoned in its present unfinished state,
and it had absorbed all his unique intellectual powers from 1912 to
1915, the years during which plans for the great work were being
elaborated and finalized. When he was informed of the disaster of
1926[2] Duchamp expressed only wry amusement, but ten years later
he spent some laborious months piecing his creation together again,
and as one by one the small fragments of glass and paint slotted into
place so was one of the most remarkable myths in the history of art
consolidated. Speaking of the breakage Duchamp later remarked
that the cracks 'brought the work back into the world',[3] and it is true
that the network of lines gives the work an air of physicality, if only
because it serves to remind the viewer of the vulnerability of its
prime matter. At the same time the restoration involved enclosing
the original work between two sheets of heavier plate glass and the
whole was encased in a new metal frame, so that the work has
acquired the character of some giant icon, battered and venerable
before its time.

The Large Glass was shown publicly only once again, at the
Museum of Modern Art during the course of 1943–4, before it
reached its final destination. In 1953 it joined the Arensberg
Collection in the Philadelphia Museum of Art, a collection rich in
the work of Duchamp's contemporaries but dedicated above all to a

*All the works by Duchamp discussed in this essay are in Philadelphia unless
otherwise indicated.

survey of his art, and there it has remained. Its condition is not good (the thin lead wires which serve to delineate most of the elements of the *Glass*, for example, have in places come loose, and much of the colour is badly faded) and it is unlikely that it will ever travel again. The projects and studies that led up to the final work were to be of cardinal importance in the emergence of the visual manifestations of Dada and Surrealism, although Duchamp himself for the most part was to keep aristocratically aloof from the most public and aggressive aspects of the two movements; the great work itself, on the other hand, although it has earned the accolade of two reconstructions by distinguished figures in the contemporary art world,[4] has in the wider sense of the word defied imitation. And yet despite its vicissitudes, its immobility, its relative inaccessibility (or partly because of these factors?) *The Large Glass* continues to emit a strange, pervasive intellectual perfume that has touched and transformed the lives and work of countless artists, many of whom have never seen the original.

Duchamp has said of it, 'The *Glass* is not to be looked at for itself but only as a function of a catalogue I never made.'[5] In fact in 1934 he published his *Green Box*, a compilation of documents, plans, sketches and notes made in connection with *The Large Glass* between 1912 and 1915 to which he added a few notes concerning his American ready-mades and some slightly later experiments in optics, which in retrospect he had come to see as significant in its genesis and elaboration.[6] Each of the slips of paper in the *Green Box* was reproduced in exact facsimile and these were then assembled in a deliberately random order, so that their arrangement varied from box to box. Although they fail, and indeed were not intended, to explain *The Large Glass* rationally, the written notes complement their great visual counterpart and they help to illuminate a work which Duchamp himself has aptly described as 'a wedding of mental and visual concepts'.

The appearance of the *Green Box* provoked Breton's beautiful essay *Phare de la Mariée* (the reference is to Baudelaire's poem *Les Phares*, in which he compares artists to beacons or lighthouses radiating shafts of light out into the surrounding darkness), which appeared for the first time in the Surrealist-biased periodical *Minotaure* in 1935. In it Breton described *The Large Glass* as 'a mechanical and cynical interpretation of the phenomenon of love', and, as he suggests, the work is concerned with the attempts of the

Duchamp,
The Bride Stripped Bare
by her Bachelors, Even,
1915–23

bride and her bachelors to consummate the physical union which they both so desire (although the bride has odd hesitations) and which, it will be seen, they both recognize themselves as incapable of achieving. But if Breton's essay has never been superceded as a sympathetic commentary on *The Large Glass* – only Octavio Paz's more recent short text rivals it in its imaginative insights[7] – this is because he was prepared to accept the fact that it was designed as an insoluble enigma. Duchamp when questioned about the work once said, 'There is no solution because there is no problem,'[8] and this quotation might perhaps be justifiably expanded to say, 'and there is no problem because the riddles that are embedded in *The Large Glass* are in any case designed in such a way that they can never be answered.' The present essay contains no magic thread to lead the reader out of a labyrinth in which it is anyway more stimulating to be lost. It can only attempt to pose some of the unanswerable questions in a slightly different light.

1 The Bride

The *Bride* is the summation and embodiment of all the female figures in Duchamp's work from the first tentative sketches of his earliest youth through to the definitive oil painting of 1912, which was only slightly simplified for incorporation into *The Large Glass*. But she has her origins most directly in two particular works, both of these, characteristically enough, very minor in appearance, since for Duchamp the casual, allusive remark is always more redolent of possibilities and of meaning than the emphatic, elaborately pondered statement. The first of these direct ancestresses of the *Bride* is a drawing, little more than a scribble, designed as an illustration or accompaniment to Jules Laforgue's poem *Encore à cet Astre*, which subsequently gave birth to two important oil paintings, the two versions of the *Nude Descending a Staircase*, the second of which represents Duchamp's first fully mature artistic statement. The signature and the date 1912 were inscribed on the drawing when Duchamp gave it to F. C. Torrey who had acquired the definitive canvas following its sensational appearance at the Armory Show in New York early in 1913; the drawing, however, clearly precedes the first, preparatory oil painting on which Duchamp was at work at the end of 1911. In so far as these two canvases (and in particular the latter) introduced a new dimension into contemporary French art, the freely pencilled image of a woman in motion (seen in the sketch as ascending rather than descending a staircase) can be regarded as the *Bride's* stylistic and technological antecedent.

Duchamp had entered the Cubist orbit during the course of 1911, in the company of his elder brothers Jacques Villon (a pseudonym), a highly gifted painter, and Duchamp-Villon, an equally talented sculptor; Villon's studio at Puteaux, on the outskirts of Paris, was soon to become an important meeting place for painters and writers moving in Cubist circles, although the true creators of the style, Picasso and Braque, remained almost entirely apart. Duchamp's work of 1911 shares many of the concerns of the Puteaux group and in particular an interest in what was to become known as the concept of 'simultaneity', a catchword in the years immediately preceding the outbreak of war. Simultaneity was interpreted in very different ways by various artists but was concerned with the representation of time, or with the crystallization of a moment of dynamic, cosmic flux. Duchamp's *Portrait*, a significant work of

Duchamp,
Nude Descending a Staircase,
***No. 2,* 1912**

1911, shows the same figure in successive stages of motion. *Sonata*, in many ways a companion piece and depicting his three sisters making music, watched over by their mother, gives the impression of being a 'memory' painting in that the figures float in a vague, undefined space; the piano is symbolized by a keyboard suspended in air, while Mme Duchamp seems to swim forward in front of the girls behind whom she is apparently standing. In both paintings the pictorial depth is restricted and the figures (and to a certain extent their surroundings) are treated in faceted, semi-transparent planes which tend to cling to the picture surface in the manner of early Cubist canvases, while the mother's face in *Sonata* combines in a somewhat schematic fashion full face and profile views. The light, lyrical colour schemes and the tentative, rather evasive handling of space, however, are peculiar to Duchamp's art, as is the humorous handling of the woman's figure in *Portrait* – as she crosses the canvas she divests herself of her clothes.

Duchamp: *The Large Glass*

But it is in the two versions of the *Nude Descending*, more than in any other of his works, that Duchamp submitted himself to the pictorial discipline which this supremely sophisticated style demanded, and it was as a result of the Cubist experience that during the following years he was able to realize convincingly his already strongly independent vision. The first of the *Nudes Descending*, although it is less fully resolved than its famous successor, comes in many ways closer to being a truly Cubist canvas than any other that Duchamp ever produced. The work is primarily a study of a figure in movement but it is dominated by a single major image, that of the nude standing on the two bottom steps. She is rendered in what is essentially a Cubist idiom in that her body has been dissected in a genuinely analytical fashion (in terms that is to say of a formalistic breakdown of her component parts) and to this extent the painting invites comparison with, for example, Picasso's canvases executed at Horta del Ebro during the summer of 1909, some of the most rigorously analytical of all his Cubist works. Other factors – the strong linear element which results in a greater fluidity of form, the feeling of transparency and the austerity of the colour harmonies in what is basically a range of earth colours, browns and siennas – would suggest that Duchamp was by now also familiar with the more highly abstracted, more hermetic phase of Cubism initiated during the course of 1910, and of which Picasso's summer canvases done at Cadaqués represented some of the first and most extreme examples. One feature which still isolates Duchamp's painting from mainline Cubism, and which makes it so extremely personal, is its interest in a cinematic depiction of successive stages of movement as opposed to the Cubists' incorporation of various viewpoints of a subject into a single, static image. This has necessitated the placing of the final figure in silhouette at right angles to the picture plane (the true Cubists rigidly avoided a purely profile view which they incorporated into the full face or three-quarter face view). Another feature is Duchamp's almost total disregard of the space around his subject; one senses that the areas to left and right of the central images have simply not interested him in any way at all, an impression confirmed by the fact that he has painted out the areas at the extreme left and right with wide black borders. Peculiar to Duchamp, too, are the elliptical forms (particularly evident in the lower legs) which seem to further define the volumes enclosed by the lines which contain them.

The compositional problems posed by the novelty of Duchamp's imagery were to be solved most coherently in the second version of the *Nude Descending a Staircase*, a work which was almost immediately recognized as one of the watersheds of twentieth-century art; and although the technical means used by Duchamp to achieve his ends still relate it to the concerns of Cubism, the work is so fully realized on its own independent terms that it can only be regarded as a totally original variant of the style. The canvas still retains a strongly perspectival passage at the top right-hand side, but successive images of the figure are now presented in a single plane only slightly angled to the picture surface (in the preparatory painting the nude seems to begin her descent down towards the spectator and then changes direction sharply in her final, most decisive stage of motion), and as in classical Cubism the entire surface is now broken down in pictorial elements of more or less equivalent weight and density, although even here, in one of Duchamp's flattest canvases, he shows little interest in forcing the images right up on to the picture plane, a characteristic concern of much contemporary French painting.

The elaborate subdivision of form, or to put it differently, the more frequent and insistent use of outlines, each of which echoes but modifies the one which precedes it, and the resultant very animated and lively breakdown of both image and picture surface can be accounted for, as Duchamp freely admitted, by the influence of chronophotography (the photographic recording of figures, animals and objects in motion) which had been invented some thirty years before but which in the early years of the century had caught the attention of the popular press. And although Duchamp appears to have been aware of this particular aspect of photography in the months before he embarked on the second *Nude Descending*, the total conviction that the work carries as a study of movement, and certain details (the pearl-like dots at the centre of the composition, for instance, which appear in chronophotographs as a result of the fact that the models carried small torches in their hands to record with light the successive movements of their hands and arms) would suggest that this was perhaps the first of Duchamp's works to effect a marriage on equal terms of the discoveries of art with those of science; and it is at least in part this fusion of disciplines that gives the work its particular originality and flavour and that makes it so pivotal in Duchamp's art. His attitude towards science was ironical and basically inimical, but he realized that to create the sort of highly intellectualized art that was his aim it must be informed and enriched by references to other sources.

Painters had been making use of the discoveries and possibilities of photography since the middle of the nineteenth century, but Duchamp's overt reliance on a specialized aspect of it must have made his *Nude Descending* seem technologically very up-to-date – a pictorial realization of Villiers de l'Isle Adam's *Eve Future*, the mechanically constructed paragon of female beauty. But because the *Nude* was to become such a scandal painting (it was one of the focal points of the Armory Show and became in subsequent years one of the most celebrated twentieth-century paintings in the Western hemisphere), critics have tended to overlook its most directly iconographical source, the poem of Laforgue which had first inspired Duchamp to recreate its mood in a graphic form. Laforgue, who belonged to the second generation of Symbolist poets, was the possessor of a double-sided talent particularly designed to appeal to Duchamp's sensibilities. His work was cosmic and philosophical in its aspirations and was informed by a pessimism and a blackness which at times seems to relate his thought as much to the nihilism of Céline and the pessimism of early Sartre as it does to the romantic *'malaise'* and despair of many of his immediate predecessors and contemporaries. At the same time his art is characterized by an ironical, equivocal, self-questioning wit and by a carefully calculated facetiousness. He delights in puns and incongruities and in a programmatic undermining of reason and logic. *Encore à Cet Astre* and the other two poems illustrated by Duchamp (all from *Le Sanglot de la Terre*) are basically concerned with the theme of sterility and impotence, with what Laforgue called the *éternulité* of human existence, although the style he uses is one of poetic understatement. In *Encore à Cet Astre* a group of mortals, ignorant and derisive, challenge the sun which is losing its warming, life-giving powers (the sun is compared to a pale, pock-marked sieve). In an imaginary dialogue the sun beams back a message of contempt, realizing that the puny creatures eons of time beneath it are doomed, animated puppets (*pantins*).

Some of the same bleak, quizzical despair is conveyed in Duchamp's work visually by the sad, falling linear rhythms and by the fact that the colour harmonies, superficially those of classical Cubism, have a sombre, leaden quality to them. What has been consistently ignored is that the *Nude Descending* is to a certain extent a 'mood' painting and it is perhaps this that sets it apart from Cubism as much as the modifications which Duchamp has imposed on a Cubist technical procedure. The *Nude Descending* is in no way a tragic painting and it would be falsifying Duchamp's original intent to dwell too deeply on its literary implications; and yet the debt to Laforgue exists in the sensation of pervasive melancholy that the canvas transmits (a month earlier Duchamp had portrayed himself as *Sad Young Man on a Train*), and also perhaps in the slightly mocking, ironic depiction of the female nude in terms of what already resembles a puppet-like agglomeration of quasi-mechanistic forms.

As early as 1914, when questioned as to whether his art was descended from that of Cézanne, Duchamp replied that whereas most of his colleagues would undoubtedly claim Cézanne as the most important of their ancestors, he personally felt a greater debt to Odilon Redon; and this was to remain an allegiance which he was still eager to acknowledge much later in life.[9] At first sight Duchamp's statement might seem puzzling. Much of his work of 1910 is obviously indebted to a study of Cézanne, whereas it is hard to find any traces of the direct influence of Redon, except perhaps in *Yvonne et Magdeleine Déchiquetées* of the early autumn of 1911, which shows four heads (or two heads each rendered twice) conveyed in strong chiaroscuro and floating against an indeterminate space. And yet Duchamp's remark is deeply revealing and testifies to the extraordinary degree of self-knowledge which conditioned his development as an artist, almost from the start. For of all the Symbolist painters Redon, perhaps more than any other, paralleled or echoed the preoccupations of his literary colleagues; and it is essential to an understanding of Duchamp's art that when his painting ceased to resemble anything else that was being produced in France (or elsewhere) in the visual field, it retained close links with the literature of the previous generation and with that of some of the most advanced and original of his contemporaries.

The imagery in the *Nude Descending a Staircase*, and the treatment of the figure as a dehumanized puppet, may owe something to Laforgue's poem which had prompted the original sketch, and the *Nude*'s slow descent also recalls *Igitur*'s progress down the steps to the crypt of his forebears.[10] But Duchamp's debt to literature was in the last analysis much more profound, much less specific. His vision was born not only out of the despair of Laforgue, who had adopted as his battle cry *'aux armes citoyens il n'y a pas de raison'*, but out of the ambiguity and deliberate hermeticism of Mallarmé, the poet he most loved, and the figure, he felt, who more than any other artist of his generation held the key to a new, intellectualized art. As Octavio Paz suggests, the work to which *The Large Glass* comes closest is *Un Coup de Dès*, Mallarmé's most ambitious experiment in which he exploited the irregular placing of words on the page and the use of different kinds of type. Duchamp realized that it was impossible to recapture the spirit and flavour of historical Symbolism which had been reflected in the work of Redon and his colleagues and he saw the element of humour in Laforgue (he particularly admired Laforgue's use of eccentric, often ironical titles) as a way out of Symbolism or as a direction in which Symbolism could be extended. He sensed, too, that the important moment in literature when the passion of the Symbolists and the so-called Decadents for the artificial met an emergent interest in the machine had not yet produced a parallel in the visual arts. Dovetailing into this literary climate and closely related to it was the emergence of science fiction, first in the works of Jules Verne, and in the 1890s Rosny and H. G. Wells, a form of literature which was also to affect Duchamp deeply if only because it touched the art of two other writers, Alfred Jarry and Raymond Roussel, to whom he acknowledged a close debt.

Although Duchamp rejected the use of the word literary in connection with his own work as being meaningless and imprecise, he stressed that he felt a greater affinity with literature than with painting. In one of the last interviews before his death he remarked, 'In France there is an old saying "Stupid like a painter", the painter was considered stupid but the poet and writer very intelligent. I wanted to be intelligent . . . I thought the ideatic a way to get away from influences.'[11] And it might be fair to say that Duchamp's unique contribution to the art of the first quarter of the twentieth century lay in the fact that to a greater extent than any of his colleagues he kept alive the fruitful dialogue between literature and the visual arts that had animated so much French nineteenth-century painting and on which the majority of his colleagues had tacitly closed the door when they acknowledged the supremacy of Cézanne, the most purely visual of the great Post-Impressionists and the most formally challenging of all nineteenth-century artists.

The *Nude Descending a Staircase* was submitted to the *Salon des Indépendants* of 1912, where it was rejected by a Cubist hanging committee, a fact that underlined the by now almost total independence of Duchamp's achievement. It is also possible that the Cubists felt that the painting might lend weight to the bid for supremacy and attention that was being made by the Italian Futurists with their great exhibition at Bernheim Jeune's Gallery (which had opened a few weeks earlier) since Duchamp's art was, like theirs, primarily concerned with rendering a sensation of movement; this suspicion is to a certain extent confirmed by the fact that the *Nude* was shown at the *Section d'Or* exhibition the same autumn, a display that showed certain Cubists making tentative gestures of reconciliation with their Italian colleagues. Duchamp was later to deny any influence of Futurism on his work at the time, and it is certainly true that when he set to work on the two versions of the *Nude* there was nothing in visual Futurism that could have offered him any kind of stimulus; it is, however, possible that he may have been aware of their early manifestos (all of which were published in France as well as in Italy) and that these may have unconsciously stimulated his imagination. Of the two painters then working in Paris to whose work Duchamp's was most comparable, one was Severini, a signatory of the initial Futurist manifesto, while the second, Léger, was sympathetic to many of their aims. But despite certain superficial similarities, Duchamp's vision was even further removed from that of Léger and the Futurists than it was from that of the true Cubists. The art of the Futurists was one of optimism strongly tinged with bombast, and they glorified and virtually deified the position of the machine in society. Duchamp's vision was not exactly pessimistic but it was passive and critical, and his anarchy was of a subtler, gentler brand. Fundamentally he viewed the machine and its effects with distrust. The Futurists had engaged in the battle of modern art with a violence and bravado that were ultimately to be self-defeating. Duchamp's development after the *Nude Descending* was to become increasingly private and in his isolation lay his strength.

Duchamp's work of 1911 still belongs, albeit peripherally, to the Cubist world; some of it is relatively large in scale and one has the sensation that during this period Duchamp was consciously trying to carve out for himself a place at the forefront of the modern movement. In 1912 there is a change of mood. It may be that the

275

rejection of the *Nude Descending a Staircase* had the effect of driving him in on himself, and it is possible, too, that he found the politics of the Paris art world (particularly ferocious in 1912 in the face of the Futurist challenge) distasteful. At any rate, the next move was towards a more hermetic, more personal art and the *Nude* was succeeded by *The King and Queen Surrounded by Swift Nudes*, painted in the spring, a subtler, more elaborate work and one which Duchamp himself came to prefer to the earlier, more controversial canvas. The *King and Queen* was executed on the back of a mildly erotic work of 1910, *Le Paradis*, which shows a crouched female nude faced by a naked man who shields his sex with his hands. The first of the sketches for the new oil, *Two Nudes: One Strong and One Swift* (titles were now playing an increasingly important part in Duchamp's work and perhaps reflect his interest in Laforgue's use of them) shows two figures in the same relative positions as in *Le Paradis*, although the male figure is set into cinematic motion in the manner of the *Nude Descending* and lunges forward towards his partner. In the next sketch, *King and Queen Traversed by Swift Nudes*, the positions of the figures are reversed and the figure of the woman has become more highly abstracted. Both figures have about them a depersonalized, sexless air, a feature already apparent in the *Nude Descending*, and owing something perhaps to Duchamp's interest in the poetry of Mallarmé and Laforgue with its hermaphroditic ideal. Both figures subsequently became static, but are connected by flowing forms that suggest some sort of sexual discharge, a feature that becomes unmistakably pronounced in the third and final study, *King and Queen Traversed by Nudes at High Speed*. In the final painting, *King and Queen Surrounded by Swift Nudes*, both figures have reached such a high degree of abstraction that it is hard to differentiate them in terms of sex. Their bodies are rendered by means of burnished, frankly metallic forms reminiscent of chess pieces, and they have about them a mysterious, hieratic air that is emphasized by the flurry of small planes that separates them, like an electric current rendered visible.

Looking at the work one has the impression that as the latent eroticism of Duchamp's vision rose to the surface of his consciousness and of his art, he felt the need to depersonalize, to abstract or to symbolize the identity and appearance of his subjects – it is perhaps not without significance that it is the female figure that is the first to assume a full disguise. The sketch still retains a tenuous stylistic

Duchamp,
***The King and Queen Surrounded by Swift Nudes*, 1912**

link with Cubism, but in terms of iconography it can be paralleled only in early twentieth-century literature. A passage from Jarry's *Messaline* could almost be used as a caption for the sketch: the Empress Messaline comes upon the acrobat Munster standing on his hands and in a provocative condition. She mistakes him for a divine presence, 'And just as Priapus himself . . . tires of balancing in front of him a great trunk – the sex of the god fell between the Empress's hands.' The exotic, hot-house atmosphere of *Messaline* evokes more immediately the jewelled imagery of Moreau rather than the mechanical, almost robot-like forms that Duchamp was evolving in his art, but *Le Surmâle*, published in 1902 a year after *Messaline* and in many ways its male counterpart, has strong science-fiction overtones and in it the machine plays an all-important part. The climax of the novel is a love scene (if such it can be called) in which the hero and heroine achieve coition eighty-two times in remarkably few hours (it is worth perhaps noting in connection with the concept of love expressed in *The Large Glass* that the participants in this incredible feat of endurance withdraw at the moment of climax, or practise *coitus interruptus*), and this is preceded by a scene in which the hero enacts a symbolical rape on a weight-testing machine which is given specifically female attributes. In turn he meets his death through an encounter with a love-making machine. The sexuality of Duchamp's work is less Rabelaisian than that of Jarry, and it was to become increasingly veiled and allusive, but he shared with Jarry a sardonic, quizzical approach to the subject and it seems likely that he derived stimulation from the work of a writer who more than any other figure of his generation formed a bridge between French literature of the nineteenth century and its subsequent manifestations in the twentieth.

The calligraphic draughtsmanship evolved by Duchamp in his studies for the *King and Queen* which had resulted in the final work in a freer, more 'overall' kind of composition and the frankly mechanomorphic imagery of the final painting, were features that were carried a step further in a remarkable series of works executed in Munich in the late summer of the same year, 1912. Two *Virgin* drawings and a little sketch which can in some ways be considered the first step towards *The Large Glass* preceded the two important oil paintings. *Virgin No. 2*, stylistically the loosest and freest and perhaps the last of the drawings to be executed, appears to have been derived from a much more naturalistic oil sketch of the previous year, *Apropos of Little Sister* (The Solomon R. Guggenheim Museum, New York), posed for by his sister Magdeleine. And if the technological origins of the *Bride* go back to the sketchy accompaniment to *Encore à Cet Astre*, this small oil sketch of his sister is the *Bride*'s most direct antecedent physically and psychologically. For in the pivotal oil painting which followed the *Virgin* drawings, the momentous *Passage from the Virgin to the Bride* (the Museum of Modern Art, New York), we witness her metamorphosis into the *Bride* herself.

The theme of sexual initiation and the psychological transposition it involves was one which had been hinted at in several works of 1911, most notably in *The Thicket*, a work finished in the early weeks of that year. It shows a heavy, mature woman who places her hand on the head of a younger, slender, virginal sister who seems to expose herself willingly to the gaze of some powerful, unseen male presence. The poses of the figures appear to have been borrowed from traditional presentation panels (often wings of altarpieces), where saints present a donor to some divinity, and there is a stylistic debt to Girieud, a now forgotten painter whom Duchamp admired.

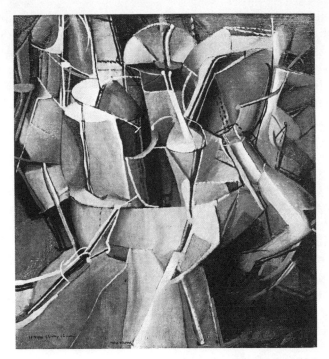

Duchamp, *Passage from the Virgin to the Bride*, 1912

The Thicket is in many ways an unsatisfactory painting; and like many other early works it suggests that Duchamp's natural talents were not primarily pictorial. A comparison with the wittily accomplished *The Bride Stripped Bare by the Bachelors* (Codier Ekstrum, New York), which probably preceded the two *Virgin* drawings, shows how far he had travelled in an astonishingly short time, both in terms of the formulation of an independent, emancipated iconography and a convincing style in which to render it. *The Thicket* still belongs fundamentally to the esoteric world of 1890s Symbolism. The Munich sketch is a totally independent statement.

In *The Bride Stripped Bare by the Bachelors* the composition is dominated by a slender female figure, the lower part of her body encased in a large cylindrical form; subsequently this was to become for Duchamp the graphic symbol of the female genitals although here it seems to act as a shield or corset, while at the *Bride*'s feet an inscription reads *Mécanique de la pudeur, pudeur mécanique*. On either side are two science-fiction male presences who point at the bridal figure a whole battery of upright phallic forms; the fact that these appear to have been derived from chronophotographs of fencers to which Duchamp once referred specifically in an interview (the successive images of the fencing foil have become the phallic barbs), accounts perhaps for some of the sadistic flavour that underlies the brilliant, mocking draughtsmanship.

Duchamp appears to have found the imagery of the drawing too explicit, and in the *Passage from the Virgin to the Bride*, the first of the Munich oils, the forms have become much more hermetic, and indeed the presence of a few relatively naturalistic members at the bottom right (a clearly legible arm attached to a headless neck) would suggest that we are not intended to 'read' the rest of the picture naturalistically or to identify its component parts in terms of specific body imagery. The forms at the left of the painting do, however, relate to the forms of *Virgin No. 2* (and also to those of the left-hand-side figure in the *King and Queen*), and shapes suggestive of an upflung arm at the top right indicate the presence of a second figure leaning back in an abandoned or satiated attitude. The cylinder that had encased the bridal figure in the drawing is now placed in the centre of the canvas as a clue to the picture's meaning, while the presence at the lower right appears to act as a witness to the ritual (it fulfils much the same function and also relates in its placing in the composition to the *Oculist Witnesses* in the *Large Glass*) and projects a strong male aura. Chronophotography had played an important role in the first sketches for the *King and Queen* and in the Munich *Bride Stripped Bare* drawing, but here there is no hint of the earlier cinematic technique and the idea of motion in terms of physical energy has been replaced by the concept of motion as the change from one psychological state of being to another, or to use a phrase employed by the painter Matta, Duchamp's art is now about the 'process of becoming'.

The final painting in the Munich series is *The Bride* herself. And having passed through the hermetic ritual of initiation she is allowed to regain a semblance of anatomical legibility; shoulder, arm and breast seem to fall naturally into place and these in turn allow us to reconstruct the empty armature of the head. The pose comes very close to that of Picasso's *Fanny Tellier* of 1910 (Museum of Modern Art, New York), one of the most celebrated of his canvases and a work which Duchamp may have known. The similarities are most probably fortuitous but a comparison of the two works serves to remind us that *The Bride* still relates at a distance to the world of Cubism and also to underline how completely mechanized Duchamp's vision has become. *The Bride* resembles nothing so much as a dressmaker's dummy stripped to its metal armature. Duchamp once remarked that she had her genesis in the figures to be seen in fair grounds, often given the attributes of bride and groom, at which visitors are invited to throw wooden balls.[12]

The dressmaker's dummy had in fact appeared in Duchamp's art in one of the cartoons of 1909, many of which are startlingly prophetic in their iconography.[13] In one of them, *Mi-Carême* (The Mary Sister Collection, New York), the standing woman is paired off against her headless, inanimate counterpart, while the wheel of the sewing machine acts as a displaced halo for the kneeling figure. In *The Bride* the 'sex' cylinder dominates once more the centre of the composition, now attached to the figure's head (a disquieting device which points forward to the displacement of the sexual organs found so frequently in Surrealist art), suggesting perhaps that sexual fantasies are the product of the mind and can be a form of intellectual as well as physical activity; in the same way one of the studies for the *Chess Players* of 1911 had shown the players' heads and arms enclosed by two larger heads (symbolized by their noses, which touch), an attempt to render graphically the idea that the true game is being played in the players' minds and not in the movement of their hands across the board. Above, to the left of *The Bride*, hangs a cylindrical form which extends mechanical tentacles towards her and evokes some of the same sadistic, science-fiction overtones conveyed by the male presences in *The Bride Stripped Bare by the Bachelors*.

The extraordinary originality of *The King and Queen Surrounded by Swift Nudes* and of the Munich series owes a great deal to a new range of intellectual and personal encounters which were conditioning Duchamp's artistic evolution. Duchamp had met Francis Picabia at the *Salon d'Automne* of 1911 and a friendship between the two men was soon struck up. Duchamp enjoyed Picabia's anarchistic sense of humour and he later observed that Picabia had been to a large extent instrumental in detaching him from the somewhat solemn world of Puteaux, where the problems of contemporary painting were discussed in serious, often highly theoretical terms.[14] Picabia's *Je Revois en Souvenir Ma Chère Udnie* of 1914 (the

Museum of Modern Art, New York), a work showing a marked influence from Duchamp, gives some idea of what the *Bride Stripped Bare by her Bachelors, Even* might have looked like had Duchamp executed it on canvas as he originally intended. Through Picabia Duchamp also often found himself in the company of Apollinaire, and although he later spoke of the poet somewhat dismissively he cannot have failed to find his company stimulating. In 1912 Duchamp took a trip with his new friends to the district in the Jura Mountains known as Zone (Apollinaire was to use the word as the title for one of his most beautiful poems), an important event in the annals of Dada since it brought together in a concentrated form the personal ingredients that were to create such a strongly proto-Dada climate in Paris during succeeding years. On the holiday Duchamp conceived his idea for the *Jura–Paris Road*, for which the original notes still exist although the work itself was never carried out; it was to have been a two-sided panel with the *Chef des Cinq Nus* (a play on the words '*seins nus*' or naked breasts) on the one side and on the other, executed in nickel and platinum, the *Enfant Phare* or *Headlight Child* (a pun on 'fanfare'). Later, in New York, Duchamp paid his poet friend a tribute by his altered ready-made *Apolinère Enameled* of 1916–17. It may have been Apollinaire who introduced Duchamp to the work of Brisset, an eccentric who had made a personal, not to say fantastical, scientific analysis of language, and whose influence Duchamp acknowledged.

Brisset felt that similar sounding words in both French and other languages really meant the same thing, a belief that led him to many bizarre and engaging conclusions (he felt, for example, that because of the similarity in sound between the word 'sexe' and the phrase 'qu'est ce que c'est que ça' he could deduce primitive man's emotions on the discovery of his reproductive organs). Brisset was acclaimed by Duchamp's writer friends as the Douanier Rousseau of contemporary literature, and just as the painters had staged a banquet for Rousseau, so the writers arranged a ceremony to honour Brisset; this took place, appropriately enough, under the statue of Rodin's *Thinker*. Duchamp was amused by Brisset's inventiveness, and his own experiments with language which were to complement increasingly his production in the visual field owe a little to the genial philologist's work.

Most important of all, however, was Duchamp's discovery of the work of Raymond Roussel, when he attended together with Picabia and Apollinaire a performance of Roussel's *Impressions d'Afrique*, an encounter that was to have, as Duchamp frequently stressed, a decisive effect on his art. The play was first staged at the Théâtre Fémina at the end of February 1911 where it ran only for a week, although it was revived at the Théâtre Antoine in May of the following year and played for some four weeks.[15] The work was originally conceived as a novel and appeared first in serialized form. *Impressions d'Afrique* could perhaps be best described as a latter-day science-fiction *Salammbô*. It is concerned with the adventures of a motley assortment of characters, shipwrecked on the shores of Africa, and half the book is devoted to describing a series of theatrical turns and displays of skill staged by the castaways to entertain themselves and their native captors, who also join in the proceedings. In its dramatic form the work was somewhat modified, and the more far-fetched of Roussel's startling inventions were obviously not practically realizable, but one suspects that Duchamp may well have been drawn to the work partly because he was entertained by the way in which the preposterous science-fiction happenings were reduced to absurdity by the equipment of a conventional Paris theatre. Later he said, 'I realized at once that I could use Roussel as an influence. I felt that as a painter it was much better to be influenced by a writer than by another painter. And Roussel showed me the way.'[16]

Reading Roussel's work with Duchamp's art in mind there are a startling number of iconographical and technical analogies between the two men's work. To begin with there is Roussel's obsession with the machine and with the human-machine analogy; one of the characters in *Impressions d'Afrique*, for example, is a woman called Louise Montalescot who breathes through a number of fine metal tubes concealed in the epaulettes of the military costume she affects, and who invents a painting machine. Some of Roussel's machines look like machines but perform human functions. A description of one of them immediately calls Duchamp's Munich series to mind: 'The work was mounted on a sort of mill-stone which, worked by a pedal, could put into motion a whole system of wheels, rods, levers and springs, which formed an inextricable metallic tangle; on one side was attached an articulated arm ending in a hand clasping a fencing foil.' Other machines perform totally fantastic, pseudo-scientific functions and one is frequently reminded that Jules Verne was Roussel's favourite author. Throughout there is a fascination with transparent, glassy, gelatinous materials. Despite its weird fantasy the book is written in a deliberately straightforward, almost prosaic, matter-of-fact style, and the play was apparently performed in this way; accounts of the production survive.

In his posthumous book *Comment j'ai Ecrit mes Livres*, which appeared in 1935, two years after his death, Roussel described how random phrases or slogans (the name and address of his bootmaker for instance), slightly altered or added to, could form the basis of a story or a poem. Another favourite technique was the arbitrary bringing together of disparate images or phrases and the subsequent formulation of relationships between them on as realistic a plane as possible. Frequently he would select two words identical in their composition except for a single letter. These words would then be put in identical sentences: one would introduce a story or a poem and the second would conclude it, so that the intervening composition or plot involved a great deal of ingenious intellectual acrobatics in order to link the two. In a sense Roussel's works are often simply gigantic puns, governed by a crazy but inexorable logic. The whole idea of *Impressions d'Afrique* was born, he tells us, out of the similarity in sound between the words 'billiard' and 'pilliard'. The pun was to become fundamental to much of Duchamp's work and often his visual images were the result of an attempt to give concrete, tangible expression to concepts that were purely linguistic. In *Impressions d'Afrique*, as in Roussel's other work, there is a deep fascination with transvestism, which can perhaps be regarded as an extension of the hermaphrodism which preoccupied so many of the Symbolist writers, and which was in turn to obsess the Surrealists. Duchamp, too, was curious to explore the borderlines of male and female sexuality and in the 1920s was to adopt a feminine pseudonym, while a collage of 1921, *Belle Haleine, Eau de Voilette*, incorporates a photograph of Duchamp disguised as a woman.

Analysing Roussel's work Michel Leiris has written: 'Aiming at an almost total detachment from everything that is nature, feeling and humanity, and working laboriously over materials apparently so gratuitous that they were not suspect to him Roussel arrived at the creation of an authentic myth.'[17] The statement might equally well be applied to Duchamp. And the comments of Roussel's distinguished analyst, Doctor Pierre Janet, are also worth recording for the indirect light they shed on Duchamp's approach. Janet writes,

'Roussel has an interesting concept of literary beauty. The work must contain nothing real, no observations on the world or the mind; nothing but completely imaginary combinations. These are already the ideas of an extra human world.'[18] Duchamp was later to stress that Roussel was important to him because of the attitude embodied in his work rather than for any concrete or visually demonstrable influence that Roussel's work had upon his own. And he was right; the significance of Roussel for him lay in the fact that the writer suggested to him the possibilities of working out his fantasies and his obsessions by the creation of abstract or dehumanized and intellectual symbols which could be manipulated verbally and visually in such a way that they would not offend his deeply fastidious sensibilities. In what is perhaps the most revealing aside he ever made Duchamp once remarked, quite simply, 'It is better to project into machines than to take it out on people.'[19]

The *Bride* marks the culminating point of the first stage in the creation of the Duchamp myth. Her transference to *The Large Glass* is fairly straightforward although she has become, as Duchamp remarks in one of the notes of the *Green Box*, more skeletal. At her base, we learn, 'is a reservoir of love gasoline (or timid-power) distributed to the motor with quite feeble cylinders'. It is interesting to speculate as to whether the motor and the reservoir have been incorporated into the forms we actually see, but in the last analysis such speculation is irrelevant for these concepts may equally well be simply embedded in the transparent glass which surrounds the bridal figure. The motor emits 'artificial sparks' which bring about her threefold blossoming or stripping. One of these appears to take place in her mind, and there is more than a suggestion that it leads to an auto-erotic climax. The second blossoming takes the form of messages she emits to her bachelors through the 'inscription on the top', whose three openings correspond to the treble blossoming. These messages in turn excite the bachelors to attempt the stripping which they partially achieve (the *Bride*'s dress, originally represented by a thin strip of glass, now rests invisibly below her on the boundaries between the two glass panels), but which they lack the freedom and vitality to pursue to its ultimate conclusions. The third stripping appears to be a combination of the other two.

The *Bride* is a slightly absurd character, and she is not particularly likeable; she is a bitch, a tease and a flirt. But she shines with the pale, impersonal beauty of some primeval moon goddess, and she carries about her an air of authority that springs from the fact that she recognizes herself as the true descendant of Flaubert's *Salammbô*, of Villier de L'Isle Adam's *Axel* and his *Eve Future*, of Mallarmé's *Hérodiade* and perhaps most immediately of Laforgue's *Salomé*. What distinguishes the *Bride* from these women of nineteenth-century fiction is her mordant sense of humour and above all her acute degree of self-knowledge. She is aware of her own absurdity and although she flaunts her sexuality so blatantly she is prepared to acknowledge its underlying frigidity. And like Mallarmé's swan in *Le Vierge, le Vivace et le Bel Aujourd'hui*, which gazes disdainfully around itself as the icy waters of the lake close in upon it, depriving it of its bodily functions, the *Bride*, in her glassy cage, miraculously preserves her dignity.

2 The Bachelors

It is one of the paradoxes of Duchamp's career (and indeed his is a career that can only be understood in terms of paradox) that while he was searching for technical solutions which would ensure the permanence of a work which was becoming increasingly ambitious iconographically and experimental in its means, he should have produced simultaneously a series of works of a highly ephemeral nature, which at the time of their creation were almost certainly not intended for posterity. These were his celebrated 'ready-mades', the objects which will perhaps prove to have been his most important contribution to the creation of a particular aesthetic climate which has conditioned a very considerable amount of subsequent artistic production. The *Bride* retained certain visual links with the world of Cubism. The *Bachelors* on the other hand belong to the world of the ready-made.

The ready-made can perhaps best be described as an object in the material, external world, most often a manufactured object, which the artist by virtue of the attention he turns upon it elevates to the symbolic status of a work of art. Its selection is obviously not a random affair and Duchamp has described his coming together with these objects as 'a kind of rendezvous'. Duchamp realized too that for the ready-made to retain its power to force upon the recipient or viewer a reappraisal of intellectual and aesthetic values it must retain a quality of rarity and he deliberately limited his output. The techniques employed in the selection or production of Duchamp's ready-mades were varied. An object could be selected on the spur of the moment but it could also be conceived in advance – a note in the *Green Box*, for example, reads 'buy a pair of tongs as a ready-made'. The ready-made could also be produced by proxy, and in 1919 Duchamp's sister Suzanne produced in Paris the *Unhappy Ready-Made*, a geometry textbook fastened to a balcony, on instructions sent to her by Duchamp from Buenos Aires. Duchamp also conceived the possibility of a reciprocal ready-made: 'Use a Rembrandt as an ironing board.' Finally there was the assisted ready-made, less pure but capable of wider psychological interpretation and for this reason the form of ready-made most venerated by the Surrealists. One of the most celebrated of these, *Why Not Sneeze?*, executed in New York in 1921, consists of small marble blocks (resembling lumps of sugar), a cuttle bone and a thermometer, all placed in a small bird cage.

Because we have lived so long with the awareness or knowledge of Duchamp's ready-mades, they have assumed an endearing familiarity to our eyes, and it is perhaps proof of their importance that history has seen fit to present the concepts embodied in them in different ways to successive generations of artists and intellectuals. Originally, however, they were conceived by Duchamp as a form of communication devoid of aesthetic enjoyment, and in later life he remarked on the fact that one of the difficulties in the creation of a ready-made lay precisely in finding objects which possessed no formally pleasing properties to the eye.[20] The original ready-mades were, furthermore, gestures of revolt against accepted artistic canons, and in many ways the most selfconsciously iconoclastic act that any artist had yet made. Because the gesture was made by an artist of stature the objects which were touched by him intellectually and physically (many of the ready-mades, such as the *Trap*, for example, a coat-rack nailed to the floor, depended on their positioning for their impact) acquired by proxy an aesthetic significance, not so much because of the aesthetic qualities unexpectedly revealed in them as by virtue of the aesthetic questions they raised. By subjecting objects to a dislocation from their normal function and material context, Duchamp forces us to look at them in a new way. In the same way the '*dépaysement*' to which the Symbolist poets subjected words in an attempt to liberate in them some hidden meaning (Maeterlinck's is perhaps the most extreme case) endowed them with certain magical qualities. The difference lies in the fact that the ready-mades are deliberately devoid of poetry. They are incantatory objects devoid of cant. Subsequently Duchamp appears to have come to view the ready-mades as works of art, just as he admitted that by seeking to be as unpoetic as possible he was secretly hoping to create poetry of a new kind, and from the start he seems to have recognized their importance. But their value lay originally in the 'higher degree of intellectuality' they represented and not in the beauty of their forms or the aesthetic pleasure embodied in the gesture that produced them.

Ultimately Duchamp was to reject the term 'anti-art' which he felt implied too positive an aesthetic attitude. He said, 'The word anti-art annoys me a little, because whether you are anti or for, it's two sides of the same thing.'[21] And indeed what isolates him from the most characteristically Dada artists is precisely the passivity of his approach. 'Irony,' he once remarked, 'is the playfulness of accepting something, mine is the irony of indifference.'[22] And again, 'While Dada was a movement of negation and, by the very fact of its negation, turned itself into an appendage of the exact thing it was negating, Picabia and I wanted to open up a corridor of humour which at once led into dream-imagery and, consequently, into Surrealism.'[23] In fact Duchamp's attitude towards Surrealism was basically the same as his attitude towards Dada. In both cases he had been a precursor and an important influence. He once said of Dada that it represented a sort of nihilism that he continued to find very sympathetic,[24] but at the same time he must have been slightly repelled by its aggressive earnestness. One suspects that he found Dada techniques lacking in subtlety, while in the same way he gracefully divorced himself from the conclusions of Surrealism when these became too programmatic and when the movement's aims involuntarily but inevitably hardened into a positive aesthetic. His own art was neither one of affirmation nor rejection, and his iconoclasm was one of sublimation and gentleness.

In a sense the ready-mades represent the culmination of a Symbolist aesthetic. Mallarmé, haunted by 'the demon of analogy', sought constantly to distance his images by substituting others which would convey similar ideas and sensations in a more allusive and suggestive way; his poems are works of art, deliberately hermetic, but immediately recognizable as such. It could be argued that Duchamp takes Mallarmé's aesthetic through to its ultimate conclusions by finding a substitute for the work of art itself. For the veiled allusions of the Symbolists, for the layers of meaning disguised in ever paler tints and so often tinged with mysticism, Duchamp substitutes, quite simply, a technique of paradox. In other words, while Mallarmé distances his image from its description by an ever-widening gulf of analogies, Duchamp produces much the same effect by an immediate short circuit of our preconceived notions about the nature of art and of the creative act. Although he was consciously trying to produce an art more purely cerebral in its conception than that of any of his contemporaries, as he was at pains to stress, he rejected the rational just as he rejected the natural, and to come to an appreciation of it the spectator must accept, as such, the paradoxes it involves.

Duchamp's first ready-mades are highly attractive as objects, although they may have seemed less immediately so to the eyes of his contemporaries. Of the *Bicycle Wheel* which in 1913 he had mounted on a white stool and placed in his studio, Duchamp later said, 'It just came about as a pleasure, something to have in my room the way you have a fire . . . except that there was no usefulness. It was a pleasant gadget, pleasant for the movement it gave.'[25] But as the idea of the ready-made developed, its connotations tended to become blacker and more disturbing and at the same time more humorous. The first ready-made to be produced after Duchamp's arrival in New York was a snow shovel entitled *In Advance of the Broken Arm* (implying that the user of the shovel may well encounter some hard, hostile substance buried under the soft snow), and this was succeeded in following years by such works as the celebrated urinal or *Fountain*, signed by R. Mutt and submitted to the New York *Indépendents* of 1917: a brief article in *Blind Man* defended the work in words which bear the imprint of Duchamp's mind: 'Whether Mr Mutt with his own hands made the fountain or not has no importance, he CHOSE it. He took an ordinary article of life, placed it so that its useful significance disappeared under the new title and point of view – created a new thought for that object.'[26] Since *Sad Young Man on a Train* of 1911 titles had played an important part in Duchamp's work (he was amused by the combination of the sounds 'triste' and 'train')[27] and now they often become an essential ingredient if the ready-made is to achieve its full significance or effect – this is true, for example, of the snow shovel – and generally speaking they tend to become more elaborate in their

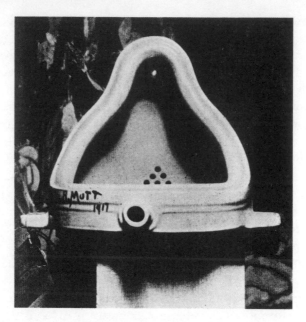

Duchamp, *Fountain*, 1917

conception. Duchamp's puns or 'verbal ready-mades' also become increasingly sophisticated and are often applied to 'assisted' ready-mades as titles. Some of these are in French and some in English and they are for obvious reasons not always translatable. This is true even in the case of *The Large Glass* itself, for in French the 'même' of the title when spoken can be interpreted as 'm'aime' or as the fact that the Bride 'loves me'.

The studies for the lower half of *The Large Glass*, or for the *Bachelor Apparatus*, and its subsequent inclusion in the work itself, introduce a further dimension into Duchamp's doctrine of paradox in that having transformed everyday objects of common usage into artefacts having artistic connotations, Duchamp was simultaneously rendering comparable objects in a painstakingly realistic or illusionistic technique. The machines of the *Bachelor Apparatus* (the *Chocolate Grinder* and the *Water Mill*) resemble the earliest ready-mades in that they have an undeniable formal elegance, although not surprisingly (since the iconography is so elaborately plotted) they also anticipate the complexity of later examples. As a prelude to the *Bachelor* machines Duchamp had executed the

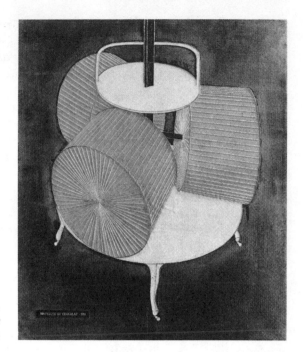

**Duchamp,
*The Chocolate
Grinder No. 2*, 1914**

delightfully witty *Coffee Mill* (Collection Mrs Robin Jones, Rio de
Janeiro), towards the end of 1911 as part of a light-hearted decorative
scheme for the kitchen of one of his brothers, a work of great
importance in that it expresses, more clearly than anything
Duchamp had hitherto produced, his fascination with the artistic
possibilities of the machine. The work parodies in a schematic
fashion the Cubists' use of a variable viewpoint, while the handle is
shown in successive motion, completed by a diagrammatic arrow;
the coffee is fed into the machine to the left of the painting and falls
(invisibly) into the drawer at the bottom, an element which still calls
to mind similar compositional devices in still lifes by Cézanne and
the Cubists. In *The Chocolate Grinder* of 1913, the first element
of the bachelor apparatus to reach concrete expression, the raw
material (the chocolate) is significantly absent and the object has
acquired an hieratic, symbolic quality which results in part from the
fact that it is divorced from its functional aspect (the ridges which
the rollers of the original, glimpsed in a confectioner's shop window
in Rouen, must have possessed in order to grip the chocolate are
missing) so that the machine is static, impotent and chocolateless.

Duchamp: *The Large Glass*

The icon-like quality is further heightened by the fact that the work is painted with a high degree of realism and in a technique of immaculate precision. Already in the *King and Queen* and in the Munich paintings Duchamp's manner had become increasingly impersonal with the paint smoothed and rubbed on to the canvas to eliminate the physical traces left by the painter's brush. Now, in *The Chocolate Grinder*, the drawing has become totally mechanical and in the process Duchamp's line has acquired a hard, spare elegance which was to be a characteristic of all the elements in the lower half of *The Large Glass*. 'I wanted to return to an absolutely dry drawing, to the creation of a dry art,' Duchamp later said, 'and what better example of this new art than mechanical drawing. I began to appreciate the value of exactitude and precision.'[28] Colour, too, has acquired a new metallic hardness.

The Cubist multiple viewpoint perspective, so wittily mocked in the *Coffee Mill*, has been replaced in *The Chocolate Grinder* by an extraordinarily skilful and lucid reversion to a traditional single viewpoint system, applied with a rigour and seriousness that recalls the art of the Quattrocento; and indeed Duchamp later came to consider that one of his most important innovations in art was the reintroduction of traditional Classical and Renaissance perspective into Post-Cubist art. A second version of *The Chocolate Grinder* emphasizes the perspectival element still further by the addition of the ridges of the rollers, achieved by the device of threading string through the canvas (the first version of the painting was to be, with one important exception, Duchamp's last essay in pure oil painting). In the first version the aggressive three-dimensionality of the machine had been counterbalanced by the adoption of a high, Cézannesque viewpoint, and by the suppression of recessive elements around the machine. In the second canvas the background has become totally flat, forcing the illusionistically rendered forms up on to the two-dimensional support, and giving them a curiously heightened air of reality. The burnished, metallic colour of the earlier version has given way, too, to harmonics that are more impersonally elegant. Within the context of *The Large Glass*, *The Chocolate Grinder*, as the notes from the *Green Box* make clear, is the symbol for the male genitals, and hence the counterpart of the bridal sex cylinder, and it occupies compositionally and symbolically much the same position in *The Large Glass* as the latter had done in the *Passage from the Virgin to the Bride*. The active role it plays in the mechanics of the *Glass* is relatively small, but it dominates the composition both by virtue of its size and by its positioning, just off centre. And once we become aware of its significance it assumes the role of a modern totem that acts as a key to the symbolism of the work as a whole.

The *Bride* is partnered not by *The Chocolate Grinder*, but by the *Nine Malic Moulds*, her bachelors, the malic of the title being, presumably, an 'adjustment' of the word 'phallic'. A definitive model on glass was executed in Paris during 1914–15. The *Malic Moulds* have their origins most directly in the robot-like apparitions flanking the bridal figure in the first Munich sketch. The number of suitors was first of all extended to eight (in a preparatory drawing) and finally to nine, 'a mathematically more agile number'. Two preparatory studies in pencil are entitled *Cemetery of Uniforms and Liveries*, and a written key to the side of the first of these enables us to identify the individual moulds in terms of their 'uniforms' as a priest, an undertaker, a policeman and so on. They are 'provisionally painted with red lead', the *Green Box* tells us, 'while waiting for each one to receive its colours, like croquet mallets'. They are hollow (the idea of the body as an empty vessel capable of receiving other substances into it was one that obsessed Duchamp from the start; for example in *Dimanches*, one of the cartoons of 1909, a young woman, obviously pregnant, pushes a pram carrying a baby thus unequivocally making a parallel between her body and the machine/container) and are destined to receive the 'illuminating gas' transmitted to them from the *Bride*'s inscription at the top. The progenitors of the moulds in the Munich sketch had bristled with phallic menace but the *Bachelors* wait passively for an erotic fulfilment which they are eventually forced to carry out on themselves: 'The bachelor grinds his chocolate himself.' The reasons for the *Bride*'s insistence on multiple partners are obscure, but her suitors perform the function of mechanical spare parts and they contribute to the sensation, cardinal to Duchamp's vision, that many possibilities are open even if none of them can lead to a definitive or totally satisfactory outcome.[29]

The first work to be executed on glass was not the *Malic Moulds* but the *Glider Containing a Water Mill (in neighbouring metals)*, begun in 1913 but finished (like the *Moulds*) in 1915 before Duchamp's departure for America; the *Glider* is unique in that of all the works on glass it alone remains unbroken. The main reason for

Duchamp: *The Large Glass*

Duchamp's adoption of glass as a support or vehicle was the result of a characteristic balance of visual stimulation and curiosity, supplemented by more purely abstract, speculative concerns. These dual aspects of artistic creativity are present in the production of all painting and sculpture, although in Duchamp's case the mind informs the eye to an unusually pronounced degree. In preceding years he had made use of a glass palette, and he had been struck by the brilliance and luminosity of pigment viewed through glass and by the fact that pressed up against the rigid, mechanically achieved surface the paint acquired a quality of impersonal perfection which he realized could ideally complement the dry, disciplined and exact form of draughtsmanship which he had achieved for the first time in *The Chocolate Grinder*. He was also intrigued by the idea that if the paint could be sealed off from behind it would not oxidize and would retain its pristine brilliance; this he achieved by pressing on to the wet paint (from behind) a layer of lead foil which isolated it from contact with the air about it. As Richard Hamilton remarks, 'The techniques of glass painting were directed at permanence.'[30] Then again glass offered an alternative to traditional canvas and stretchers and hence helped to get him away from the physicality of 'olefactory' art. A note in the *Green Box* suggests *Delay in Glass* as a 'kind of subtitle' to be thought of 'as you would say "poem in prose" or a spittoon in silver'.

During the years when Duchamp had worked with the traditional materials of the painter he had revealed himself as a painter of images, and of images whose relationship to their backgrounds and to the space around them was occasionally irrelevant and always of secondary importance, a factor that had from the start separated his concerns from those of the Cubists, who were interested in the concept of objects embedded in a spatial continuum or flux that was as pictorially significant as the objects themselves. In some works of 1911 the background had proved almost a source of irritation or embarrassment to Duchamp, who had in two instances simply painted in wide black borders at the sides of the canvas to obviate the necessity of working out a convincing background space for his images.[31] He once remarked, 'The question of painting in a background is degrading for a painter. The thing you want to express is not in the background.'[32] An image embedded in clear glass, on the other hand, accepts whatever background its situation cares to impose on it: 'with glass you can concentrate on the figure'.[33] In

294

view of Duchamp's subsequent statements about the role played by the spectator in completing for himself the inevitably imperfectly realized work of art (for he believed that between the artist's conception of a work of art and its physical realization a gap must necessarily exist) he may have been unconsciously attracted by the idea that when studying a work of art executed on glass the viewer would see himself and his surroundings to a certain extent mirrored in the object of his contemplation, thus involving a further degree of participation on his part. Jarry, in his experiments with the theatre, had toyed with the idea of a mirror backdrop which would reflect the audience behind the players' backs, thus forcing it to confront itself as part of the reality of the drama it was witnessing, and in a less extreme fashion a similar idea may have been at the back of Duchamp's mind.

Of all the elements that compose the *Bachelor Apparatus*, the *Glider* (also referred to as the 'sleigh' or 'slide' or 'chariot') approximates most closely the sort of devices found in the writings of Jarry and Roussel. One of the features of their science fiction (particularly of Roussel's) is that it is not on the whole mechanically and technologically visionary; rather it is the most ordinary objects that are made to perform the most extraordinary tasks. So too Duchamp's machines are mostly old-fashioned and out-of-date: the watermill is a relic of the nineteenth century as is the chocolate grinder. The difference between Duchamp's work and that of Roussel is that the marvels that the machines would have been made to perform in the latter's writings take place, if at all, in the case of Duchamp's art in the spectator's mind (although the *Green Box* conveys a great deal of supplementary if at times contradictory material). In *The Large Glass*, the *Glider* or *Chariot* is put into motion partly by an imaginary waterfall which strikes the *Water Mill* 'from behind the *Malic Moulds*', but more directly by a hook or weight (invisible) which falls between the *Glider* and the *Grinder* and which is 'made of a substance of oscillating density'; at one point a bottle of benedictine is suggested as an alternative. The *Glider* moves back and forth in a plane parallel to that of the glass surface. The function it plays in the overall action of *The Large Glass* is complex but, as will be seen, basically anti-climactic. In their first full incarnation the *Water Mill* and its *Glider* were inscribed on a semicircular piece of glass, bound by metal and now hinged to a wall of the Philadelphia Museum of Art. Thus for all the complicated engineering described in the *Green Box*, the movement the apparatus is allowed is one that the spectator imposes on it as he swings the glass semicircle back and forth on the axis of its supports. Its placing, next to *The Large Glass*, adds to the sense of involvement.

The complexity or intricacy of the forms of the *Water Mill* in the *Glider* demonstrate more than any other single element in *The Large Glass* Duchamp's virtuosity in the manipulation of complex effects of recession or foreshortening, and indeed the layout of the lower half of the *Glass* represents a unique perspectival *tour de force*. By the end of 1913 both plan and elevation for the *Bachelor Apparatus* were fully formulated in such a way that, to quote Richard Hamilton, 'The perspective projection onto the glass is an ideal demonstration of classical perspective, that is to say, the elements of the bachelor apparatus were first imagined as distributed on the floor behind the glass rather than as a composition on a two-dimensional surface.'[34] In fact the mathematical calculations involved in the perspectival projection, though impressive in their combined complexity and lucidity, are, as Hamilton points out, highly personal. And the spatial effect produced by the lower half of the *Glass* is ambiguous and hard to analyse. The perspectival lines all converge to an horizon that lies along the line where upper and lower panels touch. Given an effort of will on the spectator's part the various parts of the *Bachelor Apparatus* can be made to sit convincingly in this ideal illusionary space. The sensation of recession towards an horizon, however, is counteracted by the fact that forms and lines glimpsed through the glass (the line of a skirting board, for example) inevitably destroy the ideal mental projection of space, while an awareness of the *Glass*'s flatness, undestroyed and undisturbed in the areas around the various male elements, constantly forces even the most recessive and aggressively three-dimensional parts (the *Glider* and the *Chocolate Grinder*) to measure themselves up to the rigidly two-dimensional surface on which they are encrusted. We can force them back into depth and space by an effort of intellectual and visual will but they swim forward again to float, icon-like, on their glassy support.

It is characteristic of Duchamp's approach that while he was mastering various systems of scentific calculation with a view towards producing his own highly personal method of perspectival notation (in certain cases he toyed with the idea of using novel photographic procedures), he should simultaneously have been undermining the scientific basis of his art by informing it with what could perhaps best be called a sort of 'crazy mathematics', closer in many ways to Jarry's 'pataphysics' (described in *Dr Faustroll* of 1911 as the 'science of imaginary solutions') than to Pavlowski's interpretations of the fourth dimension which he was studying at the time. There had for some time been a certain amount of talk of the fourth dimension in Cubist circles though it is doubtful if any of the painters, with the possible exception of Gris, were seriously influenced by any very sophisticated or revolutionary scientific or mathematical systems of calculation. Duchamp, more than any other artist of his generation, had the bent of mind and the intellect to come to grips with the discoveries of science, and he was a friend of the amateur mathematician Maurice Princet, who was said to have introduced the subject of the fourth dimension into Cubist gatherings. But Duchamp's definition of the concept, when he formulated it, reflected his basic mistrust of science and was a characteristic blend of the ironically playful and the philosophically profound. There was no reason, he suggested, why three-dimensional objects could not be considered as the flat shadows or reflections of the fourth dimension, invisible because it could never be seen by the human eye. *The Large Glass*, he was to insist, was just such a projection of a four-dimensional object: 'the apparition of an appearance'.

One of the works to which Duchamp was particularly attached, and which more than any other single product of his art qualifies as 'pataphysical', is the *Three Standard Stoppages* of 1913. Three threads, each a metre long, were dropped from the height of a metre on to canvases stained with Prussian blue. The threads, which had taken on different configurations in the process of their descent, were then fixed to the canvases with drops of varnish, and the canvases were cut out of the stretchers and glued on to long, thin sheets of plate glass. Subsequently wooden templates or rulers were cut to conform to the three different curves, and these random curves were used to achieve the 'capillary tubes' which serve in *The Large Glass* as methods of communication between the *Malic Moulds* and the *Sieves* or *Parasols*, the forms that arch their way over the *Chocolate Grinder*; their final form is perspectively achieved from the *Network of Stoppages*, a plan view in which each of the curves was used three times, an elaborate solution to a problem which the uninitiated might suppose could have been resolved by a freehand sketch.

From a technical point of view, the *Sieves*, the *Oculist Witnesses*, the *Nine Shots*, and the *Inscription for the Top* were achieved in different ways from the other elements in *The Large Glass*. The *Sieves* are outlined, like almost all the other main elements, in lead wire, but they are coloured not with paint but with dust. The lower half of *The Large Glass* was laid face downwards on the floor, dust was allowed to accumulate for several months, and was fixed on to the *Sieves* with mastic varnish (one is reminded of Leonardo's projects for using dust as a measure of time). The forms of the *Oculist Witnesses*, the only part of *The Large Glass* which doesn't figure in the original plans, and which relate closely to an important work of 1918, *To Be Looked at (from the Other Side of the Glass) with One Eye, Close to, for Almost an Hour* (Museum of Modern Art, New York), were taken from charts used by opticians (called in French *témoins oculistes*) and put into perspective: a drawing was done on carbon paper, transferred on to a silvered area, while the silver was subsequently scraped away from between the lines to leave behind the images; originally a magnifying glass was to have been embedded in the plate glass nearby to focus the 'splashes' (invisible). The *Oculist Witnesses* serves to involve the spectator in the mechanics of *The Large Glass*: we feel ourselves placed at the central axis of the ascending circular forms which are just below the level of our heads and shoulders – so that as in Alberti's ideal perspective both the beholder and the painted things he sees will appear to be on the same plane. The *Shots*, just below and to the right of the *Inscription for the Top*, were produced by firing matches dipped in paint from a toy cannon; the holes were then bored through. The forms of the three draft pistons which form the three roughly rectangular openings of the *Inscription for the Top* were derived from photographs of a square piece of net placed in a draught and photographed three times. It is perhaps worth noticing that the two areas or features of most direct communication within the mechanics of *The Large Glass*, the *Inscription* through which the *Bride* transmits her messages, and the *Shots* fired back ultimately by the bachelors, were both elaborated from starting points that were haphazard and casual.

It must be borne in mind when looking at *The Large Glass* that just as the notes in the *Green Box* had been assembled in a deliberately random fashion, so Duchamp insisted that the elements in the *Glass* (and presumably those of the *Bachelor Apparatus* in particular) were conceived originally as being to a large extent interchangeable in their position and function.[35] Inevitably, however, as work progressed each element achieved a more particularized role within the mechanism as a whole. When asked why he had never finished the work Duchamp pleaded boredom, but he probably also felt reluctant to freeze it into completion and felt that some of the mystery and vitality of the piece would disappear (for him at least) if he realized his plans through to the letter. Towards the end of his life Duchamp was persuaded, however, to execute an etching of *The Large Glass* as it would have been completed, and with the knowledge of how these elements would have fitted into the visual scheme, it is possible, always with the help of the notes, to describe the workings (or the non-workings) of *The Large Glass* as it exists in its present incarnation. Any description, no matter how lengthy, could, however, only be partial, given the complexity of the notes and the interchangeability of ideas and imagery.

It has already been seen how the *Bride* transmits her commands or invitations to the *Bachelors* through the three *Draft Pistons* (corresponding to her treble blossoming) which are surrounded by a sort of *Milky Way*, perhaps the ectoplasmic expression of her sexual desires and processes. The *Bride*'s messages appear to induce (though not directly) a gas cast by the *Malic Moulds* into the shapes of the nine *Bachelors*; the latter, though rigid and static, are nevertheless in a state of tumescent excitement. Unable to contain themselves they allow the gas to escape through the *Capillary Tubes*, where it is frozen, cut into spangles and subsequently converted into a semi-solid fog. The spangles pass out of the *Capillary Tubes* and are fed into the *Seven Sieves*, condensing into a liquid suspension. The liquid thus produced falls into the *Toboggan* and crashes or splashes at its foot. In the last desperate attempt to achieve contact or union with the bridal apparatus the *Splashes* ascend vertically, channelled through the *Oculist Witnesses*. The *Scissors* (situated above and linked to the *Chocolate Grinder*) further control the ascent of the *Splashes* as does the circular form above the *Witnesses*, originally to have been rendered by a magnifying glass embedded in the ordinary plate glass around it, and which was to have converted some of the liquid into light energy. Subsequently the liquid is once again dispersed (some of it makes a

Sculpture of Drops, for example) and in the process partly re-excites the *Bride* to envisage once again her strippings. The main bulk of the liquid it may be supposed (the idea is suggested visually rather than verbally in the notes) succeeds in reaching the *Bride* in the *Shots*.

The *Chariot* or *Sled* running back and forth on its runners controls the cutting motion of the *Scissors*, which in turn appear to work in unison with the *Sieves*. The *Chocolate Grinder* in the meantime remains passive and static, and in its immobility achieves a status more purely symbolic than any other element in the *Glass*. The *Chariot* in motion acts also as a commentator (and hence is in some ways a voluble counterpart to the *Oculist Witnesses*) and its litanies, 'slow life', 'vicious circle', 'onanism' and so forth, are heard in the *Cemetery of Uniforms and Liveries*, so that even as the bachelor gas swells and expands in anticipation the *Bride's* partners are being informed that the game is up – it is 'check-mate'. On the surface then *The Large Glass* presents us with a tragi-comedy of frustrated physical love, with the *Bride* (as several commentators have pointed out) left literally hanging in the air.

3 The Stripping

Two works of 1911, totally different in spirit, are particularly relevant in tracing the evolution of the iconography of *The Large Glass*. The first of these, *Spring*, or *Young Man and Girl in Spring* (Collection Arturo Schwarz, Milan), was a study for a large painting subsequently destroyed, and was given by Duchamp as a wedding present to his sister Suzanne. Two somewhat emasculated nudes, male and female, face each other across a space dominated by quasi-abstract forms which, in retrospect at least, have strong sexual connotations, although the symbolism may still have been to a certain extent unconscious. There is an air of solemnity, even of ritual about the confrontation, and basically the work still belongs to the allusive world of *fin de siècle* Symbolism. *Portrait*, a slightly later work, is more progressive from a stylistic point of view, showing as it does Duchamp's assimilation of some of the devices of Cubism, and it reveals perhaps for the first time in Duchamp's work a vein of irony and self-awareness. A woman enters the painting at the top left, crosses the canvas, turns around and exits again below her point of entry, assuming in the process five different positions, an explicit statement of Duchamp's new interest in depicting motion and, in the process, of incorporating the temporal element into his art. As Duchamp's 'Dulcinea' threads her way back and forth across the picture surface she strips, or sheds her clothes (although she keeps on her hat), and Duchamp later admitted that the idea for the painting had come to him when he found himself one day mentally undressing an attractive unknown woman whom he saw in a park.[36] Embedded in the transparent, interacting planes that build up the images is a large, symbolic phallus, a subliminal anticipation of *The Chocolate Grinder*. In *Sonata*, in many ways a companion painting, the figure of Duchamp's mother is seen as a presiding genius suspended in the space above the musicians in much the same way as the *Bride* was later to hang over the *Bachelors*.

These early works of Duchamp's have about them a lyrical, tender quality, enhanced by the pale, pastel or rainbow-like tints, and tinged with an air of affectionate humour, and time has undoubtedly lent to them an aura of great distinction. On the other hand, when compared to the contemporary achievements of his great colleagues in French art it must be admitted that they look distinctly minor in appearance. The means by which Duchamp transformed himself into one of the half dozen most significant artists of his generation were derived not only through a closer study of Cubism (in the *Chess Players* and the two versions of *Nude Descending a Staircase*) but through the recognition that to express his ideas adequately he must formulate a totally new set of visual premises. In the last analysis the ideas which involved the formulation of a new optical language were the result not so much of an appreciation of contemporary painting, as of his intellectual apprehension and enjoyment of progressive French literature, both of the late nineteenth century and of the early twentieth. There is however one source for the iconography and mechanics of the *Large Glass* which remains to be explored: characteristically enough this was a system of thought that combined the written word and the visual diagram in a unique fashion.

If, as seems likely, Duchamp became interested in alchemy this would have been about the time he left Paris for Munich, or possibly even in Munich itself. The drawing of *The Bride Stripped Bare by the Bachelors*, possibly the first of all the Munich works, appears to have been derived both iconographically and compositionally from an illustration of the stripping of a virgin (or a young bride) reproduced in a treatise by the philosopher Solidonius and subsequently used in other alchemical manuals. Duchamp had the previous year produced his own first 'stripping' painting, *Portrait*, and one suspects that he would have been amused to discover a similar subject treated very graphically in an esoteric work of great learning. He seems to have realized at once that the symbolism of alchemy could help him to achieve the more abstract, more hermetic and more intellectual art towards which he was striving. A year or two later he was to remark, 'Every picture has to exist before it is put on canvas and it always loses something when it is turned into paint. I prefer to see my pictures without that muddying.'[37] Alchemy, which dealt with concepts of a cosmic and esoteric nature and yet had been forced at certain stages to render these in terms of diagrammatic visual images, held out exciting possibilities. The mixture of science and the irrational involved in alchemical thought was also of a kind exactly calculated to appeal to Duchamp. Like science fiction it must have seemed 'a way out of Symbolism'. Jung, writing of the great period of alchemy, says: 'There was no "either-or" for that age, but there did exist an intermediate realm between mind and matter, that is a realm of subtle bodies whose characteristic it is to manifest themselves in a mental as well as a material form.'[38] This defines exactly the condition to which Duchamp's art was aspiring.

Duchamp could have stumbled across alchemical writings fortuitously or he could have been led to them by his interest in Symbolism. The purest flowering of alchemy in Western Europe had taken place in the tenth and eleventh centuries when it had become almost a religion and hence had returned in a sense to its sources. In the fourteenth century it became increasingly materialistic and its apparatus correspondingly more complicated. The alchemists had always made use of sexual symbolism in the description of their methods of work and now pictorial illustrations in which the sexual symbolism was made visually very overt began to proliferate. The climate of the eighteenth century was basically unsympathetic to alchemy and it went into a marked decline; in the nineteenth century, however, a revival of interest coincided with the emergence of a series of esoteric religions often fascinated by the occult. Alchemy held an obvious fascination for the Symbolists and certain painters of the *Rose Croix*, Gustave Moreau, for example, made use of its imagery.

The concept of the stripping of the virgin or bride in alchemical literature is symbolical of the purification of the 'stone' or of the primal matter; even as the virgin is stripped of her rich bridal trappings on the night of her marriage to appear before her husband in all her transparent virginity, so the stone abandons one by one the colours which it assumed in the various processes to which it had been submitted, until it reaches a state of transparency which is the symbol of revelation and of true knowledge. Science fiction had tinged the first Munich *Bride* sketch in the form of the two robot-like *Bachelors*, but in the *Passage from the Virgin to the Bride* deeper, more mysterious forces are at work. The alchemical opus at its truest dealt not just with chemical experiments as such, but with the resolution of psychic processes and problems, expressed in a pseudo-chemical or pseudo-scientific language. So too in the *Passage from the Virgin to the Bride* these processes are described in what might be called a pseudo-pictorial language and one which Duchamp was soon to abandon in favour of an even more intellectual approach to the machine and the machine-made object.

The machines of alchemy, the mills, the distilling apparatuses and the primitive furnaces, were also of a type that would have amused Duchamp and stimulated his imagination. As in the case of Roussel's science fiction it was relatively simple, commonplace apparatus that was to produce such amazing and unbelievable results. If the illustration of the *Stripping of the Virgin* may have suggested the iconography of *The Large Glass* as a whole, it is possible that the diagrams of other alchemical works suggested to him certain forms and functions of the *Bachelor Apparatus*. The general layout of the composition of the lower half of *The Large Glass* resembles, for instance, the depiction of the *Furnace and Alembic and the Cosmic Serpent Crucified* in the *Alchimie* of Flamel, the greatest of fourteenth-century alchemists. The funnel or chimney to the left is suggestive of the shapes of individual *Bachelors*, and although the solid brick furnace is replaced in Duchamp's work by the open fretwork of the *Glider*, the *Water Mill* appears at the same point as the distilling apparatus. The fact that Duchamp may have had similar alchemical apparatus in mind when plotting the first stages of *The Large Glass* is to a certain extent confirmed by some of the very first notes of the *Green Box*. One of these, datable to 1912, describes a 'steam engine on a masonry substructure' or on 'a brick base' which forms 'a solid foundation for the bachelor-machine fat' and the same note speaks of 'the place where their eroticism is revealed (which should be one of the principal cogs in the bachelor machine)'. *The Chocolate Grinder* we know was derived from a particular counterpart seen in the shop window in Rouen, but it is just possible that Duchamp was struck by the general similarities between its form and those of the right-hand section of Flamel's diagram; the sieves, which join together in a curve, compositionally essential to the lower half of *The Large Glass*, are mysterious in their genesis and may perhaps relate to the image of the crucified serpent, an alchemical symbol of transformation and renewal.

Parallels between the tenets and language of alchemy and the iconography of *The Large Glass* abound, and although these may to a large extent be fortuitous it is also likely that certain alchemical postulates may have furnished Duchamp with a series of propositions in the manner of a chess problem laid out in writing and accompanied by a schematic diagram. Thus seven was the most important number for alchemy in ancient times, although it was subsequently extended to nine or 'a company': there are seven *Sieves* and nine *Bachelors*. The four stages of alchemy were symbolized by blackening, whitening, yellowing and reddening, although the yellowing was in later days abandoned so that the three cardinal colours of alchemy were black, white and red. The *Glass* is described in the notes first of all as 'a world in yellow', but the *Bride* is rendered in 'grisaille' or black and white and the *Bachelors* in red. In alchemy red is for the king, white for the queen at the stage at which both are ready to consummate their symbolic union which is to produce the elixir. Tarot cards, dependent on the symbolism of alchemy, use animals to caricature the human predicament in much the same way that Duchamp uses machines, and their imagery includes *The Chariot* and the *Hanged Man* or '*Le Pendu*'; the *Bride* in some of the notes is referred to as *La Pendue Femelle*. The early distillations of alchemy were made from the most despised substances, including semen, and an eighteenth-century treatise shows the products of the first distillation being offered to Luna, the female moon divinity; one is tempted to speculate whether it is not some such comparable substance that is reaching the *Bride* in the area of the *Shots*; she is referred to in the notes as an 'agricultural machine' and an 'instrument for farming', and she is, as Octavio Paz suggests, a Ceres figure, moon-like and remote, desirable but unattainable.[39]

If alchemy interested Duchamp it was because he saw in it a kind of cosmic chess, a system of speculative thought, half science half philosophy, in which ideas were constantly being formulated which by definition could never reach a definite or positive conclusion. Fundamental to alchemy was the question of the union or mating of irreconcilables, of aboveness with belowness, of air and earth, of fire and water. Duchamp had always been attracted to forms with cosmic implications, in particular the circle and spiral in rotation (the first ready-mades, the *Bicycle Wheel* and the *Bottle Rack*, are both based on the circle, a symbol or form of prime importance for the alchemist) and he may have been unconsciously attracted by the fact that the basic tenets of alchemy are archetypal in character. Alchemy for instance makes use of the myths of ancient Egypt and at times overlays them with the iconography of Christianity. In the same way Duchamp can hardly have failed to be aware of the fact that as the iconography of the *Large Glass* developed it took on similarities with traditional scenes of the Virgin's assumption, and indeed a note in the *Green Box* refers to the fact that: 'The Bachelors serving as an architectonic base for the Bride the latter becomes a sort of apotheosis of Virginity.' (One is reminded of Jarry's essay on *The Passion as an Uphill Bicycle Race*.) As in so many Assumption scenes the forms of the upper half of the composition tend to be softer, more feminine and to float in an indefinite space where perspective plays little or no part, while the male world below is rendered in forms that are strongly three-dimensional and where linear perspective often plays a strong role.

A man of extraordinary honesty, Duchamp once denied that there was any conscious use of the imagery and symbolism of alchemy in his art,[40] and it is possible that the parallels that exist are fortuitous or due to an unconscious attraction towards forms and images that are atavistic or archetypal in nature. Certainly it is true that Duchamp's 'alchemy' (and *The Large Glass* is a demonstration of alchemy if only because the most gratuitous objects and materials have been transformed into a work that is pure artistic gold), if it exists, is deeply ironic and of the same personal, deliberately dislocated brand as his science, which had been a quizzical branch of Jarry's 'pataphysics'. On the other hand it is possible that Duchamp's denial arose from the fact that he was reluctant to have too much read into his art; quite obviously it was an art of extraordinary depth and subtlety, but he was anxious that each

305

spectator should extract from it what he wished and he knew that any hard and fast explanation of *The Large Glass* was not only impossible but that an attempt to produce one could only serve to kill any true contact between himself and his viewer.

Nevertheless the analogies between his art and that of the alchemists are revealing if only because of the light they throw on the thought processes of one of the most intellectually gifted men of his age. Jung in some of the key passages of his treatise writes:

> What the symbolism of alchemy expresses is the whole problem of the so-called individuation process . . . We now realize that [alchemy] is a question of actualizing those contents of the unconscious which are outside nature, that is, not a datum of our empirical world and therefore of an *a priori* or archetypal character. The place or the medium of realization is neither mind nor matter but that intermediate realm of subtle reality which can only be adequately expressed by the symbol. The symbol is neither abstract nor concrete, neither rational nor irrational, neither real nor unreal. It is always both. It is *non vulgi*, the aristocratic preoccupation of one who is set apart.[41]

Duchamp was arguably the most aristocratic artist of his generation and unquestionably the twentieth-century symbolist *par excellence*.

Epilogue

Duchamp saw 1912 as the year in which he rejected the role of professional artist. The first version of *The Chocolate Grinder* of the following year witnessed his last essay in traditional techniques (with the important exception of *Tu m'* of 1918, a commissioned work about which Duchamp later expressed doubts) and soon after came his first experiments on glass. By 1914 the plans for *The Large Glass* were all but finalized, so that the long labour involved in its execution in a sense qualified Duchamp for the simple role of 'artisan' which he was later to claim.[42] In the late 1920s and early 1930s he appeared to be dedicating most of his interest to chess. In fact, as two major retrospective exhibitions mounted in the 1960s demonstrated,[43] he continued to work steadily throughout his life. On the other hand with the definitive abandonment of *The Large Glass* in 1923 there appears to be a diminished sense of commitment. The new experiments in optics (for he had in a sense been interested in optics all along) which were initiated in 1920 with the

Rotary Glass Plate (executed in collaboration with Man Ray) were time-consuming and have taken on a new importance in view of subsequent developments during recent decades, but they lack the depth and intensity of the studies surrounding the *Glass*: the correspondence which accompanied the creation of the beautiful *Rotary Relief* is, significantly enough, competely factual in tone in contrast to the hermetic intensity of the notes surrounding *The Large Glass*. Subsequently, as history caught up with his achievements and as new schools found in his art premonitions of their own, he wryly commented on the situation in a series of appendices or footnotes (both verbal and visual) to his earlier work. The intellectual and aesthetic paradoxes mounted.

After his death, on 2 October 1968, rumours began to circulate about an important new work on which Duchamp had been at work for some time. The following year this was installed in the Philadelphia Museum of Art and opened to the public. *Etant Donnés: 1° la Chute d'Eau, 2° le Gaz d'Eclairage*, 1946–66, is as baffling a work and as hard to analyse as *The Bride Stripped Bare by her Bachelors, Even*.[44] The title of the late work is derived from the notes of the *Green Box* and obviously the two works are deeply interrelated. The immediate sensations evoked by the two works, on the other hand, are diametrically opposed. *The Large Glass* is mysterious, hieratic, and despite the fact that the cracks have 'brought it back into the world', ultimately its remoteness places it on the other side of our experience of the material world. It is the door, the window, the looking-glass through which we glimpse a ritual that involves us obsessively but from which we are forever distanced by virtue of the hermeticism of its imagery and by the fact that at best our understanding of it can only be partial. *Etant Donnés* is mystifying precisely because of its at least partial explicitness.

Etant Donnés can only be approached through the Duchamp galleries (presided over by *The Large Glass*) of the Philadelphia Museum of Art, so that even the visitor unfamiliar with Duchamp's work has absorbed some of its complexity, its variety, its humour and its detachment before he can confront the final 'tableau'; for *Etant Donnés* could with some justification be called a 'tableau mort' of extraordinary vividness and life. At the end of a narrow, underlit room, little more than a corridor, stands an ancient, weather-worn door of wood, arched and encased in a surround of bricks. One senses at once that the door cannot be opened but one is drawn towards it as if by a magnet, and as one comes closer one becomes aware of two small holes, at eye-level, drilled through the wood. Beyond the door lies an extraordinary sight. On a plane parallel to the door and some few feet beyond it is a brick wall with a large, uneven opening punched through it. Beyond and bathed in an almost blinding light is the figure of a recumbent woman modelled with great delicacy and veracity but also slightly troubling because the illusion of three dimensionality is strong but not totally convincing (the figure is in fact in about three-quarter relief). She lies on a couch of twigs and branches and she opens her legs out towards the spectator with no false prurience or sense of shame. Her feet and ankles and most of her right arm are hidden by the brick wall and her head is shrouded by a long, continuous shock of blond hair. Her left arm is raised and in her hand she clasps a gas lamp (a jet inside an upright funnel) which glows dimly in the brilliance of light around it. Beyond the nude is a wooded landscape, rising to a low bluff, and surrounded by a blue sky, lightly ruffled by clouds. At the base of the bluff is a waterfall which flows and glints incessantly (the effect is achieved by a bent tin can which is rotated by a small motor) although its waters, one senses, are viscous and slow moving rather than clear and sparkling.

A handful of works executed during the time when *Etant Donnés* was in the making might have given some clue as to the subject matter and appearance of the final work. *Etant Donné le Gaz d' Eclairage et la Chute d'Eau* (Collection Nora Martin Lobo, Sofía) may be considered a study for the lifesize figure in the final work and is modelled in shallow relief in gesso over which vellum has been stretched, while the flesh tints are achieved in coloured pencil. The female figure *Le 'Bec Auer'*, an etching from the *Lovers* series of 1968, must have been derived directly from the already finished sculpture. Another etching, *The Bride, Stripped Bare*, taken from a photograph, shows a young woman kneeling at a prayer stool, naked, while the directness of the eroticism of Duchamp's late work is further paralleled by yet another work of the series, *Morceaux Choisis d'après Courbet*. Perhaps most remarkable of all the works related to the big Philadelphia *tableau* is *Cols Alités* (Collection Robert Lebel, Paris), a small drawing executed in 1959 which shows the *Large Glass* with a landscape background of gently swelling hills which turns the apparatus of the *Glass* quite literally into 'agricultural machinery'. To the right of the *Oculist Witnesses* and above the area of the splash is a telegraph pole, making explicit the connection between liquid and electricity.

It is hard not to view *Etant Donné* as a latter-day version of *The Bride Stripped Bare by her Bachelors, Even*. The *Bride* has been brought down to earth with a bang, but the *Bachelors* have been reduced or compressed into a gas lamp, now truly fired with the bridal gas, symbol of desire and tumescent excitement. The liquid, the water, appears to have symbolic attributes that are both male and female; the pond is deep and still, the waterfall restless and incessantly active in its downward thrust. What gives the work its power to shock is an intense physicality that exists on two levels. The body of the woman is fleshy, naturalistic and desirable. The male presence is unmistakably present and literally burning with desire and yet quite obviously abstracted and symbolized to a high degree. It is perhaps not without significance that in the sketches leading up to the *King and Queen Surrounded by Swift Nudes* it was the female form that was the first to be abstracted into a mechanistic chess piece, while late in life when the fantasy was rendered explicit it was the female who was made real while the male (Duchamp, the artist) has been, as it were, painted out of the picture, and who remains as a vestigial yet obsessive presence, half phallus, half machine.

Duchamp stressed the fact that not only the female image but *The Large Glass* as a whole was the *Bride*.[45] His attitude towards her, towards his art, was to a certain extent at least symbolized by the mechanics of the *Bachelor Apparatus*. Like Mallarmé, Duchamp appears to have been obsessed with the idea of the work of art as a symbol or substitute for the object of love or desire which cannot be touched, for to do so would break the spell. The *Large Glass* owes its depth, its never ending layers of meaning, to the fact that he saw the need to distance himself from his subject in such a way that its iconography would exist in an aesthetic realm that belonged only to it. Late in life he appears to have felt sufficiently detached to execute its three-dimensional, naturalistic (one might almost say illusionistic) counterpart. The symbolism persists but in a sense the movement has been from the world of veiled allusions and 'imaginary solutions' to a realm that relates, albeit at several removes, to the world of Surrealism. Having to such a large extent helped to create Surrealism, Duchamp in old age was perhaps prepared to accept some of its procedures. The Surrealists had dealt in terms of symbols, but, for all their love of mystery, in terms of symbols that were ultimately decipherable; a fantasy is of interest only if its possibilities can be spelt out. And yet *Etant Donnés* retains its mystery, perhaps because the symbolism is so blatant that in a sense it cancels itself out. In the same way the eroticism is stressed to the point where it transcends the purely physical or even the mentally obsessive. It has become something quite else. In conversation with Pierre Cabanne, Duchamp remarked, 'Eroticism . . . replaces if you like what other schools of literature called Symbolism, Romanticism. It could so to speak become another ism.'[46] In Duchamp's hands it has become just that. *The Large Glass* continues to preserve its enigmas intact, but it is as if having given us the literary key to a greater understanding of it by publishing the *Green Box*, Duchamp, forced to admit that he had been an artist all along,[47] felt obliged to paint and sculpt it 'back into the world' – and into art.

16

Arshile Gorky:
the Search for Self

I T WAS in 1924 that Vosdanik Adoian changed his name to Arshile
Gorky. Gorky, he was fond of remarking, was Russian for
bitterness. At first he was not sure how Arshile should be spelt and
hence signed his paintings 'A. Gorky'.[1] He claimed kinship with the
great Russian writer Maxim Gorky; and although with hindsight it
is possible to see the imprint of genius on even his earliest work, he
did nevertheless during the first half of his career attempt a series of
artistic impersonations with such total conviction that he might
with a certain amount of justification have changed his name to
Cézanne, and then to Picasso, while insisting at other moments on
his strong family likeness to Braque, Matisse, Léger, Masson and
then ultimately Miró. Gorky gave three different sites as his
birthplace; in fact the event took place in the Armenian village of
Khorkom in the province of Van, in 1904. In 1908, when Gorky was
at a particularly vulnerable age, his father fled to America to avoid
conscription into the Turkish army. After his own emigration
Gorky saw his father fairly frequently, but he never felt really at
home with him, and it is hard not to view his passionate
identification with a series of painters older than himself, often to
the brink of the effacement of his own artistic personality, as a
search for the protective father-figure he had lost as a small boy. He
used to talk of being 'with' painters: 'I was *with* Cézanne for a long
time and then naturally I was *with* Picasso.'[2]

Here is an account of his childhood and adolescence written by
his nephew: 'By the time that Gorky had begun high-school, the
Turks had massacred his four grandparents, six uncles and three
aunts. He had endured a hundred and fifty mile death march at the
end of which his mother died of starvation in his arms; he had been
in the thick of the violence of World War One, the civil war and the
Bolshevik revolution.'[3] Truly it is a tragic tale. His mother's death
occurred in 1919; after this Gorky and his younger sister found their
way to Tiflis, and eventually their childhood odyssey took them to

Arshile Gorky

Gorky,
*The Artist and his
Mother*, 1929–40

Constantinople and on to America via Greece. They arrived at Ellis Island on 26 February 1920.

The photograph of Gorky and his mother taken in Van City in 1912 Gorky kept with him until his death. He used it as the basis for the two versions of *The Artist and his Mother* (the first is in the Whitney Museum of American Art, New York), begun in the years after he had settled in New York towards the end of 1924. The second version, which was to occupy Gorky from around 1926 right through until 1942 (National Gallery of Art, Washington), is possibly the more moving because of the way in which the child's head has grown in scale and clarity while that of the mother fades and pales, as though in memory. The hands in both versions remain blurred and clumsy. Gorky was in fact a consummate draughtsman, right from the start; and yet in almost all the naturalistic figure paintings that relate to the two great canvases one senses that the hands are areas of the painting he could not face. This is particularly true of the otherwise masterly *Self Portrait* (Private Collection), probably finished in 1937 in which the artist's hands seem pathetically impotent, like bandaged stumps. The faces in these paintings are masklike and impassive; but for the hands, the painter's instruments for creation, he could find no adequate disguise.

And in a sense it might be fair tố say that if Gorky's eyes had been open and questing all along it wasn't until the early 1940s that his increasingly close and personal contacts with Surrealism unravelled the bandaged hands and allowed his talent to come spilling out in some of the most lyrical effusions of twentieth-century art. Now a wealth of childhood memories came flooding forward to feed and enrich his art. He said: 'I tell stories to myself, often, while I paint, often nothing to do with painting. Have you ever listened to a child that this is a house, this is a man and this a cow in the sunlight . . . while his crayon wanders in an apparently meaningless scrawl all over the paper? My stories are often from my childhood. My mother told me many stories while I pressed my face in her long apron with my eyes closed. She had a long white apron like the one in her portrait, and another embroidered one. Her stories and the embroideries on her apron got confused in my mind with my eyes closed. All my life her stories and her embroideries keep unravelling pictures in my memory, if I sit before a blank white canvas.'[4]

The release of his talent and the discovery of his artistic identity brought with them a period of great happiness and fulfilment. But inevitably one form of self-discovery brought with it others; the mask was off and certain aspects of what he saw he found hard to bear. The gods pursue those whom they have favoured, and during the last two years of his life Gorky experienced a sequence of accidents and disasters that seem to echo the tragedies of his childhood. His paintings became leaner, tauter and sparer; the miracle is that the lyricism remained unimpaired, although it is now informed by a new poignancy, often by a note of suppressed anguish, even of pain. His most profoundly original work was all produced within the space of some five brief years, for on 21 July 1948 he hanged himself from a beam in a barn near his Connecticut studio.

The earliest consistent group of Gorky's canvases are also the most purely Cézannesque. Although there were already quite a number of Cézanne's paintings to be seen in New York, for a young man who had not grown up with a first-hand knowledge of mainstream modern art Gorky's efforts show an astonishing command of technique and a remarkable grasp of the complexities of Cézanne's style. And Gorky seems to have sensed at once one of the profoundest and most difficult lessons that Cézanne had to teach: that the spaces between objects or landscape elements could be made to look as important, as palpable as the material substances they surround and separate. Soon, however, Gorky's use of space became highly personal; it has often been remarked that one of the hallmarks of Gorky's art is the way in which his images are not so much imposed upon the backgrounds or the space around them, but rather are defined by the way in which areas around them press forward against them, at times seeming almost to modify their contours.

These spatial sensations are already evident in the portraits, surely the most interesting and compelling of the early works. The portraits demonstrate, too, Gorky's ambition to fuse the art of the present with that of the past. Already by the late 1920s Gorky was 'with' Picasso and he clearly identified in particular with the Picasso *Self Portrait* of 1906 (Philadelphia Museum of Art) from the Gallatin Collection which was housed between 1927 and 1942 in New York University; the debt is particularly evident in the *Self Portrait* of *c.* 1937. Even Gorky's palette seems to derive from the pinks, ochres, fauns and greys of Picasso's 'rose' period, although in Gorky's hands they become sweeter, clearer – and Gorky was a natural colourist, just as he was a natural draughtsman. But in the portraits there are echoes, too, of Hittite, Sumerian and Egyptian art.

Through Picasso Gorky found his way back to Ingres; and it is very characteristic of Gorky that when he takes over an artist he also takes over his sources; there is something almost uncanny in his ability to look at one artist through another's eyes. It is revealing, too, that Gorky always had a particular love for artists' self-portraits. He was fascinated by every insight into the personalities of the artists he admired; he was obsessed, for example, by calculating at what age a painter had executed a particular work.

If the years between 1930 and 1938 are the ones in which Picasso held Gorky most completely in thrall, already by the later 1920s he had begun his immersion in Cubism. 'Has there in six centuries been a better art than Cubism? NO,' he wrote in 1931.[5] Many works of this period showed an awareness of Picasso's most recent work but also recognized his earlier more purely Synthetic Cubist manner, while Braque's final Cubist style stood behind others. Through Synthetic Cubism, Gorky taught himself how to use flatly coloured pictorial elements to emphasize a canvas's two-dimensionality while simultaneously enriching the inner spatial tensions that were so fundamental to his art. The tying of the central shapes to the edges of the canvas by the use of vertical and horizontal bands or compositional elements is, however, very particular to Gorky's work of the period; we sense, somehow, that he is afraid of allowing his imagery to exist more freely and openly in the space around it. Significantly, in certain works a note of ambiguity creeps in. Some works, which are basically still lifes, relate closely to Picasso's figure pieces.

Even in the early 1930s, while he was still sheltering so squarely behind Picasso, there are hints in Gorky's work of a nascent interest in Surrealism, a movement which Picasso had helped to create and which was persistently anxious to claim him for its own. The great invasion of Surrealist expatriates did not begin until 1939, but between 1930 and 1935 one-man shows of most of the leading Surrealist artists had been seen in New York; interest in Surrealism was further heightened by the great *Fantastic Art, Dada and Surrealism* exhibition mounted at the Museum of Modern Art in 1936. Some of Gorky's letters of the mid-1930s begin to take on a stream-of-consciousness tone; in one of them he quotes from a poem by Eluard (characteristically claiming it as his own). It was proof of the depth of his attraction to the Surrealist ethos that he was to be as deeply influenced by its literature as by its visual products. It was in any case a movement to which he had certain elective affinities. From the start he had been drawn to exploring both formal and suggestive analogies between various components and aspects of his imagery, and much of his art had been informed by a hidden, confessional quality and by that combination of the mysterious and the revelatory that the Surrealists characterized as 'the marvellous'. As de Kooning once observed, 'He had all these things before and the Surrealists told him he had it already.'[6] The Surrealists revealed Gorky to himself.

Between 1936 and 1937 the forms in Gorky's paintings begin to take on the quality of symbols, of substitutes for rather than of abstractions from actual objects. Some of the shapes Gorky uses evoke associations with birds, plants, pods and leaf forms which in turn evoke connotations of fertility. A new aura of sexuality permeates these works and this touches even the more straightforwardly representational still lifes and flower pieces of the period. The fact that Gorky was beginning to think in metamorphic terms, in terms of transforming one form or symbol into another, or of giving more than one meaning to a pictorial shape is pointed up by the fact that although these paintings now derive compositionally from Picasso's latter-day curvilinear Cubist still lifes they once again come much closer in feeling to Picasso's small figure pieces, particularly those of 1931–2, works in which Picasso was indeed briefly and most directly allied to true, mainline Surrealism. In the early 1930s Gorky himself had felt briefly the need to be 'with' de Chirico, another of the founding fathers of Surrealism, in the *Nighttime, Enigma and Nostalgia* (National Gallery of Art, Washington and Private Collection) series of 1931–4 (some of the drawings in the series derive directly from de Chirico's *Il Tempio Fatale* (Philadelphia Museum of Art) of 1913, another of the key works in the Gallatin Collection). Enigma was a favourite word not only of de Chirico's but also of Gorky's friend John Graham, a painter and writer who was to act as an important bridge between young American artists and the Surrealists in exile; and Graham may well have encouraged Gorky to look more closely at de Chirico's work.[7] Gorky was fascinated not only by de Chirico's startling confrontations of unlikely images in compositional frameworks that were strongly formalistic and themselves deeply indebted to Synthetic Cubist procedures, but also by the haunting, poetic titles he gave his works.

By the mid-1930s Gorky was sufficiently imbued with the Surrealist spirit to begin what might be described as the journey inwards and downwards. His more formalistically constructed canvases of the period are complemented by the *Khorkom* series (Private Collection), works which are often characterized by monochrome backgrounds which act as grounds or fields against which the increasingly fanciful images begin to move more freely, although the backgrounds still at times seem to be painted up against the images rather than to exist behind them. These were the first works in which Gorky began to explore associationally imagery related to his childhood memories and experiences. If some of the *Khorkom* pictures show an awareness of André Masson, one of the Surrealists who had practised automatic techniques with startling and original results, the series is even more important because it prepared Gorky for his identification with Miró to whom he was now to turn, not so much as a new father-figure and mentor, but as a blood-brother and friend.

The influence of Miró hits Gorky most squarely in the *Garden in Sochi* series (High Museum of Art, Atlanta and Private Collection) which comprises some six or seven works executed between 1940 and 1944, although Gorky had known Miró's work as early as 1928 (at the Valentine Gallery), and there are indications that he had begun to feel its impact in certain works of 1938. In 1941 New York saw the largest exhibition of Miró's work yet to be mounted, at the Museum of Modern Art. Gorky was to lean on Miró as heavily as he had relied on Cézanne and Picasso, but the nature of his debt to the Catalan was much more complex and in the final analysis possibly even more far reaching. First, and most obviously, Miró was an inspired and original colourist and he helped to release for the first time the deeply lyrical potential of Gorky's palette. Miró's identification with Catalan Romanesque ecclesiastical art and with a tradition of folk art that was still alive and flourishing must have struck affinities with Gorky's newly aroused consciousness of his Armenian heritage. Much more important, however, was the fact that during the mid-1920s, when Miró was cultivating associational thought processes and experimenting with automatic procedures in his work, his art had taken on a new dimension in that the whole question of his attitude towards his sources and his contemporaries had changed radically. Now, rather than consciously studying the works of other artists as he had done in his formative years, he found that he was able to conduct a sort of running dialogue both with his earlier sources of inspiration and with his colleagues. Thus in a single work he could metaphorically 'talk' to Bosch, to Picasso, to Kandinsky or to Klee without in any way impairing his own artistic originality or identity.

Gorky had always been as much obsessed with the art of the past as with that of the present; he frequented the Metropolitan and Frick Museums more than the Museum of Modern Art or, after it opened its doors in 1939, the Solomon R. Guggenheim Museum (then known as the Museum of Non-Objective Art). On his studio walls were reproductions of works by Piero della Francesca, Uccello, Mantegna, Bosch and Ingres. One of the reasons for his total dedication to Picasso lay in the fact that through Picasso, more than through any other twentieth-century artist, he could feel himself in touch with the art of the past to which there are so many different layers of reference in Picasso's work. And now, apart from the obvious seduction which Miró's use of colour and line exercised over him, he was drawn to him because of the element of free-flowing intercourse which Miró was able to conduct with his

317

contemporaries and his earlier sources of inspiration. He particularly loved Miró's *Dutch Interior I* of 1928 (Museum of Modern Art, New York), one of the paintings executed from postcards after a trip to Holland (the starting point for this picture was Hendrick Maertensz Sorgh's *The Lutist* of 1661), because he loved art which referred overtly to other art.

The *Garden in Sochi* pictures, above all the earlier works in the series, abound in references to Miró. Their major source of inspiration appears to have been Miró's *Still Life with Old Shoe* of 1937 (Museum of Modern Art, New York), a painting which Gorky had studied in the company of his friend de Kooning at the Pierre Matisse Gallery; and there are details which read like virtual quotes from other Miró works. But the fact remains that these paintings by Gorky are more uniquely infused by his personality, are more totally Gorky's than anything that he had yet produced. They are not paintings in the manner of Miró, as earlier works had been in the manner of Cézanne and Picasso, but dialogues with a new artist friend. Sochi is a Russian Black Sea resort, but the imagery of the works derives from recollections of Gorky's parents' home on the shore of Lake Van, and the series is in essence a continuation of the *Khorkom* theme.[8] In 1942 Gorky wrote down his memories as an accompaniment to the series: 'My father had a little garden with a few apple trees which had retired from bearing fruit. There was a ground constantly giving shade where grew incalculable amounts of wild carrots, and porcupines had made their nests. There was a blue rock half buried in the black earth with a few patches of moss placed here and there like fallen clouds. But where came all the shadows in constant battle like the lancers of Paolo Uccello's paintings? This garden was identified as the Garden of Wish Fulfilment and often I had seen my mother and other village women opening their bosoms and taking their soft and dependent breasts in their hands to rub them on the rock. Above all this stood an enormous tree all bleached under the sun, the rain, the cold, and deprived of leaves. This was the Holy Tree. I myself don't know why this tree was holy but I had witnessed many people, whoever did pass by, that would tear voluntarily a strip of their clothes and attach this to the tree. Thus through many years of the same act, like a veritable parade of banners under the pressure of wind all these personal inscriptions of signatures, very softly to my innocent ear used to give echo to the sh-h-h-sh-h of silver leaves of the poplars.'[9]

The *Sochi* pictures and all the works that followed them are rich in imagery and occasionally certain forms in them can tentatively be assigned a representational role. But now Gorky was in the world where the embroidery on his mother's apron was getting confused – confounded would perhaps be a better word – with the stories she told him, and to ascribe too literal a meaning to his images would be to falsify his art. Gorky's mind was now working freely and associatively and one set of images conjured up another and set his mind wandering down a different narrative path, while the composite images became simultaneously hardened and abstracted into freely drawn, brightly coloured shapes. The large reproductions of Uccello's battle pieces which hung in his studio (and which he sometimes used to look at upside down) attracted him particularly because the complexity of imagery and the rhythmic patterning of shapes suggested other images and rhythms to him. As he reached down into his subconscious these became fused with childhood memories and legends, like superimposed coloured transparencies out of which the final configurations came swimming or floating up to the picture surface. His dealer, Julien Levy, recalled passing on to Gorky Paul Eluard's description of how he composed his poetry, and how Gorky immediately saw the point of it: 'I hum a melody, some popular song, the most ordinary. Sometimes I sing quite loudly. But I echo very softly in my interior, filling the melody with my own errant words.'[10]

The *Garden in Sochi* paintings are still in a sense transitional works, marking the divide between works in which Gorky makes overt reference to the art of others and those in which he sings in a voice that is totally his own. In the summer of 1942 yet another dimension was added to Gorky's art when during a visit to Connecticut he began to work from nature, something he had not done for almost fifteen years. The Tate Gallery *Waterfall* (Trustees of the Tate Gallery, London), a masterpiece, datable to the winter of 1942–3, shows the fruits of this new stimulus. And 1943 is the year in which Gorky emerges as a truly great artist in his own right. The summer of this year, spent in Virginia, provoked a veritable explosion of works on paper; henceforth Gorky's drawings lead the way forward and condition the development of his paintings. Gorky was now deliberately cultivating mesmeric forms of vision. He would lie in the tall grass, staring at it for hours. Sometimes he would hold up a small object, a matchbox for example, at arm's length and invite nature to push forward and meet him there; grass, plants and trees would seem after a while to sway forward towards him, like algae bent by a current of water flowing swiftly onwards. In the undulating configurations of natural forms he saw reminiscences and echoes of art, of the old masters who hung in reproduction on his studio walls, of the European moderns whom he searched out in galleries and in art journals. And through nature he spoke to other artists in fast, free-flowing sketches. Paradoxically, by evolving a style which could enable him to record, in a single work, the crowding in upon him of the voices of any number of other artists, he was able to create a language totally his own. The importance of Surrealism for Gorky lay, in part at least, in that it forced upon him the realization that his drawings and quick, spontaneous sketches, in which he allowed both nature and other artists to speak to him in chorus, were more truly himself than his more self-consciously ambitious attempts to identify with great art by absorbing and emulating a different series of styles and manners.

Throughout his life Gorky remained receptive to new artistic encounters, although with his rediscovery of nature and through it his artistic liberation, his attitude towards his sources was subtly but also fundamentally altered. One of the first Surrealist painters to arrive in New York from Paris was the Chilean painter Matta Echaurren. Matta was some seven years younger than Gorky but his precocious talent had blossomed very quickly in Surrealist Paris and before his emigration he had already made a highly personal contribution to latter-day Surrealist painting. This lay in his dismissal of the deep perspectival dream space of Dalí and Tanguy, which had become one of the hallmarks of 1930s Surrealist painting, in favour of a space which was equally deep but which was vapourous and pocketed; through this space spin strange configurations, some with animal and some with mineral properties. Matta invented the term 'psychological morphology' to describe his work, suggesting that he wished to evolve an indefinite, mobile space that would evoke or echo psychological experience.

Gorky and Matta first met in 1940 and the relationship was to be of great importance to Gorky, both because Matta had been 'with' mainstream modernism in a much more concrete way than Gorky, and also because for the first time Gorky was to enjoy a reciprocal relationship with a Surrealist artist on whom he could lean but towards whom he could also feel paternalistic and protective; Matta

Gorky,
Waterfall, 1943

borrowed a work of Gorky's in order to study it and kept it for more than a year. Already in some of the later *Garden in Sochi* paintings the flatter, smoother areas of the most Miróesque examples are replaced by smudgy, more painterly areas of colour which appear to be embedded in and between the outlines of forms without always touching them; this is very much a feature of, for example, the Tate *Waterfall*. Since line no longer defines the boundaries of the coloured areas, line and colour now to a certain extent act independently of each other so that one gets a new sense of forms hanging and suspended in space. Miró had helped to liberate Gorky's colour sense and had quickened his sense of line, and now, through Matta, space in Gorky's work becomes freer, more experimental; henceforth Gorky was to use it in an increasingly original and inventive way.

Through the contact with Matta's work Gorky's paint effects also became thinner, more liquid and more luminous. But while Gorky's paintings often share with Matta's effects of nodules or forms and imagery floating against an indeterminate space, in Gorky's work this space also continues to push its way forward to the surface of the canvas – and this is where the heritage of Cézanne and Synthetic Cubism is so important – so that the effect is much more that of an overall dappling of colour cells or areas in which imagery and background are frequently deliberately interwoven and confounded. This is particularly noticeable in works like *How My Mother's Embroidered Apron Unfolds In My Life* (Seattle Art Museum) and *One Year the Milkweed* (National Gallery of Art, Washington) both of 1944. By evolving a type of composition in which the picture surface becomes a field over which the painter ranges freely, and in which occasionally pockets of interest and complexity occur, but in which there is no one centre of focus or interest, Gorky was making one of his most important contributions to emergent revolutionary American art – towards what American painters of the 1940s used to call an 'over-all' type of painting.

It is proof of Gorky's new stature as a painter that within his newly found originality he still felt perfectly free to turn for advice and confirmation to yet another of the mythical father-figures of twentieth-century modernism. During his student days in New York Gorky had claimed, untruthfully, to have been a student of Kandinsky's. In 1931 he wrote of Picasso, Miró and Kandinsky as representing 'the distinctive art of this century'.[11] In 1939 the opening of the Museum of Non-Objective Painting (renamed the Solomon R. Guggenheim Museum in 1952), which boasted some twenty examples of Kandinsky's work, must have rekindled his love of the work although he could also have seen Kandinsky's work elsewhere. Gorky must have recognized that like himself Kandinsky had reinvented or transformed landscape to a large extent in terms of his own inner, psychological drama. Despite the fact that Kandinsky's work is more self-conscious, more truly symbolic, more truly metaphysical, and quite obviously more highly imbued with 'Sturm und Drang', Gorky nevertheless was able to recognize in Kandinsky a father-figure with whom he could converse more freely, more joyously than he had been able to do within his attachments to painters whom he had chosen, it could be argued, precisely because they cast over him a more formalistic and authoritarian spell.

Many of the works within the unbroken succession of masterpieces produced in 1944 celebrate this new artistic relationship;

these were some of the most overtly sensuous, most relaxed and exhilarating of all Gorky's canvases. Like Kandinsky Gorky was a poet, and a fine one, too; it is worth quoting from one of his prose poems for the insights it affords Gorky's increasingly rich yet infinitely mysterious imagery: 'Ill the trees in gallow's wood, and they were enormous in the forest of repression with its foliage so thick that from dawn to dusk to dawn one did not dare to imagine that one day beyond the horizon and beyond habit there would burst a scene all sulphur and love.' Only Masson could rival Gorky in his unmasking of the limitless sexuality of nature. Gorky also recognized how the drama inherent in nature could be used as a metaphor for the human condition and experience.

The year 1944 was the one when Gorky met André Breton, the poet and writer who had been the undisputed leader of the Surrealist movement since its inception. Breton was to write the essay for the catalogue of Gorky's important one-man exhibition at the Julien Levy Gallery in New York in March 1945. The same year Breton claimed Gorky for Surrealism in a reissue of *Le Surréalisme et la Peinture*, originally published in 1928, to which he now added a chapter on Gorky's work. In the catalogue essay Breton wrote, 'Gorky is, of all the surrealist artists, the only one who maintains contact with nature – sits down to paint *before* her.'[12] Earlier the Surrealists had stressed the importance of cultivating a totally internalized form of vision.[13] Breton used the term 'hybrids' to characterize Gorky's totally new kind of imagery, echoing in turn one of his own major sources of inspiration. In his treatise *On Dreams* of 1901 Freud had written: 'The process of condensation further explains certain constituents of dreams which are peculiar to them and not found in waking ideation. What I have in mind are "collective" "composite" figures and strange "composite struc- tures" which are creations not unlike the composite animals invented by the folk imagination of the Orient.'[14] Breton's words evoke the configurations of forms we experience most evocatively of all in the two *Betrothal* canvases of 1947 (Yale University Art Gallery and Whitney Museum of American Art, New York).

In the last years of his life Gorky renounced his allegiance to Surrealism. In a letter to his sister Vartoosh he wrote: 'Surrealism is academic art under disguise and anti-aesthetic and suspicious of excellence and largely in opposition to modern art. Its claim of liberation is really restrictive because of its narrow rigidity. To its adherents the tradition of art and its quality mean little. They are drunk with psychiatric spontaneity and inexplicable dreams . . . Really they are not as earnest about painting as I should like art to be.'[15] The truth is that Gorky no longer needed the Surrealists. They had played an essential role in his evolution as an artist, but when he had discovered his own true artistic identity, in large part through their services, he also realized that a large gulf was separating him from his erstwhile mentors. He had enjoyed his first-hand contacts with the Surrealist exiles, had learnt and profited from them. But when he came face to face with them, they also lost the mythical status they had enjoyed when they were legendary figures across the ocean. Above all Gorky could not accept Surrealism's strongly anti-aesthetic bias. The Surrealists had employed art as a technique for living – Gorky saw it as a way of life. This was one of his many legacies to American artists who were about to assert the supremacy of the School of New York. Gorky was much too intelligent an observer to have been unaware of what was happening around him. Despite his diffidence he must have felt proud to realize that emergent American artists had put upon his art the seal of their allegiance, even if what they were now producing also demonstrated that artistically he remained suspended between two continents.

Outside influences continued to flood in. Critics and people who knew him well, some of whom actually watched him at work, have seen in the *Betrothals* of 1947 sources as diverse as Uccello, Ingres, Duchamp and Tanguy. But after 1944 Gorky's art was also becoming increasingly self-referential. Landscape implications once again assume some of the properties of still life, evoking memories of the *Nighttime, Enigma and Nostalgia* series of the early 1930s. The title of *Landscape Table* of 1945 (Musée National d'Art Moderne, Centre Georges Pompidou, Paris) confirms the confounding of the two genres. In the summer of 1946 Gorky had spent the days drawing out of doors and the evening drawing indoors at Crooked Run Farm in Virginia. Interior space seems to inform works like the *Study for Agony* of 1947 (Private Collection). In *The Plough and the Song* also of 1947 (Private Collection), there is on the other hand a strongly implied horizon line, and the painting has, revealingly enough, compositional affinities with his own early Cézannesque landscape.

Despite the consistency of vision and quality, the work of Gorky's final years is also in certain respects surprisingly diverse. In canvases of 1944 such as *One Year the Milkweed* line and colour are confounded to the extent that in some areas Gorky appears to be drawing over colour while in others he draws with it. This sensation persists in some of the most dappled of the late works. In other paintings line and colour now go their separate ways, although the dialogue between them remains active; this is particularly true of *Charred Beloved I* of 1946 (Collection of Mr and Mrs S. I. Newhouse Jr.). Other works, such as the *Study for Agony* (Private Collection), read almost like tinted drawings. Conversely the beautiful unfinished *Painting* of 1947 (Private Collection) indicates that certain canvases were built up colouristically and that only at a final stage was linear detail superimposed. In 1944 Gorky's use of line had been tremulous and expectant. Now it remains elastic but one has the sensation that line is being pulled tauter and tauter. In the *Betrothals* one has the feeling that if any of the pictorial relationships were even marginally altered, the linear elements and with them the pictures' whole compositional structures would snap and disintegrate. All the late work is characterized by a heightened nervosity and a feeling of piercing, valedictory sweetness, midway between pain and ecstasy.

In January of 1946 there had been a fire in the country studio that Gorky was using with the loss of some twenty-seven important canvases. In March he underwent an operation for cancer. In June 1948 he was seriously injured in a car accident; his neck was broken and his painting arm immobilized. In July there came the suicide. Shortly afterwards a friend observed that the words of Antonin Artaud on the death of Van Gogh seemed equally appropriate to Gorky: 'He sought himself all his life with a strange energy and determination. And he did not commit suicide in a fit of madness, in terror of being unsuccessful, for on the contrary he had just discovered who he was and what he was. But . . . there are days when the heart feels the impasse so strongly that it is stricken as if by sunstroke with the idea that it can no longer go on.'[16]

17

Frank Stella's *Working Space*

WHEN painters write they often do so very well and we are grateful to them for their journals, memoirs, theoretical statements, essays, lectures, pronouncements and aphorisms. But it is seldom that a major artist is prepared to commit himself publicly to a considered, large-scale survey of the art of his time, and to relate it moreover to substantial cross-sections of the art of the past. Frank Stella has done this in his Charles Eliot Norton Lectures at Harvard, with considerable erudition, great verve and genuine originality.[1]

The *Working Space* of the title is Stella's plea for the reintroduction of greater spatial expansiveness, expressiveness and experiment into contemporary art: 'What painting wants more than anything else is working space – space to grow into and expand into.' He feels – knows, indeed – that abstraction is the real, the great art of our time; but he is appalled by the dullness and flatness which he sees as characterizing so much abstract painting of recent years and which he finds shallow in every sense of the word: too 'close-valued', too conservative, too introverted, too much conditioned by technique. He believes that contemporary abstraction is also impoverished because it can relate only to pioneering abstraction and the art which immediately produced it, Impressionism and Cubism, both of which he sees as being themselves fundamentally conservative and unadventurous. The possibilities and lessons of the art of the past have been cut off from us and the cost has been devastating. Even the heroism of Mondrian is in danger of being forgotten; Barnett Newman's legacy has somehow turned to ashes. Neither is there any breath of prophecy in today's abstraction: 'We seem to be enmeshed in a difficult present.' At a subsidiary level the title of the book reflects Stella's fascination with artists' methods and the conditions in which they work – the squalors and the splendours of Caravaggio's studio at The Eight Corners in Rome, Kandinsky at his easel in Paris.

Less explicitly the book is also an apologia for the baroque in art, for an art which is spatially complex and full and which is informed by sweeping movements and gestures, by balanced dissonances and disharmonies. Stella can respond to the grave and the dignified, and there are beautiful and revealing passages on Vermeer's *Allegory of Painting* and on Caravaggio's *Madonna of the Rosary* (both in the Kunsthistorisches Museum, Vienna). But basically he is drawn to art that is extrovert or outgoing and in which there is at least potential drama. If he seems nevertheless to be more attracted by the sixteenth century than by the seventeenth, this is because revelation has come to him through Italian art; and while he responds to the element of theatre that informs much of Italian sixteenth-century art, and in particular that of Venice, he is repelled by the theatricality of much Italian art that succeeded it. Rubens is a hero partly at least because more than any other artist he learnt the lessons of Italy. But on the whole Stella is less good on art that is quiet and reflective and gives itself to us slowly. He has surprisingly little to say about Cézanne. Rothko puts in no appearance in these pages, and, even more surprisingly, neither does Braque, surely one of the two or three most spatially conscious and inventive of twentieth-century artists.

Stella's great passion and exemplar is Caravaggio. Caravaggio's painting is an enterprise that is spatially independent and self-controlled: 'Painting before Caravaggio could move backwards, it could step sideways, it could climb walls, but it could not create its own destiny.' Stella sees Caravaggio as enlarging Renaissance painting by inventing a 'more flexible container' for Venetian painterliness, a container flexible enough, moreover, to accommodate the spatially more dramatic and diagrammatically perspectival art of Rome. Since Caravaggio places his action in the middleground, the foreground tends to advance towards the spectator, inviting him to step into it. The soft, dark background areas also invite penetration; however, as Stella perceptively remarks, when in imagination we begin exploring this background space, feeling our way around the volumetrically rendered figures, after, so to speak, getting behind them we find ourselves confronting not their back views but rather their mirror images. Further on, Stella suggests that at moments Caravaggio is saying 'illusionism is still a one-way, dead-end street', and if this would have been news to Caravaggio the point is well and ingeniously argued. But to an artist whose vision was formed in the 1950s, Caravaggio also has the attraction of being simultaneously a very flat painter; the muscular interactions of the limbs of his figures create spatial tensions across the surface as well as into depth; they are eminently fleshy and tactile, but the tactility is also that of paint, of pigment applied to a two-dimensional surface. Then again Caravaggio is a supremely frontal and confrontational painter, and these qualities are reinforced by his use of a single dramatic light source which generally comes from above. Furthermore, Stella has been touched by the Greenbergian view that every painting must justify itself in its own terms, and when we think of Caravaggio we tend to think of individual paintings rather than groups or sequences of paintings, or of his development.

Stella sees Rubens as taking up and in turn expanding Caravaggio's space, while retaining Titian's painterliness and colour. Even more than Caravaggio he involves the spectator in the spatial drama of his art. Looking at certain Rubenses, 'We should see ourselves on a pedestal if we want to be true viewers of painting, because elevated on a pedestal we will surely be reminded of the space all around us – the space behind us, next to us, below us, and above us – in addition, of course, to the space in front of us, which we have so often taken as being the only space available to viewers. No one makes it clearer than Rubens how dearly painting wants to use all the space available to the human imagination.' One senses that Stella is less directly and deeply moved by Rubens than by Caravaggio because Rubens substitutes an element of artificiality for the naked realism and truthfulness of Caravaggio, and also because Stella is fundamentally most drawn to art that is capable of being developed further by others, rather than to art of total accomplishment or final realization. But he also accepts that the artificiality of Rubens is the result of the fact that he was to a large extent making painting out of and about other painting, a romantic attitude which makes him in certain respects more relevant to subsequent painting: and 'Rubens could be our perfect teacher.' (I myself feel that some of today's figurative painters would do better to stick to Caravaggio, or better still go back to Giotto.)

Although the theme of the origins, development and present dilemma of abstract art and the way in which it might be enriched by consulting the past runs throughout the six chapters of this book, the first half is directed further backwards in time, while the second half concentrates more upon the art of this century. The third chapter, on Annibale Carracci, really uses his work to throw into relief the achievements of Caravaggio and Rubens, by showing how much more open and inventive they were in consulting the work of their predecessors and mentors. The fourth chapter, entitled 'Picasso', is just as much about the origins of abstraction as about Picasso's art. Stella admires Picasso not least for his ability to pillage the art of the past; and it is indicative of Stella's ambitions that he realizes that if contemporary abstraction is ever to achieve the greatness he wants for it, it must face the challenge of the magnitude of Picasso's achievement. He quite rightly sees Picasso's Neo-Classical phase of the 1920s as a turning point in his art, although Picasso never turned his back on Cubism even temporarily, as Stella suggests, and of course it informed all his subsequent art. Stella recognizes that the Cubists used or depicted space in a new and original way, but he also feels that Cubist painting ultimately flattened out the space available to painting and that the exciting spatial possibilities implicit in it are still to be exploited and explored. His view of Cubism is somewhat blinkered because he approaches it, quite understandably, from the point of view of abstraction, from which in fact it always fought shy. At the same time, he recognizes that much of Picasso's subsequent work has the spatial thrust and vitality which can only be engendered by strongly volumetric forms forcefully and imaginatively manipulated and deployed. All great figurative painting has been reinforced by abstract, purely pictorial concerns but Picasso's work raises the question whether abstraction, always (if at times unwillingly) to a certain extent linked to representation, can function at full force without it. 'Can we get along with half the recipe?' Stella clearly believes we can, but only by competing with the richness of representational art's spatial repertoire. What he most deplores is 'the albatross' of semi-abstraction, which was 'a reality in 1920' (surely at least a decade earlier than this?) and 'is still flourishing in the 1980s'.

Stella venerates the early achievements of the great pioneering abstractionists, Mondrian, Malevich and Kandinsky, but not one of them passes through his scrutiny with colours quite at high mast. I think he is least good on Mondrian. He sees Mondrian as deriving from Impressionism and 'its surface concerns, colour, light and rhythm'. In fact the Symbolist background, filtered through the rigours of an analytic Cubist syntax, is more significant for an understanding of Mondrian; and it is simply not true to say that 'Surrender to sensation is the secret of Mondrian's success' and that 'Pure colour is the beginning of Mondrian's sensationalism.'

Far from surrendering to sensation, Mondrian dominated and suppressed it, and colour was for him an intellectual and symbolic abstraction. Stella recognizes but ultimately fails to appreciate the element of distillation that gave early abstraction its power; and it is this same distillation that has subsequently also informed many of the most moving and spiritually rich products of abstraction. He seems to find Malevich's 'breakthrough' pictures a little too schematic and arid, but he clearly responds to the element of quirkiness in Malevich's art and, I suspect, to his capacity to go to extremes. Certain reservations are expressed about Kandinsky's first abstract phase because the paint quality is too superficially seductive and not 'pushed' sufficiently hard. But we have only to look at Stella's own recent work to know that Kandinsky is ultimately to be awarded the palm; and already his early abstraction has an openness that gives us 'a bright expanding vision which in turn gives us hope that we can revive our dulled surfaces'.

If many of Stella's comments on twentieth-century art are touched by asperity, it is equally characteristic of him that he should take an original and positive view of the later works of these prophets of abstraction, works which have on the whole attracted much less critical attention. He sees the bars and grids of Mondrian's pictures as becoming increasingly free from the surfaces which they at first sight appear to define and constrict; they span the surface rather than cutting it and dividing it. And when we see them in this light they become infinitely extendable and the spaces around and behind them begin in turn to expand and float. 'It is here that abstraction is truly born again . . . With help like this anything is possible.' The best of Malevich's later, figurative work he sees as somehow optimistic, suggesting perhaps that if Malevich had recaptured his earlier visionary fervour, the products of a second phase of abstraction might have been even richer than those of his first. Kandinsky's later, harder, more difficult and convoluted work, Stella clearly sees as a storehouse of unexploited riches, largely because it is so full of movement that creates or suggests space; if much of this movement has about it a diagrammatic quality this is because Kandinsky has felt the need to try to render volumetric passages in space without the recourse to recognizable imagery.

330

'Instead of using his easel to prop up a window on the world, Kandinsky uses it as a windshield moving through the universe.'

Stella makes the point that for many American painters abstract art really began in the 1940s Understandably enough, as he homes in on the art of his immediate predecessors his judgments at times become somewhat personal. The attempt, for example, to relate Barnett Newman, who was more than any other artist a father-figure for Stella, to Kandinsky, whose work finds resonances in Stella's own recent work, is not altogether convincing; and it seems to me that as artists they have very little in common. Kandinsky's example is perhaps more relevant for Morris Louis, 'nearly the last abstract painter to hint at the potential that abstraction might have for creating a full and expansive space like that of Rubens'. He is sparing in his comments about his own contemporaries although he clearly has an affection for certain early Nolands and sees some of the rot as setting in with Olitski's bland acrylic fields. I hope he is keeping a journal; it would be worth waiting for.

Stella sees de Kooning and above all Pollock as having reintroduced into painting a sense of energy and freedom which both Impressionism and Cubism lacked. He recognizes that Pollock's greatest achievement lay in the 'overall' drip paintings and he finds parallels between their interacting skeins of paint and Mondrian's grids; their relationship to the edges of the painting is deliberately ambiguous – sometimes they seem to bind the painting to its format, at others they float up from it, liberating the space between and behind. But by implication at least Stella finds that the Cubist heritage inhibits these works and, once again, he is most excited by their potential: 'To go anywhere with the thin paint skeins that Pollock activated we have to give them more movement and definition.' Also, despite their extraordinary originality, indeed because of it, in these works Pollock destroys his own sources and contact with the past, leaving himself and other artists as it were stranded. Still, whatever the path forward may be, abstraction will have to acknowledge Pollock's achievement, if only because the relationship of his dripped configurations to the surface which supports them 'seeks to define the working space of abstract painting'.

Stella has many interesting things to say about the question of scale (as for example when he writes that it was the elimination of the palette and not of the easel that changed the face of so much

331

painting: 'The size of what one dips the brush into counts for more than the size of what one paints on'). But I wish he had said still more, and he fails to make the point that despite the effectiveness of the way in which Newman's 'zips' or vertical flairs successfully activate the surfaces of his paintings, simultaneously binding and pushing apart the monolithic coloured surfaces to their sides, ultimately it was the sheer scale on which Newman worked that defied a single viewpoint or a single reading of his pictures. And if Newman and his great contemporaries of the 1940s and 1950s gave other painters some of the 'working space' for which Stella longs, they also to a certain extent deprived much subsequent painting of a physical space in which to live. I wonder how many hundreds of thousands of vast paintings have been destroyed or are lying rolled up and neglected in studios, barns and attics across the world, and in particular the English-speaking world. I wonder, too, if the problem of an ultimate destination is not at least partly responsible for the desperation and lassitude that characterizes so much of today's large-scale abstraction.

Like Stella, I believe that most of the greatest art produced in the past forty years has been in the field of abstraction. And I too believe that much of the painting of the past two to three decades – representational as well as abstract – has ignored the fact that space is one of the richest and most emotive properties of pictorial art. But I believe there is an alternative space to the baroque, swinging, muscular space that Stella proposes, a space that works on us more slowly but which can be just as all-enveloping. This is the space created by light – light that binds and separates objects, planes and shapes, that illuminates and spreads, and that can act upon our perceptions and our senses as powerfully if not as physically as the visceral space in which Stella delights. Space through light is there in Giotto and in much Italian Renaissance painting. It found fulfilment in much Venetian sixteenth-century art, and supremely in the late work of Bellini. It informs some of Rembrandt, much of Velázquez. It is to be found in the work of Claude and in some of Poussin (an artist upon whom Stella is particularly hard). Turner was one of its greatest exponents. It was an ingredient in much nineteenth-century landscape painting and found redefinition in the late work of Monet and Cézanne. Space and light go hand in hand in the most crystalline of Braque's Cubist canvases and they were welded together into the metaphysics of his late studio paintings. For Miró (most expansive of artists) colour, light and space were at times synonymous. The space of light was Rothko's space; it is present in the Pollock of, for example, *Lavender Mist* (National Gallery of Art, Washington, DC); and it is what makes de Kooning's latest manner so elegiac and moving. I recognize, however, that Stella would perhaps find this space too slow, too conservative, too conditioned by the format which contains it, in his own words too 'boxy'.

The sixth and valedictory chapter of his book is in some respects the least satisfactory and cohesive, but it is also possibly the most important because in it Stella tells us something about his own work and how he views it. In these closing pages Stella reaffirms his enjoyment of the great abstractions of Kandinsky, Mondrian and Malevich:

> but I do have trouble with their dicta, their pleading, their impassioned defence of abstraction. My feeling is that these reasons, these theoretical underpinnings of theosophy and antimaterialism, have done abstract painting a disservice which has contributed to its present-day plight.

While Stella is so alive to and so good on the art of the past which excites him, this statement shows a startling lack of historical sense, for of course without their intellectual and ideological convictions these artists, his artistic grandparents, could never have achieved their ends. His own painting he sees as a mixture of tough, pragmatic empiricism, what he calls 'acquired New England experience' and 'half unconsciously held Mediterranean gift'. Clearly the months spent in Rome (from September 1982 to June 1983) marked an intellectual watershed for him. Renaissance painting, which had earlier seemed alien and threatening, became increasingly a challenge and an inspiration.

When Stella turns his attention to iconography he can be brilliant, as, for example, in his analysis of Titian's *Flaying of Marsyas* (State Museum, Kroměřž, Czechoslovakia), but for the most part content in art is for him a subsidiary consideration: or, to put it differently, content is something he often chooses to ignore. He makes the point that 'access to abstraction to anyone born after 1936 [the year of his own birth] is direct and unencumbered'. He believes that if abstraction is sufficiently good, sufficiently vital, it justifies itself by its appearance and presence, and there are few of us who would quarrel with that. But the fact remains that if abstraction has been with us as a central part of artistic life for three quarters of a century, artists of Stella's generation were the first who didn't have to work their way into abstraction and who hence often didn't know what their art was about. This doesn't trouble Stella: his art is about art, about life seen through art (there is a passage, for example, about how he could only see the New York environment through recent painting), and latterly very much about space. But countless abstract artists of his own and a subsequent generation have been consumed by doubts and hesitations because they have come to feel that art about art is not sufficiently self-sustaining; their gestures have become artificial or mechanical and their working spaces those of bodily routine and not of the mind and spirit. To many it is not, as Stella suggests, simply a question of sustaining pictorial energy but rather a question of looking or waiting for something to regenerate it.

Stella concludes that abstraction has its roots in a northern, realist landscape tradition – a view which has frequently been advanced. Although he deals throughout with major issues, he also for the most part elucidates them by reference to individual works of art, and here he trots out Paulus Potter's *The Young Bull* (Mauritshius, The Hague), and this simply will not do. It is a fine, touching and truthful painting but it does not support the weight of his arguments. Stella's generalizations are often contentious, generally illuminating and unfailingly stimulating. However, when he writes 'by prizing Potter over Caravaggio, Mondrian, Kandinsky and Malevich finally put nineteenth-century French painting and its source, Italian Renaissance painting, to rest', one can see what he is trying to say and admire him for the bravery of the way in which he puts it; but he also comes for the first and only time perilously close to sounding foolish. He would have been better advised to choose one of the great mystic or visionary masterpieces in which Northern art abounds; better still, he could have addressed himself to the position Courbet occupies in the history of modernism.

From Mexico to Venice
Postscript: Interview with Richard Wollheim

On the occasion of John Golding's exhibition of his paintings *Works from a Decade* at the Yale Center of British Art, New Haven, 1988

R.W. We first met in Venice in 1955. At that time, as I recall things, you were working on your thesis on Cubism, and you were also painting: but painting less strenuously than later – or, for that matter, than you had been earlier, in Mexico.

J.G. Yes, we met in the great Giorgione exhibition, in the Doge's Palace. The Cubist thesis took rather longer than I had expected; my grants ran out and I was forced to take a job as a critic for the *New Statesman*. I disliked this and it made me more than ever anxious to get back to my own painting, although of course for a long time I supported myself as an academic by teaching at the Courtauld Institute. The art-historical background is very important for me; a lot of my professional life has been as an art historian, and I still write the odd art-historical piece.

R.W. I have had the opportunity of following your work virtually since our first meeting, over a period of nearly thirty-five years, and an initial thing to say about it is that it contains two aspects which are not all that often found together in contemporary art: a strong underlying unity, and a great deal of surface change, in response to problems and challenges we shall want to talk about. In this way your career as a painter always strikes me as more like that of a traditional artist than that of a late twentieth-century artist. In so much late twentieth-century art we find either repetition all the way down or novelty all the way down. However, I don't want to talk about this general issue, which in fact is that of the pathology of contemporary art – what I think of as the widespread failure to form style. I introduced it only to contrast it with your work. Now the underlying unity in your work, is so far as it is not the unity of style, the unity imposed upon the work by the hand, the hand in the service of the eye, comes, as I see it, from its constancy of subject matter: the human body.

335

Postscript

J.G. You are quite right about the subject matter of my work. I began as a figurative artist and found my way into abstraction through moving, as it were, up and into the body imagery of my painting. Given the fact that abstract art has been with us for some seventy-five years, it never ceases to amaze me that it was only the generation of painters after my own that accepted abstraction as a language that could be immediately picked up rather than as something that had to be worked into. I think this is why abstract art has been through, and is still in a way in, a state of crisis. A lot of young artists were excited by the look of abstract art and began making abstract painting and sculpture, but then after a while they became uncertain what their work was *about*. I think it is perfectly possible to make art out of and about other art, provided you know that that is what you are doing. I myself grew up in Mexico and saw relatively little good abstract art until I began visiting New York in the very late 1940s. Apart from a few landscapes, my own first works were all figure pieces. And in one form or another the body is still always there in my work. The formats of the paintings over the past two decades have been consistently horizontal, and maybe this is why people have seen them as having connotations with landscape. This doesn't necessarily bother me – the space of landscape is for me richer and more interesting than architectural, man-made space, and I probably make use of it, indirectly. But I recognize that the body is always there in my work, that that is what my paintings are about.

R.W. Let us start with an early work. Here we see unmistakably the middle section of the human body, the male human body. The gender is not in doubt. The picture also exhibits another great theme of yours: light. The body, and light – and also a third theme, which is potent in much of your work, mystery. Mystery, as I see it, has a short-lived absence from your work in the period of the hard-edged descendents of those early torsos, and that may have been a powerful reason why you grew dissatisfied with that 'purer' kind of work. Personally, I recall the purer work with affection because you did a simplified version of one of those hard-edged images for the cover of the first English edition of *Art and its Objects*.

But to go back to the early torsos, which tell us so much about the pictures in the present exhibition, through their dissimilarities as well as through their similarities. Mystery is powerful in both groups, but in the early work it is never far away from terror, and the terror in turn comes from the penetration of the body by light. In the later work light falls on the body and explores its surface, but here it drives its way through the body, often coming at it from behind, and then generally from a single source. Light is essentially inquisitorial, and mystery comes about partly from its success, or what it uncovers about our strange interior, and partly from its failure, or what the body continues to hold secret from us. So there is the mystery of strangeness and superimposed on it, the mystery of ignorance. Do you think this is a reasonable way of describing the subject matter of these pictures?

J.G. The majority of my early single-figure pieces were male. Half the torso pieces of the 1960s were in fact female, although male and female were sometimes coupled. But there came a time when I realized that in my work I was somewhat desperately trying to find a compromise between a male and female body. This is a perfectly valid subject for art and has been explored by many artists, writers in particular; but when I realized what I was doing, I turned my back on this because I am not interested in art as self-discovery or as therapy. Hence, probably, the move to a 'purer', hard-edged art, besides the fact that there was a lot of good hard-edged painting around and I was enjoying it and responding to it. The terror you refer to in this earlier work may have something to do with personal problems I was facing; not the least of these was the fact that I was coming increasingly to recognize that I was not particularly naturally gifted as an artist. In some ways it seemed almost impertinent to try to become a painter, and yet it was the activity that most interested me. As for many, light and truth have always been associated in my mind, although I can also recognize a truth of darkness, as for example in certain attitudes towards death. So, yes, light for me was at one point inquisitorial although it no longer is. I am aware of the element of mystery you speak of, but it isn't something I consciously cultivate. Art that sets out to mystify mostly repels me. On the other hand, the very idea of art seems to me infinitely mysterious. It keeps alive certain spiritual values, but, when one actually thinks about it, it is a very odd thing to do or make, and it involves great risks at many different levels for both the practitioner and the experiencer.

Postscript

R.W. I fully understand and sympathize with the distinction you make between mystery and mystification, and when I said 'mystery', I meant mystery. But I also sympathize with your implied point that you aren't really the person to ask about mystery in your work, even though it comes from you. But I should like to stay for a moment with these early paintings, because I want to concentrate on one particular aspect of them. Not the subject matter, but something that goes along with the subject matter and provides an analogue to it. It depends on a certain optical effect which helps to carry the subject matter. These pictures have an abrasive quality, and I am thinking of this in a literal way. I don't know if you added anything to the paint in those days, but the pictures have a very gritty surface towards which the spectator then feels himself drawn. He is drawn into the surface because of this grittiness and, as he is, he starts to feel as if this grit is being rubbed across his eyes and eyelids. It is a sensation that I associate with certain pictures by Goya, particularly the single-figure pictures. They also induce it. It is a somewhat cruel effect, but the upshot is that the spectator feels that his body, as he experiences it, is twinned with the represented body. The two are allied through distress, and the distress that the spectator feels alerts him to what is happening to the body in the picture.

Now, without at this stage going further into this rather specific conception of the body, the body under inquisition, which after all is subject matter you have now left behind, I should like to ask you something about the pictorial sources you drew upon in realizing it. Someone looking at these pictures, either at the time or now, would have rather superficially thought of Francis Bacon. But in actual fact, these images, as I understand the matter, derive much more from Mexican sources. Would you like to say something about that? A great deal of your later work could be anticipated by saying that, over the years, Mexico gives way to Venice.

J.G. My first experience of contemporary art was of the Mexican Mural Movement. Orozco was my greatest source of inspiration, and I still belive he is one of the giants of the twentieth century, although his output was so incredibly uneven. One of the features of Orozco's art is the way in which his figures all seem to be in some way flayed; they wear their skeletons on the outside, like armour, although it is an armour that is useless, and he mostly seems to see

338

humanity as doomed. I sometimes get the feeling that he painted out of hatred, a sensation I also experience in front of another artist I enormously admire, Clyfford Still, although of course, in the end-products of both, the hatred is sublimated into very powerful art. In front of Orozco's work I experience the distress through empathy that you describe; and I experience it, too, in front of Bacon, much of Goya, and also when looking at a lot of El Greco. The actual grittiness of my torso pieces came, technically, from applying sand and gravel to the surfaces; this was partly to combat the gloss and stickiness of the acrylic paint I was then using, but it may also have been an unconscious attempt somehow to emulate the corrosive-ness and blackness of Orozco and other Mexican mentors. Maybe I subsequently responded so strongly to the great revolutionary American abstraction of the 1940s and 1950s because a certain amount of it owed a debt to Mexican art.

R.W. On the level of mere appearance the biggest or most abrupt change in your work was when you shifted from the early painterly, gritty manner, sombre, with very little colour, to the hard-edged representations of the body, still sometimes without colour, but sometimes with a lot of bright colour and often a rather silvery effect. But on a deeper level the really important change came later and was less immediately perceptible. It coincides with a shift from pictures that contain within their edges, or as parts of themselves, representations of the body, to pictures that in themselves or as wholes stand in for the body. This is what I call metaphorical painting – the painting is a metaphor for the body – and all the paintings in this exhibition are metaphorical paintings. They are no longer figurative paintings, we can no longer see the body in the painting, but the reference to the body is no less present. The difference is that this reference is not effected through represen-tation. These pictures are manifestly representation: we see forms or shapes arranged in depth, or with one behind, or in front of, another. But, though representational, the pictures don't represent the body. What has happened is that they have become metaphors for it. I don't want to be misunderstood. As you know, but I had better make this clear, I think that a painting can both be a metaphor for the body *and* represent it: Titian supremely. But your paintings are metaphors for the body but not representations of it. Now from this transformation your painting has acquired many benefits, many positive benefits, but there is one 'negative' benefit, a benefit by deletion, that I should like to bring up now. Abandoning figuration has resulted in the dissolution of those great centralized images which, in one way or another, presided over most of your early work. It is only with hindsight that this emerges as the major liberation it has turned out to be. Did you feel centralization to be a constricting force at the time? It seems to me that the example of Bacon, where over the years, over the decades, remorseless centralization has eroded the expressive effect of the work, might have made you wary of it. But I may be reading my own responses into your work.

J.G. Kandinsky discussed two ways of moving into abstraction, veiling and stripping or laying bare. I suppose he himself basically veiled while someone like Malevich stripped bare. The veiling process is probably easier to sustain or keep up, because the artist can continue the dialogue with his sources of inspiration, whether in the world of visual appearances or the world of ideas. But once the stripping has taken place, it leaves the artist *vis-à-vis* the reductive idea or image – whatever it is that has been laid bare – and then it is very hard to keep the dialogue up at the degree of intensity necessary to give the resulting artefact sufficient charge to make it valid or meaningful. But I think there is another, third way into abstraction, which is moving up into the image or images of an earlier mode. As I see it, Still and above all Rothko achieved their ultimate visions in this way. Newman, on the other hand, basically stripped bare, but for all his reductiveness continued to deal with developing ideas; and this was why he was so much more of an influence on other artists. Obviously I am not comparing myself in any way to these great artists, but in my own case I in a sense moved up into the centralized images of my earlier work. In the process the centralized images were abstracted, and the centralized image became the canvas itself in its entirety. The pictures themselves, as you say, became metaphors for bodies.

R.W. Before we look at the later work, I should like to ask you a question. It follows directly out of what we have been talking about and is something that troubles many people, though it also troubles them that it does. They think that it is puerile or unsophisticated. But Clement Greenberg, to his credit, has always felt that abstract painters should never lose sight of the fact that they deny themselves things that figurative painters could make use of. Abstraction, in other words, involves loss: though – and this is the crucial point – not necessarily overall loss. You are doing something different from what Signorelli or Veronese or Poussin or Manet did. They are all painters whom you admire, yet there is no conceivable way in which you could straightforwardly combine what you do with what they did. But how do you experience the fact that you have denied yourself part of what was available to them? There are, I am sure, many ways of experiencing the loss – including denying it – but I am sure that everyone who admires your work will be interested in any answer you have to this question.

J.G. The loss is in terms of possibilities. Reading a stimulating book full of new ideas or confronting a new and exciting visual situation, either in terms of other art or in external reality, seldom helps in the way that it can with figurative art, or even in 'veiled' abstraction. Visually the body offers fewer possibilities for reinvention than nature does, so painters who have worked their way into abstraction through landscape are in a sense in a more open and receptive situation. Interestingly enough I can't think of any abstract artists whose work interests me who have worked their way into abstraction through still life. Mondrian was interested in still life, but it was the landscapes and in particular the seascapes that got him into abstraction. Malevich's still-life abstractions are really just a misunderstanding of Cubism, and it was through the body that he achieved his really significant abstraction. Kandinsky did it through the figure in landscape. In the case of both the 'stripping bare' and 'moving up' processes, it becomes a very confrontational situation for the artist and the viewer; and the danger, for the artist, is that the picture/image becomes self-referential and repetitive.

If you do a painting of a figure or of figures in a landscape, for example, the possibilities are endless: you can move the figure about in space, make it larger or smaller and so forth. But if you have produced an abstract painting by moving up into body imagery and the picture itself has become the image, it becomes extremely difficult to reinvent the image, to visualize it in different situations or in different surroundings as you can constantly when you are working in a figurative idiom. I see Malevich's *Black Square* very much in terms of body imagery. But if it was, as he saw it, a *tabula rasa*, it was also in certain respects a dead end, the end of a process.

He had to look for new themes through which he could work himself back into abstraction, and he did it through aerial photographs and so forth; for a while there was much more variety in his abstractions – many more possibilities – though he produced no image that was as powerful as the *Black Square*; then of course he ended up with the *White Square*. Pollock, after he had found his way into abstraction, subsequently tried to revive or repeat the *processes* by which he had got himself there, not always so totally successfully the second time round. I think a very high proportion of abstract artists, more particularly those who have found their way into abstraction through figure work, and even more particularly those who have done so through the single figure, have at certain times felt it difficult to renew themselves and their art. I think Rothko was ultimately and tragically very much aware of this.

To get back to a question you asked earlier: I confronted the centralized images in earlier works by moving right into them. The individual images had become simultaneously so flat and so centralized that they seemed almost like pictures within a picture. I was faced with the alternative of expanding the space or the areas around the image in order to be able to move the image about more, to destroy the centralization, or else of moving up into the image, making the image the picture and subsequently looking for ways to fill the picture-image with light and space. The movement up into the imagery was and still is in some ways liberating and exhilarating, but it has also shut endless doors, endless possibilities. I spend a lot of time looking at other painting and it is possibly my greatest pleasure; but it saddens me that I can now very seldom respond to its stimulus in my own work in the way that I would like to. I love the paintings in the National Gallery, but I can now very seldom draw on them directly in my own work in the way that many of my figurative painter friends do. On the other hand, I often try to echo in my own work the emotional or psychological chords that individual works of the past strike in me, and I can be very directly inspired by colour combinations, effects of light and so forth. When the El Greco *View of Toledo* was on loan to the National Gallery, for example, I thought how good it would be if an abstract painter could produce a painting that was so mysterious and so totally dark and nocturnal and yet so full of light.

R.W. Now there is one issue which, as far as I can see, is, historically at any rate, much associated with the rise of abstraction, though perhaps only accidentally so: and that is the disappearance, the attenuation, of detail, at least detachable or significant detail. You could, of course, excise a portion of a Pollock, but it wouldn't really be detachable detail. There isn't detail in Rothko, though the jagged edges of the rectangles invariably come to engross our attention. Detail abounds in one abstract painter whom I admire more than you do: Hans Hofmann, particularly in his very late work, the *Renate* paintings. Now, *your* work displays detail. Now, what do you feel about this tendency in so much twentieth-century painting, abstract and non-abstract, which has the effect of squeezing out localized attention? Do you feel it's just the end of one historical tendency, or is it something graver than that?

J.G. I wonder if it isn't more a question of incident than of detail. In Impressionist painting, for example, there is for the most part very little detail, but there are a lot of incidental effects in the handling of paint, and because of this one enjoys looking at them close to as well as from the greater distance from which they were meant to be viewed; small sections of the paintings reproduce very well. I think the question of the abolition of detail is as relevant to a lot of contemporary figurative work as it is to almost all contemporary abstract art. An artist like Bacon achieves some of his effects by playing off small touches of detail against large empty areas, or, in his best work, large empty spaces. But there isn't all that much detail in late Picasso or in, for example, an artist like Baselitz, although there is quite a lot of incident in the paint effects. One of the legacies of heroic mid-century abstraction to subsequent figurative art was the legacy of the large-scale format, and this has posed problems. Artists whose imaginative powers rely on very specific use of imagery and hence often on detail then find it hard to incorporate it into, so to speak, the grander scope of things; and it often looks fussy or lost – this happens, for instance, in a lot of the big Clementes. The detail or incident in Hofmann probably comes because he enjoyed pushing paint about, while many of his colleagues in contemporary American art were more involved in making large physical and symbolic gestures. The incident in my own paint effects comes from the fact that I work the pictures over very long periods, and the traces of earlier marks and configurations build up and coagulate into little pockets of interest that aren't immediately apparent when seen from a distance; but I like being able to go up to a picture and to enjoy bits of it close to after having apprehended it as a whole. Maybe one of the reasons that contemporary art in general makes less use of detail or incident is that viewers, even serious ones, spend less time actually looking at individual works than they used to.

R.W. Let me try and be more precise. How I think of detail is as something that makes a distinct contribution to the whole. The leading idea here is that detail works in a picture in a way analogous to the way a word is used in a sentence. A word makes a distinct contribution to the meaning of a sentence, even though there are many words – 'and', 'very', 'is' – whose meaning it would be extremely hard to give outside the context of a sentence. Of course this is only an analogy here, just because, as I am always so insistent, pictorial meaning and linguistic meaning are such very different things. Now let's take a painting of yours for an example. Take *Body*: a passage that I think of as detail is to be found against the right edge, about half way down, isolated by narrow pale bands. It is cavernous, with a split or fissure, above a lot of far space. We can identify the contribution that this makes to the picture – though remove the passage from the picture and who knows what the passage would look like? In your painting, as I see it, detail often centres around incident – to use your distinction. The successor to the abrasive surface, which we talked about earlier, is constituted by smallish passages in which the paint (as you say) coagulates. They remind me of somewhat similar passages, very differently produced, which we find in de Kooning: passages which I have described as resembling the breast of a tiny bird. Why I think of these as successors to the abrasive surfaces is that they too draw the spectator towards them – and this effect has a great deal to do with their segmentation into detail. They *compel* isolated attention, as I see it.

J.G. Yes, I was probably underplaying the role of what I called incident in my work. Earlier on I very consciously enjoyed playing off more elaborately worked passages of paint against larger, emptier, or more broadly handled areas. It is something that I now do much less consciously, but it is still very central to how I work and to the effects I want to achieve. As centres of focus or interest begin to form or grow, I often make them into cells or pockets by catching them up in a linear net, or by reinforcing the contours of areas around them. It is a process of affirmation and cancellation because sometimes the whole surface becomes too busy and pocketed and then I have to get rid of the detail or incident, or at least some of it, in favour of recapturing the broader effects. As you say, or imply, it is a question of ensuring that details, areas one can home in on when one moves up close to a painting, simultaneously fall into place within the totality of the picture when one moves back from it. In the case of *Body*, the banded spatial cells at the right are in fact less highly worked than the denser red areas to the left where there was much more of the process of cancellation and reaffirmation; because of this the smallish superimposed colour patches and touches are more separate and read more as detail and this effect is reinforced by catching them up in the pale bands or flares. The more vaporous treatment of the space at the right seems to balance the matted space of the rest of the picture and is in a sense an escape for the eye. I do appreciate your point that in a lot of more recent abstraction every mark and gesture seems to be at the service of the painting as a whole, no matter how small or broken it may be, and because of this the eye is not invited to enjoy or explore individual areas of the surface.

R.W. You've talked just now of the bands or flares in your pictures. You've anticipated me. I think that anyone, on looking at the body of work in this exhibition as a whole, will eventually become aware of the three factors I've isolated: the body, light, mystery. But someone wanting to come to grips with the actual surfaces would most likely start by trying to grasp the role of the one recurrent morphological feature in the pictures, and that is the bands – and the gap between the bands. Leaving aside their genesis, where they come from, how do you think of their evolution over the ten years of work that this exhibition covers? This would give the spectator a way of ordering the pictures.

J.G. I find it hard to separate the functions of the bands in the paintings from their genesis. I spoke of the way the figures in Orozco's paintings seem to wear their skeletons on the outside. The white bands or flares in my painting are a distant legacy from him in that they are the paintings' bones or substructures.

Originally, after I had moved into abstraction, I divided the canvases into two or three simple geometric shapes which had for me the quality of presences. The flares or bands articulated the edges of the shapes; they helped to separate the shapes while the geometry of the compositions held the paintings together. Then the relationship of the bands to the shapes became more complicated; bands began getting into the shapes, animating and modifying them. As a result of this I sensed how I could get more light into the pictures. I have for a very long time been obsessed with the way in which Braque compresses or accordion-pleats space up on to the canvas, so that a painting of an interior can seem to contain more space within it than the actual interior to which it is related. By multiplying the bands, I think I was instinctively trying to pleat more light into the paintings. And of course when light shifts it makes one more aware of space too, so that as there was more light in the paintings and more variety of light, I think the paintings got more spatial, too – or at least I hope so. Originally the pleating of light was on an upright axis, and basically it still is; I think that for most people the upright emphasis is more evocative of the human presence than the horizontal. At one point light in my painting became increasingly pocketed, and the bands began to bend and interlace to contain the pockets of light. And in order to get more light into the paintings, I began folding it in more different directions or axes. But when there is too much horizontal pleating or folding, the pictures begin to acquire horizon lines and to look like surrogate landscapes and I have to wipe them out and begin again.

R.W. One question that interests me about your paintings is point of view. When we look at a painting of yours, are we looking at an image that sticks up in front of us – like the painting itself does – or are we looking down on something, or do our points of view (as I suspect) shift? The question I'm asking is one that descends from Monet's *Nymphéas*, which in this respect at any rate were precursors of abstraction. Otherwise I regard this as an exaggerated issue. There, I feel, we look down on to the watery surface for about the upper two-thirds of the picture; then, as our eyes reach the lower one-third, we find ourselves looking back into the water from a point barely above it. I take it that one thing that this achieves is that it preserves the traditional idea of the bottom versus the top of the picture. Would you like to say where you stand on this? Do you think of yourself as organizing a picture with a top and a bottom, or one which has four sides with nothing directional about them – like a swimming pool looked at from above? Or do you feel a tension between these two perspectives on to the work – if you do, how do you adjudicate between them? 'Adjudicate' is of course an artificial word, but that's why I use it. Because what we are doing here is trying to make explicit something that is executed implicitly. And why not? It always seems to me a perfectly legitimate thing to do.

J.G. Maybe it is the scale of the *Nymphéas* that induces the ambiguities. The edge of the water Monet was looking down on, or had looked down on, he painted at eye level and so we experience it as though just above them, as you say. The larger sheets of water that were receding from him horizontally he had to look down on in imagination; and after he had, so to speak, picked them up and put them on the upright canvas, we seem to be suspended over them as if we were looking at them from a high bridge but also quite close to. One doesn't – or at least I don't – get the same ambiguous reading from the smaller water paintings. When the vast format became one of the hallmarks of American abstract painting of the late 1940s and 1950s, all kinds of odd things happened. For instance, I get sensations almost of vertigo in front of certain Clyfford Stills; the tops of the paintings are often quite high above one's head, but the eye rushes up their surfaces at such a speed that one can somehow sense oneself at the top of the pictures and about to fall off them. (Tintoretto sometimes gives me visual vertigo, but this is because of the high viewpoints he uses and because the space in his work often seems to spin.) I don't know where Still placed himself when he was studying his own work, but I imagine it was relatively close to. Then when we got used to the idea of having very big modern paintings around, a lot of people unconsciously began treating them as if they were smaller pictures by trying to 'hold them down'. I think that this is why the Newman exhibition at the Tate in 1972 had such a surprisingly poor reception. One went into these enormous galleries and saw people standing too far back from the works.

I suppose the fact that I sometimes stand and work my paintings upside down but couldn't ever look at them on their sides confirms the fact that I see them as having a top and bottom, very definitely. After a few elements have been laid in, I tend to begin the pleating process I spoke of at the top and bottom. Because the tops and bottoms are more articulated than the sides, the sides are more open and expansive; the eye can drift off the sides sometimes but seldom off the top or bottom. But I do work the paintings on the floor a lot when I want to paint very wetly, and then I walk round them in all directions, although the canvas always remains stretched up because the exact format is crucial to me. I suspect that when painters work on the floor, they tend to work more quickly, partly because they are to a certain extent working blind in that they can't totally appreciate what they have done until the canvas is dry and can be studied vertically against the wall. So, basically, I see the images as sticking up in front of me, or in front of the viewer, but there is also something of the swimming pool about them because of the technique, the way they are executed.

R.W. With what someone coming fresh to this exhibition is bound to think of as unnatural restraint, we haven't so far talked about your concern with colour. Colour is such a salient aspect of your painting. It has great meaning for you and great appeal. I deliberately put it like that to bring out its twice-over appearance in your work. And you have a striking natural sensitivity to colour compared not only to myself – I have rather defective colour vision – but to almost everyone else.

I propose starting with something I remember from a review written by the Israeli painter Arikah. It has somehow stuck in my mind. He asked why it was that almost all critics in writing about a painter's work described it in the vernacular of colour instead of in the language of pigment. Of course this was in part malice, or a way of saying that art critics aren't technically qualified to write about art, but there is a way of taking it straight, and, if we do, then I think that it's most interesting taken on the most general level. Then it is pointing out that colour gets into painting only through the manipulation of pigment: something which people who approach painting through slides of painting can effectively overlook. Because slides make paintings approximate to stained glass. But there is also – or could be – a normative aspect to the remark. Painting, it might be saying, is profounder, or most itself, when it emphasizes the materials of colour. Florentine painting, for all its great beauty, is constantly haunted by the aetherealization of colour: of course, in some cases, the beauty and the aetherealization of colour go together, one arises out of the other. I suppose the historical truth of the matter is that this aetherealization could be fully overcome only with the introduction of oil paint and the emergence of the brush stroke; in effect, Venice. I think we should talk about Venice, and your work certainly invites it. But before we take this up, let us take up an issue, a distinct issue, but one which is the mirror image of colour as materiality: and that is materiality as colour. It seems to me that within painters to whom the materiality is something enormously important, there is a difference between those to whom this stuff is essentially coloured, and is so even when they drain it of brightness, and those for whom the stuff is not like that at all. Rembrandt, for instance, for whom matter is essentially tangible. This struck me so forcefully the other day in Vienna looking at the Titians. There we have a painter for whom colour is materialized and, at the same time additionally, the materiality is something essentially coloured. I looked at a number of early Titians, middle Titians, and then at the great late *Nymph and Shepherd*. Now there is no more colour in this painting, I imagine, than in, say, a late Rembrandt self-portrait. Yet even at his most tenebrist, Titian still strikes me as a painter who, in loading the canvas with matter, is encrusting it with colour, even if maximally muted colour. In other words, he remains the opposite of Rembrandt.

Now I would like to ask you two questions. Is there anything you can say about colour in your work – or is it too close to you, like the element of mystery I raised earlier? And how do the colour and pigment fit together in your scheme of things? More particularly, there is this issue: you use acrylic, and yet, as far as I can see, you seem to get out of acrylic something rather like what the Venetians got out of the newly discovered oil paint.

J.G. I think colour is the hardest aspect of painting to analyse or talk about. On the one hand it can often be the most immediately physical and emotive aspect of painting and on the other it is the most elusive and intangible; it also provokes a more subjective response in spectators, I suspect, than any other pictorial property. It strikes me as interesting and possibly revealing that whereas one can think of endless artists who were natural-born draughtsmen – Degas and Picasso, to name only two, come instantly to mind – many artists whom one thinks of as colourists only became really great colourists in mid-career or relatively late in life. There are marvellous colouristic passages in Delacroix's *Massacre at Scio*, but the painting as a whole isn't a colouristic marvel in the way that later works of his are. Similarly, it seems to me that Bonnard didn't truly hit his stride as a colourist until the 1920s when he was well into middle age. Matisse was a natural colourist, but even so it took him quite a time to find his feet.

The question of colour as a substance baffles me somewhat. When you talk of the aetherealization of colour in Florentine art, I suppose you mean that it has so little substance to it – it can be beautiful and can move us, but it is seldom the painter's primary concern or vehicle. Bellini must somehow be a test case here because even in his late work his colour retains some residual feeling of 'fill in'; one is always so aware of the contours of forms, and yet colour is what is carrying the pictures more than anything else. Of course he had oil paint, but he was applying it lightly and smoothly so that, although light seems to flood the pictures from various directions on our side of the canvas, the pictures also seem to be lit from behind. I imagine that for him light and colour had become more or less synonymous, and except in pictures that are totally tenebrist it is always a bit hard to separate the two. Titian is so much more physical and emotive. But what is interesting is the way in which the sensuous quality of the pigment and colour, even its sensuality, becomes sublimated. We become increasingly aware of the tactility of the paint, and of the paint as colour, and yet also increasingly aware of the fact that it isn't itself at all, that it is just pure emotion. I wonder if it would be fair to say that he felt in terms of colour. Latterly, and as his eyesight deteriorated, he was able to endow very dark paintings, the tenebrist paintings you speak of like *Nymph and Shepherd* and the London National Gallery *The Death of Actaeon*, with colouristic sensations, even though there is relatively little colour in them.

Although Veronese's colour is so incredibly rich and sumptuous, I think he used colour much more intellectually and self-consciously. Maybe he thought rather than felt in colour. And one can learn so much from him. Last time I stood in front of the *Feast in the House of Levi* in the Accademia, I all of a sudden realized how he was structuring those vast expanses in terms of his reds; red, for me, is the most static of colours. If you mentally remove the other colours from this painting, the reds are still giving you the painting's structure or basic composition. I don't think you could ever mentally remove a colour from a Titian. I am also intrigued by the way Veronese can use a very small amount of a particular colour and yet make it pervade a picture; one can think 'that is a very blue painting', and yet on examination one finds there is relatively little blue pigment in it. His use of drapery is extraordinary too. Drapery sometimes seems to convey more of the movement and drama of what he is saying than the bodies underneath – drapery as metaphor, I suppose.

In this century the painter who has got most out of colour is of course Matisse. Sometimes he invents new light sensations with it, as he did in his Fauve work, sometimes he recreates natural light with it, and sometimes he uses it decoratively, or simply as itself, for the pleasure it gives the eye – I see some of the paintings of the 1930s in this way. He could also use colour very physically in the sense of making one so aware of pigment and colour as matter, while at other times – and in these instances colour seems to take us over even more completely – there seems to be very little of the actual stuff on the canvas. These are the Matisses that emanate most light. A lot of contemporary abstraction is very bright but gives out very little light. Occasionally it actually cannibalizes the light around it. These works look wonderfully stimulating and alive when one first encounters them, but after a while one's eyes feel dry and drained.

I myself am obsessed by the properties of pure pigment, which is why I work so much in pastel. There is no binding medium, or virtually none, so that there is nothing getting between you and the pure colour sensation; and the moment you rub it on to a white support, colour seems to be lit up not only from behind but from within – the colour is very much there, but it is also in a sense insubstantial because there is hardly any matter to it. In my own work I see colour and light as totally interdependent. I would never put one colour down next to another simply to make one or other or both more telling and vivid. Rather, colours initiate dialogues which produce light sensations which in turn echo or induce psychological experience. To this extent the paintings are about states of mind, although I suppose in a sense everybody's paintings are, in one way or another. In the paintings I use acrylic because of its quick-drying properties; also it can be used very wetly without becoming too thin or insubstantial. As I have said, the paintings are worked on for very long periods, and in the process they become very elaborately built up. If I were working in oils it would take that much longer for me to finish a painting, years rather than months. But acrylic can be very unpleasant as a substance, and it can also look like an unpleasant synthetic skin, which of course is what it is. Then again acrylic paints, in England at least, as opposed to oil paints, are very underpigmented; because of this they can be simultaneously garish but dull. To combat this I do a lot of glazing; one can, for example, make a cobalt blue more resonant or more spatial by glazing it over another blue that has a lot of purple in it, or even over a Venetian red. As the colours become more layered, they become more physically palpable but also more luminous so that paradoxically they lose some of their physicality. I realize that I have, largely unconsciously, tried to use the glazing and layering possibilities of acrylic to achieve something that corresponds or approximates to the way the Venetians used oils. The colour and light in Venetian painting continues to move me in a way that colour and light in more recent painting, which means as much to me in other ways, does not.

R.W. I think that it is crucial for a spectator of your work to bear in mind what you say about Veronese and drapery. I think that it is a failure to recognize the way you are implicitly drawing on these effects of Veronese's – light falling not directly on the body but on drapery, or an outer coating of the body – that leads people off on a tangent to assimilate your work to landscape. And that reminds me to go back to something you said at the beginning. In agreeing that your painting always retained its reference to the body, you said that some people thought it derived from landscape, and you said that, though this wasn't right, you didn't mind. You said that 'it didn't bother you'. I'll now confess that this amazed me. I think of you as an extremely tolerant person, and I think that is a characteristic of yours that is to some degree formative of your painting: it makes your painting unhectoring, indeed unrhetorical, and I personally find this quality so exhilarating in an art world full of manifestos and denunciations and declarations of intent, disguised as paintings. Nevertheless – and I may be taking you too literally here – I wonder how it is that you cannot mind being misunderstood. Of course I can see how you might think that what you're doing could get through to people at one level, unconsciously or preconsciously, even when at another level they conceptualize it to themselves incorrectly. However, isn't there a real danger in these false conceptualizations? I say this partly for a particular reason: and that is I think it's becoming increasingly clear that the New York School has suffered so much from critics just saying what they wanted about the artists, and the artists, or some artists, for one reason or another, not challenging them. But, as I say, I may be reading too much into a casual remark of yours.

J.G. The whole question of the ways in which abstract art can be 'read' is so vexed. Undoubtedly people's response to abstract art is even more subjective than their response to figurative painting. I remember Frank Stella writing in *Working Space* that he 'had trouble' with what he called the 'underpinnings' of pioneer abstraction; in a sense this is an odd thing to say because without their ideological and intellectual underpinnings the artists would never have achieved their ends or got themselves visually where they did. On the other hand, I don't think that one has to be aware of their interest in theosophy or the fourth dimension, for example, to sense that their work has content and is profound.

I said earlier that when my paintings began to look like surrogate landscapes I wiped them out; and if I thought that people saw them as surrogate landscapes, this would worry me. But if people see certain landscape connotations in the work, this doesn't trouble me. Turner's light is often straightforwardly naturalistic, of course, and he is the British painter who has most influenced me, although it is also true that I respond most to the most visionary and most abstract of his works. Cézanne haunts me; I am particularly obsessed by the late landscapes, and I would like to think that some of their space had got indirectly into my work, even if my own imagery does derive ultimately from the body. I think that artists got very brain-washed by the insistence on flatness in so much abstract art, and for that matter so much figurative art, of the 1940s and 1950s. The painting that I am drawn to most of all is painting that is very flat but also very full of space. Late Bellini means as much to me as any painting in the world; it is very flat because it tends to be very frontal, and the overlapping images are so tightly bonded to the surface; but the paintings are also full of space that comes through light even more than through perspective. I agree with you about it being wrong for artists to allow critics to falsify their work and that they should speak up for themselves, although while one can think of artists who have written marvellously well, one can think of others who would have been better advised to remain silent. Today I think it is the art impresarios more than critics who tend to interpret or misinterpret artists' work for them.

R.W. Now there is one point I'd like to end on. You think of your pictures in terms of their succeeding or not, of their 'working' or not. What is it for you for a picture to work? Let's – if you like – take the painting here that you like best: can you say why? I don't mean conclusively – but can you say something about why?

J.G. Well, quite obviously the pictures have to work in the straightforward way of complying with visual, formalistic criteria. They sometimes do this at a fairly early stage in their evolution, but the ones that do so are in fact often the ones I have to work on longest. There is no one painting in the exhibition that I like best, so can I take the painting that on recent visits to my studio is the one that I think you liked best? I often give my pictures titles only in order to be able to identify them quickly in my mind after they have left the studio. Sometimes a title suggests itself to me as I am working on a painting; this is the case, for example, with the painting called *Echo*, which incidentally, despite the fact that the greens immediately evoke associations with foliage, I see in terms of body imagery – the white, columnar form is somehow to me very female, and so I gave the picture the name of a nymph. But the picture I am talking about, which we have already mentioned, is predominantly red. When I asked you if you could think of a title for it, you suggested I call it simply *Body*; so I did. It was a picture that began very well; it had a nice swinging movement to it, and a couple of painter friends who saw it urged me to leave it as it was. But after a while it seemed to me to be all surface, both in the sense that it didn't have enough space and depth to it visually, but also in that it looked exactly the same every time I pulled it out, so that after a while it seemed psychologically flat too. I went back into the painting and worked it over a period of some months. I kept losing it; after altering aspects or elements in it, the picture looked awkward or inconclusive, but it was also becoming more layered in every sense. Then I put it aside again. Subsequently I reworked it yet again, quite quickly, and it got back to looking more like it originally had, but I could now look at it for longish spells without getting bored with it. I like the way it seems to move from right to left and yet the eye ends up in the middle of it. To this extent, although there is a lot of movement in the picture, it is also quite firm and steady, even quite still. It is in certain respects a visceral painting, and several people have seen suggestions of body imagery in it.

Notes

1 Guillaume Apollinaire: the Painters' Friend

1 The articles, occasioned by a Picasso exhibition at the Galerie Serrurier, appeared in the April issue of *La Revue Immoraliste* and in *La Plume*, 15 May 1905.

2 In a preface to the catalogue of the exhibition at the Galerie Serrurier.

3 Approximately ninety per cent of Apollinaire's writings on art dates from 1904 to 1914, when the critic's career was interrupted by the war.

4 However, only in a letter of 1917, published by the *Mercure de France*, did Apollinaire suggest that Cubism was not the exclusive creation of Picasso, but rather the result of his collaboration with Braque.

5 There is a reference to this in the various cartoons by Picasso which show Apollinaire wearing the papal tiara. The most completely 'papal' of these is reproduced in André Billy, *Guillaume Apollinaire*, Seghers, Paris, 1956.

6 It was Mollet who introduced Apollinaire to Picasso.

7 In *Je dis tout*, 12 October 1907.

8 The article was published in the December issue, under the title *Henri Matisse*.

9 This was, in fact, a preface to the *Cercle d'Art Moderne* exhibition held in Le Havre in June 1908. It appeared in article form in *Le Feu*, 1 July 1908 and was later incorporated with some changes into *The Cubist Painters*.

10 The manuscript for the poem is dated 5 November 1907. The poem appeared for the first time in *La Phalange*, 15 November 1907.

11 See Alfred Barr, *Picasso, Fifty Years of His Art*, Museum of Modern Art, New York, 1946, p. 57.

12 Apollinaire's association with Géry-Piéret led to his false arrest in 1911 on charges of collusion with the thief of the *Mona Lisa*.

13 Published under the title *Guillaume Apollinaire: Chroniques d'Art 1902–18*, Gallimard, Paris, 1960.

14 Originally intended to be published merely as a collection of little essays entitled MEDITATIONS ESTHETIQUES with *Les peintres cubistes* as a subtitle, but the printer by mistake reversed the use of capitals and thus the emphasis.

15 In *L'Intransigeant*, 20 April 1911.

16 Delaunay's article, entitled *Réalité, Peinture Pure*, appeared in the December issue of Apollinaire's own new periodical, *Les Soirées de Paris*.

17 This part was an adaptation of the speech delivered at the *Section d'Or*; it comprises the bulk of Section VII.

18 In *L'Intransigeant*, 7 February 1912, and in *Le Petit Bleu*, 9 February 1912.

19 The idea of the Paris trip had originally been Severini's. Upon their return to Italy the Futurist painters either destroyed their earlier work or reworked it in the light of Cubist discoveries.

20 In the *Revue Blanche*, 1 April 1903.

21 In *Je dis tout*, 12 October 1907. Jourdain had rejected many late Cézannes in favour of works from the earlier, constructive phase.

22 This appeared as *Lettre de Paris* in *Le Passant*, Brussels, 25 November 1911.

23 The review discusses the *Société Nouvelle* and appeared in *L'Intransigeant*, 11 March 1911.

24 In an article published in *L'Esprit Nouveau*, 26 October 1924, a special issue dedicated to Apollinaire.

25 Done by Marcel Duchamp.

26 Quoted from Cecily Mackworth in *Guillaume Apollinaire and the Cubist Life*, London, 1961, p. 98.

27 Apollinaire later used the name as the title of one of his most beautiful poems.

28 Notes from the trip are in *The Green Book*, Paris, 1934.

29 In March 1916, Apollinaire received a severe head wound.

30 *Le 30ᵉ Salon des Indépendants* in *Les Soirées de Paris*, 15 March 1914.

31 *Nouveaux peintres*, *Paris Journal*, 14 July 1914.

32 In *La Phalange*, 15 February 1908.

33 Programme notes to *Parade*, Paris, May 1917.

34 Apollinaire died from an attack of Spanish flu in addition to complications resulting from his war injury.

35 There is some doubt whether the portrait under discussion is Zervos, *Picasso* (Editions Cahiers d'Art, Paris, 1949) III pl. 26, no. 75 or no. 76, erroneously dated 1917 by Zervos. No. 76 seems to be the more likely one, since it is a less romantic work and shows Picasso in a more serious, questioning mood. Picasso originally told Roland Penrose that he had executed one self-portrait at this time (Roland Penrose, *Picasso, His Life and Work*, London, 1958, pp. 205–6) but he later told John Richardson that he had done two self-portraits (information received from Mr Richardson).

Notes

2 Fauvism and the School of Chatou: Post-Impressionism in Crisis

1 Paul Sérusier, *ABC de la Peinture*, published together with Maurice Denis's *Paul Sérusier, sa Vie, son Œuvre*, Paris, 1942, p. 42.
2 Ibid., p. 43.
3 Maurice Denis, 'Définition du Néo-Traditionisme' in *Art et Critique*, Paris, 23 and 30 August 1890. Reprinted in *Théories – Du Symbolisme au Classicisme*, Paris, 1964, p. 33.
4 Maurice Genevoix, *Vlaminck*, Paris, 1954, p. 13.
5 Maurice Catinat, *Les Bords de la Seine avec Renoir et Maupassant, L'Ecole de Chatou*, Paris, 1952.
6 Maurice de Vlaminck, *Dangerous Corner* (translated by Michael Ross), London, 1961, p. 74.
7 Ibid., p. 74.
8 Ibid., p. 147.
9 André Derain, *Lettres à Vlaminck*, Paris, 1955.
10 Ibid., p. 44.
11 Ibid., p. 98.
12 Marcel Sauvage, *Vlaminck, sa Vie et son Message*, Geneva, 1956.
13 André Derain, *Lettres à Vlaminck*, Paris, 1955, pp. 154–5.
14 Gaston Diehl, *Les Fauves*, Paris, 1971.
15 See *The Tate Gallery Catalogue: The Foreign Paintings*, London, 1959, pp. 64–5.
16 Ellen Oppler, *Fauvism Re-examined*, New York/London, 1974, p. 104. John Elderfield, *Fauvism*, Museum of Modern Art, New York, 1976, p. 35.
17 Maurice Denis, 'L'influence de Gauguin', in *L'Occident*, October 1903, reprinted in *Théories*, Paris, 1964, pp. 50–4.
18 Richard Griffiths, *The Reactionary Revolution*, London, 1966.
19 Charles Chassé, *Les Nabis et leur Temps*, Paris, 1960, p. 56.
20 Paul Sérusier, *ABC de la Peinture*, 3rd edn, Paris, 1950 (contains a 'correspondance inédite' collected by Mme P. Sérusier and annotated by Mlle H. Boutaric), pp. 39–42.
21 Ibid., pp. 39–42.
22 André Derain, *Lettres à Vlaminck*, Paris, 1955, p. 147.
23 Maurice de Vlaminck, *Dangerous Corner*, London, 1961, p. 76.
24 Ibid., p. 15.
25 Jean-Paul Crespelle, *Vlaminck*, Paris, 1958.
26 André Derain, *Lettres à Vlaminck*, Paris, 1955, p. 150.

3 Two New Views of Matisse: a Book and an Exhibition

1 See the references to Matisse in Breton's collected art criticism published as *Le Surréalisme et la Peinture*, Paris, 1965.
2 Jean Cocteau, *Le Rappel à l'Ordre*, Paris, 1926, pp. 98–9.
3 A. Ozenfant, *Mémoires 1886–1962*, Paris, 1968, pp. 215–16.
4 Roger Fry, *Henri Matisse*, Paris and New York, 1930.
5 Jack Flam's *Matisse: the Man and his Art 1869–1918*, London, complements both Barr's and Schneider's monographs.
6 Quoted in G. Duthuit, *Les Fauves: Braque, Derain, Van Dongen, Dufy, Friesz, Manguin, Marquet, Matisse, Puy, Vlaminck*, Geneva, 1949, p. 170.
7 John Elderfield, *Henri Matisse: A Retrospective*, New York and London, 1992, with assistance from Beatrice Kernan and Judith Cousins. 480 pages including 295 plates in colour, 95 plates in black and white and 150 black and white figures.

4 Pioneering Cubism

1 Wilhelm Uhde, *Picasso et la Tradition Française: Notes sur la Peinture Actuelle*, Paris, 1928, p. 39.
2 For Braque's most explicit statements about the role of space in his art, see Dora Vallier, 'Braque, la peinture et nous', *Cahiers d'Art*, 1, Paris, 1954.
3 D. H. Kahnweiler, *Der Weg zum Kubismus*, Munich, 1920, p. 27.
4 Max Morise, 'Les yeux enchantés', *La Révolution Surréaliste*, 1, 1 December 1924.
5 André Breton, *Le Surréalisme et la Peinture*, (new edition 1928–1963), Paris, 1965, p. 6.
6 John Richardson, *Georges Braque*, 1959, London, p. 26.
7 Ibid., p. 27.
8 Kahnweiler often repeated this story to me.

5 Still-Life Lives

1 Simon Schama, *The Embarrassment of Riches*, London, 1987.
2 Jean Sutherland Boggs, *Picasso and Things*, Cleveland Museum of Art, 1992, p. 54.
3 See William Rubin, 'From narrative to iconic in Picasso: the buried allegory in *Bread and Fruitdish on a Table* and the role of *Demoiselles d'Avignon*', *Art Bulletin*, LXV, (4), December 1983.
4 Picasso, *Collected Writings*, London, 1989.
5 Interview with Angel Ferran, *La Publicitat*, Barcelona, 19 October 1926.
6 Jaime Sabartés, *Portraits et Souvenirs*, Paris, 1946, p. 125.
7 Picasso, *Collected Writings*, London, 1989, p. XXIX.
8 Ibid., p. XI.
9 *Picasso/Apollinaire Correspondence*, (ed.) Pierre Caizergues and Hélène Seckel, Paris, 1992, p. 77.
10 Christian Zervos, 'Conversation avec

Picasso', *Cahiers d'Art*, Paris, 1935, 1, (10), pp. 173–8.

11 Daniel-Henry Kahnweiler, 'Le sujet chez Picasso', *Verve*, 25–6, Paris, 1951.

12 Picasso, *Collected Writings*, London, 1989, p. 9.

13 Ibid., p. 44.

14 Jean Sutherland Boggs, *Picasso and Things*, Cleveland Museum of Art, 1992, p. 330.

15 Gertrude Stein, *Picasso*, Paris, 1938, p. 1.

16 *Transition*, Paris, 4 July 1927. Reprinted in amended form in *Portraits and Prayers*, New York, 1934.

17 Quoted in *Picasso and Braque, Pioneering Cubism*, MOMA, New York, 1989, p. 389.

18 *The Collected Writings of Juan Gris 1913–1927*, from an appendix to Daniel-Henry Kahnweiler's *Juan Gris: His Life and Work*, translated by Douglas Cooper, London, 1947.

19 *Letters of Juan Gris*, (ed.) Douglas Cooper, London, 1956, p. 36.

20 Ibid., p. 104.

21 Kahnweiler, see note 11, p. 138.

22 Ibid., p. 138.

23 Quoted in Jean Leymarie, 'Braque's journey', in *Georges Braque*, Solomon R. Guggenheim Museum, New York, 1988, p. 15.

24 *Letters*, see note 19.

6 Two Picasso Exhibitions: Early and Late

1 The catalogue in two volumes, produced by the Musée Picasso, Paris, and edited by Hélène Seckel. It contains essays by Leo Steinberg, William Rubin, Pierre Daix, and a chronology by the editor and Judith Cousins. Hélène Seckel also brings together virtually every scrap of information relating to the *Demoiselles* up to 1939 when it entered its present home.

2 For a discussion of the literature on *Guernica*, see

Herschel B. Chipp *Picasso's Guernica*, University of California Press, 1989, and Ellen C. Oppler (ed.), *Picasso's Guernica*, Norton, 1987.

3 Fernande Olivier, *Picasso et ses amis*, Paris, 1933; *Souvenirs Intimes Ecrits pour Picasso*, Paris, 1988.

4 See catalogue of the exhibition under discussion, 2, p. 471, fn. 36.

5 Ibid., p. 654.

6 Ibid., p. 670.

7 Ibid., p. 650.

8 Gertrude Stein, *Picasso*, Paris, 1938, p. 18.

9 Catalogue, 2, pp. 685–6.

10 Ibid., p. 688.

11 Ibid., pp. 658–68. In the years between 1955, when I first went to see him, and his death in 1979, Kahnweiler often talked to me of the *Demoiselles*.

12 Ibid., pp. 376–8.

13 Ibid., p. 585.

14 Ibid., p. 590.

15 Ibid., p. 614. (The Advisory Committee of the Museum of Modern Art is clearly echoing Barr's views.)

16 Ron Johnson, 'Picasso's *Demoiselles d'Avignon* and the Theatre of the Absurd', *Arts Magazine*, 55 (2), October 1980; Rolf Laessoe, 'A source for Picasso's *Les Demoiselles d'Avignon*', *Gazette des Beaux Arts*, CX, October 1987; John Richardson, 'Picasso's apocalyptic whorehouse', *The New York Review of Books*, 23 April 1987.

17 John Richardson, 'L'époque Jacqueline', in *Le Dernier Picasso, 1953–1973*, Centre Georges Pompidou, Paris, 1988, pp. 55–75.

18 André Malraux, *La Tête d'Obsidienne*, Paris, 1974, pp. 18–19.

19 See Michael Leja, '''Le vieux marcheur'' and ''les deux risques'': Picasso, prostitution, venereal disease, and maternity, 1899–1907', *Art History*, 1, March 1985.

20 Leo Steinberg's *Le Bordel Philosophique*, originally published in 1972, was reprinted in the catalogue of the exhibition under discussion, with slight modifications, pp. 319–67.

21 Douglas Cooper, *Connaissance des Arts*, 257, July 1973, p. 23.

22 *Le Dernier Picasso*, fn. 17. The selectors were Marie-Laure Bernadac, Isabelle Monod Fontaine and David Sylvester.

23 Françoise Gilot and Carlton Lake, *Life with Picasso*, London, 1965, Penguin, 1966, p. 201.

24 Picasso in conversation with Pierre Daix, quoted by Richardson in the catalogue of the exhibition under discussion, p. 57.

25 Roland Penrose, *Picasso, his Life and Work*, 1958, revised 3rd edn, University of California Press, p. 396.

26 David Sylvester, 'Fin de partie', in *Le Dernier Picasso*, pp. 134–5.

27 Roland Penrose, *Picasso, his Life and Work*, 1958, p. 420.

28 *Le Dernier Picasso*, p. 35.

29 *Les Demoiselles d'Avignon*, (see note 1), 2, p. 587.

30 See John Richardson, 'L'époque Jacqueline', in *Le Dernier Picasso*, pp. 55–75.

31 Gilot and Lake, *Life with Picasso*, 1966, p. 120.

32 Brassaï, 'The master at 90', *New York Times Magazine*, 24 October 1971.

33 Picasso to Roland Penrose who repeated the remark to me.

34 Aragon, *Henri Matisse, a novel*, 1, London, 1972, p. 153.

35 Hélène Parmelin, *Picasso dit*, Paris, 1966, p. 151.

36 José L. Barrio Garay, in his introduction to *Picasso in Milwaukee*, Milwaukee Art Center, October 1970 to January 1971.

37 John Richardson, 'L'époque Jacqueline', in *Le Dernier Picasso*, p. 72.

38 David Sylvester in conversation with me.

Notes

7 Léger and the Heroism of Modern Life

1 English translation by Jonathan Mayne, *Baudelaire, Art in Paris 1845–1862*, London, 1965, p. 32.

2 This lecture was printed in *Les Soirées de Paris*, June 1914, as 'Les réalisations picturales actuelles'. It is included in *Les Fonctions de la Peinture*, a collection of Léger's essays published by Editions Gonthier, Paris, 1965.

3 Quoted in the catalogue of the 1956 Léger memorial exhibition at the Musée des Arts Décoratifs, Paris, p. 27.

4 Léger discussed the work of Cézanne in a lecture given at the Académie Wasilief on 5 May 1913. The lecture subsequently appeared in successive issues of *Montjoie* (29 May, 14 and 29 June 1913) as 'Les origines de la peinture et sa valeur représentative'. It is also included in *Les Fonctions de la Peinture*.

5 The influence of Futurism on Léger's thought becomes very clear in the second of the Académie Wasilief lectures 'Les Réalisations Picturales Actuelles'. Severini, in *Tutta la Vita di un Pittore* (published in Italy in 1946), tells us that Léger contemplated joining the Futurist movement officially, but was put off from doing so by his dislike of Marinetti.

6 In an article by 'La Palette', *Paris Journal*, 19 November 1911.

7 'Everybody is so fond of quoting that remark of mine, "I don't seek, I find".' Françoise Gilot and Carlton Lake, *Life with Picasso*, London, 1966. p. 189.

8 Quoted in the 1956 catalogue, see note 3, p. 114.

9 Malevich, *Essays on Art, 1915–1933*, 2, London, 1969, p. 67.

10 *De Stijl*, no. 9, 2nd year, 1919, p. 101. The statement had been first published a couple of months earlier, in the February–March issue of *Valori Plastici*.

11 *De Stijl*, no. 12, 2nd year, 1919, p. 457.

12 Mondrian *Le Néo-Plasticisme*, Paris, 1920.

13 'Note sur la Vie Plastique Actuelle', first published in a German translation in *Das Kunstblatt*, Berlin, 1923. It is reprinted in the original French in *Les Fonctions de la Peinture*.

14 Ozenfant, *Mémoires, 1886–1962*, Séghers, Paris, 1968, p. 517.

15 1918 is the date generally accepted for the meeting between Ozenfant and Jeanneret, but Ozenfant, (*Mémoires* p. 101) says that they met in May 1917; this may perhaps be an error of memory, or a slip on his part. Léger met Jeanneret/Le Corbusier in 1920. The exact date of his meeting with Ozenfant is not known but it was probably at more or less the same time. In 1924 Léger and Ozenfant together opened a painting school.

16 Reyner Banham, *Theory and Design in the First Machine Age*, London, 1960, p. 207.

17 The quotations in this paragraph are drawn from *Après le Cubisme*, Paris, 1918, 'Le Purisme', published in *L'Esprit Nouveau*, 4, January 1921, and *La Peinture Moderne*, Paris, 1925.

18 See *The Letters of Juan Gris*, (ed.) D. Cooper and published by D. H. Kahnweiler, London, 1956, pp. 104–6, and Ozenfant, *Mémoires*, pp. 132–4.

19 Quoted in the 1956 catalogue, see note 3, p. 162.

20 Ibid., p. 32.

21 Ernst, *Beyond Painting*, New York, 1948, p. 13.

22 'Couleur dans le Monde', *Europe*, 16 May 1938, p. 112.

8 Ozenfant

1 Ozenfant, *Mémoires, 1886–1962*, Paris, 1968, p. 586.

2 Ibid., p. 87.

3 Ozenfant and Jeanneret, *Après le Cubisme*, Paris, 1918, p. 56.

4 Ozenfant, *Mémoires*, pp. 90–1, 133–4.

5 *Art*, Paris, 1928.

6 Ozenfant, *Mémoires*, p. 115.

9 Futurism in Venice

1 Many, though by no means all, of the Futurist manifestos are reprinted in the *Archivi del Futurismo*, (ed.) Maria Drudi Gambillo and Teresa Fiori, Rome, 1, 1958, 2, 1962.

2 *Archivi*, 1, p. 475.

3 Founding Manifesto.

4 *Poesia*, 7, Milan, August 1905, p. 11.

5 *La Ville Charnelle*, Paris, 1908, pp. 167–72.

6 *Le Monoplane du Pape* was first published in Paris in 1912 but became better known in its Italian version, published under the aegis of *Poesia*.

7 Letter of 12 April 1912, *Archivi*, 1, pp. 237–8.

8 Although the piece became known as *Zang Tumb Tumb*, it was originally published as *Zang Tumb Tuuum Adrianopoli*, October 1912, *Parole in Libertá*, Poesia, Milan, 1914.

9 *Poesia*, Milan, 1916.

10 *Archivi*, 1, p. 225.

11 'Arte libera e pittura Futurista', *La Voce*, 25, 22 June 1911.

12 *La Voce*, 34, 24 August 1911.

13 Letter from Boccioni to Balla, month unknown, 1915, *Archivi*, 1, pp. 365–6.

14 Quoted in Caroline Tisdall and Angelo Bozzoli, *Futurism*, London, 1977, p. 69.

10 Supreme Suprematist (Malevich)

1 The exhibition was selected and curated by Angelica Zander Rudenstine.

2 The largest selection of Malevich's writings which includes most of the major texts published in Russia during his lifetime is *Essays on Art 1915–1935*, 1 and 2, (ed.) Troels Andersen with translations by Zenia Glowacki-Prus and Arnold McMillin, London, 1968.
3 Léger, 'Les origines de la peinture et sa valeur représentative', *Montjoie*, Paris, May–June, 1913; 'Les réalisations picturales actuelles', *Les Soirées de Paris*, Paris, June 1914.
4 See Pierre Daix and Joan Rosselet, *Picasso, The Cubist Years, 1907–1916*, London, Thames and Hudson, 1979, Catalogue number 332.
5 *On New Systems of Art*, 1919. Malevich's misunderstanding of Cubism is underlined in the first manifesto when he writes, 'The very object itself, together with its essence, purpose, sense of fullness of its presentation the Cubists thought were also unnecessary.'
6 Malevich, *God is not Cast Down*, 1920.
7 Howard Hinton, *The Fourth Dimension*, New York and London, 1904. See also Susan Compton, 'Malevich and the Fourth Dimension', *Studio International*, London, April 1974.
8 Malevich, *From Cubism to Suprematism, The New Realism in Painting*, subsequently reissued as *From Cubism and Futurism to Suprematism. The New Realism in Painting*, 1916.
9 For a slightly more detailed discussion of this painting, see my own 'The Black Square', *Studio International*, London, March/April 1975.
10 From the initial manifesto.
11 Published as an appendix to *Essays on Art*, 2, pp. 147–54.
12 Avenarius, *Philosophie als Denken der Welt gemässe dem Princip des kleinsten Kraftmasses*, Leipzig, 1876, p. 6.

13 Malevich, *Non-Objective Creation and Suprematism*, 1919.
14 *Suprematism, 34 Drawings*, 1920.
15 *Suprematism in World Reconstruction*, 1920. (Republished in *El Lissitzky* by Sophie Kueppers-Lissitzky, London, 1968).
16 Quoted in Ronald Hunt, 'The constructivist ethos: Russia 1913–32', *Art Forum*, New York, September/October 1967.
17 The drawing, probably dating from 1923–4, is in the State Russian Museum.

11 White Magic: Brancusi
1 Paul Herbé, 'Visite à Brancusi', *Architecture d'aujourd'hui*, Paris, April 1946, p. 54.
2 Quoted in Sidney Geist's preface to the Brancusi exhibition held at the Solomon R. Guggenheim Museum, New York, 1969, pp. 23–34.
3 Quoted in Radu Varia, *Brancusi*, Rizzoli, 1987, p. 60.
4 Quoted in Pontus Hulten, Natalia Dumitresco and Alexandre Istrati, *Brancusi*, Paris, 1988, p. 64.
5 Ibid., p. 65.
6 Peter Neagoe, *The Saint of Montparnasse*, Philadelphia and New York, Chilton, 1965.
7 See Varia, *Brancusi*, p. 109 and Hulten *et al.*, *Brancusi*, p. 66.
8 The photographs described are reproduced in Hulten *et al.*, *Brancusi*, p. 101 and p. 257.
9 Ibid., p. 132.
10 Quoted in Sidney Geist, *Brancusi, a Study of the Sculpture*, Hacker Books, 1983 (a revised edition of Geist's 1967 monograph).
11 Barbu Brezianu, *Brancusi in Romania*, Editura Academica Republicii Socialiste Romania, Bucharest, 1976.
12 See Geist, *Brancusi, a Study of the Sculpture*.
13 Varia, *Brancusi*, p. 15.
14 Hulten *et al.*, *Brancusi*, p. 247.

15 Ibid., p. 120.
16 The books under discussion are those by Varia, and by Hulten *et al.*
17 Varia, *Brancusi*, p. 17.
18 Ibid., p. 24.
19 Ibid., p. 11.
20 Ibid., p. 50.
21 Varia, 'The meaning and identity of Tirgu Jiu', in *Brancusi*, pp. 268–85. Brancusi refused to sign *The Table of the Kiss* and some Brancusi scholars question its status as a work of art and see it rather as an example of Brancusi's manufacture of furniture.
22 Hulten *et al.*, *Brancusi*.
23 *Brancusi*, ibid., p. 242.
24 Ibid., p. 154.
25 Varia, *Brancusi*, pp. 285–92.
26 Ibid., p. 292.
27 Ibid., p. 292.

12 Picasso's *Góngora*
1 In 1989 Aurum Press brought out an invaluable edition of Picasso's *Collected Writings*, edited by Marie-Laure Bernadac and Christine Piot. See also Lydia Gasman's PhD thesis of 1981, *Mystery, Magic and Love in Picasso, 1925–1938*, published by Yale University Press in 1986.
2 Brassaï, *Picasso and Co.*, London, Thames and Hudson, 1967, p. 128.
3 Kahnweiler told me this story.
4 Félicien Fagus, 'L'invasion Espagnole: Picasso', *La Revue Blanche*, 15 July 1901, pp. 464–5.
5 Z. Milner, 'Góngora et Mallarmé', *L'Esprit Nouveau*, 3, 1922, p. 285.
6 Pierre Reverdy, *Self Defence*, Paris, 1919, reprinted in *Oeuvres Complètes*, (ed.) Etienne-Allain Hubert, Paris, 1975.
7 André Breton, *What is Surrealism?* London, 1936, English translation by David Gascoyne, p. 25. Original French edition, *Qu'est que c'est le Surréalisme?*, Brussels, 1934.

Notes

8 Robert Desnos, *Réflexions sur la Poésie, Domaine Public*, Gallimard, Paris, · 1953, p. 403.

9 See for example Breton's comments on Picasso's work in *Combat*, Paris, 6 November 1961.

10 Gerald Brenan, *The Literature of the Spanish People*, Penguin Books, 1963, p. 224.

11 Published in *Poetry, East*, Spring–Summer, 1984.

13 Picasso and Surrealism

1 This was the first of a series of articles by Breton which came out in book form (with further additions) as *Le Surréalisme et la Peinture*, Paris, 1928. The word Surrealism is for the most part not capitalized in the original documents. For the sake of continuity a capital letter will be used throughout this essay.

2 A. Breton, 'Pablo Picasso', *Combat*, Paris, 6 November 1961. The original French reads 'sur le plan onirique et imaginatif'.

3 W. S. Rubin, *Dada and Surrealist Art*, New York, 1968, p. 279. The phrase was originally Breton's.

4 *Documents*, 2, Paris, 1930.

5 Quoted by Brassaï, *Picasso and Co.*, London, 1967, p. 28.

6 Brassaï, p. 27, says that the works by Picasso at the first Surrealist exhibition were lent by collectors without his knowledge. Sir Roland Penrose in *Picasso, His Life and Work*, London, 1958, p. 229, says Picasso agreed to have his work shown and this seems more likely.

7 For the problems involved in an exact dating of the *Three Dancers* see R. Alley, *The Three Dancers*, Charlton Lectures on Art, Newcastle upon Tyne, 1967.

8 Since 1972 when this essay was written critics have tended to focus on the iconographic, erotic and psychological implications of the *Demoiselles*. (See my own review of the 1988 *Demoiselles* exhibition in this volume.)

9 *Magazine of Art*, New York, 1937, pp. 236–9. Graham, Russian by birth and American by naturalization, spent much time in Paris and moved in Surrealist circles.

10 For a fuller analysis of *The Three Dancers* see the Tate Gallery *Report*, 1964–5, pp. 7–12. The passages on *The Three Dancers* were written by Lawrence Gowing and my own analysis and understanding of the picture are much indebted to him.

11 R. Alley, *The Three Dancers*, p. 11.

12 Picasso told Françoise Gilot that a friend of his youth had committed suicide for love of Germaine Pichot. Casagemas had shot himself after first trying to kill a young woman with whom he was obsessed. In the police files her first name is given as Laure, but it seems likely that it was the same woman. See F. Gilot and Carlton Lake, *Life with Picasso*, London, 1966, p. 75, and G. Daix and P. Boudaille, *Picasso 1900–1906*, Neuchâtel, 1966, p. 338.

13 'Picasso étudié par le Docteur Jung', *Cahiers d'Art*, 7th year, 8–10, Paris, 1932, p. 352. Jung's article printed here in a somewhat abbreviated form, was originally commissioned by the *Neue Zürcher Zeitung* on the occasion of the Picasso exhibition held at the Zürich Kunsthaus.

14 For the influence of tribal art on Picasso's art in the Synthetic Cubist phase see J. Golding, *Cubism, 1907– 14*, 2nd edn, London, 1968, pp. 123–5.

15 The mask is reproduced as plate 113 (p. 83) of *Picasso 1881–1973*, (eds) R. Penrose and J. Golding, Elek, 1973, in which this essay originally appeared and also in *Primitivism in the Twentieth Century*, (ed.) William Rubin, 2 vols., Museum of Modern Art, New York, 1984, p. 135.

16 E. Nesfield, *The Primitive Sources of Surrealism*, unpublished MA report submitted to the Courtauld Institute of Art, London University, 1970, pp. 23– 4. This essay is heavily indebted to Elizabeth Cowling's (née Nesfield) researches for many of the comparisons between Picasso's work and primitive sources.

17 L. Gowing, *The Three Dancers*, pp. 10–11.

18 Breton, *What is Surrealism?*, London, 1936 (Eng. translation by David Gascoyne), p. 25. Original French edition, *Qu'est que c'est le Surréalisme?*, Brussels, 1934.

19 *Combat*, Paris, 6 November 1961. Breton sees affinities with Surrealism in 'some of (Picasso's) work of 1923– 24, a number of works of 1928–30, the metal constructions of 1933, the semi-automatic poems of 1935 and up till *Le Désir attrapé par la queue* of 1943'. But he gives pre-eminence to the pre-war constructions.

20 Breton refers to this painting in his 1925 article. Eluard mentions it in 'Je Parle de ce qui Est Bien', *Cahiers d'Art*, 7–10, Paris, 1935. The canvas was also shown at the International Surrealist Exhibition at the New Burlington Galleries, London, 1936.

21 Tériade, who was steeped in the movement's aesthetic, writes: 'D'autre part, elle (l'écriture) relie l'aesthétique surréaliste au langage primitif, à ce langage par signes dont on connaît de si étonnantes schématisations,' *Cahiers d'Art*, 5th year, 2, Paris, 1930, p. 74.

22 The attitude of the

Surrealists to *Mercure* and its place in Picasso's work at the time is discussed by Peter Ibsen in *Interactions between Miró and Picasso: 1924–1932*, unpublished MA report submitted to the Courtauld Institute of Art, London University, 1970, pp. 8–9.

23 *Picasso*, Paris, 1938, p. 37.

24 See P. Waldberg, *Max Ernst*, Paris, 1958, p. 25 and p. 150.

25 Zervos in *Cahiers d'Art*, Paris, July 1926, quotes Picasso as having said: 'J'ai assez donné a mon tour d'en prendre aux autres'; Picasso appears to have been referring to his relations with his younger colleagues.

26 *Le Surréalisme et la Peinture, suivi de Genèse et Perspective Artistique du Surréalisme et de Fragments Inédits*, New York, 1945. (This is an expanded version of the 1928 book.)

27 Miró's enthusiasm for neolithic art is discussed at some length in R. Doepel's *Aspects of Joan Miró's Stylistic Development*, unpublished MA report submitted to the Courtauld Institute of Art, London University, 1967.

28 Charts of Easter Island hieroglyphs were printed in *Cahiers d'Art*, 2–3, 1929. Zervos, its editor, was a friend of Picasso and the Surrealists, and when articles and reproductions of different art forms appear in his periodical (and in other Surrealist or Surrealist-biased magazines such as *Documents* and *Minotaure*) it was often as a result of the painters' and writers' enthusiasm.

29 The first work in which Picasso appears to have made deliberate play of reversing the axes of the features (as opposed to tilting them slightly as he was doing in the years before 1914) is the *Harlequin* of 1924, Zervos, V, 328.

30 R. Rosenblum, 'Picasso and the anatomy of eroticism', in *Studies in Erotic Art*, (eds) T. Bowie and C. Christensen, New York, 1970, p. 341. This present essay owes a great deal to Professor Rosenblum's pioneering study.

31 Preface to an exhibition of Oceanic art held at the Galerie Andrée Olive, Paris, 1948. Reprinted in *La Clé des Champs*, Paris (?), 1953.

32 See in particular the *Embracing Couple* of this year, Zervos, *Picasso*, V, 460 (catalogued by Zervos as *Femme Assise*).

33 See Zervos, VIII, 57–9. *Minotaure*, 2nd year, 7, Paris, 1935, published an article with illustrations of the praying mantis.

34 Other works, in particular Zervos, V, 115, seem to make specific reference to predatory marine forms.

35 Rubin, *Dada and Surrealist Art*, reproduces both works, thus underlining their affinities with Surrealism.

36 I now feel that I originally misread this picture when I saw the mysterious figure at the left as possibly being the painter himself; this is surely the model while the stick-like figure to the right is the painter.

37 Authorized statement by Picasso published in the catalogue of the 1955 exhibition held at the Musée des Arts Décoratifs, Paris, 1955. The statement appears between nos. 40 and 41 of the catalogue.

38 J. Richardson, *Pablo Picasso*, London, 1964, p. 60.

39 *Cahiers d'Art*, 10th year, Paris, 1935, 7–10.

40 Both these fragments are from *Cahiers d'Art*. The appearance of Picasso's collected writings, *Picasso, Ecrits*, Paris, 1989, (eds) Marie-Laure Bernadac and Christine Piot, has made it obvious to many people, including myself, that Picasso was in fact a major poet and writer.

41 See Rosenblum, *Studies in Erotic Art*, p. 348.

42 In 'Fragments of a Lecture given at Madrid at the Residencia de Estudiantes', published in *La Révolution Surréaliste*, 4, Paris, 1925.

43 See Nesfield, *The Primitive Sources of Surrealism*, p. 29.

44 Rubin, *Dada and Surrealist Art*, p. 284.

45 I have come to realize that the Surrealists' attitude towards the Classic past was in fact complex. See Elizabeth Cowling, 'Proudly we claim him as one of us; Breton, Picasso and the Surrealist movement', *Art History*, March 1985, pp. 82–105.

46 In its second issue of 1929, *Documents* published an article on *L'Apocalypse de Saint-Sever* by Georges Bataille, with five illustrations including one of the Flood. The strong, somewhat crude colour of Picasso's *Crucifixion* suggests that Picasso might even have seen the original. Both Bataille and Tériade, whom Picasso was seeing at the time, had contacts with the Bibliothèque Nationale.

47 R. Kaufmann, 'Picasso's Crucifixion of 1930', *The Burlington Magazine*, September 1969, pp. 553–61.

48 Miró's painting was reproduced in *La Révolution Surréaliste*, October 1926. Picasso's first studies for the *Crucifixion* were executed before February–March 1927 when they were reproduced as recent drawings in *Cahiers d'Art*, 2. Rubin, *Dada and Surrealist Art*, p. 283, suggests that *An Anatomy* comes out of Giacometti's *Objets Mobiles et Muets*.

49 In the section on Dali in *What is Surrealism?*, p. 27, Breton writes, 'Dali is like a man who hesitates between talent and genius or as one might once have said, between vice and virtue.'

Notes

14 The Blind Mirror: André Breton and Painting

1 All quotes in his essay are taken from this original 1928 book form of Le Surréalisme et la Peinture.

2 See in particular Elizabeth Legge, Conscious Sources of the Unconscious: Ernst's use of psychoanalytic themes and imagery, 1921–1924, PhD thesis, University of London, 1985.

3 Dawn Ades, Dali, Thames and Hudson, 1982, p. 65.

4 Preface to the Dali exhibition at the Goemans Gallery, Paris, 1929.

15 Duchamp: The Large Glass

1 The exhibition was organized by Duchamp and Katherine Dreier.

2 Duchamp was in France at the time of the breakage and only discovered it several years later when the packing case containing the work was removed from storage.

3 Lawrence D. Steefel, The Position of La Mariée Mise à Nu par ses Célibataires, Même (1915–23) in the Stylistic and Iconographic Development of the Art of Marcel Duchamp, unpublished PhD thesis, Princeton, 1960, p. 22. The statement was made in 1956.

4 The first of these was made by Ulf Linde for the Moderna Museet in Stockholm in 1961. The second, by Richard Hamilton and now in the collection of William Copley, was begun in 1965 and finished the following year.

5 Robert Lebel, Marcel Duchamp, London, 1959, (English translation by George Heard Hamilton), p. 67.

6 In 1914 Duchamp had published a first, smaller collection of notes of which only five copies were issued. This is generally known as the Box of 1914.

7 Octavio Paz, Marcel Duchamp or the Castle of Purity, London, 1970, (translated from the Spanish by Donald Gardner). The pages of this short book are not numbered.

8 Quoted by Calvin Tomkins in Ahead of the Game, London, 1968, p. 58. (First published in America as The Bride and the Bachelors, 1962.) The remark was made to George Heard Hamilton.

9 Quoted in Walter Pach, Queer Thing Painting. New York, 1935. The statement was made to Torrey in Paris before the war. He made the same statement to the author in 1956.

10 The point is made by Paz, Marcel Duchamp or the Castle of Purity.

11 'I propose to strain the laws of physics', Art News, New York, December 1968; the text of an interview with Francis Roberts which took place on the occasion of the Duchamp retrospective at Pasadena in 1963.

12 To the author in 1956.

13 Very few of these (perhaps none) were executed to commission so that both the ideas and the visual images are Duchamp's own.

14 Pierre Cabanne, Entretiens avec Marcel Duchamp, Paris, 1967, pp. 52–3. (Published in America as Conversations With Marcel Duchamp, The Viking Press, 1971.)

15 Cabanne, ibid., in his interview refers to the visit to Roussel's play as having taken place in 1911 and Duchamp appears to have tacitly agreed.

16 Duchamp, interview in Museum of Modern Art Bulletin, New York, XII, 4–5, 1946.

17 Michel Leiris, 'Concepts of reality in the work of Raymond Roussel', Art and Literature, 2, Lausanne, Summer 1964, p. 20.

18 Ibid., p. 12.

19 Steefel, see note 3, p. 301, fn. 20.

20 Interview with Francis Roberts, see note 11.

21 Ibid.

22 Quoted in Harriet and Sydney Janis, 'Duchamp Anti-Artist', View, V, 1, New York, March 1945, p. 23.

23 Paz, Marcel Duchamp or the Castle of Purity, London, 1970.

24 Museum of Modern Art Bulletin interview, see note 16.

25 Calvin Tomkins, see note 8, p. 29.

26 Blind Man, 2, New York, May 1917.

27 Pierre Cabanne, see note 14, p. 47.

28 Quoted in James Nelson (ed.), 'Marcel Duchamp', Conversations with the Elder Wise Men of Our Day, New York, 1958, p. 92.

29 In Jarry's Le Surmâle during the course of the orgiastic love scene seven prostitutes are kept waiting in an adjacent room, again almost as 'spare parts', in case the heroine needs a replacement.

30 The Almost Complete Works of Marcel Duchamp, Catalogue for the Arts Council exhibition held at the Tate Gallery, London, 1966, p. 51.

31 In the oil sketch for Chess Players, Musée d'Art Moderne, Paris, and in the first version of the Nude Descending a Staircase, in Philadelphia.

32 Interview with Francis Roberts, see note 11.

33 Ibid.

34 The Almost Complete Works of Marcel Duchamp, p. 45, see note 30.

35 Duchamp stressed this point in his conversations with Steefel, see note 3, p. 27. 'Duchamp has stated that he consciously wished to create an effect comparable to the paramagnetic process, where each form could be interchanged with any

other and still belong to
many contexts.'
36 To the author.
37 Walter Pach, see note 9.
38 C. G. Jung, *Psychology and
Alchemy*, London, 1953,
(first published in Zürich in
1944), pp. 266–7.
39 Paz, *Marcel Duchamp or
the Castle of Purity*,
London, 1970.
40 Lebel, *Marcel Duchamp*,
London, 1959, p. 73.
41 Jung, *Psychology and
Alchemy*, London, 1953,
pp. 269–70.
42 Talking about his
experiments in optics with
the author, Duchamp
referred to himself as
'simply an artisan'.
43 The first of these was at
the Pasadena Art Museum
in 1963, the second at the
Tate Gallery in 1966.
44 *Etant Donnés* is the subject
of a revealing essay by
Anne d'Harnoncourt and
Walter Hopps, published by
the Philadelphia Museum
of Art in 1969.
45 Steefel, see note 3, p. 164.
46 Cabanne, see note 14,
pp. 166–7.
47 In 1961 Duchamp said,
'I'm nothing else but an
artist, I'm sure, and
delighted to be.' Quoted in
an interview by Richard

Hamilton for the British
Broadcasting Corporation,
27 September 1961.

**16 Arshile Gorky:
the Search for Self**
1 Gorky hesitated between
Archel, Archele and
Arshile before settling for
Arshile. Gorky he at first
sometimes spelt Gorki.
2 Julien Levy, *Arshile Gorky*,
New York, 1966, p. 56.
3 Karlen Mooradian, 'The
unknown Gorky', *Art
News*, 66, September 1967,
pp. 52–3, 66–8.
4 Quoted in Levy, see note 2,
pp. 34–5.
5 Arshile Gorky, 'Stuart
Davis', *Creative Art*, 9,
September 1931,
pp. 212–17.
6 Jim M. Jordan and Robert
Goldwater, *The Painting of
Arshile Gorky, A Critical
Catalogue*, New York and
London, 1982, p. 27.
7 Ibid., p. 43.
8 Gorky once acknowledged
that 'Sochi' should really be
'Khorkom', but that he had
used Sochi because
'Americans prefer names of
places more "popularly"
known.' Quoted by Jordan,
see note 6, p. 66.
9 Gorky's prose poem is
dated 26 June 1942 and

was written when the
Museum of Modern Art
acquired the Sochi picture
in this exhibition. The
manuscript is on deposit in
the Archives Collection of
the Museum and is quoted
in Ethel Schwabacher,
Arshile Gorky, New York,
1957, p. 66.
10 Quoted in Levy, see note 2,
p. 24.
11 In his article on Stuart
Davis. See note 5.
12 André Breton, *The Eye
Spring: Arshile Gorky*,
Julien Levy Gallery, New
York, March 1945.
13 See for example the
opening passages of *Le
Surréalisme et la Peinture*.
14 Sigmund Freud, *On
Dreams*, standard edition,
London, 1953, V,
pp. 651–2.
15 Karlen Mooradian, *The
Letters of Arshile Gorky*,
Ararat, 1971, p. 30.
16 Elaine de Kooning, 'Gorky:
painter of his own legend',
Art News, 49, January
1951, pp. 38–41.

**17 Frank Stella's *Working
Space***
1 All quotations are taken
from Frank Stella, *Working
Space*, Harvard, 1986.

List of Illustrations
(References are to page numbers)

$(75\frac{1}{2} \times 44\frac{7}{8}$ in$)$. The Pushkin Museum of Fine Arts, Moscow
72 Pablo Picasso *The Accordionist* 1911. Oil on canvas. 130×89.5 cm $(51\frac{1}{4} \times 35\frac{1}{4}$ in$)$. The Solomon R. Guggenheim Museum, New York
72 Georges Braque *Man with a Guitar* 1911. Oil on canvas. 116.2×80.9 cm $(45\frac{3}{4} \times 31\frac{7}{8}$ in$)$. The Museum of Modern Art, New York. Acquired through the Lillie P. Bliss Bequest
77 Georges Braque *The Pedestal Table* 1913. Oil on canvas. 91×71 cm $(36 \times 28$ in$)$. Heinz Berggruen Collection, Geneva
82 Pablo Picasso *Still Life with Death's Head* 1907. Oil on canvas. 115×88 cm $(45\frac{1}{4} \times 34\frac{5}{8}$ in$)$. The Hermitage Museum, St Petersburg
85 Pablo Picasso *Still Life with Jug and Apples* 1919. Oil on canvas. 65×43.5 cm $(25\frac{1}{2} \times 17\frac{1}{8}$ in$)$. Musée Picasso, Paris
91 Juan Gris *Still Life with Fruit Dish* 1914. Papier collé with canvas, oil paint and coloured chalks. 92×64.7 cm $(36\frac{1}{4} \times 25\frac{1}{2}$ in$)$. State Museum Kröller Müller, Otterlo, The Netherlands
91 Juan Gris *Still Life with Siphon* 1916. Triplex wood with oak upper layer. 73×116 cm $(28\frac{3}{4} \times 45\frac{3}{4}$ in$)$. State Museum Kröller Müller, Otterlo, The Netherlands
100 Pablo Picasso *Les Demoiselles d'Avignon* 1907. Oil on canvas. 243.9×233.7 cm $(96 \times 92$ in$)$. The Museum of Modern Art, New York. Acquired through the Lillie P. Bliss Bequest
115 Pablo Picasso *Mother and Child* 1971. Oil on canvas. 162×130 cm $(63\frac{3}{4} \times 51\frac{1}{4}$ in$)$. Musée Picasso, Paris
125 Fernand Léger *La Ville* 1919. Oil on canvas. 231×298.5 cm $(91 \times 117\frac{1}{2}$ in$)$. Philadelphia Museum of Art, A. E. Gallatin Collection

135 Fernand Léger *Mouvements à Billes* 1926. Oil on canvas. 146×114 cm $(57\frac{1}{2} \times 45$ in$)$. Kunstmuseum, Basle. La Roche Bequest
146 Amédée Ozenfant *Nacres I* 1926. Oil on canvas. 100×81 cm $(39\frac{3}{8} \times 32$ in$)$. Musée National d'Art Moderne, Centre Georges Pompidou, Paris
161 Umberto Boccioni *States of Mind: The Farewells* 1911. Oil on canvas. 70.5×96.2 cm $(27\frac{3}{4} \times 37\frac{7}{8}$ in$)$. The Museum of Modern Art, New York. Gift of Nelson A. Rockefeller, 1979
161 Umberto Boccioni *Matéria* 1912. Oil on canvas. 225×150 cm $(88\frac{1}{2} \times 59$ in$)$. Mattioli Collection, Milan
163 Giacomo Balla *Speeding Car and Light* 1913. Oil on paper. 84×109 cm $(33 \times 43$ in$)$. Moderna Museet, Stockholm
174 Kasimir Malevich *Taking in the Rye* 1912. Oil on canvas. 72×74.4 cm $(28\frac{3}{8} \times 29\frac{3}{8}$ in$)$. Stedelijk Museum, Amsterdam
179 Kasimir Malevich *Suprematist Painting, Eight Red Rectangles* 1915. Oil on canvas. 57.5×48.5 cm $(22\frac{5}{8} \times 19$ in$)$. Stedelijk Museum, Amsterdam
192 Constantin Brancusi *Maiastra* 1915. Marble. Height 61.9 cm $(24\frac{3}{8}$ in$)$. Philadelphia Museum of Art. Louise and Walter Arensberg Collection
197 Constantin Brancusi *Endless Column* 1920. Plaster. Height 6.03m $(19$ ft $9\frac{1}{2}$ in$)$. Musée National d'Art Moderne, Paris. Brancusi Studio. © Photo R.M.N.
213 Pablo Picasso *The Three Dancers* 1925. Oil on canvas. 215.3×142.2 cm $(84\frac{3}{4} \times 56$ in$)$. Tate Gallery, London
221 Pablo Picasso *La Femme en Chemise* 1913. Oil on canvas. 148×99 cm $(58\frac{1}{4} \times 39$ in$)$. Mrs Victor W. Ganz Collection, New York
254 Giorgio de Chirico *The Child's Brain* 1914. Oil on

canvas. 80.8×64.7 cm $(31\frac{7}{8} \times 25\frac{1}{2}$ in$)$. Moderna Museet, Stockholm
267 Marcel Duchamp *The Bride Stripped Bare by her Bachelors, Even* 1915–23. Oil, varnish, lead foil, lead wire, and dust on two glass panels (cracked), each mounted between two glass panels, with five glass strips, aluminium foil, and a wood and steel frame. 277.5×175.9 cm $(109\frac{1}{4} \times 69\frac{1}{4}$ in$)$. Philadelphia Museum of Art. Katherine S. Dreier Bequest
269 Marcel Duchamp *Nude Descending a Staircase No. 2* 1912. Oil on canvas. 146×89 cm $(57\frac{1}{2} \times 35$ in$)$. Philadelphia Museum of Art. Louise and Walter Arensberg Collection
277 Marcel Duchamp *The King and Queen Surrounded by Swift Nudes* 1912. Oil on canvas. 114.5×128.5 cm $(45 \times 50\frac{1}{2}$ in$)$. Philadelphia Museum of Art. Louise and Walter Arensberg Collection
279 Marcel Duchamp *Passage from the Virgin to the Bride* 1912. Oil on canvas. 59.4×54 cm $(23\frac{3}{8} \times 21\frac{1}{4}$ in$)$. The Museum of Modern Art, New York, Purchase. 1945
290 Marcel Duchamp *Fountain* 1917. Readymade: porcelain urinal. Height 62.5 cm $(24\frac{5}{8}$ in$)$. Original lost
291 Marcel Duchamp *The Chocolate Grinder No. 2* 1914. Oil and thread on canvas. 65×54 cm $(25\frac{1}{2} \times 21\frac{1}{4}$ in$)$. Philadelphia Museum of Art. Louise and Walter Arensberg Collection
312 Arshile Gorky *The Artist and his Mother* 1929–40. Oil on canvas. 152.4×127 cm $(60 \times 50$ in$)$. © 1993 National Gallery of Art, Washington. Ailsa Mellon Bruce Fund $(1979.13.1)$
321 Arshile Gorky *Waterfall* 1943. Oil on canvas. 153.7×113 cm $(60\frac{1}{2} \times 44\frac{1}{2}$ in$)$. Tate Gallery, London

Sources

Guillaume Apollinaire: The Painters' Friend was originally delivered as a lecture at the Courtauld Institute in 1962. The following year it was published in an edited form by the Baltimore Museum of Art under the title *Guillaume Apollinaire and the Art of the Twentieth Century*. The original version is used here.

Fauvism and the School of Chatou: Post-Impressionism in Crisis was delivered as a lecture at the British Academy in 1980 and published by the British Academy in the same year. Some detailed analysis of individual pictures has been deleted.

Two New Views of Matisse: a Book and an Exhibition brings together a book review that appeared in *The New York Review of Books* (*The Golden Age*) on 31 January 1985, and a review of the Matisse exhibition mounted by the Museum of Modern Art, New York, in 1992, published in *The Burlington Magazine*, in December 1992.

Pioneering Cubism, Still-Life Lives and *Two Picasso Exhibitions: Early and Late* were published (under different titles) by *The New York Review of Books* in the issues of 31 May 1990, 14 and 28 January 1993, and 21 July 1988 respectively. A section

dealing with the symposium mounted by MOMA in connection with the *Pioneering Cubism* exhibition has been deleted.

Léger and the Heroism of Modern Life was written for the catalogue of the exhibition *Léger and Purist Paris*, organized by John Golding and Christopher Green, and held at the Tate Gallery in 1970.

Ozenfant was written for the catalogue of the exhibition mounted in New York at Knoedler's in 1973.

Futurism in Venice appeared in *The New York Review of Books* on 14 August 1986 under the title *The Futurist Past*.

Supreme Suprematist (Malevich) was published in *The New York Review of Books* on 17 January 1991. The essay published here incorporates some additional material from the author's *The Black Square*, Studio International, April 1975.

White Magic: Brancusi was published by *The New York Review of Books* on 4 February 1988.

Picasso's Góngora was published in *The New York Review of Books* on 12 November 1985.

Picasso and Surrealism was published in *Picasso 1881–1973*, (eds) Roland Penrose and John Golding, Paul Elek, London, 1973.

The Blind Mirror: André Breton and Painting was delivered as a lecture to the Association of Art Historians in 1981.

Duchamp: The Large Glass was published in the 'Art in Context' series, Penguin, 1973.

Arshile Gorky: the Search for Self was published in the catalogue to the Gorky exhibition, *Arshile Gorky, 1904–1948*, held at the Whitechapel Art Gallery, London, in 1990.

Frank Stella's Working Space was published in *The Times Literary Supplement* on 27 March 1987.

From Mexico to Venice, Postscript: Interview with Richard Wollheim appeared in the catalogue for *John Golding: Works from a Decade*, Yale Center for British Art, New Haven, 1989.

All previously published texts which appear in this book have been readjusted for publication.

Index

366

Index

12535 Dillow A17160
£28 —